T0301864

Continuous Auditing with AI in the Public Sector

The effectiveness of internal audit activities is important for the sustainability of change in the public sector. In this sense, the tools and techniques used and the level of competencies of public sector auditors are decisive. This book deals with the effects of current technological developments in the public sector on auditing and risk management activities. Therefore, it is a resource for public internal auditors to create a digital audit strategy based on artificial intelligence (AI) and blockchain-based applications. Institutionalisation of their structures is important for public sector internal auditors. For this, basic requirements, future expectations, and best practices are explained. The digital business model is presented to produce value-added audit findings and outputs that guide public internal auditors and all digital-era stakeholders. This book is a pioneering work based on continuous auditing/continuous monitoring approaches using various AI and blockchain-based tools and techniques.

There is nothing more valuable to the success of a public internal auditor than a detailed understanding of the business. The important lesson in developing business knowledge, especially in the new audit universe emerging with digital transformation, is that all auditors must understand that they never finish learning about business processes, risks, and control points in the digital era.

They must constantly push themselves to be motivated and learn about the business operations they audit to implement new audit approaches powered by AI. In addition to obtaining up-to-date business information from process owners and stakeholders, public auditors responsible for conducting an AI-based continuous audit programme should also look inside their departments for a different perspective on business information that impacts continuous audit programme phase details and has the potential to add value. It should be noted that the additional source of information begins with your individual audit experience, digital skills, and qualifications.

Security, Audit and Leadership Series

Series Editor: Dan Swanson, Dan Swanson and Associates, Ltd., Winnipeg, Manitoba, Canada

The *Security, Audit and Leadership Series* publishes leading-edge books on critical subjects facing security and audit executives as well as business leaders. Key topics addressed include Leadership, Cybersecurity, Security Leadership, Privacy, Strategic Risk Management, Auditing IT, Audit Management and Leadership

The Security Leader's Communication Playbook: Bridging the Gap between Security and the Business
Jeffrey W. Brown

Modern Management and Leadership: Best Practice Essentials with CISO/CSO Applications
Mark Tarallo

Rising from the Mailroom to the Boardroom: Unique Insights for Governance, Risk, Compliance and Audit Leaders
Bruce Turner

Operational Auditing: Principles and Techniques for a Changing World (Second Edition)
Hernan Murdock

CyRM℠: Mastering the Management of Cybersecurity
David X Martin

Why CISOs Fail (Second Edition)
Barak Engel

Riding the Wave: Applying Project Management Science in the Field of Emergency Management
Andrew Boyarsky

The Shortest Hour: An Applied Approach to Boardroom Governance of Cybersecurity
Lee Parrish

Global Audit Leadership: A Practical Approach to Leading a Global Internal Audit (GIA) Function in a Constantly Changing Internal and External Landscape
Audley L. Bell

Construction Audit: Building a Solid Foundation
Denise Cicchella

Continuous Auditing with AI in the Public Sector
Lourens J. Erasmus and Sezer Bozkuş Kahyaoğlu

For more information about this series, please visit: www.routledge.com/Internal-Audit-and-IT-Audit/book-series/CRCINTAUDITA

Continuous Auditing with AI in the Public Sector

Edited by
Lourens J. Erasmus and
Sezer Bozkuş Kahyaoğlu

CRC Press
Taylor & Francis Group
Boca Raton London New York

CRC Press is an imprint of the
Taylor & Francis Group, an informa business

Designed cover image: © Shutterstock

First edition published 2025
by CRC Press
2385 NW Executive Center Drive, Suite 320, Boca Raton FL 33431

and by CRC Press
4 Park Square, Milton Park, Abingdon, Oxon, OX14 4RN

CRC Press is an imprint of Taylor & Francis Group, LLC

Library of Congress Cataloging-in-Publication Data
Names: Erasmus, Lourens, editor. | Kahyaoglu, Sezer Bozkus, editor.
Title: Continuous auditing with AI in the public sector / edited by
Lourens Erasmus and Sezer Bozkus Kahyaoglu.
Other titles: Continuous auditing with artificial intelligence in the public sector
Description: First edition. | Boca Raton : CRC Press, 2024. |
Series: Security, audit and leadership series |
Includes bibliographical references and index.
Identifiers: LCCN 2024012497 (print) | LCCN 2024012498 (ebook) |
ISBN 9781032465197 (hardback) | ISBN 9781032466651 (paperback) |
ISBN 9781003382706 (ebook)
Subjects: LCSH: Auditing–Technological innovations. |
Artificial intelligence–Financial applications.
Classification: LCC HF5667 .C5898 2024 (print) |
LCC HF5667 (ebook) | DDC 657/.45–dc23/eng/20240515
LC record available at https://lccn.loc.gov/2024012497
LC ebook record available at https://lccn.loc.gov/2024012498

ISBN: 978-1-032-46519-7 (hbk)
ISBN: 978-1-032-46665-1 (pbk)
ISBN: 978-1-003-38270-6 (ebk)

DOI: 10.1201/9781003382706

Typeset in Sabon
by Newgen Publishing UK

Contents

Foreword 1

This book addresses the needs of the 21st-century evolution of assurance methods in particular the consideration of AI and its application in the public sector where the environmental rigidities may be less constraining because of the lack of profit motive and the needs of public need. There is also a need for changing the methodologies of public reporting toward a consideration not only of current financial status but also two main dimensions which are quality of service and maintenance of infrastructure (Bora, Duan, Vasarhelyi, Zhang, Dai 2021).

The economy has drastically evolved over the last two decades and even more so since Fra Luca Pacioli summarized and formalized the double-entry system used by Venetian merchants since the beginning of the millennium (Sangster and Scataglinibelghitar 2010). From records and formal agreements necessary to manage businesses with physical assets, we have transitioned into an economy characterized by digital value (Dardani et al. 2024) and numerous virtual processes, investments, and assets. In this environment, traditional measurement (accounting/financial statements) and validation (auditing/assurance) methods are inadequate and need to be rethought.

However, the development of new entity measurement and report assurance methods has been slow due to regulatory rigidity and a lack of awareness about the impact of innovation. These methods are urgently needed as traditional business measurement models become increasingly obsolete, leading to market valuations of leading tech companies often much larger than their total assets. Consequently, the assurance of outdated numbers diminishes the value of audit reports.

Since the 1980s, the concept of continuous auditing (Vasarhelyi and Halper 1991) has been proposed and illustrated at large companies such as AT&T (Vasarhelyi, Halper, and Fritz 1991) and Unibanco, but its practice has remained limited. Today, the notion of an annual report with quarterly updates seems outdated in a world where automated, software-based trades account for 50–80% of stock transactions (Pei and Vasarhelyi 2020). These trades generally ignore balance sheet numbers, instead focus on fluctuations in other values such as price, volume, and peer company performance, among many confidentially kept variables.

Another major development is the emergence of big data that encompasses a wide set of variables (Brown-Liburd, Cheong, Vasarhelyi, and Wang 2019; Cheong et al. 2022; Yan, Appelbaum, Kogan, Vasarhelyi 2023). Corporations, pressed by competitive and management compensation issues, are very reluctant to disclose more detailed data and are helped dramatically by the consolidation of subsidiaries that hide the value of wealth-generating sub-entities.

To develop better business measurement models, public sector entities—free from the pressures of management compensation and competitive data suppression—have begun leveraging modern technology to create increasingly rich, though not fully validated, open data repositories. Despite facing corporate resistance and conservative standard setters, these entities are pioneering the use of data in ways that can significantly enhance the accuracy and effectiveness of business metrics.

For instance, several countries and organizations have made substantial progress in this domain:

- US:
  - USA.gov Data: Provides a broad range of government data and statistics.
  - Census Bureau Data: U.S. demographic data, population statistics, economic information.
  - Environmental Protection Agency (EPA) Data: Environmental data, including air quality, water quality, and chemical safety.
  - NASA Open Data: Data from NASA's various missions and research projects.

- Brazil:
  - Portal Brasileiro de Dados Abertos: The official open data portal of the Brazilian government.
  - Instituto Brasileiro de Geografia e Estatística (IBGE): Offers extensive data on demographics, economy, geography, and social indicators.
  - Banco Central do Brasil: Provides data on the Brazilian economy.

- Turkey:
  - Turkish Statistical Institute (TurkStat): Offers extensive data on demographics, economy, health, and education.
  - Republic of Turkey Open Data Portal: The official open data portal of the Turkish government.
  - Central Bank of the Republic of Turkey (CBRT): Provides data on the Turkish economy.
- Other countries and organizations:
  - UK Government Open Data: Various datasets from the UK government.
  - World Bank Open Data: Global development data and statistics.
  - European Union Open Data Portal: Data from the institutions and agencies of the European Union.
  - United Nations Data: A wide array of data on global economic, social, financial, and environmental issues.

These repositories provide a wealth of information across multiple fields, including demographics, health, environment, economics, and more. They enable intensive usage of exogenous variables in the creation of machine learning models, facilitating advanced data analytics and business intelligence.

Additionally, data simulation environments have become essential tools for machine learning studies, providing synthetic data for training and testing algorithms. Popular data simulator environments include:

- SimPy: A process-based discrete-event simulation framework.
- OpenAI Gym: A toolkit for developing and comparing reinforcement learning algorithms.
- CARLA: An open-source simulator for autonomous driving research.

- Unity ML-Agents: A toolkit for training intelligent agents using the Unity game engine.
- Gazebo: A 3D dynamic simulator for testing robot algorithms.
- AirSim: A simulator for drones and cars, built on Unreal Engine.
- Mujoco: A physics engine for research in robotics and biomechanics.

These tools aid in the development and testing of machine learning algorithms by simulating real-world scenarios and generating synthetic data.

Artificial intelligence (AI) is a very broad concept and includes several key components, such as machine learning (including supervised learning, unsupervised learning, semi-supervised learning, and reinforcement learning), deep learning, natural language processing, computer version, robotics, and expert systems.

Consequently, continuous monitoring of near real-time reporting by public entities presents great potential. This can be achieved by integrating the vast amount of already disclosed data, simulation tools, and thousands of AI algorithms, many of which are available in Python and R libraries. For example:

Entity	Potential project	AI to be used	Description
State government	Continuous reporting of checks paid	Machine learning	Apply unsupervised anomaly detection on the paycheck data to identify abnormal payment patterns.
State government	Continuous reporting of contracts requested, signed, and paid	Natural language processing, machine learning, blockchain	Improve the reliability and independence of audit evidence through blockchain technology, and continuously monitor contract status using machine learning. Utilize natural language processing to automatically manage large volumes of contract data.
Public service counters	Continuous monitoring of service satisfaction	Computer version, machine learning	Continuously monitor and analyze customer traffic at service counters using surveillance data to increase, decrease, or redirect counter availability as needed.
Federal government	Continuous reporting of procurement projects	Machine learning, deep learning, natural language processing	Continuously monitor procurement patterns and analyze potential collusions between vendors, government employees, and other stakeholders.
Tax authority	Continuous audit of tax risk using invoice data	Natural language processing, machine learning	Automatically detect inconsistencies between invoice data from tax authorities and company records to identify tax risks.

This book explores how current technological advancements, particularly in AI and blockchain, impact public sector auditing and risk management. As internal auditors seek to develop a digital audit strategy, understanding these technologies is crucial. AI accompanied by continuous audit could enhance audit processes through advanced data analytics and predictive modeling, allowing auditors to identify risks and anomalies more effectively. Blockchain, on the other hand, provides a secure and transparent ledger of transactions, which enhances the reliability and independence of audit evidence. By leveraging blockchain, auditors can ensure that records are tamper-proof and verifiable, reducing the risk of fraud and errors. This book serves as a comprehensive guide for public internal auditors, offering insights into integrating these technologies into their audit practices. It provides practical examples and case studies to illustrate the transformative potential of AI and blockchain in creating a more robust and efficient audit framework.

Miklos A Vasarhelyi
Qing Huang

REFERENCES

Brown-Liburd, H., Cheong, A., Vasarhelyi, M. A., & Wang, X. (2019). Measuring with exogenous data (MED), and government economic monitoring (GEM). *Journal of Emerging Technologies in Accounting*, 16(1), 1–19.

Bora, I., Duan, H. K., Vasarhelyi, M. A., Zhang, C., & Dai, J. (2021). The transformation of government accountability and reporting. *Journal of Emerging Technologies in Accounting*, 18(2), 1–21.

Cheong, A., Duan, H. K., Huang, Q., Vasarhelyi, M. A., & Zhang, C. A. (2022). The rise of accounting: Making accounting information relevant again with exogenous data. *Journal of Emerging Technologies in Accounting*, 19(1), 1–20.

Dardani, M. A., Gu, Y., Hu, H., Medinets, A. F., Palmon, D., & Vasarhelyi, M. A. (2024). Rethinking the standard-setting process: The role of intangibles. *Journal of Emerging Technologies in Accounting*, 21(1), 9–28.

Pei, D., & Vasarhelyi, M. A. (2020). Big data and algorithmic trading against periodic and tangible asset reporting: The need for U-XBRL. *International Journal of Accounting Information Systems*, 37, 100453.

Sangster, A., & Scataglinibelghitar, G. (2010). Luca Pacioli: The father of accounting education. *Accounting Education: an international journal*, 19(4), 423–438.

Vasarhelyi, M., Halper, F. B. & Fritz, R. (1991). *The Continuous Audit of Online Systems*. Released AT&T Bell Laboratories document, 110–125.

Vasarhelyi, M. A., & Halper, F. B. (1991). The continuous audit of online systems. *Auditing: A Journal of Practice & Theory*, 10(1), 110–125.

Vasarhelyi, M. A., Halper, F. B., & Ezawa, K. J. (1991). The continuous process audit system: A UNIX-based auditing tool. *The EDP Auditor Journal*, 3(3), 85–91.

Yan, Z., Appelbaum, D., Kogan, A., & Vasarhelyi, M. A. (2023). Teaching predictive audit data analytic techniques: Time-series forecasting with transactional and exogenous data. *Journal of Emerging Technologies in Accounting*, 20(1), 169–194.

Foreword 2

The accounting profession has been in the limelight over the last few decades, commencing with the Enron and WorldCom scandals in the early 2000s, which spilt over to various private and public sector scandals. Consistently, accountants and auditors (both internal and external) are in the media – sometimes due to doing an excellent job, but all too often also due to misconduct. The profession must restore public trust as one of the most prominent accountability measures within the business environment. In the past, it was difficult for auditors to provide a comprehensive and detailed overview of all business activities. Rightfully said by the previous CEO of the Global Institute of Internal Auditors (IIA) with over 200,000 members worldwide, Richard Chambers, in 2014: "We can audit anything, but not everything." This is purely based on the number of activities within an organisation where assurance must be provided. However, with continuous auditing, where various ICT tools and techniques, including AI, can be used to ensure timely and relevant reporting, this statement by Chambers is no longer true. With continuous auditing, systems can be programmed to draft management reports and auditors can "continuously" interrogate these to identify potential problems. However, the question remains: How well is continuous auditing embedded in organisations, and more specifically, the public sector? And to what extent is AI used to assist in continuous auditing?

This book reports on research conducted on the incorporation of continuous auditing using AI within the public sector environment, especially for internal auditing. Laying a foundation in Chapter 1, key terms are contextualised, and the scope and aim of the research are explained. Chapter 2 builds further on the foundation of the book by providing background information on AI within the accounting profession, specifically accounting and auditing practices. New approaches and developments, based on the scholarly body of knowledge, are debated, guiding the future of using AI within continuous auditing. Specifically, blockchain-based accounting systems that support the core values of auditing and facilitate the implementation of international auditing standards are presented in Chapter 3. Applying the continuous auditing approaches and developments within a public sector environment, it was necessary to investigate current innovations, especially in AI, within public sector audit ecosystems. As reported in Chapter 4, this was done on the basis of global best practices, leading to the identification of potential benefits and challenges. When delving into the audit process, Chapter 5 supports the need that an audit should be performed based on algorithms, again supporting the notion of continuous auditing within the public sector. However, due to the nature of this sector, policy recommendations are proposed.

Due to this changing landscape of auditing, the competence of auditors is questioned in Chapter 6, especially public sector internal auditors. As a foundation, the future internal audit organisational structure is debated, leading to guidance for internal auditors on how to remain effective and still be "trusted advisors" in the digital environment, providing value-adding reports to all relevant stakeholders. Internal auditors should thus take cognisance of reporting tools using AI as provided in Chapter 7. Various tools are analysed, and the value of each is provided. Chapter 8 specifically speaks of the skills required by public sector internal auditors to be able to perform their duties professionally within the digital environment. Challenges, opportunities, and threats are highlighted, leading to potential policy recommendations.

Due to the ever-changing landscape in which auditors operate, the Covid-19 pandemic that affected the world, the business environment, and governments is used as an example to illustrate how continuous auditing can be extremely effective in Chapter 9. Using continuous auditing, it was possible that remote control and audit and risk management could be maintained during lockdown periods. Various advanced and new developments, advantages, and future continuation are debated, leading to potential policy implementations. Another aspect that is in the limelight due to the profession's link to scandals is the role of professional ethics. In Chapter 10, the ethical perspective of conducting audits within a digital public sector environment is debated. "Grey areas" are highlighted; potential violations and AI abuse are presented, including the actions that are expected of an ethical professional auditor should such activities be identified. Finally, in Chapter 11, the impact of AI on sustainable internal auditing within the public sector is presented, guiding how this can be achieved.

The book concludes with a comprehensive analysis and summary of the issues highlighted, leading to potential policy changes. With continuous auditing within the digital age no longer an option, but a necessity to remain relevant, this book will add value to any internal auditor – from entry-level internal auditors who usually conduct internal audit engagements to chief audit executives who are mainly responsible for the strategic direction of the internal audit function. Additionally, by adding to the scholarly body of knowledge, postgraduate students, academia, and researchers will benefit from the new information presented. The IIA, the global professional body, could use the information to improve its guidance to its members worldwide.

Philna Coetzee
Department of Auditing
Faculty of Economics and Finance
Tshwane University of Technology
Pretoria, South Africa

Editors

Lourens J. Erasmus is a Professor in the Department of Financial Governance at the College of Accounting Sciences at the University of South Africa (UNISA), Pretoria. His fields of academic interest include public sector financial governance and internal auditing. Lourens is Commissioner of the Financial and Fiscal Commission of South Africa, the Chairperson of the Education Committee of the Southern African Institute of Government Auditors (SAIGA), and the Treasurer of the Research Ethics Committee Association of Southern Africa. Lourens is a rated researcher and Editor-in-Chief of the *Southern African Journal of Accountability and Auditing Research* (SAJAAR). He is an associate editor of the Scopus-listed *South African Journal of Accounting Research* (SAJAR) and project leader of the registered Engaged Scholarship project, Continuous Auditing in Public Sector Internal Auditing (CAPIA).

Sezer Bozkuş Kahyaoğlu (CIA, CFE, CFSA, CRMA, CICP, CPA) is an Associate Professor of Finance at the Bakırçay University in Izmir, Türkiye, and an Academic Associate of the University of South Africa (UNISA), Pretoria, and the University of Johannesburg. Her research interests include applied econometrics, time series analysis, financial markets and instruments, AI, blockchain, sustainability, corporate governance, risk management, fraud accounting, auditing, ethics, coaching, mentoring, and natural language processing (NLP). Sezer is the Associate Editor of two indexed journals and the AI Book Series Editor at Springer. She is a steering committee member at the Good Governance Academy Research Forum and a co-founding member of the registered Engaged Scholarship project, Continuous Auditing in Public Sector Internal Auditing (CAPIA).

Contributors

Babalwa Ceki
Department of Accounting
University of South Africa (UNISA)
Pretoria, South Africa

Lourens J. Erasmus
Department of Financial Governance
College of Accounting Sciences
University of South Africa (UNISA)
Pretoria, South Africa

Sezer Bozkuş Kahyaoğlu
Department of Accounting and Finance
Bakırçay University
Izmir, Türkiye

Cameron Modisane
College of Accounting Sciences
University of South Africa (UNISA)
Pretoria, South Africa

Ilse Morgan
Department of Auditing
University of South Africa (UNISA)
Pretoria, South Africa

Georges Naoufal
Audit, Evaluation, and Risk Branch
Canada Revenue Agency
Ottawa, Ontario, Canada

Thakane E. Rampai
Department of Auditing
University of Pretoria (UP)
Pretoria, South Africa

Louis A. Smidt
Department of Auditing
Tshwane University of Technology
Pretoria, South Africa

Léandi Steenkamp
Department of Accounting and Auditing
Central University of Technology, Free State
Bloemfontein, South Africa

Acknowledgement of peer reviewers

A blind peer-review process was followed prepublication where international experts scientifically reviewed allocated chapters. The authors and editors of this book wish to thank all the reviewers for their time and expert contributions to ensure the quality of the content presented.

Independent International Review Panel

Dr Razia Abdieva, Kyrgyz-Turkish Manas University, Kyrgyzstan
Assoc. Prof. Aidi Ahmi, Universiti Utara Malaysia, Malaysia
Dr Elif Ay, Dokuz Eylul University, Türkiye
Prof. Damira Baigonushova, Kyrgyz-Turkish Manas University, Kyrgyzstan
Assoc. Prof. Ramazan Ekinci, Izmir Bakircay University, Türkiye
Assoc. Prof. Hany Elbardan, Bournemouth University, England
Prof. Houdini Fourie, Nelson Mandela University, South Africa
Dr Junus Ganiev, Kyrgyz-Turkish Manas University, Kyrgyzstan
Dr Ayşegül Dumlu Kırkpınar, Izmir Katip Çelebi University, Türkiye
Dr Mario Labuschagne, Nelson Mandela University, South Africa
Prof. Rui Pedro Figueiredo Marques, Universidade de Aveiro – ISCA-UA, Portugal
Mr Siswe Nyenyiso, Nelson Mandela University, South Africa
Dr Lethiwe Nzama, University of Johannesburg, South Africa
Prof. Vahap Tecim, Dokuz Eylul University, Türkiye
Prof. Aynura Turdaliyeva, Kyrgyz-Turkish Manas University, Kyrgyzstan
Prof. Timucin Yalcinkaya, Dokuz Eylul University, Türkiye

Chapter 1

An assessment of the prospects of digital transformation in public sector internal auditing

How far will artificial intelligence go?

Lourens J. Erasmus and Sezer Bozkuş Kahyaoğlu

1.1 INTRODUCTION

Recent developments, described as the data revolution (Kitchin, 2014; Witz et al., 2019), owing to the impact of technological innovations, can be constructive or destructive. The important point here is the acceptance that change and technological innovations are inevitable and irreversible. Differences in readiness and adaptation to change and innovation affect whether it is perceived as constructive or destructive (Coskun & Bozkuş Kahyaoğlu, 2023). Therefore, organisations need to consider this perspective of "acceptance maturity" when making strategic plans while benefiting from tools and techniques that can detect risks early (Chen & Ahn, 2017).

The topics examined in this book are generally discussed based on examples and good practices in the public sector, in particular. When we compare the public sector with other sectors, it will be revealed why these changes and innovations should be made (Witz et al., 2019). While explaining the effects of developments in the public sector, Köse (2023) draws attention to the rapid increase and ageing of the population in the world, as an example of why change and innovation need to be constant. In addition, it is observed that women and "Generation Z" have emerged as a divergent style in the increasing international e commerce and digitalised markets (ACCA & IFAC, 2020; Deloitte, 2021). Mega social trends (OECD, 2019a) such as increasing cross-border migration, urbanisation, construction of smart cities, mounting populism, and the rise of the middle class, all fuelled by global conflicts, are observed around the world (WEF, 2024). These observations do not only trigger technological innovations but also change the fundamental paradigms in the world we live in exacerbated by mega environmental trends, such as global warming and climate change, food and water scarcity, and increasing energy demands. Consistent technological developments such as an increase in internet use, artificial intelligence, and machine learning are forcing society to adapt to a digitalised environment. This change in the fundamental paradigms on how we operate directly affects our social world and the structure of public administration. Accordingly, it forces senior management and all organisations to rethink the radically renewed management approaches and practices stemming from the COVID-19 pandemic (OECD, 2019b; UN, 2022; Witz et al., 2019).

Considering the ambitious goals that most developing countries pursue within the ambit of scarce resources, it is critical to observe the level of measures taken to use public resources effectively and efficiently (OECD, 2019a). Given the circumstances, the functionality of internal audit, internal control, and risk management mechanisms with an integrated approach are important catalysts to increase social value (Coşkun & Bozkuş Kahyaoğlu,

2023; Köse, 2023). When evaluated from an increased social value perspective, the audit, internal control, and risk management infrastructure of the public sector must be designed to adapt to current technological developments and innovations (Deloitte, 2017; Oxford Insight, 2022). Currently, it is inevitable to make full use of technology and establish the necessary audit and control mechanisms. The latest addition in new technology is the implementation and acceleration of audit fieldwork and control activities in near real-time and from a remote location, made possible by artificial intelligence and blockchain-based techniques (Deloitte, 2019).

In this chapter, an introduction is made to "the elements of the next-generation audit" (Figure 1.1) and the topics covered in the chapters of this book (Figure 1.2). The conceptual framework is presented considering the cause-and-effect relationship and implications for the public sector by justifying the scope of the chapters.

The need for next-generation auditing emerges entirely within the framework of the requirements of the emerging business world (KPMG, 2023; Lemann & Thor, 2020; Protiviti, 2021). The most fundamental feature of this new business world is its rapid digital transformation process based on technological advancements such as artificial intelligence, machine learning, robotic process automation, and blockchain. Hence, in the fast-changing and transforming business world, the business model becomes digital. This digital business model determines new risks, business processes, and strategic goals with an approach that triggers radical change (KPMG, 2023; OECD, 2021). Institutions must harness the benefits

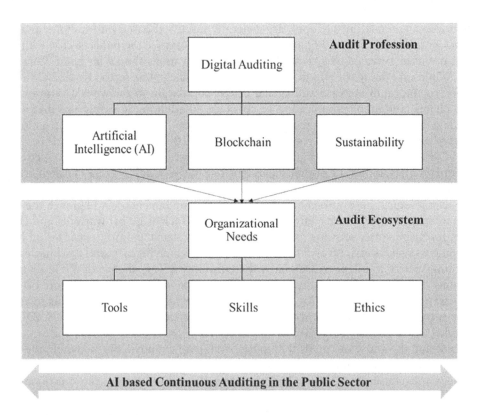

Figure 1.1 The scope of work.

Source: Prepared by the authors.

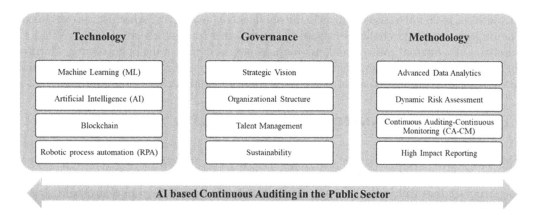

Figure 1.2 The elements of the next-generation audit in the public sector.

Source: Prepared by the authors by adapting from Protiviti (2021) and Oxford Insights (2022).

of internal audit, internal control, and risk management mechanisms to ensure full compliance with this business process, assurance, and early detection of risks. In this book study, based on examples from the public sector, the basic requirements are discussed to reveal the expected benefit of internal auditing within the framework of this radical change.[1]

It could be argued that the audit profession is undergoing a significant transformation in the business world, and the public sector is at the heart of this transformation. Institutions striving to achieve strategic goals in an environment of rapid development and intense competition must have the ability to early diagnose the risks provided by audit and control activities to produce value-added work. The important point here is that conventional audit, internal control, and risk management techniques are being replaced by innovative approaches that benefit from the power of advanced technologies and comprehensive big data analytics (Coşkun & Bozkuş Kahyaoğlu, 2023; Kitchein, 2014; Wirtz et al., 2019). Such a big data analytics and data revolution comes in the form of the integration of predictive data analytics and continuous auditing and continuous monitoring (CA-CM). With the advantages it provides, it paves the way for a more efficient, proactive, and risk-oriented audit and real-time monitoring process in all economic sectors.

In this book, the effects of artificial intelligence on auditing in the public sector and the prospects of continuous audit applications, based on artificial intelligence, are analysed. Public sector internal auditing is evaluated in all its aspects and the impacts of technological developments are discussed. In each chapter of our book, in-depth information and application examples corresponding to the scope given in Figure 1.2 are shared. Thus, the structure of the "audit profession" and the "dynamics of the audit ecosystem" are revealed. The quality and effectiveness of assurance services are of critical importance to carrying out activities in the public sector on an effective, efficient, economical, and ethical (4Es) basis (KPMG, 2023; OECD, 2019a; PwC, 2019). This book aims to contribute to audit professionals and all stakeholders in the public sector.

The topics in this introductory chapter are briefly presented as follows: Firstly, the recent developments and current situation regarding digital transformation in the public sector are presented. This assessment is important for a good understanding of the basis of the topics presented in the chapters of our book. Secondly, the challenges and opportunities encountered in digital transformation in the public sector governance structure are explained. The opportunities and challenges presented within this framework are directly related to internal audit, internal control, and risk management activities in the public sector. Thirdly, the development areas of internal auditing in the public sector based on technology and continuous auditing shaped according to new tools and approaches are emphasised.

1.2 THE DIGITAL TRANSFORMATION PROCESS IN THE PUBLIC SECTOR

Although digital transformation is defined as a process, it is rather a structural change. Structural changes refer to the elements or infrastructure that determine the knowledge and structure that will lead to change in its entirety (Coşkun & Bozkuş Kahyaoğlu, 2023; Matthess & Kunkel, 2020). This infrastructure covers the whole of the rules, plans, recording, and reporting standards that are formed during the production of required information. This process of "knowledge production" can also be defined as a "knowledge system". In this context, digital transformation represents a cultural transformation in itself, where the knowledge structure and system will change completely (PwC, 2019; Oxford Insight, 2019). The most significant impact of this change will manifest itself in the public sector, where existing processes will be implemented at the highest level. Along with all the factors that determine the size of the public sector, this transformation is observed from the smallest to the largest unit. The fact that the public sector is composed of different areas and has different service units creates complexity in the implementation of digital transformation and the technological knowledge structure that will form the infrastructure of quantum, neuro-finance, and various artificial intelligence-based algorithms (Bozkuş Kahyaoğlu et al., 2023).

One of the important elements in the activities of the public sector is the implementation of business processes as well as the supervision of the conformity of these processes. Since this new audit approach requires risk-based auditing in itself, it consists of continuous and real-time auditing, as well as internal auditing, internal control, and risk management (KPMG, 2023; Protiviti, 2021). Thus, the new audit approach will turn into a structure where artificial intelligence is the basic infrastructure. Digital transformation here can be defined as the implementation of artificial intelligence applications to audit processes (Bozkuş Kahyaoğlu, 2019). However, as mentioned before, the transformation of the auditor performing the audit activity will also gain importance as an important influencing factor in this transformation process. This process requires re-establishing the auditor's general professional knowledge, technical skill sets, and infrastructure and transforming the auditor's perspective accordingly (Esmeray, 2023).

When the general view of the public sector in the world is examined, it can be said that a significant development based on approaches to digitalisation and smart applications has emerged. In this context, governments have begun to increasingly transform into "digital governments" (OECD, 2021), and while this transformation process is rapidly progressing in most countries, some developing countries are making comprehensive project plans for digital transformation in their government policy and structure. The areas subject to these transformation projects are based on rapid developments in the field of the internet, social media, mobile technologies and devices, smart technologies, and more recently, digital technologies such as robotics, blockchain, and artificial intelligence. Thus, this new technological tool, technique, and system infrastructure fundamentally offer governments a wide range of innovative opportunities. However, governments that begin to use these new technologies are being forced to change their core functions, institutional structures, operational processes, activities, and relationships with all external stakeholders, including their citizens, the business world, and civil society (Chen & Ahn, 2017). Behind the state of adopting new infrastructure, in addition to the technological developments that accelerated with the COVID-19 pandemic, is the emergence of enormous volumes of big data that governments can use, especially due to the rapid developments provided by smart technologies and devices.

Ensuring the implementation and adaptation of digital transformation for all countries in the world brings with it policy coordination and cooperation at an international level. Hence, it is known that institutions such as the World Bank, United Nations (UN), Organisation for Economic Co-operation and Development (OECD), and European Union (EU) constantly monitor the digital transformation process and maturity level of states. Performance evaluations are made within a framework of relevant criteria, and maturity levels are determined with the help of indices such as the World Bank's GovTech Maturity Index (2022), the UN's e-Government Development Index (2022), Oxford Insight's (2022) Government AI Readiness Index, and OECD's (2019b) Digital Government Development Index.

The main tools of digital transformation are based on artificial intelligence and blockchain technologies. Through digital transformation applications based on artificial intelligence and blockchain technologies, a significant increase in the performance of public administration can be achieved, with a significant reduction in cost. It provides unique opportunities to ensure high accuracy and consistency in decision-making, audit, and risk management processes in public administration. For example, a study conducted by Deloitte (2019) for the public sector reveals that automating workflows with artificial intelligence will save up to 30% of the time of government employees. If we were to count the advantages provided by technological innovations, especially artificial intelligence, a very long list could emerge. In the context of their impact on the public sector, positive developments in service standards together with the effective and efficient use of public resources are an inevitable element that increases satisfaction among citizens. For this reason, artificial intelligence applications are given priority and a prominent place in the strategic plans and policies of all states and governments (Lehmann & Thor, 2020). However, it may be appropriate to mention the challenges encountered when an objective evaluation is made.

1.3 THE CHALLENGES OF DIGITAL TRANSFORMATION IN THE PUBLIC SECTOR

Compared to the digital transformation process in the private sector, pursuing digital transformation in the public sector is more complex and challenging. The main reason can be summarised as follows. It is accepted that the private sector's digital transformation process is based on a decision-making mechanism that is generally "profit-oriented" and based on "cost-benefit analysis" (ACCA & IFAC, 2020; Bozkuş Kahyaoğlu et al., 2023). However, this approach is not valid in the public sector. Instead, digital transformation in the public sector is carried out with an accessible approach with a wide coverage area that can meet national strategic goals and citizens' needs (Deliotte, 2017). All activities of the public sector must be carried out within the legal framework, and digital transformation must be made transparent, accountable, and auditable by the public supervisory institutions, i.e., Court of Accounts. Therefore, it is important to ensure legal compliance, data security, and reliability while providing services to all citizens in the digital environment.

The service range of the public sector must cover all citizens, and therefore, digital transformation is expected to be achieved with a more comprehensive approach and a

Social Effects	Technological Effects	Ethical Effects	Legal & Compliance Effects
• Workforce transformation and Human to Machine interactions	• System and data integrity issues in relation to the designing expert systems.	• Discrimination and moral issues in relation to the human & machine judgements.	• Privacy and safety issues related to Management of autonomous & smart systems.

Figure 1.3 Challenges to artificial intelligence applications in the public sector.
Source: Adapted from Wirtz et al. (2019).

user-friendly design. One of the most sensitive issues in the public sector digital transformation process is cyber security within the framework of data security (Sundberg, 2023).

Challenges to artificial intelligence applications are addressed in four main areas in the literature regarding the public sector (Wirtz et al., 2019). These can be examined within the framework of social effects, technological effects, ethical effects, and legal compliance effects, as shown in Figure 1.3.

Although the classification given in Figure 1.3 is taken as a basis for the public sector challenges, it should not be forgotten that there is a transmission between these factors and internal dependencies that should be considered when determining policy. In other words, although it is not easy for the public sector to overcome these four key challenges in the short term, there is a significant awareness among all states globally (OECD, 2021, World Bank, 2019, 2020, 2022). The difference in practice and the maturity level reached in terms of artificial intelligence implementation is also closely related to the difficulties of the countries in terms of economic and trained manpower.

The point that should be taken into consideration here is that the public sector can contribute to the widespread use of artificial intelligence applications at the social level in a safe and ethical context, within the framework of its powers to determine policies and make surveillance mandatory on a national basis (Munoko et al., 2020). Improving the education system and training, a better equipped labour force is key for both the public sector and the private sector. In this respect, internal audit, internal control, and risk management mechanisms must be functional in the public sector to create successful artificial intelligence-based projects and digital service delivery standards in a short time by using resources effectively and efficiently (Sundberg, 2023).

It is necessary to use advanced audit tools and techniques to test the functionality of internal audit, internal control, and risk management mechanisms in the public sector and to provide assurance to the governments. As a result of the good governance structure of the public sector and the increase in the technological maturity level, internal audits in the public sector need to adapt to the environment and even be one step ahead of those being audited (Köse, 2023; Esmeray, 2023; Steenkamp et al., 2023).

Recently, a situation has emerged in which it is accepted that the perspective on auditing has changed in the understanding of modern public administration and that traditional audit tools and techniques are insufficient. This means that with digital transformation in the public sector, there is also a need for the digitalisation of auditing. This is generally named by audit professionals within the umbrella of the "Next Generation Audit" (KPMG, 2023; Protiviti, 2021). The connection between good governance in the public sector and the next-generation audit is presented in Figure 1.4.

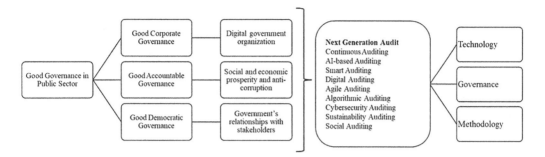

Figure 1.4 Connection between elements of good governance and next-generation audit in the public sector.

Source: Prepared by the authors by adapting from Protiviti (2021), Oxford Insights (2022), and Wirtz et al. (2019).

Current developments and affecting factors regarding the application of digital auditing are discussed systematically in the following chapters of this book. In this chapter, a general overview is given on how to redesign internal auditing in the public sector, and the basic framework is presented as preparation for in-depth discussions in subsequent chapters.

1.4 THE REDESIGNING OF INTERNAL AUDITING IN THE PUBLIC SECTOR

While there are such comprehensive changes and digital transformations in the public sector, inevitably, the structure of public sector internal auditing will change (Coşkun & Bozkuş Kahyaoğlu, 2023; Köse, 2023). However, the cumbersome movement of the public sector within the framework of compliance with the legislation and its large scale appears to be a situation that slows things down. The major priority for the governments can be defined as the functionality and good governance of the public sector mechanism as the key to success here. In this respect, having a good internal audit, internal control, and risk management infrastructure contributes to speeding up the process and providing an effective and efficient working environment; it can also play a role in the early diagnosis of possible risks, including cyber-risks and climate risks (KPMG, 2023; Protiviti, 2021; PwC, 2019). In this process, which we can describe as the digitalisation of auditing, the scope of auditing, planning, fieldwork, and the tools and techniques used must change. For this effort towards digital auditing to achieve its goal, the basic elements listed below must be appropriately included in the process and actively used by competent auditors. Thus, it is possible to carry out strategic goals and policies in a stable manner in the public sector, and the capacity of auditing to produce value-added work can be demonstrated (Esmeray, 2023; Lemann & Thor, 2020).

The need for digital transformation in auditing emerges as a global necessity. The most obvious evidence of this is the comprehensive change made by the Institute of Internal Auditors (IIA) in international internal audit standards as of 2023 (Esmeray, 2023). It aims to improve the process of generating added value by conducting the audit with the help of advanced technology, increasing its contribution to the good governance process, and increasing the scope of reporting standards and quality of communication with stakeholders.

Within the framework of digitalisation of auditing and audit processes, auditors need to renew themselves and increase their compliance levels on the following aspects. Beyond being a choice for the auditors, this is now becoming a necessity after the COVID-19 pandemic. It means that the processes and transactions that are essential for auditing are digitalised and turned into big data, so it is not appropriate for auditors to audit with traditional methods (Deliotte, 2019; Kitchin, 2014). This situation requires the public sector audit to be redesigned and this redesign has to be based on the following basic elements.

1.4.1 Big data analytics

With the effect of digitalisation, data accumulation in every field is increasing rapidly, contributing to the formation of big data. The important point here is that the audit should change its investigation and testing tools and techniques by considering the structure and characteristics of big data.

The key features of big data and the need for auditing to use new approaches and techniques are explained in detail in the following chapters of our book. In this context, it must be acknowledged that the audits that were previously based on sampling and process-based are no longer sufficient for the public sector. Instead, it is important to implement continuous auditing supported by big data analytics covering all data as shown in Figure 1.5. To fully realise this digital approach in the public sector, auditors must have the necessary technical knowledge. In other words, the level of "technology literacy" should be increased (Esmeray,

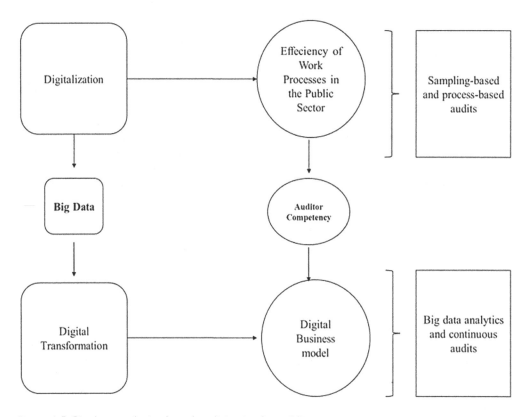

Figure 1.5 Big data analytics-based auditing in the public sector.

Source: Coşkun and Bozkuş Kahyaoğlu (2023).

2023; KPMG, 2023; Protiviti, 2021; Köse, 2023). This requires auditors to attach greater importance to continuous professional development.

1.4.2 Artificial intelligence

It is recognised that even though a clear definition of artificial intelligence cannot be made, at the current point, it requires steps towards the institutionalisation of human-machine relations (Mckinsey, 2016; Schou & Hjelholt, 2018). This approach is the basic condition for the safe start of artificial intelligence applications, especially in the public sector. By meeting the condition of establishing human-machine relations, it may be possible for the audit to reach the competence to audit artificial intelligence and at the same time to carry out more effective audits using artificial intelligence. Therefore, since our book provides a theoretical framework and practical information based on artificial intelligence and blockchain implementation in the public sector auditing from start to finish, we will not go into further detail here. The point we would like to bring to the attention is that the value-added information that all our colleagues may need to be able to audit artificial intelligence and use artificial intelligence as a basic tool in audits is presented to our readers with a systematic approach by a team composed of both the academics and professionals with in-depth field experience.

It should be noted that involving audit activities in the artificial intelligence generation process is a crucial need from start to finish of artificial intelligence projects. This audit approach ensures that applications are reliable and transparent. Involving audit activities is also a fundamental need to overcome ethical problems, which have been an important topic of discussion recently, and to produce permanent solutions.

1.4.3 Blockchain

Although blockchain applications, which can be considered a "hidden hero" among technological developments, have entered our lives recently, since 2009 compared to other innovations, it can be stated that its impact areas are increasing day by day. It creates a significant potential for corporate applications in the public sector, based on the opportunities offered by the perception of trust and transparency that the blockchain infrastructure inherently provides (Consensys, 2023). In this book, new auditing approaches and techniques based on blockchain are presented in detail in one of the chapters. In this respect, it contributes to the audit and risk management literature.

1.4.4 Sustainability

The 17 goals, which emerged as a "global emergency call" under the leadership of the UN and were put forward as a solution to the dangers affecting individuals, societies, the next generations, and the whole of nature, constitute the conceptual framework of sustainability. Despite the international decisions taken, strict steps towards global legal regulation, and social responsibility support from non-governmental organisations, sustainability practices in the public sector are just the beginning. The audit in the public sector can be used as a strategic tool to ensure that this sustainability implementation process progresses quickly and effectively (Zhang & Shanyue, 2023).

Compared to other types of auditing, sustainability auditing, reporting, and monitoring of measurements can be considered quite new. Hence, the public sector, which is responsible to determine sustainability standards and policies, to expect others to comply with sustainable development goals (SDGs) and act responsibly, must first set a "role model" by complying with their own requirements in their public services. This can be expressed as a strategic vision that supports credibility, trust, and institutional maturity indicators (UN, 2022).

1.5 CONCLUDING REMARKS

In this introductory chapter, where the issue of digital transformation in public sector internal auditing is discussed, the current situation assessment and future expectations are emphasised. It should be noted that correctly understanding the factors that affect the success and/or failure of the digital transformation process, especially at the corporate level, and producing solutions are critical for the effective use of resources and corporate sustainability in the public sector.

In this respect, audit findings and recommendations can show us a strategic direction and support this digital transformation process in the public sector. Based on this: To understand where the source of the problem comes from, it is critical that internal audit, internal control, and risk management mechanisms designed following corporate governance principles and international auditing and reporting standards are functional.

It is recommended to benefit from the audit function in early diagnosis of key risks to be encountered here. Auditors can play an active role, especially in determining new types of risks that newly installed artificial intelligence-based public systems and smart services may pose. For this, the auditor must be competent and have the knowledge of technological infrastructure and equipment to follow and internalise innovations and direct the corporate strategy on digitalisation and sustainability issues.

NOTE

1 This discussion becomes more understandable in the context of the Technology Acceptance Model (TAM). Because, in the context of corporate governance principles, how institutions that want to achieve their strategic goals use technology and what their perceptions are, are decisive. For further details: the Technology-Organization-Environment Framework (TOE) (Amini & Bakri, 2015).

REFERENCES

ACCA & IFAC (2020). Ground-breakers: gen Z and the future of accountancy. www.accaglobal.com/content/dam/ACCA_Global/professional-insights/groundbreakers-gen-z/PI-GEN%20Z-GROUNDBREAKERS.pdf

Amini, M., & Bakri, A. (2015). Cloud Computing Adoption by SMEs in the Malaysia: A Multiperspective Framework Based on DOI Theory and TOE Framework. *Journal of Information Technology & Information Systems Research (JITISR)*, 9(2), 121–135.

Bozkuş Kahyaoğlu, S. (2019). An Analysis on the Implementation of New Approaches and Techniques in the Auditing of Business Processes Based on Blockchain Technologies. Editors; Prof. Burak DARICI & Dr. Fatih AYHAN. Cyrptocurrencies in all Aspects, Peterlang Publications. An analysis on the implementation of new approaches and techniques in the auditing of business processes based on blockchain technologies (bakircay.edu.tr)

Bozkus Kahyaoglu, S., Durst, S. & Coskun, E. (2023). To Digitalize or Not? Covid Effect in Medium Sized Companies Based on Three Cases. *EDPACS Journal*, 68(4). www.tandfonline.com/doi/abs/10.1080/07366981.2023.2260612

Chen, Y. & Ahn, M.J. (eds.) (2017). *Routledge Handbook on Information Technology in Government*. London: Routledge.

Consensys (2023). Blockchain in government and the public sector. https://consensys.io/blockchain-use-cases/government-and-the-public-sector

Coşkun, E. & Bozkuş Kahyaoğlu, S. (2023). Dijital Dönüşüm ve Denetimin Dönüşümünde Dijital Teknolojilerin Rolü: Fırsatlar ve Tehditler, Digital Transformation and the Role of Digital Technologies in the Transformation of Audit: Opportunities and Threats. *Kamu Yönetiminde Denetim: Temel Paradigmalar, Değişim ve Yeni Yönelişler, Audit in Public Administration: Basic Paradigms, Change and New Directions*. Editors. Murat Önder & Hacı Ömer Köse. Ankara, Türkiye: Sayıştay Publications, pp. 35–63.

Deloitte (2017). How much time and money can AI save government?. The Deloitte Center for Government Insights. www2.deloitte.com/content/dam/insights/us/articles/3834_How-much-time-and-money-can-AI-save-government/DUP_How-much-time-and-money-can-AI-save-government.pdf

Deloitte (2019). How to redesign government work for the future A step-by-step guide to optimizing human-machine collaboration in the public sector A report from the Deloitte Center for Government Insights in collaboration with the Harvard Kennedy School. www2.deloitte.com/xe/en/insights/industry/public-sector/job-automation-future-of-work-in-government.html

Deloitte (2021). Understanding generation Z in the workplace, new employee engagement tactics for changing demographics. www2.deloitte.com/us/en/pages/consumer-business/articles/understanding-generation-z-in-the-workplace.html

Esmeray, A. (2023). İç Denetim Standartlarında Vizyon Değişimi: Üçlü Savunma Hattı Bakış Açısının Dönüşümüne Olan İhtiyaç. *Editörler Bozkuş Kahyaoğlu ve Kurt, KÜRESEL İÇ DENETİM STANDARTLARI: YENİLENEN KAVRAMLAR VE DEĞİŞİM ALANLARI. Vision Change in Internal Auditing Standards: The Need for Transformation of the Triple Lines of Defense Perspective*. Editors. Bozkuş Kahyaoğlu & Kurt, Global Internal Audit Standards: Renewed Concepts and Areas of Change. Ankara: Gazikitabevi. pp.19–40.

Kitchin, R. (2014). *The Data Revolution: Big Data, Open Data, Data Infrastructures & Their Consequences*. London: Sage.

Köse, H.Ö. (2023). Kamu Yönetiminde Denetimin İşlevleri, Dinamikleri ve Geleceği. Functions, Dynamics and Future of Auditing in Public Administration. *Kamu Yönetiminde Denetim: Temel Paradigmalar, Değişim ve Yeni Yönelişler, Audit in Public Administration: Basic Paradigms, Change and New Directions*. Editors. Murat Önder & Hacı Ömer Köse. Ankara, Türkiye: Sayıştay Publications. pp. 35–63.

KPMG (2023). All eyes on: transforming the audit with AI, By Sebastian Stöckle, Head of Innovation, Global Audit, KPMG International. https://kpmg.com/xx/en/blogs/home/posts/2023/02/all-eyes-on-transforming-the-audit-with-ai.html

Lehmann, D. & Thor, M. (2020). The Next Generation of Internal Audit Harnessing Value from Innovation and Transformation. *CPA Journal*, February, 2020. www.cpajournal.com/2020/02/18/the-next-generation-of-internal-audit/

Matthess, M. & Kunkel, S. (2020). Structural Change and Digitalization in Developing Countries: Conceptually Linking the Two Transformations. *Technology in Society*, 63, 101428. www.sciencedirect.com/science/article/pii/S0160791X20303973

McKinsey (2016). The "how" of transformation. www.mckinsey.com/industries/retail/our-insights/the-how-of-transformation#/

Munoko, I., Brown-Liburd, H.L. & Vasarhelyi, M. (2020). The Ethical Implications of Using Artificial Intelligence in Auditing. *Journal of Business Ethics*, 167, 1–26.

OECD (2019a). Effective multi-level public investment. www.oecd.org/effective-public-investment-toolkit/Full_report_Effective_Public_Investment.pdf

OECD (2019b). OECD's Digital Government Development Index. https://goingdigital.oecd.org/en/indicator/58

OECD (2021). Digital government: progress towards digital competence and maturity. https://doi.org/10.1787/1c258f55-en, 9789264964068 (EPUB), www.oecd-ilibrary.org/sites/2bed4623-en/index.html?itemId=/content/component/2bed4623-en#fig10-1

Oxford Insight (2019). The next generation of anti-corruption tools: Big data, open data & artificial intelligence. https://oxfordinsights.com/wp-content/uploads/2024/02/Researchreport2019_TheNextGenerationofAnti-CorruptionTools_BigDataOpenDataArtificialIntelligence.pdf

Oxford Insight (2022). Government AI Readiness Index. www.unido.org/sites/default/files/files/2023-01/Government_AI_Readiness_2022_FV.pdf

Protiviti (2021). The next-generation internal audit journey needs to begin now. www.protiviti.com/sites/default/files/2022-07/next-generation-internal-audit-journey-begins-now-protiviti.pdf

PwC (2019). The future of audit. www.pwc.co.uk/who-we-are/future-of-audit/pwc-future-of-audit-report-july-2019.pdf

Schou, J. & Hjelholt, M. (2018). *Digitalization and Public Sector Transformations*. Cham: Springer.

Steenkamp, L., Smidt, L.A., Kahyaoğlu, S.B. & Coderre, D. (2023). A Maturity Level Assessment of the Use of Technology by Internal Audit Functions: A Comparative Analysis of the Federal Government of Canada. *The EDP Audit, Control, and Security Newsletter*, 68(1), 1–41. http://doi.org/10.1080/07366981.2023.2229986

Sundberg Leif (2023). Towards the Digital Risk Society: A Review. *Human Affairs Journal*. https://doi.org/10.1515/humaff-2023-0057. www.degruyter.com/document/doi/10.1515/humaff-2023-0057/html

UN (2022). UN's e-Government Development Index. https://publicadministration.un.org/egovkb/en-us/data-center

Wirtz Bernd, W., Weyerer Jan, C. & Carolin, G. (2019). Artificial Intelligence and the Public Sector – Applications and Challenges. *International Journal of Public Administration*, 42(7). www.tandfonline.com/doi/full/10.1080/01900692.2018.1498103.

World Bank (2019). Digital Government Readiness Assessment Questionnaire, January 2019, Washington, DC.

World Bank (2020). Digital Government Readiness Assessment Toolkit: Guidelines for Task Teams, Washington, DC.

World Bank (2022). GovTech Maturity Index (GTMI). www.worldbank.org/en/data/interactive/2022/10/21/govtech-maturity-index-gtmi-data-dashboard

World Economic Forum (WEF) (2024). Global Risk Report. www3.weforum.org/docs/WEF_The_Global_Risks_Report_2024.pdf

Zhang, Y. & Jin, S. (2023). How Does Digital Transformation Increase Corporate Sustainability? The Moderating Role of Top Management Teams. *Systems*, 11(7), 355. https://doi.org/10.3390/systems11070355

Chapter 2

Background information about AI in accounting and auditing practice

Cameron Modisane

2.1 INTRODUCTION

The traditional approach to auditing has changed in recent years due to certain developments in the global financial environment and new risks that have emerged. The advancement of technology in how accounting transactions are processed allowed the accounting and auditing professions to evolve in the manner that business is conducted. (Byrnes et al., 2018). In today's digital space, financial statements are drawn up with the use of emerging technology tools.

Auditors and accountants need to embrace these technologies to help them with the auditing and accounting processes. The process to automise and to digitise accounting and auditing processes has not fully matured to date. As previously stated by Tan and Low (2019), the use of technological advances such as artificial intelligence (AI) has had a great impact on innovation and disruption to how work is conducted. Accountants, auditors, and those charged with the responsibility of guidelines and norms will be greatly impacted by advanced technology for the processing and recording of transactions. Financial transactions and recording procedure document the entire process from initiation to reconciliation and reporting (Coyne and McMickle, 2017; Fuller and Markelevich, 2020).

The use of AI is growing, and organisations are seeing huge positive results with the increase of spectrum of human cognitive and functional outcomes. According to Keenoy (1958), AI systems in the accounting and auditing professions have been employed for decades and the AI impact will continue over time due to improvements in information technology (IT). With authoritative data processing and analytical capability, AI is significantly altering the traditional audit processes and procedures (Thibodeau, 2003). Furthermore, the use of AI-based tool is growing at rapid pace, which is also impacting on the auditing process (Conick, 2017). Due to large volumes of structured, semi-structured, and non-structured data, providing the evaluation of corporate financial and non-financial results is more difficult (Lam, 2004; Baldwin et al., 2006). AI-augmented audit tools create more trust and provide higher quality audits (Alles and Gray, 2020).

AI-enabled technology can be utilised to analyse big data, by collating and summarising data from various sources, providing auditors with relevant and appropriate evidence. This data collated can be used in judgements, complementing their judgement capability, and providing more informed decisions to give clients with advanced levels of assurance. More importantly, AI-based auditing tools and techniques are important in data analysis, such as data extraction, validation, and comparison (Hsu and Lin, 2016; Lin, 2017); this means that AI-enabled technology can extract textual information from multifaceted electronic records and data (Deloitte, 2015).

DOI: 10.1201/9781003382706-2

With the advancing economic necessities of countries which was followed by a drastic development and evolution in IT, this inevitable trend has led to substantial improvements in the accounting industry and its growth (Luo et al., 2018). The reliance on smart systems and software applications in the areas of financial reporting, auditing, and other accounting areas increased (Vlacic et al., 2021). In the last few decades, there has been a steady technological improvement meant at developing "artificially intelligent" computer systems. The idea of AI and its use has been debated in academic and business circles. This has been done through the introduction of advanced technologies that eventually provide drastic changes in processes and reorganisation all economic sectors to invest funds in the various sectors (Lin, 2021).

The fast-paced improvement of AI has resulted in universal attention due to the great positive impact that AI-enabled technology has on the world over. The impact of AI has been felt and seen on people's daily lives. According to Geisel (2018), it is expected that there would be job losses and replacement due to the work done by robots in the upcoming years. This would impact accounting professionals, especially those performing repetitive tasks. The financial institutions such as banks have moved to automate some of their business processes in order to maintain a competitive edge to ensure long-term survival (Oláh et al., 2020).

2.2 HISTORICAL PERSPECTIVE AND THE EMERGENCE OF AI

Artificial intelligence (AI) is a wide-ranging term that includes technologies that enable computer systems and machines to operate in a "smart" manner. Organisations are spending millions in AI advancement and systems to mechanise, enhance, or imitate human behaviour, and analytical and/or decision-making and the accounting profession should be in a position to fully implement organisational AI programmes. The AI idea creation dates to the 1950s, since there have been technological updates and improvements that happened later in the 1980s and 1990s. The term AI refers to any that enables computers to imitate human intelligence, and this includes deep learning and machine learning.

The 1980s signify the history of the use of AI systems and methods in the accounting profession. Terms such as deep learning, cognitive processing, machine learning, and augmented intelligence are all associated with AI. These can be used interchangeably, and these terms and concepts encompass AI. The most comprehensive definition of McCarthy came up with a comprehensive definition of artificial intelligence in 1956. John McCarthy, who is seen as the father of AI, defined it as "the science and engineering of making intelligent machines, especially intelligent computer programmes" (McCarthy et al., 1956). AI is about allowing a computer to behave like a human using a computer-controlled robot by making use of software think intelligently as a human being does (McCarthy et al., 1956). The study of AI can be done through learning how the human brain functions, how problems are resolved by humans, and the manner in which decisions are being made. This ultimately forms the basis of creating intelligent software and systems through the use of AI. In the 2000s, Hallevy (2013) added that AI could bring a new dimension and create new markets in the area of technology and systems. Makridakis (2017) further added that there are opportunities in the area of accounting and AI specialisation where a form of collaboration could exist. This is where AI applications can be used through pairing experts in accounting for the growth in research and development around AI technology. The implementation of technology and systems such as AI is the step in the right direction towards operational efficiency and effectiveness in accounting and auditing activities (Pedrosa et al., 2020).

2.3 ARTIFICIAL INTELLIGENCE DEFINED

According to the Organization for Economic Co-operation and Development (OECD), AI is "a machine-based system that for explicit or implicit objectives infers, from the input it receives, how to generate outputs, such as predictions, content, recommendations, or decisions." (Russel et al., 2023).

AI is the ability for computer machines or application systems software to display some form of human intelligence. Current AI tools and applications behave like living humans in that they are modified to feel, think, and react like us. There will be benefits of AI by accountants according to the Association of Chartered Certified Accountants (ACCA) in that AI-enabled application will reduce the repetitive tasks of bookkeeping and financial transaction entries. This will further assist accountants to provide high-value services and focus on strategic matters and more advisory services (Baldwin et al., 2006).

Academic research of AI in the audit profession is also improving due to the advances being made in technology. The definition of AI has widened today than earlier. For example, the definition cited by Sutton, Holt, and Arnold (2016) separates accounting-related AI into knowledge-based systems and machine learning, which does not include all the technologies. In their outline, Issa, Sun, and Vasarhelyi (2017) choose to only focus on expert systems and neural networks (Issa, Sun, and Vasarhelyi, 2017).

According to Hirst (2014) and Taghizadeh et al. (2013), intelligent systems with AI should have the ability to enforce compliance with the numerous rules, regulations, and organisational policies. AI systems will also assess employee performance and influence HR decisions. There are some fears concerning AI, as there are those who believe it may invade human privacy by analysing human behaviour and lifestyle patterns through its "machine learning" aspect (Hirst, 2014). Accountants are concerned about the safety of their future careers as this technology advances and becomes more powerful. There is concern that perhaps AI might make the professional jobs currently being done by accountants redundant. The access to date has also been increased by the technology improvement which will also increase the effectiveness and efficiency of accountants based on financial information they receive. Therefore, with the more accurate and comprehensive data received, this will ultimately improve the decision-making process of accountants (Hansen and Messier, 1987; Suton, 2016).

Haenlein and Kaplan (2019) described AI to be the capability of a computer application to correctly interpret outside data, study from it, and apply what it has been studied to achieve specific objectives and assignments through variable adaptation. Zhang et al. (2020) defines AI as the outcome of the progressive utilisation of machine learning (ML) and big data technology to study past events and predict the future using large volumes of data. Lee and Tajudeen (2020) stated that AI gives the opportunity for the computer system to acquire from their error, adjust to new input, and perform humanlike jobs. Massive volumes of data can be analysed using modern AI technologies, creating patterns in the data more recognisable. Chukwudi et al. (2018) defined artificial intelligence as the study of how to enable computer systems execute tasks better than human beings.

Shukla and Vijay (2013) describe that AI is a subset of computer science, which deal with making computer systems exhibit a kind of intelligence and its study. AI is about those computer systems that can study new concepts and activities and use them to interpret data and make conclusions. AI can also analyse an audio language or understand a visual scene and execute a task. AI makes use of human intelligence and the study of concepts that will allow computer machines capable of recreation similar to known human responses, given the human ability to comprehend, interpret, and conclude (Shukla and Vijay, 2013). Furthermore, Haenlein and Kaplan (2019) described AI as a computer system that comprehends and understands sounds and varied dialects, has the ability to come up with solutions for problems, can diagnose medical ailments, direct road traffic, play games like chess, and can imitate human behaviour.

AI is a computer system that has the capability to execute activities that are ordinarily linked with living things. In addition, Kitsios and Kamariotou (2021) also describe AI as that area of study that portrays the ability of ML and mimicking humans and learns the skill to react to some behaviours also known as artificial intelligence. At the same time, Poola (2017) defines it as creating more complex intricate computer systems that can outperform humans in numerous ways. Payne et al. (2021) indicate that AI has the ability to alter human life in multiple ways which includes finance, communications, medical services, privacy, security, manpower, wars, and even ethics, among others. The AI specialisation has also been viewed as an academic arena that explores how to develop computers and computer systems that can perform and behave in a smart and sophisticated fashion. The AI technologies and systems software have affected the financial sector by altering the manner of how transactions are processed. There have been several ways and approaches that have been carried out to advance the value creation by implementing new technologies and integration of AI with financial services (Gomber et al., 2018).

According to Duan, Edwards, and Dwivedi (2019), AI emerges from an intelligent dimension that requires computer systems to function in the manner humans are anticipated to operate after research and work. AI can be explained in three dimensions which include expert systems, knowledge representation and inference, and ML.

Kwak et al. (2021) and Kerzel (2021) posited that expert systems are tools and application that work together to create new solutions for challenges that need specialised knowledge and expertise. It is a group of AI software adopted in the 1980s, reaching a degree of skill with the ability of replacing human specialisation in a certain area of decision-making. Expert systems are often used for AI technology. This includes computer programming system that imitates the manner an expert in a certain field thinks (Chukwudi et al., 2018).

Fraij et al.'s (2021) knowledge representation and inference (KRI) means that the AI system should have the artificial ability of acclimatising to its environment, obtaining knowledge that explains this environment, and keeping knowledge in a manner that allows for agile and appropriate response to any stimulus created by the environment. Succinctly, it means the method of knowledge representation and the manner of acquiring it. The knowledge representation and procedural inference has shown the capability of intelligent systems to acclimatise with its environment, knowledge generation and storage, ease of reflection, and utilisation of time needed. KRI is a critical component of intelligent data processing, especially if the large volumes of data is enormous or the data itself is complicated. The skill to unscramble problems largely depends on the knowledge available in the arena and the increase in the volume of data. In modern times, there has been a need for an intelligence data system that can process data quickly and efficiently. Therefore, logic being used to understand activities and tasks through analysis and interpretation (Arnau et al., 2013). The representations of knowledge is shown when AI is used to demonstrate how knowledge is processed using computer systems and programme thinking which forms part of AI displaying smart behaviour (Greenman, 2017). It also indicates the purpose of knowledge representation and logic in realising the interrelationship between human knowledge and its illustration through computer programming languages (Fraij et al., 2021).

Bertomeu et al. (2021) defines machine learning (ML) as a multiplex, multidisciplinary field of research and progress that incorporates various techniques from AI, computer science, analytical statistics, and biology. ML can be utilised with the purpose of expanding services and products for their clients (Bertomeu et al., 2021). ML has been described as one of the important categories of AI which means systematising and refining the process of studying computer systems based on their knowledges without being programmed, and without human aid, and by building first learning models using data and several algorithms, which depend on the nucleus of data (Bertomeu et al., 2021).

2.4 STRATEGIC IMPORTANCE OF AI TO THE ACCOUNTING AND AUDITING PROFESSION

There are strategic benefits of using AI in the practice of accounting and auditing. Raji and Buolamwini (2019) posited that several auditing and accounting processes that previously needed manual labour are now computerised by AI, which contains data entry procedures. AI systems, unlike human auditors, can investigate 100% of data, develop audit tests, and document scripts. The computerised analysis of accounting entries is one method that AI changes auditing. The key benefit of using AI in creating automatic accounting entries is that human error is reduced. Fraudulent transactions can be detected through the use of AI and an alert can be raised at head office which can ultimately decrease human intervention (Moffitt et al., 2018). Furthermore, Khamis (2021) adds that AI can improve overall operational efficiency in the audit process and achieve better outcomes.

AI is an important tool that can assist in the reduction of costs through efficiency and effectiveness of audits. AI has proven to be a sensible tool for decreasing the chance of human error. AI can be used as a new opportunity and technique to improve their auditing process. The risk of a material misstatement is one of the components that need to be analysed as part of the audit process. Financial statements are probably to be materially misstated if financial consequences are not appropriately written in the audit file. Puthukulam et al. (2021) adds that AI systems recognise cases of suspected threats and the risk of fraud, as also shown by the study, and help with professional scepticism and judgement. The study shows that AI assists in detecting errors and frauds by employing predictive analysis techniques (Puthukulam et al., 2021).

By using AI techniques, the user can exponentially improve and increase the information spread process by virtue of expanding the transmission momentum, thereby bringing down the transmission cost and conquering a number of bottlenecks in challenges (Griffin, 2016; AI Topics, 2016). The large volumes of data provided by various sources of data and the limitless computing power of cloud computing break the bottleneck that limits advances of AI and allow for the application of the deep learning algorithm. The deep learning allows for the execution of various ML systems and increases the scale of the AI research. Deep learning has already been included in various programmes. Therefore, AI can be seen of as a "container" of the human knowledge. Therefore, the creation of the deep learning algorithms and techniques will increase this "container" to the level that people cannot foretell (Demski, 2007; Greenman, 2017).

IT tools and techniques have been extensively used by accounting and auditing in the business environment. Accounting systems and financial modelling software have applied IT to enhance the work which has shown to be favourable in the investigative facets of accounting. Nonetheless, the speed of IT application by the accounting profession was seen as slow due to the conventional manner of its early adopters. By the late 1990s, the accounting profession was forced to computerise its processes and procedures as a tool of increasing their efficiency, ultimately, to challenge the competition and decrease the expenses (Manson et al., 2001).

According to Al-Aroud (2020), the audit profession has considerably evolved over time due to technological advancements. A large portion of these updates in this profession have already been seen. This includes an increase in the number and complexity of the auditing rules, several changes in the norms and values of professional ethics, an enhanced quality of the audit work, increasing competition among the audit firms, decreased audit fees, and establishment of new services to the clients (e.g., financial, and computing advice). Furthermore, this profession has seen the expansion of new audit types and services. All these considerations in totality have made the auditing profession increasingly competitive than ever before. Consequently, the new techniques and tools offered by IT and AI have been universally accepted by auditors. The auditor's decision-making process has increased and made more reliable to process data and information in a fast-paced manner. Accordingly, audit efficiency and quality has improved over time (Silver et al., 2016; Sun and Vasarhelyi, 2016).

2.5 TECHNOLOGY TRAINING OF ACCOUNTANTS AND AUDITORS

With the introduction of AI-based technology in the accounting and auditing processes, the professional staff and the accounting personnel do not only require professional knowledge in accounting and auditing, but they also require knowing the IT and advance skill in practice of the accounting systems software and data management to adapt to the developments and the associated changes in the work conditions. The training and education programmes of the accounting students in the universities require amendment and enhancement to infuse these IT knowledge and skill (Al-Aroud, 2020). The college or university graduates are the main workforce of the accounting and auditing profession in the future; therefore, it is important that these institutions make parallel adjustments and updates to their accounting education programmes. The course currently offered and the training programmes lack the required IT knowledge and skills with an AI focus and devote limited time to innovation of accounting principles. The lack of IT knowledge and skills results in the inability to meet the requirements from industry in terms of employability (Al-Aroud, 2020).

Since numerous accounting entries will sooner or later be computerised, the role of the auditor will change, concentrating on gaining engineering and IT knowledge and skills (Kokina and Davenport, 2017; Schmitz and Leoni, 2019). Furthermore, the professional hierarchy will experience organisational variations, reducing a substantial category of repetitive and redundant activities. These shifts will lessen the positions of several employees, specifically accounting technicians or junior-level (entry-level) auditors. Accordingly, professional audit firms will also endure the big challenge of making organisational transformations. Hence, professionals will require to amend their firms' organisational configurations to give the latest and current accountancy services; activities will become the new normal. Beyond this, they must advance staff roles and responsibilities that previously were not there. The latest staffing model of accounting and audit organisations will be vastly disturbed.

Management was introduced to IT accounting, and audit organisations' management might need to prepare themselves by initially obtaining knowledge about the new technologies' synergic properties on the function's going concern. Further to this, audit firms must accelerate the application of AI techniques and the provision of huge databases. The technology surroundings need a considerably complex management method to manage the individual tools and organise their functions to provide the most efficient, effective outcomes to both clients and accounting organisations. Additional management strategies for accepting technological advances might comprise of internal requirements regarding attaining and employing new expertise or hiring skilled people with specific industry knowledge and specific technical expertise, as well as acceptance of partially remote work.

The training and educational role profile of staff in accounting and auditing firms are shifting. Organisations will require to pool resources or engage IT knowledge and skills to properly realise the latest emerging technologies such as AI. Once these tools have been properly implemented, organisations in the accounting profession will advance multilevel consulting models, need fewer junior employees, and use skilled staff with varied industrial expertise. Organisations will continue by adjusting to new technologies, by implementing business and operating models that allow the digitisation and transformation of activities, by appreciating technology and obtaining computer and technological expertise, and by working effectively with experts in numerous areas to produce added service value.

According to Luo et al. (2018), there is currently limited knowledge in terms of how exactly emerging technology tools could impact auditors' methods. Just as accountants and auditors require to think about AI, they also need to think how the cloud considers big data (Luo et al., 2018). The limited adequate training in computerised auditing and limited understanding of special functions of audit software by audit staff are the main limitations to implementing emerging technology techniques for audit software in the audit process (Abou-El-Sood et al., 2015; Thottoli, 2021). The next generation of auditors require to be adequately trained to be ready to work with technology successfully and efficiently as financial auditing uses more on automation, AI, and machine learning. They will need to be trained in these emerging technologies.

Qualified auditors' IT and auditing expertise are becoming more and more critical for retaining the reliability of computerised systems (Adeyemi et al., 2014). The traditional method of auditing has changed visibly among auditors because of the current developments in technology. The latest innovative enterprise resource planning (ERP) systems are expanding the usage of online business transactions by stakeholders, as well as the use of the cloud and the harried communication and availability of e-data for provisioning by auditors and boards of directors (Byrnes et al., 2018).

The current auditors who are making use of AI to assist them in their audits will require extensive training in these technologies. Audit firms need to be prepared to invest in training their audit staff to ensure that they do not get left behind and become redundant as the world is transforming. AI is bringing about these new reforms and transformations in the auditing profession. Possessing the correct and the required skills will be key to ensuring survival in the current business world that is undergoing changes due to AI.

2.6 EMERGING IT TECHNOLOGIES IN ACCOUNTING AND AUDITING – BLOCKCHAIN, DATA MINING, RPA, AI, AND DEEP LEARNING

According to Noordin et al. (2022), the improvement of advanced technology such as AI, data analytics, ML, and blockchain technologies has an important impact on auditors, accountants, and auditing firms. The Association of Chartered Certified Accountants (ACCA; 2019) is backed by the fact that the technology possesses the ability to transform the audit but also at the degree of the data analysis that impose the finality of this process.

These analyses are based on large volumes of data (i.e., big data), at the level where data analysis procedures are occurring in a sequence due to the IT impact on processes. This impact can be viewed as a prospect for auditors; it also involves challenges created mainly by blockchain technology (Farcane and Deliu, 2020) and the advent of smart contracts, for example. The impact of IT through AI tools develops big data, robotic process automation (RPA), data analytics, predictive analytics, ML, and blockchain, in financial audit assignments. RPA adds to the computerisation of repetitive and well-recognised work procedures comprising of AI algorithms. While blockchain allows, through the characteristics of transparency and discretion of transactions, immediate authentication of data updates or fraud attempts, ML, which is seen as a branch of AI, allows the creation of algorithms to ensure a learning procedure for computer application. In a study by Lee and Tujudeen (2020), it was found that the use of AI-based accounting software assisted to store invoice images together with fully computerising the records management system process.

A consideration is made by these technologies for accounting and auditing profession, such as AI, RPA, ML through deep learning, and blockchain. Technological progress in the accounting and auditing profession is as a result of opportunities presented by the imaginative invention, blockchain, which adds to improving the quality of audit process delivery and accomplishing the degree of reporting needed by professional regulators, information users, and auditors (Rozario and Thomas, 2019).

This would also remove the presence of intermediaries and costs required to authenticate transactions, the blockchain enables access to customer data, in terms of assisting to support productivity and usefulness (Rozario and Thomas, 2019), by reducing the level of detail and cost of the audit engagement. Based on the presence of intelligent contracts, which characterise the blockchain, auditors can depend on the files underlying the resulting financial entries.

Although the presence of software with a certain level of decision-making intelligence and even predictive behaviour is well-acknowledged (Kuenkaikaew, 2013), AI applications are not so prevalent as to develop a problem in financial audit, given the substantial potential for revolutionising this profession. AI is seen as an overarching term for several technologies that can be merged in a different way. A number of experts are of the view that AI has made significant progress in recent years, but it is improbable to claim an approach to this phase (Johnson, 2018). It is widely accepted that, in addition to computerising procedures belonging to AI, analytical processes and audit examinations are undertaken that are analysed through data analytics (AICPA, 2018; ISACA, 2018). Data analytics is about the whole entire methodology and procedures followed and not parts of the analysis process, being seen as a multidisciplinary field. Analytical review, from planning the audit stage, entails analysing, linking, and validating changes between accounts, the correlation between financial information (e.g., balance sheet information, profit and loss account, treasury statement, accounting policies, and explanatory notes) and non-financial (e.g., information about business model, main risks, or information on key performance indicators).

RPA is a computerisation with business processes and principles founded on robots and AI. RPA computerises routine, traditional work tasks that would require access from different sources (e.g., from the SAP IT system, excel, client-auditor platform), by eliminating the human element from the process (ACCA, 2019). The advance that the system uses is learning human activities and replicating them seamlessly. This would be done by following certain type of predetermined rules for the activity. The software system would automate certain financial tasks such as bank reconciliations, reviewing the correctness of accounting balances. The integration of RPA into the financial systems and audit processes would improve the efficiency of work (Gartner, 2019).

2.7 PRIOR RESEARCH ON THE IMPLEMENTATION OF AI ON ACCOUNTING AND AUDITING OPERATIONS

According to a study by Issa et al. (2017), there was a proposal on various areas of AI-related research to investigate where this emerging technology is most prevalent. This study describes a sequence of the changes in the research questions aimed at better understanding the AI-driven transformation of the current world of audit into the assurance of the future. In the papers by Bai (2017), it was described that the current stance of the implementation of AI in the area of audit and assurance services in the four big global accounting firms analyses the impact of AI on the audit industry and the relevant auditing practitioners and regulators who are mandated with regulations and laws for the industry regulations.

Another study of Kokina and Davenport (2017) detailed an outline of the advent of AI in accounting and auditing and examined today's abilities of cognitive technologies and the consequences these technologies will have on the audit process in its entirety and the humans who execute these audits. The study by Gusai (2019) examined the significance of artificial learning in accounting and auditing areas and measured the level of forthcomings regarding AI in auditing and accounting in general. The key findings from this study paved a way for an enhanced favourable environment in the field of accounting and auditing. The advancement of AI can help human efforts in the workplace environment. Greenman (2017) explored the influence of AI on the accounting profession. In this study, it was found that AI is an important tool that will give accounting professionals the required tools and the ability to enhance the efficiency and effectiveness of their work. The recurring tasks of book-keeping or process-driven assignments are more likely to be substituted with a computerised technology than the higher value specialties that involve professional judgement. It is said that the newer generation of accounting professionals need to fully appreciate technology and be geared up to work alongside AI.

Li and Zheng's (2018) article focused on how to take advantage of AI to avoid accounting irregularities and to develop a positive impact on accounting information quality; this study analysed how AI affects the accounting personnel. The focus of this article was how AI could influence accounting personnel and it would improve the work done by accountants. Luo et al.'s (2018) study took the use of AI in the accounting profession as a research object, the development of accounting-related technologies and challenges that are faced by the industry and how they could be addressed in future. Chukwudi et al.'s (2018) study aim was to investigate the impact of AI on the performance of accounting processes among accounting firms in Southeast Nigeria. The findings of the investigation indicated that smart systems have a great effect on the performance of accounting function of accounting firms in Southeast Nigeria. The study concluded that the implementation of AI had a positive effect on the performance of accounting operations.

Technology has advanced over the years and accounting firms and audit professionals are taking advantage on the use of AI to aid the entire audit process. The audit programmes that are developed by auditors need to reflect the use of AI to ensure that they remain relevant and keep abreast with the latest trends. The AI technology might need to be tailored specifically to meet the needs of audit professionals. At the same time, the accounting operations will thus be improved due to the use of this technology.

2.8 ARTIFICIAL INTELLIGENCE (AI) IMPACT ON THE ACCOUNTING ORGANISATION

AI is synthetic astuteness or computer system communication that replicates intellectual functions. Those reactive AI systems are the elementary form of AI that is post-event normative. This kind of AI "reacts" to certain activities with pre-programmed responses. A restrained memory AI system is obtained from a knowledgebase which is past learned information, stored data, or events. The system or technology is engineered to "learn" from an event that occurred in the past. It is a "future class AI product" to replicate human-like actions and responses in proper context. This future form of AI will have self-guided thoughts and reactions which the current accountants and auditors can take advantage of (Reynoso, 2019).

Accounting firms that have implemented AI in their processes have had sufficient time to shift their focus by analysing and interpreting the outcomes to meet the customer's urgent needs and giving more counsel. With the use of AI, progress will be made to include machine-based learning where the accuracy rate of report will be improved with little human involvement. A study of over 3,000 business executives performed by MIT Boston Consulting Group showed that over 80% of managers are of the view that AI provides competitive advantage, and 79% are of the view that the AI will enhance the company's productivity (Ovaska-Few, 2017).

Roetzer (2014) states that AI has the ability of computers and system to exhibit or replicate a sense of cognitive intelligence. The introduction of AI has become a valuable asset for business, including the accounting profession where the professionals would also need to be trained in the area of technology. Therefore, accounting professionals in firms would need to enhance their IT skills and knowledge to leverage for the effect AI has on accounting processes. The correct technical skills are required for accounting professionals also to have great scope for AI applications (Roetzer, 2014).

Sutton et al. (2016) studied the environment of accounting and auditing problems and the requirement for the use of computerisation. Based on this investigation, auditing is a field that is intrigued using automation. Auditors must deal with vagueness and incomplete financial information, but the audit conclusions that are finalised and documented are usually recurring. United States (2016) examined the utilisation of smart systems in major accounting firms. Accounting firms usually make use of expert systems mostly to eliminate time and costs while auditors have more time to take critical audit decisions. Expert systems can assist to facilitate accuracy and correctness of financial information which will result in the improvement of the pace of how the work is done and completed. The study also found that, accountants are sceptical regarding the integrity of the financial data provided by computerisation. The deficiency in knowledge of big data and the analysis of the data could create inappropriate results; accountants may not be able to analyse and interpret the results accurately. This makes it important for these professionals to be adequately trained in these areas.

2.9 BENEFITS OF USING AI IN THE AUDIT PROCESS

The use of AI-based technology in audit process gives auditors the chance to automate the auditing procedures from stage to stage (Moffitt et al., 2018). This can be affected from the pre-engagement stage to the presentation of an audit report's opinion; effectiveness is critical at each stage (Kokina and Davenport, 2017). Using AI technology adds the enhancement of the accuracy and efficiency throughout the audit process (Kaplan and Haenlein, 2019). The implementation of AI assists in correctly improving a company's accounting operations even more (Kaplan and Haenlein, 2019). The use of AI technology can help in the identification of potential issues with a company's financial statements and has helped to identify potential fraud on a company's accounting records (Chassignol et al., 2018). There is also a benefit of identifying potential challenges with a company's accounting processes and practices that need to be improved. AI is a useful tool that can assist to make audits more efficient and cost-effective. Companies that have used AI have proven that it is a positive and trusted way of decreasing the risk of human error. AI should be considered if firms are planning to be innovative in their audit processes.

The other benefit of using AI according to Raji and Buolamwini (2019) is that several auditing practices that previously needed traditional labour are now computerised by AI, which includes data entry processes. The benefit of using AI systems is that 100% of the data can be tested through generating audit tests and the writing of scripts. The computerised analysis of accounting entries assists in reducing human errors through the use of AI tools. Another benefit is that AI can quickly identify any issues of fraud that may occur. This also decreases the human intervention required for accounting entries (Moffitt et al., 2018). Overall, AI is an effective tool that helps with efficiency and usefulness of audit assignments. The risk of material misstatement may be reduced through the use of AI which is an improvement of the auditing process. Auditors are a part of their work; they need to evaluate the risk of material misstatement. If there is financial mismanagement and there is no adequate record keeping, the risk of material mistake is likely to increase. AI tools are beneficial to detect irregularities later if illicit transactions and/or other anomalies are not identified immediately. Salem (2012) adds that AI could be used to detect any areas of fraud that could be found in financial transactions. High-risk transactions could be readily discovered by using AI-based auditing technologies which benefit in improving the auditing process. AI allows for testing of the entire population without the use of sampling where risk could occur, thus reducing the risk of non-detection/discovery.

Therefore, the integration of AI into the audit process reduces the repetitive tasks and makes it easier for auditors to analyse large volumes of data and to have a thorough view of the business operations (Kokina and Davenport, 2017). Auditors can now spend their energies on activities that are valuable and generate revenue as well (Luo et al., 2018). The literature has shown that organisations who invest in AI technology produced quality audit results where there is a decrease in the number of misstatements for issued audits. The computerisation of a number of financial transactions has provided the audit teams with greater insights into the business they are auditing which have proven to be cost-effective as well (Hassan, 2022). Through automation of certain duties, errors can also easily be detected through the audit process. This therefore becomes important when accurate financial is required for the audit process (Omoteso, 2012).

Another study by Gentner et al. (2018) indicated that AI is used as a tool in auditing to identify errors and mistakes in financial reports at a fast pace. The identification of patterns and making prediction using AI by auditors improves the auditing process. Nwakaego and Ikechukwu (2015) indicated that AI-enabled auditing software can assist to perform complex audits in short space of time in an effective manner that is cost-efficient and better than humans with minimal errors. According to Lin and Hazelbaker (2019), AI has proven that meaningful financial data will be produced through the improved quality of accounting entries. At the same time, Nickerson (2019) agreed that AI new jobs could be created, and productivity levels would increase as well through the use of AI technology. Audit professionals can spend more time focusing on more complex activities and other business objectives while the routine tasks can be done by AI-based technology (Lin and Hazelbaker, 2019). According to a report by the ACCA, the work done by accountants could be repurposed to focus on advisory, consultative, and growth planning roles instead of routine tasks of bookkeeping and transaction recording to services (Jariwala, 2015). AI is transforming the manner in which audits are being done as per Hemin (2017), and AI can assist with improving the communication and collaboration between auditors and other stakeholders within an organisation (Hassan, 2022).

According to Gentner et al. (2018), the other benefit of AI is that the reports produced can be customised and tailored to meet the organisational needs to assist in decision-making process through the use of data analysis. Al-Aroud (2020) indicated that AI technologies are key in terms of the growth and future of the auditing profession. Deniz and Sorenson (2022) indicated that several organisations are including AI as part of their business process and there implementation therefore is improving the financial information that is extracted from these systems. Auditors are now required to better understand AI systems which can have an impact on the substance underlying the financial information.

2.10 KEY LESSONS LEARNED FROM ADOPTING AI TECHNOLOGIES

The background provided in this chapter provides practitioners and researchers with ideas and reasons why an organisation should be adopting this disruptive technology of AI to their auditing and accounting processes. This chapter also contributes to the body of knowledge of AI's contribution to the quality of auditing and accounting practices. AI can be used to assist in auditing, and concurrently, auditors can increase their technical skills regardless of which type of audit firm they work for. Many organisations can consider adopting AI to improve work speed and quality. There should be a focus on training auditors to keep pace with technological advancements in AI applications in collecting audit guides, representing knowledge, and controlling the search for such evidence within databases. Big data, RPA, data analytics, predictive analytics, ML, and blockchain are tenets of AI, and these generally help in improving the processes and quality of reporting in auditing and accounting practices. The following key lessons are learned from organisations that are adopting AI in their accounting and auditing practice:

- The use of AI gradually increased over the years since its emergence in the early 1950s;
- AI research has increased and expanded over the years;
- AI is that section of computer science that uses intelligent and smart systems to simulate human behaviour;
- The AI tools and techniques have been used by a number of business organisations;
- The accounting and auditing professions have noted the strategic importance of using AI for the benefit of the profession;
- AI can use 100% of the data to test accounting entries; this assists to limit risk associated with human error;
- Accountants and auditors alike will be required to upskill themselves with IT knowledge to enable them to use AI effectively;
- The next generation of auditors' and accountants' profile is changing due to the introduction of AI in the audit process; therefore, the educational needs will change as well;

- Cognitive technologies are used in accounting and auditing which have assisted in the efficiency and effectiveness of work done by professionals;
- AI has had a positive impact on the accounting and the auditing professions due to improved quality of information and accuracy of data that is processed by smart technologies;
- Auditors and accountants can now focus on other strategic matters of advising their clients instead of performing routine tasks that can now be performed by AI-enabled technologies;
- Financial reports are generated faster using AI technology; decision-making by accountants and auditors is now expedited; and
- AI technologies are key and important for the growth and the future of the accounting and auditing profession as they provide improvement and effectiveness of work done by professionals.

REFERENCES

Abou-El-Sood, H., Kotb, A. and Allam, A. (2015). Exploring auditors' perceptions of the usage and importance of audit information technology. *International Journal of Auditing*, 19(3), 252–266.

ACCA. (2019). Audit and technology. Retrieved online: www.accaglobal.com/content/dam/ACCA _Global/professionalinsights/audit-and-tech/pi-audit-andtechnology.pdf (Accessed on 1 June 2023).

Adeyemi, S.B., Mohammed, A.K., Ogundeji, M.G. and Oladipupo, M.T. (2014). Audit technology tools and business process assurance: Assessment of auditors' perspective in Nigeria. *Universal Journal of Industrial and Business Management*, 2(4), 93–102.

AI Topics. (2016). Brief history of artificial intelligence. Retrieved from http://aitopics.org/topic/brief-historiestimelines (Accessed on 23 June 2023).

AICPA and CIMA. (2018). Audit risk alert: General accounting and auditing developments 2018/ 19. Retrieved online: https://books.google.ro/books?id=Rpg9DwAAQBAJ&printsec=frontco ver&dq=inauthor:%22AICPA%22&hl=ro&sa=X&ved=0ahUKEwi81_vQzoDnAhVBZlAKH ehxAecQ6AEIKDAA#v=onepa ge&q&f=false (Accessed 2 April 2023).

Al-Aroud, S.F. (2020). The impact of audit evidence of artificial technologies. *Academy of Accounting and Financial Studies Journal*, 24(Special Issue 2), 1–11.

Alles, M.G. and Gray, G.L. (2020). Will the medium become the message? A framework for understanding the coming automation of the audit process. *Journal of Information Systems*, 34(2), 109–130.

Arnau, D., Arevalillo-Herráez, M., Puig, L. & González-Calero, J.A. (2013). Fundamentals of the design and the operation of an intelligent tutoring system for the learning of the arithmetical and algebraic way of solving word problems, *Computers & Education*, 63, 119–130. https:// doi.org/10.1016/j.compedu.2012.11.020

Bai, G.H. (2017). Research on the Application and Influence of Auditing Artificial Intelligence. *DEStech Transactions on Social Science, Education and Human Science*.

Baldwin, A.A., Brown, C.E. and Trinkle, B.S. (2006). Opportunities for artificial intelligence development in the accounting domain: The case for auditing. *Intelligent Systems in Accounting, Finance and Management*, 14, 77–86. https://doi.org/10.1002/isaf.277

Bertomeu, J., Cheynel, E., Floyd, E. and Pan, W. (2021). Using machine learning to detect misstatements. *Review of Accounting Studies*, 26(2), 468–519.

Byrnes, P.E., Al-Awadhi, A., Gullvist, B., Brown-Liburd, H., Teeter, R., Warren, J.D. and Vasarhelyi, M. (2018). Evolution of auditing: From the traditional approach to the future audit 1, in Chan, D.Y., Chiu, V. and Vasarhelyi, M.A. (Eds), *Continuous Auditing (Rutgers Studies in Accounting Analytics)*, Emerald Publishing, Bingley, pp. 285–297.

Chassignol, M., Khoroshavin, A., Klimova, A. and Bilyatdinova, A. (2018). Artificial Intelligence trends in education: A narrative overview. *Procedia Computer Science*, *136*, 16–24.

Chukwudi, O., Echefu, S., Boniface, U. & Victoria, C. (2018). Effect of artificial intelligence on the performance of accounting operations among accounting firms in South-East Nigeria. *Asian Journal of Economics, Business and Accounting*, *7*, 1–11. https://doi.org/10.9734/AJEBA/2018/41641

Conick, H. (2017). The past, present and future of AI in marketing. *Marketing News*, *51*(1), 26–35.

Coyne, J.G., & McMickle, P.L. (2017). Can Blockchains Serve an Accounting Purpose? *Journal of Emerging Technologies in Accounting*, *14*(2), 101–111. https://doi.org/10.2308/jeta-51910

Deloitte. (2015). Disruption ahead: Deloitte's point of view on IBM Watson. Retrieved online: www2.deloitte.com/content/dam/Deloitte/us/Documents/about-deloitte/us-ibm-watson-client.pdf (Accessed on 23 June 2023).

Demski, J.S. (2007). Is accounting an academic discipline? *Accounting Horizons*, *21*(2), 153.

Deniz, A. and Sorenson, J. (2022). Artificial intelligence and the auditor: Are you ready? Retrieved online: https://idea.caseware.com/ai-auditor-are-you-ready/ (Accessed on 3 June 2023).

Duan, Y., Edwards, S. and Dwivedi, K. (2019). Artificial intelligence for decision making in the era of Big Data–evolution, challenges and research agenda. *International Journal of Information Management*, *48*, 63–71.

Farcane, N. and Deliu, D. (2020). Stakes and challenges regarding the financial auditor's activity in the blockchain era. *Audit Financiar*, *XVIII*(1(157)/2020), 154–181.

Fraij, J., Haddad, H. and Aburumman, N. (2021). The quality of accounting information system, firm size, sector type as a case study from Jordan. *International Business Management*, *15*(2), 30–38.

Fuller, S.H. & Markelevich, A. 2020. Should accountants care about blockchain? *Journal of Corporate Accounting & Finance*, *31*, 34–46. https://doi.org/10.1002/jcaf.22424

Gartner. (2019). Why audit leaders need to adopt RPA. Retrieved online: www.gartner.com/smarterwithgartner/why-audit-leaders-need-to-adopt-rpa/ (Accessed 3 May 2023).

Geisel, A. (2018). The current and future impact of artificial intelligence on business. *International Journal of Scientific and Technology Research*, *7*(5), 116–122.

Gentner, D., Stelzer, B., Ramosaj, B. and Brecht, L. (2018). Strategic foresight of future b2b customer opportunities through machine learning. *Technology Innovation Management Review*, *8*, 5–17.

Gomber, P., Kauffman, R.J., Parker, C. and Weber, B.W. (2018). On the fintech revolution: Interpreting the forces of innovation, disruption, and transformation in financial services. *Journal of Management Information Systems*, *35*(1), 220–265.

Greenman, C. (2017). Exploring the impact of artificial intelligence on the accounting profession. *Journal of Research in Business Economics and Management*, *8*(3), 116–122.

Griffin, O. (2016). How artificial intelligence will impact accounting. *Economia*. www.icaew.com/technical/technology/artificial-intelligence/artificial-intelligence-articles/how-artificial-intelligence-will-impact-accounting

Gusai, O.P. (2019). Robot human interaction: Role of artificial intelligence in accounting and auditing. *Indian Journal of Accounting*, *51*(1), 59–62.

Haenlein, M. and Kaplan, A. (2019). A brief history of artificial intelligence: On the past, present, and future of artificial intelligence. *California Management Review*, *61*(4), 5–14.

Hallevy, G. (2013). *When Robots Kill: Artificial Intelligence under Criminal Law*. University Press of New England, Lebanon, NH.

Hansen, J.V. and Messier, W.F. (1987). Expert systems in auditing: The state of the art. *Auditing: A Journal of Practice and Theory*, *7*(1), 94–105.

Hassan, R.A. (2022). Artificial intelligence (AI) in accounting & auditing: A literature review. *Open Journal of Business and Management*, *10*, 440–465.

Hemin, A.Q. (2017). Will artificial intelligence brighten or threaten the future science, ethics, and society. Retrieved online: www.researchgate.net/publication/323535179_Will_Artificial_Intelligence_Brighten_or (Accessed on 13 August 2023).

Hirst, T. (2014). Does technological innovation increase unemployment? World Economic Forum.

Hsu, Y.S. and Lin, S.J. (2016). An emerging hybrid mechanism for information disclosure forecasting. *International Journal of Machine Learning and Cybernetics*, 7, 943–952. https://doi.org/10.1007/s13042-014-0295-4

ISACA. (2018). Impacts of blockchain on the auditing profession, Vol. 5. Retrieved online: www.isaca.org/Journal/archives/2018/Volume-5/Pages/impacts-of-Blockchain-on-the-auditingprofessionaspx (Accessed 11 May 2023)

Issa, H., Sun, T. and Vasarhelyi, M.A. (2017). Research ideas for artificial intelligence in auditing: The formalization of audit and workforce supplementation. *Journal of Emerging Technologies in Accounting*, 13(2), 1–20.

Jariwala, H.V. (2015). Analysis of financial literacy level of retail individual investors of Gujarat State and its effect on investment decision. *Journal of Business & Finance Librarianship*, 20, 133–158.

Johnson, S. (2018). Human-like A.I. will emerge in 5 to 10 years, say experts. Retrieved online: https://bigthink.com/surprising-science/computerssmart- as-humans-5-years (Accessed 11 June 2023).

Kaplan, A. and Haenlein, M. (2019). Siri, Siri, in my hand: Who's the fairest in the land? On the interpretations, illustrations, and implications of Artificial Intelligence. *Business Horizons*, 62, 15–25.

Keenoy, C.L. (1958). The impact of automation on the field of accounting. *Accounting Review*, 33(2), 230–236.

Kerzel, U. (2021). Enterprise AI canvas integrating artificial intelligence into business. *Applied Artificial Intelligence*, 35(1), 1–12.

Khamis, A. (2021). The impact of artificial intelligence in auditing and accounting decision making. www.researchgate.net/publication/352166419_The_Impact_of_Artificial_Intelligence_inAuditing_and_Accounting_Decision_Making (Accessed online on 23 May 2023).

Kitsios, F. and Kamariotou, M. (2021). Artificial intelligence and business strategy towards digital transformation: A research agenda. *Sustainability*, 13(4), 2025–2039.

Kokina, J. and Davenport, T.H. (2017). The emergence of artificial intelligence: How automation is changing auditing. *Journal of Emerging Technologies in Accounting*, 14(1), 115–122.

Kuenkaikaew, S. (2013). Predictive Audit Data Analytics: Evolving to a New Era. PhD dissertation, Rutgers Business School, Newark.

Kwak, W., Shi, Y. and Lee, F. (2021). Data mining applications in accounting and finance context, in Lee, C. F. and Lee, J. C. (Eds), *Handbook of Financial Econometrics, Mathematics, Statistics, and Machine Learning*, World Scientific, New Jersey NY, pp. 823–857.

Lam, M. (2004). Neural network techniques for financial performance prediction: Integrating fundamental and technical analysis. *Decision Support Systems*, 37(4), 567–581. https://doi.org/10.1016/S0167-9236(03)00088-5

Lee, C.S. and Tajudeen, F.P. (2020). Usage and impact of artificial intelligence on accounting: 213 evidence from Malaysian organisations. *Asian Journal of Business and Accounting*, 13, 213–240.

Li, Z. and Zheng, L. (2018). The impact of artificial intelligence on accounting, in *2018 4th International Conference on Social Science and Higher Education (ICSSHE 2018)*. Atlantis Press.

Lin, P. and Hazelbaker, T. (2019). Meeting the challenge of artificial intelligence. *CPA Journal*, 89, 48–52. Retrieved online: www.cpajournal.com/2019/07/03/meeting-the-challenge-of-artificial-intelligence/ (Accessed on 27 July 2023).

Lin, S.J. (2017). Integrated artificial intelligence-based resizing strategy and multiple criteria decision-making technique to form a management decision in an imbalanced environment. *International Journal of Machine Learning and Cybernetics*, 8, 1981–1992. https://doi.org/10.1007/s13042-016-0574-3

Lin, S.J. (2021). Integrated artificial intelligence and visualization technique for enhanced management decision in today's turbulent business environments. *Cybernetics and Systems*, 52(4), 274–292.

Luo, J., Meng, Q. and Cai, Y. (2018). Analysis of the impact of artificial intelligence application on the development of accounting industry. *Open Journal of Business and Management*, 6(4), 850–856.

Makridakis, S. (2017). The forthcoming artificial intelligence (AI) revolution: Its impact on society and firms'. *Futures*, *90*, 47–60.

Manson, S., McCartney, S. and Sherer, M. (2001). Audit automation as control within audit firms. *Accounting, Auditing & Accountability Journal*, *14*(1), 109–130.

McCarthy, J., Minsky, M., Shannon, C.E., Rochester, N. and Dartmouth College. (1956). A proposal for the Dartmouth summer research project on artificial intelligence. *AI Magazine*. https://doi.org/10.1609/aimag.v27i4.1904

Moffitt, K.C., Rozario, A.M. and Vasarhelyi, M.A. 2018. Robotic process automation for auditing. *Journal of Emerging Technologies in Accounting*, *15*, 1–10.

Nickerson, M.A. (2019). AI: New risks and rewards. Retrieved online: https://sfmagazine.com/post-entry/april2019-ai-new-risksand-rewards (Accessed on 18 July 2023).

Noordin, N., Hussainey, K. and Hayek, A. (2022). The use of artificial intelligence and audit quality: An analysis from the perspectives of external auditors in the UAE. *Journal of Risk and Financial Management*, *15*(8), 1–14.

Nwakaego, D.A. and Ikechukwu, O.I. (2015). The effect of accounts payable ratio on the financial performance of food and beverages manufacturing companies in Nigeria. *Journal of Research in Business and Management*, *3*, 15–21.

Oláh, J., Aburumman, N., Popp, J., Khan, M.A., Haddad, H. and Kitukutha, H. (2020). Impact of Industry 4.0 on environmental sustainability. *Sustainability*, *12*(11), 46–74.

Omoteso, K. (2012). The application of artificial intelligence in auditing: Looking back to the future. *Expert Systems with Applications*, *39*, 8490–8495.

Ovaska-Few, S. (2017). How artificial intelligence is changing accounting. *Journal of Accountancy*. Retrieved online at: www.journalofaccountancy.com/newsletters/2017/oct/artificial-intelligence-changing-accounting.html (Accessed on 24 June 2023).

Payne, M., Peltier, J. and Barger, V.A. (2021). Enhancing the value co-creation process: Artificial intelligence and mobile banking service platforms. *Journal of Research in Interactive Marketing*, *15*(1), 68–85.

Pedrosa, I., Costa, C.J. and Aparicio, M. (2020). Determinants adoption of computer-assisted auditing tools (CAATs). *Cognition, Technology and Work*, *22*(3), 565–583.

Poola, I. (2017). How artificial intelligence in impacting real life every day. *International Journal of Advance Research and Development*, *2*(10), 35–49.

Puthukulam, G., Ravikumar, A., Sharma, R.V. and Meesaala, K.M. (2021). Auditors' perception on the impact of artificial intelligence on professional skepticism and judgment in Oman. *Universal Journal of Accounting and Finance*, *9*, 1184–1190.

Raji, I. and Buolamwini, J. (2019). Actionable Auditing: Investigating the Impact of Publicly Naming Biased Performance Results of Commercial AI Products. Paper presented at the 2019 AAAI/ACM Conference on Artificial Intelligence, Ethics, and Society, Honolulu, HI, USA, January 27–28.

Reynoso, R. (2019). Four types of artificial intelligence, Learn.G.2Crowd. Retrieved online at: https://learn.g2crowd.com/types-of-artificial-intelligence (Accessed on 24 June 2023).

Roetzer, P. (2014). *The Marketing Performance Code: Strategies and Technologies to Build and Measure Business Success*. John Wiley & Sons, Inc., Hoboken, NJ.

Rozario, A.M. and Thomas, C. (2019). Reengineering the audit with blockchain and smart contracts. *Journal of Emerging Technologies in Accounting*, *16*(1), 21–35.

Russel, S., Perset, K. & Grobelnik, M. (2023). Updates to the OECD's definition of an AI system explained. Retrieved online at: https://oecd.ai/en/wonk/ai-system-definition-update

Salem, M. (2012). An Overview of Research on Auditor's Responsibility to Detect Fraud on Financial Statements. *Journal of Global Business Management*, *8*(2), 218.

Schmitz, J. and Leoni, G. (2019). Accounting and Auditing at the Time of Blockchain Technology: A Research Agenda. *Australian Accounting Review*, *29*, 331–342. https://doi.org/10.1111/auar.12286

Shukla, S. and Vijay, J.F. (2013). Applicability of artificial intelligence in different fields of life. *International Journal of Scientific Engineering and Research*, *1*(1), 29–39.

Silver, D., Huang, A., Maddison, C.J., Guez, A., Sifre, L., Van Den Driessche, G. and Dieleman, S. (2016). Mastering the game of Go with deep neural networks and tree search. *Nature, 529*(7587), 484–489.

Sun, T. and Vasarhelyi, M. (2016). Sentiment features of conference calls and internal control quality: An application of deep learning technology. Working paper, The State University of New Jersey.

Sutton, S.G., Holt, M. and Arnold, V. (2016). "The reports of my death are greatly exaggerated" – Artificial intelligence research in accounting. *International Journal of Accounting Information Systems. Research Symposium on Information Integrity & Information Systems Assurance, 22,* 60–73.

Taghizadeh, A., Mohammad, R., Dariush, S. and Jafar, M. (2013). Artificial intelligence, its abilities and challenges. *International Journal of Business and Behavioral Sciences, 3*(12), 30–34.

Tan, B.S. and Low, K.Y. (2019). Blockchain as the database engine in the accounting system. *Australian Accounting Review, 29*(2), 312–318.

Thibodeau, J.C. (2003). The development and transferability of task knowledge. *Auditing: A Journal of Practice and Theory, 22*(1), 47–67. https://doi.org/10.2308/aud.2003.22.1.47.

Thottoli, M.M. (2021). Impact of information communication technology competency among auditing professionals. *Accounting Analysis Auditing, 8*(2), 38–47.

United States. (2016). *Artificial Intelligence, Automation, and the Economy.* Executive Office of the President, Washington, DC.

Vlacic, B., Corbo, L., Silva, S.C. and Dabic, M. (2021). The evolving role of artificial intelligence in marketing: A review and research agenda. *Journal of Business Research, 134*(5), 187–203.

Zhang, Y., Xiong, F., Xie, Y., Fan, X. and Gu, H. (2020). The impact of artificial intelligence and blockchain on the accounting profession. *IEEE Access, 8,* 110461–110477.

Chapter 3

New auditing perspectives for a blockchain-based accounting system in the public sector

Ilse Morgan

3.1 INTRODUCTION: BACKGROUND AND DRIVING FORCES

Using blockchain technology can improve information gathering, distribution, and governance across all industries (Bambara & Allen, 2018), and as a result, has become increasingly popular in the accounting and auditing professions (Kabir et al., 2022; Kahyaoglu Bozkuş & Aksoy, 2021). Blockchain technology offers a reliable and transparent method of recording and verifying transactions and is recognised as a shared and irreversible data structure (Burns, Steele, Cohen & Ramamoorti, 2020; Ferri, Spano & Ginesti, 2021; Kahyaoglu Bozkuş & Aksoy, 2021).

Ferri et al. (2021) support the view that substantial technological advancements have been a key driver in adopting blockchain in accounting and auditing. Ferri et al. (2021) further note that introducing blockchain technology enhances the reliability of auditing procedures and improves the overall accounting and audit processes in terms of efficiency and effectiveness (Burns et al., 2020; Cangemi, 2021; Sastry, Lee & Teoh, 2021).

The evolution of information and communication technologies and the automation of the audit process (Ferri et al., 2021) resulted in a significant reduction in the time spent on account reconciliations (Han, Shiwakoti, Jarvis, Mordi & Botchie, 2023), confirmation from external sources, observation of processes, inquiries, and source document verification. When implementing blockchain in the public sector, it is essential to consider factors such as auditability, transparency, traceability, and decentralisation, which could benefit the auditing profession greatly when used correctly (Dai & Vasarhelyi, 2017; Guo, Chen, Li, Li & Lu, 2022).

As a result of auditing the distributed ledger technology (DLT) in blockchain, the accounting and financial reporting standards and regulations are bound to be impacted, as stated by Cangemi (2021). DLT securely replicates, shares, and synchronises data across a distributed computer network using cryptography and consensus algorithms, ensuring data accuracy and integrity without a central authority (Aghili, 2023). New reporting standards and regulations are required with additional controls to address the new risks and weaknesses highlighted by the audit and risk assessment processes, as also pointed out by Cangemi (2021) and Aghili (2023).

3.2 DEVELOPMENT OF BLOCKCHAIN TECHNOLOGY AND THE MODERNISATION OF PUBLIC SECTOR ACCOUNTING SYSTEMS (TECHNOLOGY)

Blockchain was initially introduced as a distributed ledger for storing and sharing cryptocurrency transactions that share blocks across a peer-to-peer (P2P) network (Batubara,

DOI: 10.1201/9781003382706-3

Ubacht & Janssen, 2019; Liu, Yu, Li, Ji & Leung, 2020). The blocks in the chain include a secure, unique hash value that cryptographically commits to its contents, a timestamp, and the previous hash value and transaction details (Berryhill, Bourgery & Hanson, 2018; ECA, 2020). Every node also holds a copy of the blocks in the network to ensure integrity (Batubara et al., 2019).

Blockchain is defined as a decentralised, distributed digital and immutable ledger (Bambara & Allen, 2018; Liu et al., 2020; Kahyaoglu Bozkuş & Aksoy, 2021; Peng, 2022) used for recording transactions across several devices or computers, resulting in lower operational costs (Bambara & Allen, 2018; Berryhill et al., 2018). The distributed ledger is considered to be a more trustworthy ledger, preventing the retroactive or unauthorised change of records or transactions (Berryhill et al., 2018; Ferri et al., 2021) without changing all the subsequent blocks accordingly (Ferri et al., 2021).

Blockchain technology introduced the triple-entry accounting system bookkeeping to prevent transaction fraud and minimise errors (Dai & Vasarhelyi, 2017; Burns et al., 2020). The triple-entry system automates the accounting function in terms of *"recognition, measurement, presentation and disclosure"* of transactions (Aghili, 2023:65). This third entry into a blockchain could enhance transparency and security in the public sector through the *"self-verifying accounting information system"* (Dai & Vasarhelyi, 2017:66). This accounting system enables continuous data sharing, transaction visibility (transparency) and reporting for related entities and stakeholders (Dai & Vasarhelyi, 2017; Burns et al., 2020). The public sector with a blockchain financial system based on algorithms offers real-time access to financial statements for internal and external stakeholders (Dai & Vasarhelyi, 2017; Yermack, 2017; Burns et al., 2020; Kahyaoglu Bozkuş & Aksoy, 2021).

The triple-entry blockchain accounting solution offers transparency and reduces audit time and associated costs while enhancing operational efficiency and accountability within the public sector (Dai & Vasarhelyi, 2017; Mosteanu & Faccia, 2020; Muller, 2021; Aghili, 2023). A blockchain-based accounting system significantly affects the role of the related audit and assurance processes, with the potential for enhanced audit efficiency and effectiveness and related reports (Aghili, 2023:63).

Blockchain technology can be implemented as a global governance tool using a public blockchain in a distributed and decentralised manner (Bambara & Allen, 2018; Aghili, 2023), enabling centralised governance and enhancing transparency and accountability through distributed ledger architecture, cryptography, and consensus mechanisms (Liu et al., 2020). Blockchain technology contributes to data security, traceability, and transparency by being available to all participants within a governance structure or network with full disclosure of all changes (Dai & Vasarhelyi, 2017; Bambara & Allen, 2018; O'Leary, 2018; Yermack, 2019; Burns et al., 2020; Ferri et al., 2021; Kahyaoglu Bozkuş & Aksoy, 2021). The transaction is not stored in the database of a central authority but by each user as a node in a blockchain network (Dai & Vasarhelyi, 2017; Berryhill et al., 2018), such as a public and shared network, which anyone can join with no restrictions on participation (Liu et al., 2020).

Blockchain can be classified into four main types of blockchain technology, i.e., public, consortium, private, and hybrid (Peng, 2022:34).

I   **Public (unpermissioned/permissionless ledgers)** (Berryhill et al., 2018; Guo et al., 2022; Aghili, 2023) – Anyone can maintain and access data in the open public blockchain system (Liu et al., 2020) and the applications are easy to use. The system operates fully decentralised without being controlled by a specific organisation (Paul, Sarkar

& Mukherjee, 2014; Burns et al., 2020). Transactions in a public blockchain are open and anonymous (Aghili, 2023), and each node on the blockchain participates in the authorising process by "*sending, receiving, monitoring, and verifying the transactions*" (Liu et al., 2020:10). Such openness may cause concerns regarding the privacy and security of transactions (Liu et al., 2020).

II **Consortium** – The system is semi-private and open to only consortium members gaining access through registration and authorisation (Liu et al., 2020; Aghili, 2023). Unlike public blockchains, the consortium blockchain does not authorise all nodes to "*send, receive*", monitor, or validate transactions (Liu et al., 2020:10).

III **Private (permissioned ledgers)** are mostly closed, and only authorised nodes can join and "*participate in the blockchain*" (Liu et al., 2020:10). This multichain ledger system can be used by organisations, individuals, or government institutions (Dinh, Wang, Chen, Liu & Tan, 2017). Using private ledgers can enhance auditability but cannot completely resolve the trust issues relating to "*security and privacy*" (Liu et al., 2020:6). Berryhill et al. (2018) noted that permissioned ledgers might be the most suitable for the public sector to enhance accountability due to transparent transactions to all stakeholders without unauthorised individuals having access to transact (Liu et al., 2020).

IV **Hybrid blockchains** involve private and public ledgers, but access is customised and controlled by a single institution, providing increased "*security and flexible*" implementation (Aghili, 2023:265). Adopting a stand-alone or hybrid system requires identifying appropriate and trustworthy agents, serving as nodes for transaction verification, with a certain portion of trustworthy and non-corruptible nodes needed depending on the network's consensus algorithm to maintain data record integrity (WEF, 2020:32).

For a transaction to be recorded and verified, the majority of nodes in all these network transactions must be reviewed and authenticated through predefined rules created within smart contracts (Berryhill et al., 2018; Aghili, 2023).

3.2.1 Smart contracts in blockchain

Smart contracts are digital transaction protocols encoded on a blockchain to verify, control, and self-execute an agreement if all the parties meet predefined rules (Dai & Vasarhelyi, 2017; Liu et al., 2020). Auditors need to understand how smart contracts and other artificial intelligence (AI) applications are being used and ensure that they have been adequately designed and implemented. Smart contracts are automated or "*self-executing contracts*" (Berryhill et al., 2018:19), coded on the blockchain by using computerised algorithms or programs (Bambara & Allen, 2018; Peng, 2022). The seller and buyer's contractual terms or agreements are directly encoded to produce transparent and real-time information (Berryhill et al., 2018; Han et al., 2023), e.g., the electronic identification mechanism within electronic funds transfers (EFT) (inter-bank payments). Thus, combining blockchain with smart contracts allows for more "*security*", confidence, and assurance in record-keeping and monitoring (Bambara & Allen, 2018).

Integrating AI, blockchain, and automated decision-making can add additional value to business processes in the public sector that involve multiple stakeholders (Burns et al., 2020; Liu et al., 2020). AI models embedded in smart contracts within the blockchain can automate processes and enforce business logic based on predefined rules and conditions (Han et al., 2023), such as recommending expired products for recall, executing transactions, resolving disputes, and selecting sustainable shipping methods in supply chain management (Dai & Vasarhelyi, 2017). These capabilities in smart contracts produce a "*digital workflow*" (Berryhill et al., 2018:19) or audit trail mechanism within the network (Regueiro, Seco, Gutiérrez-Agüero, Urquizu & Mansell, 2021) and can "*remove friction between agencies*"; reduce fraud and errors; and increase speed, effectiveness, and efficiency (Berryhill et al., 2018; Dai & Vasarhelyi, 2017).

Machine learning (ML) techniques and smart contracts can be applied within data analytics to automate data processing, perform complex calculations, and trigger actions based on specific events (Liu et al., 2020). Similarly, accounting standards and policies could be automated through smart contracts encoded into the software (Dai & Vasarhelyi, 2017). Dai and Vasarhelyi (2017:72) further suggest that smart contracts can enhance AI by incorporating "*big data and predictive analytics*" within the public sector's accounting processes, thereby enhancing its effectiveness for decision-making and reporting purposes (Burns et al., 2020).

3.2.2 Blockchain and other AI applications

While blockchain securely stores encrypted data through a decentralised, distributed, and immutable ledger (Liu et al., 2020), AI serves as the brain or system responsible for analysing the collected data and making decisions accordingly (Peng, 2022). AI can rapidly read, interpret, and analyse data within blockchain, transforming the future of information systems by producing automated decision-making or "*group intelligence*" (Peng, 2022:115). Blockchain helps AI scale large volumes of data by providing more trustworthy and transparent data and actionable information, potentially enhancing accountability and security in digital transactions, reporting, and results (Liu et al., 2020).

The various AI applications that can be combined with blockchain in the public sector accounting and information systems are:

I **Supply chain management** – Keeping track of assets or inventory (Xu, Chen & Kou, 2019) as they change ownership or location by recording essential events and agreements through relevant and timely data stored on the blockchain. All the required quality assurance standards (Xu et al., 2019) can be continuously monitored by accurately documenting each step in the supply chain, thereby ensuring a transparent and traceable audit trail (Aghili, 2023; Han et al., 2023).

II **Internet of Things (IoT) and Internet of Service (IoS)** – IoT involves multiple devices being interconnected through networking and computing capabilities, thus allowing for data "*collection, analysis, and sharing*" (Liu et al., 2020:11). It can be effectively utilised in applications such as smart healthcare, logistics, smart homes and cities, and agriculture (Liu et al., 2020) and is therefore very useful in the public sector. Devices connected to the Internet can utilise blockchain as a reliable and accessible storage alternative by using smart contracts to facilitate globally distributed computing capabilities (Dai & Vasarhelyi, 2017; Liu et al., 2020). Devices can rely on the blockchain for secure software and configuration update notifications. Delegated access control can be implemented, including physical or remote access control for device locking and unlocking or updates. The IoT is still in its initial stage and is primarily used for real-time data collection, remote monitoring, and control systems (Dai & Vasarhelyi, 2017). As technology becomes smarter and AI is integrated into more applications, the IoTs will transform into a network of autonomous devices

(Bambara & Allen, 2018). These smart devices will have the ability to communicate with each other and make independent, intelligent, and real-time decisions, removing the need for human intervention or interpretation (Dai & Vasarhelyi, 2017; Bambara & Allen, 2018).

III **Metered access to resources and services** – Monitoring can be provided by IoT or IoS devices and related smart contracts in blockchain for utility usage, e.g., electricity or municipal services (Liu et al., 2020).

IV **Digital rights and intellectual property (IP) management** – A blockchain can provide a trusted registry of digital assets (media) or other intellectual property and can manage, delegate, or transfer access and rights to information for those assets (Vyas et al., 2022). Note that media are not necessarily stored on the blockchain itself due to limited storage capacity.

V **Verification and proof of existence and identity management** – A blockchain can record evidence of the existence of data or documents by creating a timestamped record of a cryptographic hash of the document contents. The timestamped record can represent the authentication or witnessing of corresponding physical documents by trusted third parties (Aghili, 2023).

VI **Interdivisional accounting** – In the public sector, the different sectors and departments have different regulatory or governance needs to control their internal accounting and to share accounting information or reports with other departments.

VII **Machine learning (ML) and AI** – Blockchain and ML can be integrated by using AI to replace human judgement in terms of data recording, processing, and analysis to improve "*communications and networking systems*" (Liu et al., 2020:5) and decision-making (Burns et al., 2020). Liu et al. (2020:6) further suggest that blockchain can enhance ML "*for data sharing, security and privacy, decentralised intelligence*", and reliable decision-making. Additionally, ML can enhance "*blockchain for energy and resource efficiency, scalability, and intelligent smart contracts*" (Liu et al., 2020:26). Blockchain can function more efficiently if ML is used to detect and prevent theft, fraud, and illegal transactions on the blockchain and "*create and execute*" complex smart contracts for greater effectiveness (Liu et al., 2020:7).

VIII **Robotic process automation (RPA) and intelligent process automation (IPA)** – RPA software can function on other applications and software to automate tasks that require human reasoning and decision-making from structured data and deterministic processes (Moffitt et al., 2018; Zhang, 2019). To manage inference-based processes for problem-solving and decision-making, IPA combines AI applications with RPA (Zhang, 2019), which is mainly used in the banking and insurance industries (ECA, 2020). The automated tasks could include data extraction, classifications, and analysis. Although underexplored in accounting and auditing processes, RPA and IPA enable the automation of audits due to the AI applications in accounting, consequently expanding the scope to continuous auditing (ECA, 2020).

IX **Data management and analysis** – Blockchain can create a metadata layer for decentralised data sharing and analytics. Although large datasets are unlikely to be stored on them, a blockchain can help discover and integrate those datasets and data analytics services (Burns et al., 2020). Access control mechanisms implemented on a blockchain could allow public data sources to be integrated more easily with private datasets and data analysis services.

3.2.3 Blockchain and data analytics technology

Storing and managing data through blockchain technology can potentially enhance the security, transparency, and reliability of *"real-time and verifiable"* data used for the purpose of data analytics (Dai & Vasarhelyi, 2017:64; Liu et al., 2020). The processes automation and business logic through smart contracts further enhance the efficiency and effectiveness of data analytics for continuous assurance purposes (Dai & Vasarhelyi, 2017).

Blockchain technology adds to the utilisation of data analytics by providing secure and transparent data that is available to everyone in the network under a pseudonym (Muller, 2021; Kahyaoglu Bozkuş & Aksoy, 2021). The combination of big data and blockchain technology presents various opportunities in the public sector, enabling data governance, traceability, and fraud detection and enhancing data privacy, security, reliability, and transparency (Dai & Vasarhelyi, 2017; Liu et al., 2020; Muheidat, Pater, Tammisetty, Tawalbeh & Tawalbeh, 2021).

While there are still some technical challenges to overcome (Liu et al., 2020), the potential benefits of combining these two technologies are significant in effectively conducting continuous audits. Big data and blockchain technology are two emerging fields that have the potential to revolutionise the way we store, manage, and analyse data (Liu et al., 2020).

Blockchain affects data and data analytics in the following ways that impact the continuous audit process:

I **Data immutability:** A key feature of blockchain is storing sensitive or critical data, such as financial records, healthcare data or supply chain data, in an immutable and *"tamper-proof"* way (Dai & Vasarhelyi, 2017:73; Liu et al., 2020; Berryhill et al., 2018). Using blockchain technology to store data can ensure that data is protected from unauthorised access or manipulation and it cannot be altered when it is updated (Muller, 2021). The cryptographic hash total or value function ensures that any changes will be disclosed to the network (Muller, 2021).

II **Data source and traceability:** Blockchain technology provides a way to track the origin of the data, ensure its authenticity and provide a layer of evidential support (Regueiro et al., 2021). This is particularly important in industries such as health and food supply chains, where it is critical to ensure that data has not been tampered with or altered. By using blockchain technology to track the source of data or an item (Lee, Fiedler & Mautz, 2018), the public sector can improve transparency and trust in their data.

III **Data privacy and security:** Blockchain technology provides enhanced data privacy and security through user control, allowing users to keep access to their data encrypted (Liu et al., 2020). This is particularly important in the healthcare sector, where patient data must be kept secure and confidential (Liu et al., 2020). Using blockchain technology for data storage and management gives assurance to government departments that their data is secured and protected. Integrating big data and blockchain increases the value of the technology by using stored and secure data and real-time information for predictive analytics (Liu et al., 2020; Peng, 2022).

IV **Data sharing:** Blockchain technology can also be used to enable secure and transparent data sharing between different parties (Liu et al., 2020). This is especially useful in financial or supply chain management, giving multiple parties access to the same data (Hewa, Ylianttila & Liyanage, 2021). Using blockchain to share data, public sector departments can ensure data security and accessibility only to authorised parties (Hewa et al., 2021).

V **Immutable data storage:** Blockchain's ability to store data in a secure, decentralised, and immutable way (Liu et al., 2020; Berryhill et al., 2018) makes it an ideal solution for storing large amounts of transactional data that need to be tamper-proof, e.g., financial records or supply chain data. By using blockchain technology to store big data, government departments can protect their data from unauthorised access or manipulation (Liu et al., 2020). However, blockchain is not a database equipped to store large amounts of general data (Berryhill et al., 2018).

VI **Scalability and performance:** One of the challenges of using blockchain technology for big data is scalability and performance (Berryhill et al., 2018). Blockchain networks can become slow and inefficient as the size of the network grows. However, solutions such as "*sharding*" and "*off-chain*" scaling can assist in improving the performance of blockchain networks for big data applications (Liu et al., 2020).

VII **Data analytics:** Big data is generally used as a source for data analytics and ML applications, with the blockchain providing secure and reliable data (Liu et al., 2020). By using blockchain technology to store big data, government departments can ensure that their data is accurate and tamper-proof (Liu et al., 2020), which is critical for ML algorithms that rely on clean and reliable data.

Auditors in the public sector need to understand blockchain technology and how transactions are recorded, how the system is secured, and how data is verified before auditing a blockchain-based accounting system (Dai & Vasarhelyi, 2017). It further requires carefully and continuously evaluating the control environment, related technologies and applications, data integrity, and third-party data sources.

Auditors need to know the benefits but also be aware of all the potential risks and weaknesses associated with using blockchain in the public sector and ensure that the system functions correctly. The risks, characteristics, challenges, and processes when conducting a continuous audit in a blockchain-based accounting system in the public sector are investigated in the sections that follow.

3.3 ACCESS TO INFORMATION AND TRANSPARENCY FOR ENHANCED ACCOUNTABILITY

Access to information and transparency are critical components of accountability in any institution or system (Zúñiga, 2018; Koene et al., 2019). Transparency involves the openness and clearness of information "*for public scrutiny*" (Tõnurist & Hanson, n.d.:108; Ginsberg, Carey, Halchin & Keegan, 2012; Office of the Auditor-General New Zealand [OAG-NZ], 2016). A transparent system allows for information to be readily available, understandable, and presented in a way that facilitates accountability (Ginsberg et al., 2012; OECD, 2016; Zúñiga, 2018; Gabriel et al., 2019; Liu et al., 2020). The World Economic Forum (WEF) believes that the use of blockchain technology within the global supply chains might provide opportunities to increase trust and "*transparency by reducing discretionary decision-making*" (WEF, 2020:21). The WEF suggests that blockchain technology will enable decentralised, distributed, and secure file storage and transfer of information (WEF, 2020:6, 30, 36), providing transparent records of transactions and activities. Blockchain could be an effective tracking mechanism for monitoring transactions that can increase data integrity, security, and transparency (Dai & Vasarhelyi, 2017), thereby empowering all stakeholders and reducing costs to the taxpayer from government corruption (WEF, 2020:6, 30, 36).

To further enhance accountability in the public sector, it would be beneficial to implement more stringent legislative requirements that mandate transparent public data, communication and reporting of all decision-making activities, performance information, and transactions (IIA, 2019). Since the blockchain ledger is shared with all nodes within the network, it ensures transparency and avoids a single point of failure (Vyas et al., 2022; Aghili, 2023). Transparency, however, includes providing clear and concise financial statements, disclosures of significant accounting policies, and explanations of any unusual transactions or events. In addition, auditors may also need access to other information such as minutes of meetings, contracts, and other relevant documentation to assess the effectiveness of the control environment and compliance and risk management processes. Sufficient and continual access to information can maintain the credibility of the audit report (IIA, 2019). Transparency is important because it allows stakeholders to understand the basis for the auditors' findings presented in the audit report and to assess the credibility of the report.

The use of AI and ML within blockchain has the potential to increase due diligence and monitoring by improving the accuracy, availability, and transparency of data; the effectiveness and efficiency of operations; and the identification of regulatory gaps (Burns et al., 2020; WEF, 2020; Kossow, Windwehr & Jenkins, 2021). In blockchain-enabled ML systems, data is recorded on a tamper-proof, datapoint-by-datapoint basis, providing a simple way for continuously auditing automated decisions (Burns et al., 2020). Blockchain can further ensure the reliability of the data and ML models through its "transparent accountability and auditability features" and provide a traceable audit trail of the "*ML decision-making processes*" (Burns et al., 2020; Liu et al., 2020:6–7).

3.4 BENEFITS AND FEATURES OF BLOCKCHAIN-BASED AUDITS

Blockchain can significantly change the audit process by providing a more secure, transparent, and efficient way of verifying, analysing, and continuously auditing financial and other types of data (Burns et al., 2020). Blockchain-based audits involve using blockchain technology to verify, analyse, and audit financial data and transactions on a continuous basis (Burns et al., 2020). Auditors in the public sector need to understand blockchain technology and how transactions are recorded (Lee et al., 2018), how the system is secured, and how data is verified before auditing a blockchain-based accounting system (Dai & Vasarhelyi, 2017). It further requires carefully evaluating the control environment, related technologies and applications, data integrity, and third-party data sources. Auditors need to know the benefits but also be aware of all the potential risks, weaknesses, and challenges associated with using blockchain in the public sector and ensure that the system functions correctly (Lee et al., 2018).

Key features and benefits of blockchain-based audits:

I **Increased transparency:** Blockchain offers a secure and transparent method of recording transactions that cannot be altered (Liu et al., 2020; Aghili, 2023; Han, Shiwakoti, Jarvis, Mordi & Botchie, 2023). By using blockchain technology to record financial transactions, auditors can easily verify the accuracy of financial statements and ensure that there are no discrepancies or errors (Han et al., 2023) on a continuous basis. Increased transparency is possible using the triple-entry accounting system, promising improved efficiency and trust (Dai & Vasarhelyi, 2017; Yermack, 2017). Transparency is enhanced by providing evidential support in audits or reviews by maintaining a record of supporting documents and the related transaction details (i.e., date and user details) (Aghili, 2023). These improved transparency mechanisms within the audit process effectively manage and mitigate audit risks while also generating quality reports (Dai & Vasarhelyi, 2017).

II **Improved data security:** Blockchain technology provides enhanced data security by allowing users to control access to their data and keep it encrypted (Liu et al., 2020). This is particularly important in industries such as finance, where sensitive financial data must be kept secure and confidential.

III **Enhanced audit trail:** Blockchain technology provides an enhanced and detailed audit trail by recording all transactions in a secure and immutable way (ECA, 2020; Sastry et al., 2021; Han et al., 2023). This makes it easy for auditors to continuously trace the transaction flow and verify that all transactions are properly authorised and completely recorded (Dai & Vasarhelyi, 2017; Kozlowski, 2018). The audit trail embedded in the blockchain is an AI transparency mechanism implemented through smart contracts (Regueiro et al., 2021; Aghili, 2023). The data stored in the blockchain cannot be altered (Burns et al., 2020), ensuring the integrity and traceability of audit evidence, as it is distributed and verified across multiple nodes (Lee et al., 2018; Regueiro et al., 2021), making fraud prevention and detection almost unnecessary (Burns et al., 2020; Liu et al., 2020). Blockchain technology further guarantees the reliability and authenticity of audit evidence by keeping an unchangeable record of origin, which means non-repudiation is ensured (Regueiro et al., 2021).

IV **Automation of audit processes:** Smart contracts can be used to automate audit processes and perform continuous audits in real-time (Kozlowski, 2018), leaving an audit trail on the blockchain (Han et al., 2023). Smart contracts can be programmed to verify financial transactions and flag any irregularities, making the audit process more efficient and effective (Kozlowski, 2018; Han et al., 2023).

V **Increased efficiency and reduced costs:** Blockchain technology benefits the audit process through automation, e.g., and reconciliation and provides a tamper-proof audit trail (Sastry et al., 2021; Han et al., 2023). This can further reduce human error and the time and costs associated with traditional audit processes (Kokina et al., 2017; Han et al., 2023). Extracting an increased amount of data for continuous audit purposes in terms of data analysis can be made easier by using blockchain (ECA, 2020; Han et al., 2023).

The technical and regulatory challenges (par 3.7 and 3.8) relating to blockchain technology will, however, affect general adoption in the audit industry and the public sector and need to be addressed through regulatory standards, policies, and procedures (Bambara & Allen, 2018).

3.5 THE BLOCKCHAIN-BASED AUDIT PROCESS

Auditing blockchain architecture requires a comprehensive and multi-disciplinary approach considering technical and non-technical (regulatory or qualitative) factors. Auditors should comprehensively understand blockchain (Lee et al., 2018) and the relevant compliance and regulatory framework within the public sector, as well as the ability to analyse complex technical systems on a more continuous basis.

3.5.1 Understanding the blockchain technology and environment

The public sector auditor must obtain an understanding of the purpose, nature, and characteristics of the blockchain-based accounting system and identify the key business and financial processes, the transactions involved, the control environment, and the risks (Lee et al., 2018). The auditor further needs to understand the type of blockchain (public or private), the consensus mechanism, the smart contracts, the governance structure, and the roles and responsibilities of the participants. Assessing the blockchain architecture typically involves analysing the design and implementation of a blockchain system to ensure its reliability (credibility), security, and compliance with policies, industry best practices, and relevant laws and regulations. The blockchain platform has five distinct layers, i.e., the data, network, consensus, smart contract, and application layer (Liu et al., 2020; Peng, 2022). The transactional data within the data layer can be "*generated from different applications*" (Liu et al., 2020:8).

Auditors need to be aware of all the potential risks and weaknesses associated with using blockchain in the public sector and ensure that the system functions correctly.

3.5.2 Assessing the risks and evaluating controls related to blockchain

Blockchain technologies, AI, and smart contracts have inherent risks that may pose challenges in the public sector in terms of governance and risk management processes, related controls, and legal and regulatory compliance (Bambara & Allen, 2018; Burns et al., 2020). Standards and regulations within a governance framework are required for control, oversight, and monitoring of these risks and to implement blockchain and related AI effectively (Bambara & Allen, 2018; ECA, 2020). The auditor must continuously assess the risks and the design and implementation of controls within the blockchain system to mitigate the identified risks (Dai & Vasarhelyi, 2017; Lee et al., 2018). These controls may include access controls, encryption, monitoring, reconciliation, cryptographic mechanisms, smart contract code reviews, authentication, authorisation, verification, and permission settings.

The risks related to a blockchain-based accounting system in the public sector are:

I **Performance (flexibility management)**: Currently, the performance of blockchain technology may hinder its application in specific domains, e.g., banking and payment services, especially those that demand high transaction processing rates (Bambara & Allen, 2018). Blockchain technology is still limited in adequately processing thousands of transactions per second (Bambara & Allen, 2018; Liu et al., 2020), especially considering the extent of the public sector's operations. Continuously auditing and monitoring these operations is necessary to improve assurance services (ECA, 2020).

II **Network architecture**: The sustainable network architecture of a blockchain system is another critical area to consider. Auditors should examine the network topology for resilience, fault tolerance, and sufficient backup mechanisms for disaster recovery purposes (Aghili, 2023).

III **Interoperability**: Achieving interoperability between different blockchain implementations is essential to facilitate continuous communication and interface between various blockchain networks (Burns et al., 2020). Such interfacing improves optimisation through increased intelligence and being more informative (Dai & Vasarhelyi, 2017), but there could be limitations due to a possible lack of operating standards

(Bambara & Allen, 2018) and adequate resources. However, blockchain establishes direct communication for users in a P2P network without the intervention of an agent, thus enhancing data *"security and privacy"* and reducing the related resources and cost implications (Liu et al., 2020:4, 5).

IV **Data privacy and security:** Blockchain systems store sensitive data, and auditors should continuously assess the security measures that are in place to protect that data (Aghili, 2023). Security measures include reviewing the encryption protocols used to secure data in transit and at rest and access controls to prevent unauthorised access.

V **Consensus mechanisms:** The consensus mechanism used by a blockchain network is critical to its security and reliability (Burns et al., 2020). Auditors should examine the consensus algorithm used by the network and continuously assess its vulnerability to cyber-attacks (Burns et al., 2020), system failure, and its ability to handle high volumes of transactions (Aghili, 2023).

VI **Cryptography algorithms:** The cryptographic algorithms and protocols used by the blockchain ensure data security in terms of *"confidentiality, integrity and authentication"* (Aghili, 2023:23). The auditor should continuously analyse this to ensure its robustness and include examining the encryption methods used to secure transactions and the hashing algorithms used to generate block hashes.

VII **Scalability:** Blockchain networks require each node to be continuously aware of every single *"transaction occurring globally"* (Bambara & Allen, 2018:85; Liu et al., 2020). This requirement can create scalability challenges and put a strain on the network (Burns et al., 2020). The goal is to achieve higher transaction efficiency (Liu et al., 2020) without compromising the *"decentralisation and security"* that blockchain networks provide (Bambara & Allen, 2018:85).

VIII **Smart contracts:** Smart contracts are integral to the architecture of blockchain and can be hacked by rewriting the ledger, altering the smart contracts, and introducing new smart contracts (Burns et al., 2020; Vyas, 2022). Auditors should continuously assess the design and implementation of the underlying code to ensure they are secure and free from such vulnerabilities (Aghili, 2023). This assurance includes analysing the code for potential flaws and reviewing the contract's functionality to ensure it operates as intended (Aghili, 2023).

IX **Authenticity, complexity, legal compliance, and viability:** Blockchain enables reliable and transparent data in AI systems, enhancing the confidence of stakeholders in the quality and validity of AI algorithms (Liu et al., 2020:28). Depending on the use, the blockchain may be subject to legal and regulatory requirements (Bambara & Allen, 2018; Aghili, 2023).

3.5.3 Conducting the audit

The auditor must clearly define the audit objectives and the scope of the audit after identifying the risks related to the audit and the assessment of the control environment. The scope of the audit will depend on the risk assessment and the weaknesses identified in the internal controls. Auditors should also assess whether the system meets all the relevant compliance requirements, regulations, or data protection laws on a continuous basis.

Continuous auditing uses automated tools and technologies to assess and verify transactions and data in real-time or *"near real-time"*, providing assurance of the reliability, accuracy, and completeness of the information recorded in a blockchain system (Dai & Vasarhelyi, 2017). Continuous auditing is an automated process to continually collect data from systems supporting the business processes (Deloitte, 2010). Continuous auditing further provides ongoing and more timely assessment of risks and controls using information technology (IT), especially in larger quantities of "*transactions or big data*" (IIA, 2015:1). Another benefit of using continuous auditing and data analytics within the blockchain and other technologies is the cost-effectiveness and increased audit efficiency and audit coverage (ECA, 2020).

The following are examples of audit procedures that could be performed but do not represent a comprehensive list of procedures:

- Verify the data integrity to ensure that the data on the blockchain has not been tampered with and matches the corresponding off-chain records, reports, or financial statements.
- Verify the authenticity and validity of the transactions and blocks using cryptographic techniques such as digital signatures and hash functions to verify the accuracy and completeness of transactions.
- Verify that transactions are properly authorised and executed according to required policies and procedures.
- Review applicable smart contracts used within the accounting system by reviewing their potential weaknesses, functionality, and security.
- Verify that the smart contracts execute the business logic and rules on the blockchain in compliance with the relevant regulations, policies, procedures, and standards.
- Analyse the blockchain network's activity logs, transaction history, and mining processes to obtain insights into the system's performance and potential anomalies.
- Identify and investigate any exception reports for irregularities or discrepancies in the data or transactions and conduct a comprehensive evaluation to identify the root cause and potential impact.
- Review the blockchain-based accounting system for compliance with relevant financial regulations, reporting standards, and related requirements.
- Review compliance with applicable data privacy and protection laws.
- Engage with key stakeholders involved in the blockchain network to understand their roles, permissions, and responsibilities.

Consider involving blockchain experts and auditors who have experience in auditing blockchain systems, depending on the complexity of the blockchain technology.

3.5.4 Reporting on the audit

Auditors should present the findings and recommendations in an audit report and clearly communicate any identified weaknesses or areas of improvement to the relevant parties.

3.6 TECHNICAL CHALLENGES IN BLOCKCHAIN-BASED AUDITS

Auditing in a blockchain environment presents several technical challenges that need to be addressed before the technology can be widely adopted in the auditing industry.

I **Interoperability and integration:** Blockchain technology is currently fragmented, with multiple blockchain platforms, protocols, and other existing systems (Burns et al., 2020). This makes it difficult to ensure interoperability between different blockchains and to verify data integrity across different platforms.

II **Scalability:** Blockchain technology is still in the development phase and still needs to achieve the scalability required for widespread adoption (Burns et al., 2020). As the number of transactions on a blockchain increases, the network can become slow, unmanageable, and costly (Bambara & Allen, 2018; Burns et al., 2020), which can impact the efficiency and accuracy of an audit. Hence, a need for continuous audits.

III **Smart contract complexity:** Smart contracts, as self-executing contracts coded on the blockchain (Burns et al., 2020) and designed to automate processes and enforce business logic based on predefined rules, can be "*incorrectly developed or manipulated*" (Burns et al., 2020:11). Smart contracts can be complex (Liu et al., 2020), and their implementation requires expertise in programming and continuous monitoring. Smart contracts could introduce elements of subjectivity, fairness, and good faith into their logic, but this cannot yet be readily translated or verified for reasonableness (Bambara & Allen, 2018; Vyas, 2022:238).

Addressing the abovementioned challenges is essential in effectively adopting blockchain and smart contracts to achieve their full potential in the public sector and related sectors (Bambara & Allen, 2018).

3.7 LEGAL IMPLICATIONS AND REGULATORY CHALLENGES WHEN AUDITING BLOCKCHAIN IN THE PUBLIC SECTOR

Blockchain-based audits in the public sector require careful attention to the legal matters (Bambara & Allen, 2018), such as standardisation in fragmented systems, regulatory oversight, data privacy, smart contracts, and "*cross-border transactions*" (Aghili, 2023:11). The legal matters pose regulatory challenges that need to be resolved by collaboration between regulators and auditors. A clear and consistent regulatory framework is essential for ensuring the reliability and accuracy of blockchain-based audits.

The regulatory matters that need to be addressed are:

I **Governance:** Blockchain technology and the "*decision-making processes embedded in smart contracts*" rely on a decentralised governance model that can create challenges relating to decision-making and accountability (Kozlowski, 2018:307; Burns et al., 2020). Auditors need to ensure that they have a clear understanding of the governance model, policies, and procedures to verify the accuracy and reliability of data and transactions (Bambara & Allen, 2018; Kozlowski, 2018).

II **Lack of standardisation:** There is currently no standardisation of blockchain technology and its implementation. This can create challenges for auditors in assessing the reliability and accuracy of the data recorded on a particular blockchain. Regulators may need to develop standards and guidelines for blockchain implementation and use, as well as related accounting and auditing standards (Kozlowski, 2018).

III **Regulatory oversight and compliance:** Public sector departments are subject to specific regulations and compliance requirements. Auditors need to give assurance that blockchain technology used in the public sector complies with relevant regulations, such as financial regulations (e.g., International Financial Reporting Standards (IFRS), procurement or supply chain laws, or government auditing standards). Regulators need to develop a governance framework to oversee the use of blockchain technology in auditing to address data privacy, security, and regulatory compliance.

IV **Cross-border transactions:** Blockchain technology allows for cross-border transactions without the need for intermediaries. This presents challenges in terms of regulatory compliance across different jurisdictions (Burns et al., 2020).

V **Data privacy:** While blockchain technology provides enhanced data security, the challenges in terms of privacy (Burns et al., 2020; Berryhill et al., 2018) involve the storage and processing of data, which may include personal or sensitive information (Bambara & Allen, 2018). Auditors must ensure compliance with the data protection laws and privacy regulations of the specific country, e.g., the General Data Protection Regulation (GDPR) or relevant local data privacy regulations when auditing blockchain systems that manage personal data (Bambara & Allen, 2018).

VI **Legal validity and enforceability:** Auditors should consider the legal validity and enforceability of transactions and smart contracts recorded on the blockchain (Bambara & Allen, 2018; Liu et al., 2020). This includes assessing whether the blockchain system complies with applicable legal frameworks, contract requirements, and electronic signature laws.

VII **Intellectual property (IP) rights:** Auditors should consider intellectual property rights associated with blockchain systems, including copyrights, patents, or trademarks (Bambara & Allen, 2018). It is important to ensure that using blockchain in the public sector should not infringe on any IP rights.

VIII **Liability and dispute resolution:** Auditors should assess the liability framework in case of errors, omissions, or disputes related to the blockchain system. It is important to consider mechanisms for dispute resolution and establish contractual agreements and terms of reference that outline the responsibilities and liabilities of all parties involved (Bambara & Allen, 2018).

IX **Open-source records and transparency:** The public sector is often subject to open records laws and transparency requirements (Bambara & Allen, 2018). Auditors need to ensure that blockchain technology being used in the public sector aligns with transparency obligations and allows for appropriate public access to information while maintaining data privacy and security.

Auditors conducting blockchain audits in the public sector should work closely with legal experts familiar with the relevant laws and regulations to ensure compliance and address any legal implications associated with auditing blockchain systems.

3.8 CONCLUDING REMARKS/LESSONS LEARNT

This chapter explored the use of continuous auditing and related IT tools in the public sector in a blockchain-based accounting environment. It provided an overview of blockchain technology and other AI applications in the public sector, such as ML and smart contracts. It also discussed how blockchain can enable the modernisation of public sector accounting systems by improving data quality, security, and efficiency. The chapter explained smart contracts and how they can automate decision-making and enforce rules on the blockchain and examined the benefits and challenges of using smart contracts in the public sector, such as transparency, accountability, and validity. The integration of blockchain with other AI applications, such as ML, IoT, IoS, RPA, IPA, and data analytics, was explored. Suggestions were provided on how these applications can enhance the performance and functionality of blockchain systems in the public sector, such as data analysis, fraud detection, and continuous monitoring. The chapter described how blockchain could provide a reliable and verifiable source of data for data analytics and promote the use of continuous auditing in the public sector by providing real-time insights and predictive analytics.

The chapter discussed how blockchain can improve access to information and transparency in the public sector to enhance the accountability and trust of public sector stakeholders. The benefits and features of blockchain-based audits in the public sector were highlighted, and the main steps of the audit were outlined. Basic examples of audit procedures to obtain sufficient audit evidence from the blockchain system under audit were provided. The technical challenges that auditors may face when conducting blockchain-based audits in the public sector were highlighted. The legal implications and regulatory challenges when auditing blockchain in the public sector were also identified.

The future trends and research directions for continuous auditing in a blockchain-based accounting environment in the public sector suggest that continuous auditing and blockchain has yet to be actively used in the public sector, and the practical implications of the adoption should be further researched.

REFERENCES

Aghili, S. (2023). *The auditor's guide to blockchain technology*. Taylor & Francis.

Bambara, J.J., & Allen, P.R. (2018). *Blockchain: A practical guide to developing business, law, and technology solutions*. McGraw-Hill Education.

Batubara, F.R., Ubacht, J., & Janssen, M. (2019). Unravelling transparency and accountability in blockchain. Proceedings of the 20th Annual International Conference on Digital Government Research, June, 204–213. https://doi.org/10.1145/3325112.3325262.

Berryhill, J., Bourgery, T., & Hanson, A. (2018). OECD Working Papers on Public Governance No. 28: Blockchains Unchained: Blockchain Technology and Its Use in the Public Sector. https://dx.doi.org/10.1787/3c32c429-en.

Burns, J., Steele, A., Cohen, E.E., & Ramamoorti, S. (2020). *COSO. Blockchain and internal control*. Deloitte.

Cangemi, M.P. (2021). Blockchain and internal control: The COSO perspective: An introduction and brief review. *EDPACS*, 64(1), 14–19 https://doi.org/10.1080/07366981.2021.1892708.

Dai, J., & Vasarhelyi, M.A. (2017). Toward blockchain-based accounting and assurance. *Journal of Information System*, 31(3), 5–21. https://doi.org/10.2308/isys-51804.

Deloitte. (2020). Continuous monitoring and continuous auditing – Deloitte US. www2.deloitte.com/content/dam/Deloitte/us/Documents/audit/us-aers-continuous-monitoring-and-continuous-auditing-whitepaper-102910.pdf.

Dinh, T.T.A., Wang, J., Chen, G., Liu, R., & Tan, K.L. (2017). BLOCKBENCH: A framework for analyzing private blockchains. [online]. *The 2017 ACM International Conference*, 5(12), 205–209. Available from: https://arxiv.org/pdf/1703.04057.pdf [Accessed 13 June 2023].

European Court of Auditors (ECA). (2020). Big data & digital audit. www.eca.europa.eu/en/Pages/news.aspx?nid=13396.

Ferri, L., Spano, R., & Ginesti, G. (2021). Ascertaining auditors' intentions to use blockchain technology: Evidence from the Big 4 accountancy firms in Italy. *Meditari Accountancy Research*, 29(5), 1063–1087 http://dx.doi.org/10.1108/MEDAR-03-2020-0829.

Gabriel, A.G., Ramos, V.B., & Marasigan, J.T. (2019). Transparency and accountability in local governance: The nexus between democracy and public service delivery in the Philippines. *Public Policy and Administration Research*, 9(7). https://doi.org/10.7176/PPAR.

Ginsberg, W., Carey, M.P., Halchin, L.E., & Keegan, N. (2012). Government Transparency and Secrecy: An examination of meaning and its use in the Executive Branch [online]. Congressional Research Services, 14 November 2012. Available from: https://fas.org/sgp/crs/secrecy/R42817.pdf [Accessed 20 November 2020].

Guo, L., Chen, J., Li, S., Li, Y., & Lu, J. (2022). A blockchain and IoT based lightweight framework for enabling information transparency in supply chain finance. *Digital Communications and Networks*, 8(4), 576–587. https://doi.org/10.1016/j.dcan.2022.03.020.

Han, H., Shiwakoti, R.K., Jarvis, R., Mordi, C., & Botchie, D. (2023). Accounting and auditing with blockchain technology and artificial intelligence: A literature review. *International Journal of Accounting Information Systems*, 48(2023), 100598 https://doi.org/10.1016/j.accinf.2022.100 598.

Hewa, T., Ylianttila, M., & Liyanage, M. (2021). Survey on blockchain based smart contracts: Applications, opportunities and challenges. *Journal of Network and Computer Applications*, 177(2021), 102857. https://doi.org/10.1016/j.jnca.2020.102857

Institute of Internal Auditors (IIA). (2015). Global Technology Audit Guide (GTAG) 3. Continuous auditing: Coordinating Continuous Auditing and Monitoring to Provide Continuous Assurance. gtag-3-continuous-auditing-2nd-edition.pdf (theiia.org)

Institute of Internal Auditors (IIA). (2019). *Unique aspects of internal auditing in the public sector.* Institute of Internal Auditors.

Kabir, M.R., Sobhani, F.A., Mohamed, N., & Ashrafi, D.M. (2022). Impact of integrity and internal audit transparency on audit quality: The moderating role of blockchain. *Management and Accounting Review*, 21, 1 www.researchgate.net/publication/358125543.

Kahyaoglu Bozkuş, S., & Aksoy, T. (2021). Survey on blockchain based accounting and finance algorithms using bibliometric approach. In *Accounting and Finance Innovations*, Edited by Nizar M. Alshari. IntechOpen. http://dx.doi.org/10.5772/intechopen.98207.

Koene, A., Clifton, C., Hatada, Y., Webb, H., Patel, M., Machado, C., LaViolette, J., Richardson, R., & Reisman, D. (2019). *A governance framework for algorithmic accountability and transparency.* EPRS. https://doi.org/10.2861/59990.

Kokina, J., Mancha, R., & Pachamanova, D. (2017). Blockchain: Emergent industry adoption and implications for accounting. *Journal of Emerging Technologies in Accounting*, 14(2), 91–100. https://doi.org/10.2308/jeta-51911.

Kossow, N., Windwehr, S., & Jenkins, M. (2021). Algorithmic transparency and accountability. [online]. Available from: https://knowledgehub.transparency.org/assets/uploads/kproducts/Algo rithmic-Transparency_2021.pdf [Accessed 4 July 2023].

Kozlowski, S. (2018). An audit ecosystem to support blockchain-based accounting and assurance. *Continuous Auditing*, 12 March 2018, 299–313. https://doi.org/10.1108/978-1-78743-413-420181015.

Lee, L., Fiedler, K., & Mautz, R. (2018). Internal audit and the blockchain. [online]. 24 September 2018. Available from: https://internalauditor.theiia.org/en/articles/2018/september/internal-audit-and-the-blockchain/ [Accessed 26 October 2023].

Liu, F., Yu, F.R., Li, X., Ji, H., & Leung, V.C.M. (2020). *Blockchain and machine learning for communications and networking systems.* IEEE. https://doi.org/10.1109/COMST.2020.2975911.

Moffitt, K.C., Rozario, A.M., & Vasarhelyi, M.A. (2018). Robotic process automation for auditing. *Journal of Emerging Technologies in Accounting*, 15(1), 1–10. https://doi.org/10.2308/ jeta-10589.

Mosteanu, N.R., & Faccia, A. (2020). Digital systems and new challenges of financial management-FinTech, XBRL, blockchain and cryptocurrencies. [online]. *Quality-Access to Success*, 21(174), 159–166. Available from: https://pure.coventry.ac.uk/ws/portalfiles/portal/30597575/Binder3_ 1_.pdf [Accessed 16 June 2023].

Muheidat, F., Pater, D., Tammisetty, S., Tawalbeh, L.A., & Tawalbeh, M. (2021). Emerging concepts using blockchain and big data. [online]. *Procedia Computer Science*, 198(2022), 15–22. Available from: https://creativecommons.org/licenses/by-nc-nd/4.0 [Accessed 4 March 2022].

Muller, S. (2021). The new ecosystem of the digital age – Impact of blockchain technology on the accounting environment and financial statement fraud detection. Masters Dissertation. ISCTE Business School.

O'Leary, D.E. (2018). Open information enterprise transactions: Business intelligence and wash and spoof transactions in blockchain and social commerce. *Intelligent Systems in Accounting, Finance and Management*, 25(3), 148–158. https://0-doi-org.oasis.unisa.ac.za/10.1002/isaf.1438.

OECD. (2016). *Governance of regulators' practices: Accountability, transparency and co-ordination, the governance of regulators*. OECD Publishing. http://dx.doi.org/10.1787/9789264255388-en.

Office of the Auditor-General New Zealand (OAG-NZ). (2016). Part 2: Understanding public sector accountability [online]. Available from: https://oag.parliament.nz/2016/accountability/part2.htm [Accessed 29 October 2020].

Paul, G., Sarkar, P., & Mukherjee, S. (2014). Towards a more democratic mining in bitcoins. *International Conference on Information Systems Security*, 14(7), 120–123. https://link.springer.com/chapter/10.1007/978-3-319-13841-1_11.

Peng, S. (2022). *Blockchain for big data – AI, IoT and cloud perspectives*. Taylor & Francis Group.

Regueiro, C., Seco, I., Gutiérrez-Agüero, I., Urquizu, B., & Mansell, J. (2021). A blockchain-based audit trail mechanism: Design and implementation. *Algorithms*, 14, 341. https://doi.org/10.3390/a14120341.

Sastry, S., Lee, T.H., & Teoh, M.T.T. (2021). The use of blockchain technology and data analytics in the audit profession. *Quantum Journal of Social Sciences and Humanities*, 2(4), 67–86. www.qjssh.com.

Tõnurist, P., & Hanson, A. (n.d). OECD. Anticipatory innovation governance shaping the future through proactive policy making. [online]. Available from: www.oecd-ilibrary.org/docserver/cce14d80-en.pdf?expires=1698490230&id=id&accname=guest&checksum=51183EDB8B0BB46537F6725E2B1F8DA1 [Accessed 25 October 2023].

Vyas, S., Shukla, V.K., Gupta, S., & Prasad, A. (2022). *Blockchain technology exploring opportunities, challenges, and applications*. CRC Press Taylor & Francis Group.

World Economic Forum (WEF). (2020). Exploring Blockchain Technology for Government Transparency: Blockchain-Based Public Procurement to Reduce Corruption [online]. Available from: www3.weforum.org/docs/WEF_Blockchain_Government_Transparency_Report.pdf [Accessed 29 July 2020].

Xu, M., Chen, X., & Kou, G. (2019). A systematic review of blockchain. *Financial Innovation*, 2019(5), 27. https://doi.org/10.1186/s40854-019-0147.

Yermack, D. (2017). Corporate governance and blockchains. *Review of Finance*, 2017, 7–31. https://doi.org/10.1093/rof/rfw074.

Yermack, D. (2019). Blockchain technology's potential in the financial system. [online]. Available from: www.frbatlanta.org/-/media/documents/news/conferences/2019/0519-financial-markets-conference/papers/yermack_policysession-one_blockchain-technology-potential-in-the-financialsystem.pdf [Accessed 23 October 2023].

Zhang, C. (2019). Intelligent process automation in audit. *Journal of Emerging Technologies in Accounting*. https://doi.org/10.2308/jeta-52653.

Zúñiga, N. (2018). Does more transparency improve accountability? U4 Anti-Corruption Resource Centre [online]. *Transparency International*. Available from: www.u4.no/publications/does-more-transparency-improve-accountability [Accessed 2 July 2020].

Chapter 4

The innovations in the public sector internal audit ecosystem

Louis A. Smidt and Léandi Steenkamp

4.1 INTRODUCTION

This chapter focuses on how the innovations in the world affect the developments in audit activities and audit innovations. The position of the public audit ecosystem among the different ecosystems that emerged with the effect of digitalisation is evaluated. In particular, the definition of the audit ecosystem is made, and how the audit innovations cause effects here is explained with a broad perspective. Thus, the significant aspects that can add value to public sector auditing are presented to professionals and stakeholders in the digital era. Depending on technological developments, the structure of the audit ecosystem is changing, and it is necessary to support it with a comprehensive digitalisation strategy. The public sector audit innovation examples are determined based on different countries' best practices. These cases are analysed, and the benefits and future challenges are explained. Especially in the public sector, the strategic interaction areas that the innovations in the audit ecosystem can cause are examined, and policy recommendations are presented.

4.2 DEFINING THE PUBLIC AUDIT ECOSYSTEM

An audit ecosystem was defined as a "holistic approach to the design and development of a technology-driven framework to provide overall management and control of the audit technology components employed, and coordination of the activities of the participants involved" (Kozlowski, 2018). The growth in the use of technology and digital dependencies has significantly impacted how organisations and business processes are run. Organisations had to adapt to a transformed control environment in order to fulfil their business objectives, which in turn exposed them to cyber vulnerabilities during their daily operations (World Economic Forum, 2022). An ecosystem approach enables automated audit functions to adapt to evolving environments (Kozlowski, 2018). The public audit ecosystem's major stakeholders include government departments or state-owned entities, external auditors, regulators, standard-setting bodies, and the public (Lino et al., 2023; Murphy et al., 2022; Tetteh et al., 2023). Government departments or state-owned entities are responsible for appropriately managing public funds and resources to service the public and the respective country. They are held accountable for their actions through independent audits that the appointed external auditors conduct. The external auditors' mandate is to provide an independent view of the accuracy of the financial statements of these government departments as well as any compliance issues that these government departments must adhere to as defined by the regulators. The regulators oversee the public audit process to ensure that the audits are conducted with independence, integrity, and objectivity. Furthermore, to ensure

DOI: 10.1201/9781003382706-4

that the financial reporting is undertaken consistently and comparable between the different government departments of a respective country, the standard-setting bodies must define the accounting standards and guidelines for public sector financial reporting. The public is also one of the key stakeholders in the public audit ecosystem. It is vested in ensuring that government departments manage and coordinate public funding responsibly to benefit the public and the country. The public can also hold government agencies and auditors accountable for their actions (Lino et al., 2023; Murphy et al., 2022; Tetteh et al., 2023).

In this digital era, the public sector ecosystem must conduct its duties as far as possible within the control environments dominated by large volumes of data. This evolvement and adoption of technology, specifically artificial intelligence (AI), has not only impacted the public sector but has brought about a significant change in various sectors and business industries. The adoption of AI in the following sectors serves as examples:

- Automobile manufacturers that build self-driving vehicles.
- Online search engines that provide focused search results.
- Social media organisations that use AI for face recognition on social media pages.
- The retail industry provides tailor-made experiences for their customers in line with their buying habits.
- Logistics companies benefit from the most economical routes planned and calculated with AI.
- Governments that can utilise AI for predictive purposes, such as epidemics.
- Marketing organisations can provide customised content to their customers in real-time (Fedyk et al., 2022; Lino et al., 2023; The Institute of Internal Auditors (IIA), 2017a,b; The Institute of Internal Auditors Global, 2017).

This advancement and adoption of technology, specifically AI and its resulting impact, is also no different for the internal audit profession and its role within the public audit ecosystem as it relates to AI (Farcane and Deliu, 2020; The Institute of Internal Auditors (IIA), 2017a,b; The Institute of Internal Auditors Global, 2017). The Institute of Internal Auditors (IIA) in their report (2017) *Global Perspectives and Insights: The IIA's Artificial Intelligence Auditing Framework (Practical Applications, Part B)* defines the role of the internal audit function related to AI as follows: *"help an organization evaluate, understand, and communicate the degree to which artificial intelligence will affect (negative or positive) on the organization's ability to create value in the short, medium, or long term"*.

For this purpose, the Institute of Internal Auditors (IIA) has developed an AI Auditing Framework (The Institute of Internal Auditors (IIA), 2017a,b; The Institute of Internal Auditors Global, 2017). Figure 4.1 illustrates the interaction of the internal audit function with the use of the AI framework in delivering on its mandate to its various stakeholders.

The AI framework, as depicted in Figure 4.1, is comprised of three main aspects and seven associated elements (Al-Okaily et al., 2022; Lino et al., 2023; Nair, 2022; The Institute of Internal Auditors, 2017):

AI Strategy

- Cyber Resilience – As more organisations and public sector departments increase their reliance on AI that uses algorithms from large volumes of data, it becomes increasingly essential for organisations and public sector departments to ensure their cyber vulnerabilities are adequately and effectively managed.

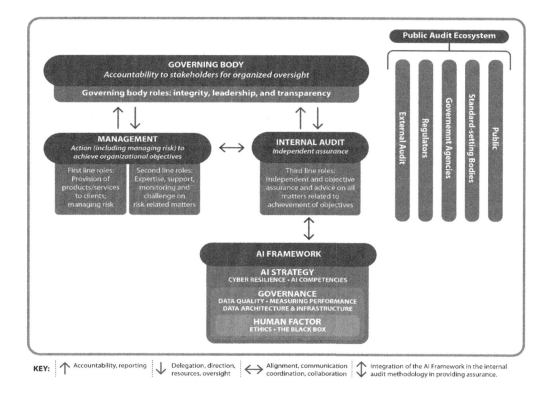

Figure 4.1 Interaction of the internal audit AI framework.

Source: Adapted from The Institute of Internal Auditors (IIA), 2017; The Institute of Internal Auditors, 2017; The Institute of Internal Auditors Global, 2017.

- AI Competencies – To ensure an effective AI solution, organisations and public sector departments will require technically skilled staff.

Governance

- Data Quality – AI algorithms are built on large volumes of data. The accuracy, completeness, and reliability of the data are therefore critical.
- Measuring Performance – With the adoption of AI in business processes, it becomes an integral part of the business process and the associated objectives. Management is tasked to closely monitor and integrate its performance measures by including its AI initiatives.
- Data architecture and infrastructure – The data's confidentiality, integrity, and availability are critical. In addition, the data ownership policies must also be clearly defined and adhered to for the AI governance to be effective.

Human Factor

- Ethics – The fact that humans prepare the AI algorithms emphasises the importance of ethical conduct. Human errors and bias may be integrated into the AI algorithm if not adequately managed and controlled.

- The black box – This refers to the ability of certain types of AI machines that can learn by themselves or communicate with other machines. The black box will increasingly become more of a challenge as the different types of AI become more sophisticated and complex.

The internal audit function, in its systematic, disciplined approach, will have to embrace the opportunities that are available with the integration of technology in its internal audit methodology in delivering on its AI mandate, which is to *"help an organization evaluate, understand, and communicate the degree to which artificial intelligence will have an effect (negative or positive) on the organization's ability to create value in the short, medium, or long term"*.

The advancements in technology have forced internal audit functions to become more creative in offering their assurance and advisory services. The modern internal audit functions have been able to adapt to the needs of the public sector and its stakeholders by utilising various technological tools such as data analytics software, blockchain, and artificial intelligence. These innovations are clear indications of how the internal audit function is keeping up with the increasing expectations of its stakeholders (Al-Okaily et al., 2022; Nair, 2022; The Institute of Internal Auditors Global, 2017).

4.3 AUDIT INNOVATIONS

Dynamic control environments require dynamic tools and techniques to enable assurance providers to execute their mandate in an effective and efficient manner. It is necessary for the internal audit function to adopt innovative techniques to provide assurance in e-government environments (refer to Section 4.4). This is also echoed in the words of David Coderre (2009),

> Internal auditors cannot stand by and watch as the business world embraces new technology. The tools and techniques used in the past are no longer adequate; we need to restock our toolboxes with a variety of software to meet the challenges of auditing in today's business environment.

Auditing plays a key role in providing assurance within public sector governance. Its mandate is to provide objective assessments as to whether public resources are managed effectively and in a responsible manner. Auditors help public sector organisations achieve accountability and integrity, improve operations, and instil confidence among citizens and stakeholders through their independent assurance and advisory activities. As a result, the public sector's responsibilities of oversight, insight, and foresight are also supported through the auditor's independent assessments. *Oversight* refers to providing assurance whether public sector entities conduct their day-to-day activities as intended and identify any areas of possible public corruption. *Insight* enables decision-makers to make informed decisions through the auditor's independent assessment of public sector programs, policies, operations, and results. Auditors provide *foresight* to members of management and other stakeholders within the public sector by providing them with trends and outliers and emerging risks that may occur (The Institute of Internal Auditors, 2012).

The internal audit function can provide *oversight*, *insight*, and *foresight* to the public sector risk landscape through enabling tools and technologies such as data analytics software, blockchain, and AI. Internal audit functions are undergoing a major transformation, as traditional audit techniques are no longer adequate for conducting internal audit engagements. To continue as a value-adding assurance function within their organisations, internal audit teams must integrate technology-enabled tools into their audit methodologies (Smidt, 2016).

The IIA (The Institute of Internal Auditors, 2012; The Institute of Internal Auditors Global, 2012) defines data analytics as follows:

> "Data analytics" is not a technology program, but technology does enable more effective and efficient use of data analytics. Data analytics can be used in tandem with tools such as artificial intelligence (AI), machine learning and robotic process automation (RPA).
>   Types of analytics include:
>
> - Descriptive analytics, which covers the details of past performance and may include year-over-year or month-over-month changes in sales, revenue, pricing, inventory, customers, visitors, or other trends or changes that have already occurred.
> - Diagnostic analytics, which examines the factors behind a trend or result.
> - Predictive analytics, which uses predictive modelling to discern what might happen in the future.
> - Prescriptive analytics, which assesses potential outcomes and identifies the next best actions based on analysis of existing data.

The fast-paced, complex, and evolving risk landscape compels the internal audit function to respond to their stakeholders' expectations by providing especially predictive and prescriptive analytics in the execution of its duties (Deloitte, 2017; Ernst & Young Global Limited, 2019). Reviewing the definitions provided above with regard to the different types of analytics, the application of the use of diagnostic, predictive, and prescriptive analytics should enable the internal audit function to provide greater *insight* and *foresight* with regard to the underlying control environments in which the organisation operates. The *Mission Statement of Internal Audit*, as defined in the International Professional Practices Framework (IPPF), also highlights the requirement of the internal audit function to provide risk-based and objective assurance, advice, and *insight* to enhance and protect organisational value (The Institute of Internal Audit, 2016). In order for the internal audit function to be successful with the implementation of innovative tools and techniques, they also need to ensure that their work aligns with the needs of the organisation or the control environment that is under evaluation. Deloitte (2017) proposes a view of the "four I's of Internal Audit Innovation".

Integrated: The implementation of innovative methods in a relevant and timely manner by the internal audit function to provide real-time advice and insights to the organisation's stakeholders is dependent on the internal audit function's integration into the goals of the business and the strategy for achieving those goals.

Iterative: Innovative ideas often result in being iterative after successive attempts have been realised. These iterations allow the internal audit function to explore new approaches as they learn through experience, and it assists in building trust with their stakeholders prior to implementing innovative ideas. This iteration also assists in managing the expectation gap between what the internal audit function can provide through its innovative methods and that of its stakeholders' expectations.

Incremental: The rapid and ever-evolving use and implementation of technology have a significant impact on the manner in which the internal audit function conducts its work. The ideal manner in responding to this evolvement is to introduce and adopt innovative ideas in an incremental or gradual manner. This incremental approach enables the internal audit function to revisit specific aspects of its work with the objective of understanding cause and effect and isolating ways to improve continually.

Independent: The internal audit function should always ensure that it protects its independence and objectivity when collaborating its innovative ideas with its various stakeholders. No innovative idea is worth compromising the independence and objectivity of the internal audit function.

4.4 A BRIEF OVERVIEW OF E-GOVERNMENTS

The evolvement of information and communication technologies (ICTs) such as AI, machine learning (ML), Internet of things (IoT), smartphones, mobile Internet, open data, cloud computing, social media, blockchain, and big data over the last decade has been key in the transformation of the practices of governments, businesses, and society at large (Goede, 2019; Han et al., 2023; Hujran et al., 2023; Al Sayegh et al., 2023). Consequently, this gave rise to the emergence of e-governments. E-government refers to the improvement in the quality of its service offering to its citizens at large through the use and application of information and communication technologies (Gasco-Hernandez et al., 2022; Hujran et al., 2023; Al Sayegh et al., 2023; Thottoli et al., 2019). This should allow more opportunities for the active participation of citizens in their government's interests. In the dynamic landscape of public sector internal audit, continuous innovation has become the cornerstone of enhancing accountability, transparency, and efficiency.

The evolution of internal audit practices aligns with the transformative journey of public administration in the digital age. Together, these components propel the public sector into a new era of heightened effectiveness and responsiveness, reshaping the landscape of public accountability and governance. Four types of e-governments can be classified based on their interactions between government agencies and members of the public. The four types of e-governments are government-to-citizen (G2C), government-to-business (G2B), government-to-employee (G2E), and government-to-government (G2G) (Epstein, 2022; Pérez-Morote et al., 2020; Al Sayegh et al., 2023). These are briefly discussed below:

Government-to-citizen – A key attribute of the G2C model is the availability of information and online access to public services for citizens. These can include services such as licence renewals, filing of income taxes, school registration, health-care information, libraries, and birth or marriage certificates for the citizens (Epstein, 2022; Lim and Kamaruddin, 2023; Al Sayegh et al., 2023).

Government-to-business – This type of e-government platform is related to the use of the internet, buying and selling of goods and services (e-procurement), the announcement of new regulations, and the distribution of applicable policies. Through G2B, businesses are enabled to, amongst others, apply for business registration, renew licences, obtain permits, or pay taxes. A further benefit of G2B is the enhanced efficiency of business transactions, resulting in informed decision-making and better data on business transactions and taxes (Epstein, 2022; Lim and Kamaruddin, 2023; Al Sayegh et al., 2023).

Government-to-employee – Although this type of e-government platform also includes the functionalities of the G2C model, it includes additional features only available to government employees. These may include, amongst others, human resource training to enable the government employees to be more efficient in the conduct of their work, payroll information, access and renewal of employment contracts, and it allows for the application of work permits for expatriate staff (Epstein, 2022; Lim and Kamaruddin, 2023; Al Sayegh et al., 2023).

Government-to-government – The G2G government type refers to the integration between agencies and bureaus and includes the interaction between national and state governments. This integration of services enables citizens to access a centralised government portal, resulting in time efficiencies for citizens as they are then able to access multiple services from a single platform (Epstein, 2022; Lim and Kamaruddin, 2023; Al Sayegh et al., 2023).

The transformation and implementation of e-governments, however, remains a challenge despite the associated advantages that can be derived from the implementation thereof

Table 4.1 Summary of selected major studies that explored the use and adoption of e-governments

Year of study's publication	Authors	Title of study	Key findings	Country
2023	Al Sayegh et al. (2023)	Factors affecting e-government adoption in the UAE public sector organisations: The knowledge management perspective	The following factors influence e-government adoption: • Short-term job performance • Long-term job performance • Client impact • Leadership support • Employee training • Organisational preparedness	United Arab Emirates (UAE)
2023	Hujran et al. (2023)	Examining the antecedents and outcomes of smart government usage: An integrated model	• Performance expectancy has the strongest influence on e-government usage • Facilitating conditions has the lowest influence on e-government usage • Personalisation has no significant impact on e-government usage	United Arab Emirates (UAE)
2023	Lim and Kamaruddin (2023)	Violated factors in building citizen-centric e-government websites: insights from the performance of the federal, state, and local government websites in Malaysia	• Openness of funding and expenditure records on government websites were major elements that influenced the notion of citizen-centric e-government	Malaysia

(Continued)

Table 4.1 (Continued)

Year of study's publication	Authors	Title of study	Key findings	Country
2022	Gasco-Hernandez et al. (2022)	The role of organizational capacity to foster digital transformation in local governments: The case of three European smart cities	• Having a clearly defined strategy driven by management is a key factor in the digital transformation of becoming a smart city • Collaboration initiatives between different types of organisations to assist in the funding of transitioning to a smart city is also a key factor	Europe
2022	Epstein (2022)	Two decades of e-government diffusion among local governments in the United States	• Cities with larger populations displayed a greater offering and use of e-government services • Broadband access by citizens had, to a lesser extent, an impact on the use and offering of e-government services • The wealth status of citizens did not have a significant impact on the usage of e-government services	United States of America
2020	Glyptis et al. (2020)	E-government implementation challenges in small countries: The project manager's perspective	The following factors influence e-government adoption: • Financial position of a country • E-readiness of a country • Infrastructure facilities and technological innovations for effective knowledge management and communication • Political and legal frameworks • Organisational and institutional aspects • Socio-cultural aspects	Cyprus

Source: Authors' own deduction.

(Glyptis et al., 2020). Table 4.1 provides a summary of selected major studies that highlight certain key characteristics to be considered for countries and their governments to ensure successful implementation and adoption of e-governments.

Contributing factors to the use and adoption of e-governments can also be attributed to trust, information transparency, and cost implications to transform (Gasco-Hernandez et al., 2022; Hujran et al., 2023; Lim and Kamaruddin, 2023; Al Sayegh et al., 2023). Reviewing the information in Table 4.1, it is evident that the technological innovations and adoption thereof in the public sector are influenced by various factors. It is inevitable for government departments or state-owned entities to stay abreast with the fast-paced evolution of ICTs to succeed in their mandate to service its citizens at large. Notwithstanding these factors, as indicated in Table 4.1, there is an upward trend in the adoption of e-government services (Epstein, 2022; Gasco-Hernandez et al., 2022; Glyptis et al., 2020; Hujran et al., 2023; Al Sayegh et al., 2023).

As the public sector e-government maturity improves over time, it is of utmost importance that internal audit functions that provide assurance services in the public sector must adapt and evolve with the times. Internal audit functions fixated on traditional techniques risk obsolescence. Internal audit functions that embrace innovative technology tools, such as generalised audit software (GAS), AI, blockchain, and data analytics, can produce valuable insights to stakeholders in an efficient manner. By adopting and implementing these technologies, internal audit functions aim to reach a more advanced level of maturity. This allows for continuous testing of controls as routine analytics become embedded in client systems (refer to Section 4.3).

4.5 BENEFITS AND FUTURE CHALLENGES

The adoption and implementation of AI bring with it a number of benefits to organisations' business processes. However, it also has its associated challenges. Key challenges for organisations to take note of with the adoption and implementation of AI in a business era that is dominated by large volumes of data are data integrity and cybersecurity. In other words, the confidentiality, integrity, and availability of data are of utmost importance in an environment where technology tools have been implemented (Smidt et al., 2018). In their study, conducted on the *Current State and Challenges in the Implementation of Smart Robotic Process Automation in Accounting and Auditing*, Gotthardt et al. (2020) also point out, amongst others, the importance of data quality and data integrity together with the associated skills required for AI to be implemented and operating effectively within organisations. The following serve as examples of the benefits that can potentially be derived with the effective adoption and implementation of AI (Fedyk et al., 2022; Gotthardt et al., 2020; Ormond, 2023; Raji et al., 2022; Sousa et al., 2019; The Institute of Internal Auditors, 2017a,b):

- Compressed data processing cycles.
- Limited processing errors by replacing human actions with automated, repeatable machine actions.
- Reduced labour time and costs as a result of the replacement of time-intensive activities with time-efficient activities such as the automation of business processes.
- The protection of human lives that might otherwise be exposed to dangerous situations using drones or robots instead of humans.
- Proactive decision-making by members of management as a result of the predictive analytic capabilities associated with using AI.
- Improvement in revenue and an expansion of market share through AI initiatives.

In contrast with these associated benefits, there are also several challenges to take note of with the adoption and implementation of AI. The following serve as examples (Fedyk et al., 2022; Gotthardt et al., 2020; Ormond, 2023; Sousa et al., 2019; The Institute of Internal Auditors, 2017a,b; La Torre et al., 2019):

- Human biases that are introduced in the AI technology that go undetected.
- Human logic processing errors that are implemented in the AI technology.
- Poor quality results or outputs from the AI technology due to inadequate testing and validation of the AI results.
- Reputational damage caused by the implementation of AI technology also results in adverse financial implications for the organisation.
- Customers or employees may resist the adoption or acceptance of the organisation's AI strategy.
- Organisations may lose market share if they do not stay abreast of all the latest technology to remain competitive, for example, with the adoption of AI in their business processes.
- The investment in AI (technology infrastructure, research and development, and talent acquisition) may not yield an acceptable return on investment (ROI).

These challenges and opportunities hold equally true for the internal audit function. With the rapid advancement of technology, the internal audit function is confronted with control environments that are dominated by large scales of data. In other words, the modern-day internal audit function will heavily rely on data. Therefore, adopting AI and its capability to provide predictions from large volumes of data puts the internal audit function at the centre of technology's impact in delivering on its mandate (Fedyk et al., 2022). According to their study, "*Is Artificial Intelligence Improving the Audit Process*", AI is widely used in audits, with a highly centralised and top-down adoption in the sector. The main focus of AI is to improve audit quality through improved anomaly identification and fraud detection, enhanced risk assessment, and the ability to shift human labour to more advanced and high-risk areas. Although AI investments made by auditors are critical for audit quality, clients' AI investments play a much smaller role. The adoption of AI has led to significant shifts in labour demand and composition, including the elimination of lower-level tasks. However, the primary barrier to the widespread adoption of AI is the onboarding and training of skilled human capital.

Reflecting on the IIA's AI framework that was introduced in Section 4.2, from an organisational perspective, members of management will have to ensure that they have implemented controls and action plans to manage the potential risks facing the aspects of (1) AI strategy; (2) governance; and (3) human factor. Failure to do so could have significant implications for organisations and the public audit ecosystem in the achievement of their objectives.

From an internal audit function perspective, if they want to remain relevant and to be seen as one of the key assurance providers to management and its various stakeholders, they will have to ensure that they embrace the technology offering and must ensure that they upskill themselves to keep on delivering on its mandate in an effective and efficient manner.

4.6 POLICY RECOMMENDATIONS

The growth in AI governance globally is on the rise, with Europe, Asia, and North America setting the trend (Belli et al., 2023; Dwivedi et al., 2023; Eke et al., 2023; Filgueiras, 2023; Jones, 2023). With the increased use and adoption of AI coupled with the associated benefits and challenges related to the adoption and use of AI, as discussed in Section 4.5, it is not surprising to see this need for more stringent AI policy regulation. Wakunuma et al. (2022) reiterates the importance of AI governance due to the social and ethical concerns associated with the use and application thereof. They highlight specifically the concerns related to privacy, autonomy, anonymity, and dependency, amongst others, which can only be governed through regulatory policies and applicable laws.

Europe is following a holistic and comprehensive approach regarding AI regulation at both the European Union (EU) and Council of Europe levels. The EU has been very successful with its previous guidance that was developed on the General Data Protection Regulation (GDPR), which has become the industry norm for many countries. The EU hopes that the development and implementation of their AI Act will also be seen as the global benchmark for the adoption and use of AI. Their purpose with the AI Act is to *"strengthen significantly the Union's role to help shape global norms and standards and promote trustworthy AI that is consistent with Union values and interests"* (Belli et al., 2023; Dwivedi et al., 2023; Eke et al., 2023; Feldstein, 2023).

The United States has a few initiatives to regulate the adoption and use of AI:

- The Federal Trade Commission (FTC) published guidelines for the implementation of AI, which include existing guidelines regarding automated decision-making systems such as the Fair Credit Reporting Act (FCRA) and the Equal Credit Opportunity Act (ECOA).
- The US Department of Defence (DoD) has adopted a set of AI principles that should be applied in combat and non-combat situations. These principles provide guidance specifically in the areas of responsibility, equitability, traceability, reliability, and governability.
- The US Food and Drug Administration (FDA) also highlighted the need for regulation in this area through their "Artificial Intelligence and Machine Learning (AI/ML) Software as a Medical Device Action Plan". It is the aim that a regulatory framework exists that: *"Could enable the FDA and manufacturers to evaluate and monitor a software product from its premarket development to post-market performance. This approach could allow for the FDA's regulatory oversight to embrace the iterative improvement power of artificial intelligence and machine learning-based software as a medical device while assuring patient safety"*.
- The above-mentioned initiatives are also supported by certain legislative initiatives, such as the Algorithmic Accountability Act of 2022 (Belli et al., 2023; Dwivedi et al., 2023; Filgueiras, 2023).

Another international development was brought about by the Chinese regulation on algorithmic recommendation systems. This regulation came into effect on 1 March 2022 and has as its aim to guide the use and impact of algorithmic recommendation systems. This regulation is intended to provide a standard for more transparency in the use of AI. It is important, for example, to have user notifications that provide clear criteria for recommendations and distinguish between algorithmically generated/synthetic information. There should be orders for the implementation of mechanisms of manual intervention and autonomous user choice. The use of information control, ranking, and presentation must be regulated in various ways to prevent manipulative recommendations. Additionally, a registry and categorisation system should be created to manage algorithms put on the market. The UK government has also published an algorithmic transparency standard for their public sector environment (Belli et al., 2023; Eke et al., 2023; Roberts et al., 2021).

Reviewing the regulatory policies and guidance that are implemented by Europe, Asia, and North America that are leading the way in terms of AI policy regulation, it is evident that governing the responsible use of AI has become a matter of strategic importance for both developed and developing countries (Belli et al., 2023). The adoption and use of AI have moral and ethical implications, and therefore, it becomes inevitable for countries to issue regulatory policies and guidelines that will enable countries to use AI in a responsible manner in managing the risks associated with its use but to also take hold of the benefits that it offers. The internal audit function as an independent assurance provider has an important role by ensuring that it includes the evaluation of AI regulations on its risk register as part of its mandate on AI (refer to Sections 4.2 and 4.3).

4.7 CONCLUSION

The process of auditing in the public sector should be continuous to provide assurance to stakeholders regarding the effectiveness of governance, risk management, and controls. As the business environment is uncertain and risk is constantly evolving, internal audit functions are expected to anticipate future risk events that may affect public sector organisations' objectives. These functions will have to operate within control environments that are increasingly dominated by artificial intelligence, technology, and big data. Therefore, stakeholders will increasingly demand more meaningful results and analyses of the effectiveness of their respective control environments. Refer to Sections 4.3 and 4.4 for more information on the increased pressures that internal audit functions in the public sector industry will face.

Corporate scandals have become increasingly common in recent years, affecting both private and public sector industries. As a result, internal audit departments' chief audit executives must be proactive in preparing their teams for the future. They need to adopt technology-enabled tools to reduce the risk of becoming obsolete and continue delivering valuable insights to stakeholders.

In addition to ensuring that their internal audit functions are effective and efficient, senior audit officials and chief audit executives must also take up leadership responsibilities and advance their internal audit functions to a level of maturity that integrates technology-enabled tools like data analytics software, blockchain, and AI into their audit methodologies.

The modern internal audit function must acknowledge that the integration and use of technology-based tools like data analytics software, blockchain, and AI for data analysis is no longer optional but essential. Eventually, the implementation of these tools will be driven by necessity rather than personal choice, transforming their internal audit processes.

REFERENCES

Al Sayegh, A.J., Ahmad, S.Z., AlFaqeeh, K.M. and Singh, S.K. (2023), "Factors affecting e-government adoption in the UAE public sector organisations: The knowledge management perspective", *Journal of Knowledge Management*, Vol. 27 No. 3, pp. 717–737, doi: 10.1108/JKM-09-2021-0681.

Al-Okaily, M., Alqudah, H.M., Al-Qudah, A.A. and Alkhwaldi, A.F. (2022), "Examining the critical factors of computer-assisted audit tools and techniques adoption in the post-COVID-19 period: Internal auditors perspective", *VINE Journal of Information and Knowledge Management Systems*, doi: 10.1108/VJIKMS-12-2021-0311.

Belli, L., Curzi, Y. and Gaspar, W.B. (2023), "AI regulation in Brazil: Advancements, flows, and need to learn from the data protection experience", *Computer Law and Security Review*, Vol. 48 No. October 2021, p. 105767, doi: 10.1016/j.clsr.2022.105767.

Coderre, D. (2009), *Internal Audit: Efficiency through Automation*, John Wiley & Sons, Inc.

de Sousa, W.G., de Melo, E.R.P., Bermejo, P.H.D.S., Farias, R.A.S. and Gomes, A.O. (2019), "How and where is artificial intelligence in the public sector going? A literature review and research agenda", *Government Information Quarterly*, Vol. 36 No. 4, p. 101392, doi: 10.1016/j.giq.2019.07.004.

Deloitte. (2017), *Internal Audit Innovation: Structured Methods to Unlock New Value*, Deloitte.

Dwivedi, Y.K., Kshetri, N., Hughes, L., Slade, E.L., Jeyaraj, A., Kar, A.K., Baabdullah, A.M., et al. (2023), " 'So what if ChatGPT wrote it?' Multidisciplinary perspectives on opportunities, challenges and implications of generative conversational AI for research, practice and policy", *International Journal of Information Management*, Vol. 71 No. March, doi: 10.1016/j.ijinfomgt.2023.102642.

Eke, D.O., Akintoye, S. and Wakunuma, K. (Eds.). (2023), *Responsible AI in Africa: Challenges and Opportunities*, Palgrave Macmillan.

Epstein, B. (2022), "Two decades of e-government diffusion among local governments in the United States", *Government Information Quarterly*, Vol. 39 No. 2, p. 101665, doi: 10.1016/j.giq.2021.101665.

Ernst & Young Global Limited. (2019), *Five Considerations to Disrupt the Internal Audit Risk Assessment Process*. Ernst & Young Global Limited.

Farcane, N. and Deliu, D. (2020), "Stakes and challenges regarding the financial auditor's activity in the blockchain era", *Audit Financiar*, Vol. 18 No. 157, pp. 154–181, doi: 10.20869/auditf/2020/157/004.

Fedyk, A., Hodson, J., Khimich, N. and Fedyk, T. (2022), "Is artificial intelligence improving the audit process?", *Review of Accounting Studies*, Vol. 27 No. 3, pp. 938–985, doi: 10.1007/s11142-022-09697-x.

Feldstein, S. (2023), "Evaluating Europe's push to enact AI regulations: How will this influence global norms?", *Democratization*, Vol. 0 No. 0, pp. 1–18, doi: 10.1080/13510347.2023.2196068.

Filgueiras, F. (2023), "Designing artificial intelligence policy: Comparing design spaces in Latin America", *Latin American Policy*, Vol. 14 No. 1, pp. 5–21, doi: 10.1111/lamp.12282.

Gasco-Hernandez, M., Nasi, G., Cucciniello, M. and Hiedemann, A.M. (2022), "The role of organizational capacity to foster digital transformation in local governments: The case of three European smart cities", *Urban Governance*, Vol. 2 No. 2, pp. 236–246, doi: 10.1016/j.ugj.2022.09.005.

Glyptis, L., Christofi, M., Vrontis, D., Del Giudice, M., Dimitriou, S. and Michael, P. (2020), "E-government implementation challenges in small countries: The project manager's perspective", *Technological Forecasting and Social Change*, Vol. 152 No. December 2019, doi: 10.1016/j.techfore.2019.119880.

Goede, M. (2019), "E-Estonia: The e-government cases of Estonia, Singapore, and Curaçao", *Archives of Business Research*, Vol. 7 No. 2, pp. 216–227, doi: 10.14738/abr.72.6174.

Gotthardt, M., Koivulaakso, D., Paksoy, O., Saramo, C., Martikainen, M. and Lehner, O. (2020), "Current state and challenges in the implementation of smart robotic process automation in accounting and auditing", *ACRN Journal of Finance and Risk Perspectives*, Vol. 9 No. 1, pp. 90–102, doi: 10.35944/JOFRP.2020.9.1.007.

Han, H., Shiwakoti, R.K., Jarvis, R., Mordi, C. and Botchie, D. (2023), "Accounting and auditing with blockchain technology and artificial Intelligence: A literature review", *International Journal of Accounting Information Systems*, , Vol. 48 No. November 2022, p. 100598, doi: 10.1016/j.accinf.2022.100598.

Hujran, O., Al-Debei, M.M., Al-Adwan, A.S., Alarabiat, A. and Altarawneh, N. (2023), "Examining the antecedents and outcomes of smart government usage: An integrated model", *Government Information Quarterly*, Vol. 40 No. 1, p. 101783, doi: 10.1016/j.giq.2022.101783.

Jones, E. (2023), "Digital disruption: Artificial intelligence and international trade policy", *Oxford Review of Economic Policy*, Vol. 39 No. 1, pp. 70–84, doi: 10.1093/oxrep/grac049.

Kozlowski, S. (2018), "An audit ecosystem to support blockchain-based accounting and assurance", *Continuous Auditing*, pp. 299–313, doi: 10.1108/978-1-78743-413-420181015.

La Torre, M., Botes, V.L., Dumay, J. and Odendaal, E. (2019), "Protecting a new Achilles heel: The role of auditors within the practice of data protection", *Managerial Auditing Journal*, Vol. 36 No. 2, pp. 218–239, doi: 10.1108/MAJ-03-2018-1836.

Lim, S.B. and Kamaruddin, K.A. (2023), "Violated factors in building citizen-centric e-government websites: Insights from the performance of the federal, state and local governments websites in Malaysia", *Journal of Systems and Information Technology*, Vol. 3, pp. 109–132, doi: 10.1108/jsit-12-2021-0262.

Lino, A.F., Azevedo, R.R. de and Belote, G.S. (2023), "The influence of public sector audit digitalisation on local government budget planning: Evidence from Brazil", *Journal of Public Budgeting, Accounting and Financial Management*, doi: 10.1108/JPBAFM-05-2022-0090.

Murphy, P., Lakoma, K., Eckersley, P., Dom, B.K. and Jones, M. (2022), "Public goods, public value and public audit: The Redmond review and English local government", *Public Money and Management*, doi: 10.1080/09540962.2022.2126644.

Nair, B. (2022), "The evolution of internal audit in a digital-first environment", *ISACA Industry News*, available at: www.isaca.org/resources/news-and-trends/industry-news/2022/the-evolution-of-internal-audit-in-a-digital-first-environment (accessed 19 December 2022).

Ormond, E. (2023), "Artificial intelligence in South Africa comes with special dilemmas – plus the usual risks", *The Conversation*, available at: https://theconversation.com/artificial-intelligence-in-south-africa-comes-with-special-dilemmas-plus-the-usual-risks-194277 (accessed 31 January 2023).

Pérez-Morote, R., Pontones-Rosa, C. and Núñez-Chicharro, M. (2020), "The effects of e-government evaluation, trust and the digital divide in the levels of e-government use in European countries", *Technological Forecasting and Social Change*, Vol. 154 No. July 2019, p. 119973, doi: 10.1016/j.techfore.2020.119973.

Raji, I.D., Xu, P., Honigsberg, C. and Ho, D. (2022), *Outsider Oversight: Designing a Third Party Audit Ecosystem for AI Governance*, AIES 2022 – Proceedings of the 2022 AAAI/ACM Conference on AI, Ethics, and Society, Vol. 1, Association for Computing Machinery, doi: 10.1145/3514094.3534181.

Roberts, H., Cowls, J., Morley, J., Taddeo, M., Wang, V. and Floridi, L. (2021), "The Chinese approach to artificial intelligence: An analysis of policy, ethics, and regulation", *AI and Society*, Vol. 36 No. 1, pp. 59–77, doi: 10.1007/s00146-020-00992-2.

Smidt, L.A. (2016), *A Maturity Level Assessment of the Use of Generalised Audit Software by Internal Audit Functions in the South African Banking Industry*, University of the Free State.

Smidt, L.A., Ahmi, A., Steenkamp, L., van der Nest, D.P. and Lubbe, D. (2018), "A maturity-level assessment of generalised audit software: Internal audit functions in Australia", *Australian Accounting Review*, Vol. 29 No. 3, pp. 1–16, doi: 10.1111/auar.12252.

Tetteh, L.A., Agyenim-Boateng, C. and Simpson, S.N.Y. (2023), "Institutional pressures and strategic response to auditing implementation of sustainable development goals: The role of public sector auditors", *Journal of Applied Accounting Research*, Vol. 24 No. 2, pp. 403–423, doi: 10.1108/JAAR-05-2022-0101.

The Institute of Internal Audit. (2016), "Mission of Internal Audit", *The Institute of Internal Audit*, available at: www.theiia.org/en/standards/mission-of-internal-audit/ (accessed 16 May 2023).

The Institute of Internal Auditors (IIA). (2012), *Global Technology Audit Guide (GTAG®) 1 Information Technology Risk and Controls*, Global Technology Audit Guide (GTAG®), Vol. 2nd Edition. The Institute of Internal Auditors.

The Institute of Internal Auditors (IIA). (2017a), "Implementation Guides – International Professional Practices Framework (IPPF)", pp. 1–181.

The Institute of Internal Auditors (IIA). (2017b), "Understanding and Auditing Big Data", *Ippf*, pp. 1–49.

The Institute of Internal Auditors Global. (2012), *Supplemental Guidance: Auditing in Public Sector Governance*, The Institute of Internal Auditors.

The Institute of Internal Auditors Global. (2017), *The IIA's Artificial Intelligence Auditing Framework: Practical Applications Part A*, Global Perspectives and Insights.

Thottoli, M.M., Thomas, K.V. and Ahmed, E.R. (2019), "Qualitative analysis on information communication technology and auditing practices of accounting professionals", *Journal of Information and Computational Science*, Vol. 9 No. 9, pp. 529–537.

Wakunuma, K., Ogoh, G., Eke, D.O. and Akintoye, S. (2022), "Responsible AI, SDGs, and AI governance in Africa", *2022 IST-Africa Conference, IST-Africa 2022*, No. May, doi: 10.23919/IST-Africa56635.2022.9845598.

World Economic Forum. (2022), *The Global Risks Report 2022*, *World Economic Forum*, 17th Edition, World Economic Forum.

Chapter 5

The emergence of algorithmic auditing in the public sector

Ilse Morgan

5.1 INTRODUCTION: BACKGROUND AND DRIVING FORCES

Algorithmic systems such as artificial intelligence (AI), blockchain, and machine learning (ML) hold tremendous potential to improve human rights and democracy in societies (Ebers & Gamito, 2021), provided they are used appropriately (Koene et al., 2019). AI is a sophisticated algorithmic system capable of analysing information, exhibiting intelligent behaviour, and autonomously taking action to achieve specific objectives (European Commission [EC], 2019).

The use of automated decision-making processes within AI systems is becoming more prevalent (Ebers & Gamito, 2021; Waldman & Martin, 2022), both in the public and private sectors, having a potentially significant impact on society (Koene et al., 2019; Hayes, van de Poel & Steen, 2022; Minkkinen, Laine & Mäntymäki, 2022). However, AI systems can be vulnerable to exploitation, whether it is done intentionally or unintentionally, to the detriment of certain stakeholders or population groups (Ebers & Gamito, 2021).

As a result, the regulatory, ethical, and security implications associated with algorithmic systems have gained significant importance in both business and society due to the rapid advancement of AI and the associated risks (Brown, Davidovic & Hasan, 2021; Koshiyama et al., 2021). This further increased the focus on important considerations such as privacy, accountability, transparency, fairness, and security within these systems (EC, 2019; Koshiyama et al., 2021). These systems can cause adverse outcomes such as biases (Brown et al., 2021), discrimination, inefficiencies, and unclear decision-making when algorithmic systems lack transparency and accountability (Bannister & Connolly, 2020; Kossow et al., 2021). The lack of transparency and accountability within the public sector can erode trust in these systems and negatively impact society and the economy (Koene et al., 2019).

Rocco (2022) identified two main pillars of justice, i.e., substantial and procedural fairness, in achieving good governance that applies to AI. However, one of the most concerning limitations of algorithmic systems is the lack of transparency, as Koene et al. (2019) highlighted. The lack of transparent information raises concerns about the effectiveness of traditional governance frameworks for implementing transparency and accountability mechanisms in public sector systems (Koene et al., 2019). These systems can be complex and use ML, causing their behaviour to be influenced not only by their initial design but also by the data they were trained on and the input (source data) they receive (Burrell, 2016; Kossow et al., 2021).

Using algorithmic systems in the digital economy has globally far-reaching implications (Koene et al., 2019) for governments and related industries. To effectively govern these systems, it is essential to create international dialogue and collaboration between both

 DOI: 10.1201/9781003382706-5

developed and developing countries (Koene et al., 2019). Furthermore, there is a need to establish a new framework for international coordination that promotes accountability and transparency in algorithmic systems (Koene et al., 2019; Bannister & Connolly, 2020).

Due to these algorithms playing a critical role in decision-making and producing specific outcomes, establishing effective governance frameworks, regulations, and standards is crucial to prevent potential risks caused by automated or technology-driven decision-making (Koshiyama et al., 2021; Schneider, Abraham, Meske & Vom Brocke, 2022). To mitigate potential risks and achieve effective consequence management, it is essential to establish algorithmic transparency and accountability mechanisms (Koene et al., 2019; Cobbe, Lee & Singh, 2021).

Algorithmic transparency and accountability mechanisms can lead to more scientifically rigorous algorithmic audits, ensuring that algorithms and AI systems are audited thoroughly, continuously, and objectively (Koene et al., 2019). This may further lead to improvements in AI and algorithmic systems (Koene et al., 2019), making it possible to identify and manage biases, errors, and weaknesses in the algorithms' design or implementation. With adequate standards and frameworks, audit or assurance functions will have adequate criteria against which to measure performance or results effectively (Koene et al., 2019).

Algorithmic auditing is the assurance process of evaluating the algorithms (Koshiyama et al., 2021) and automated decision-making systems used in various applications, including those powered by AI. Algorithmic audits are based on transparent standards and can help uncover shortcomings in AI and algorithmic systems and suggest improvements by understanding the underlying processes, data, and decision-making mechanisms. Additionally, algorithmic audits offer a means of verifying compliance with regulations (OGL, 2022) and ensuring that ethical considerations are upheld. Inadequate assurance processes can lead to a lack of accountability, insufficient corrective measures, and no recourse for compensation (Koene et al., 2019) in the case of harm caused by algorithmic decisions. Consequently, internal auditors need to conduct algorithmic audits continuously.

5.1.1 Definition and overview of algorithms and algorithmic systems

An algorithm is a predetermined and well-defined set or sequence of computer instructions used to solve a specific problem or perform a computation (Koshiyama et al., 2021). From a data-centric perspective, an algorithm transforms the descriptive data of a problem into a format consistent with a solution (Hayes et al., 2022). Algorithmic systems use recommender algorithms in ML to analyse attributes and patterns to achieve specific outcomes, such as enhancing efficiencies, executing sophisticated procedures, or facilitating "*evidence-based policymaking*" (Koene et al., 2019:71).

According to Koshiyama et al. (2021:3), an algorithm consists of three main components or elements: data, model architecture, and development. *Data* includes the "*input, output, and simulation environment*" (ecosystem); *model architecture* comprises the "*objective function, formulation, parameters and hyperparameters*" of the algorithm; and *development* involves the designing, documenting, building the algorithm, and "*preparing data for training*" (Brown et al., 2021:2) and implementing the "*infrastructure and open-source libraries*" of the algorithm (Koshiyama et al., 2021:3).

Algorithms with AI systems are used by most computers and smart devices for automated decision-making and processing of data (Association for Computing Machinery [ACM], 2017). With the rise of data analytics and big data, algorithms can now be used to make institutional decisions based on the detection, interpretation, analysis, and presentation of meaningful patterns in data (ACM, 2017). Data analytics has become especially useful in organisations with large data sets (ACM, 2017; Breslow, Hagstroem, Mikkelsen & Robu, 2017), specifically the public sector, and depends on statistical analysis, software, programming, and operational analysis to measure performance.

AI has enabled computers to imitate intelligent human behaviour and is a branch of computer science, creating machines capable of simulating intelligent behaviour (Merriam-Webster, 2020). Algorithms are designed by humans and draw on data produced by humans that contain errors and biases (ACM, 2017; Waldman & Martin, 2022). Likewise, algorithms can be flawed if based on incorrect data. When the public sector uses algorithms without transparency, accountability, and adequate oversight, stakeholders can be at risk, increasing existing bias and inefficiencies. Biases, corruption, and inequalities can be perpetuated by the creators of the algorithms and systems by manipulating the underlying data (Kossow et al., 2021). Detecting algorithmic biases is difficult and can cause harm (AI Now, 2018).

AI algorithms can either be static by performing predetermined fixed actions or dynamic by advancing through ML (Koshiyama et al., 2021). Algorithms are categorised into *“computational statistics (e.g., Monte Carlo methods), complex systems (e.g., agent-based systems)”*, AI, and ML *(e.g., “artificial neural networks”)* (Koshiyama et al., 2021:5). Dynamic algorithms, also known as *“intelligent”* algorithms, are more complex and require increased regulations due to *“testing and verification challenges”* (Koshiyama et al., 2021:5).

An algorithmic or AI system is a set or collection of algorithms that replicate various forms of *“learning, reasoning, knowledge, and decision-making”* (Koshiyama et al., 2021:5), and the following three categories of AI systems are identified:

I   *Knowledge-based (heuristic) or rule-based learning systems* follow an *“if-then logic”* (Kossow et al., 2021:5; Koshiyama et al., 2021:5–6). Limitations of rule-based learning systems include the inability of the application to handle unforeseen situations or new information due to predefined instructions (Kossow et al., 2021; Koshiyama et al., 2021:5–6).

II *Evolutionary algorithms or metaheuristics algorithms* are a group of algorithms that can find the best solution and mechanisms for a complex problem by imitating natural evolution (Brownlee, 2011:91; Koshiyama et al., 2021:5–6). They use a set of suitable and *“adaptive”* methods that work with many possible solutions at once, e.g., *“genetic algorithms or genetic programming”* (Brownlee, 2011:91).

III *Machine learning (ML) algorithms* are AI systems that continuously learn without requiring additional programming, being able to adapt and *“improve through experience”* as new data is introduced (Kossow et al., 2021:5; Koshiyama et al., 2021; Rocco, 2022:4).

Similar to the “Big Data” phase, the algorithmic decision-making and evaluation phase is referred to as *“Big Algo (algorithm)”*, which holds excellent opportunities for the public sector and related institutions (Koshiyama et al., 2021:2). With algorithms and algorithmic systems having a greater impact on our lives, researchers and practitioners have embraced the 5Vs methodology to address the associated implications and challenges (Brundage, Avin, Wang, Belfield, Krueger & Hadfield, 2020; Liu, Wei & Gao, 2020; Koshiyama et al., 2021):

Volume: The significant increase in data generated and processed by algorithms highlights the need for effective data management and analysis strategies.

Velocity: The data collection and processing rate emphasises the need for real-time decision-making and response mechanisms with limited human interventions.

Variety: The diverse types and data sources used by algorithms, ranging from structured to unstructured data, require adaptable approaches for managing and interpreting the information.

Veracity: The accuracy, reliability, regulatory compliance, fairness, and trustworthiness of the data used in algorithmic systems, highlighting the importance of data quality assurance.

Value: The value and insights derived from algorithms and the data being processed highlight the importance of ensuring that algorithmic systems generate meaningful and beneficial outcomes, i.e., new services and cost-savings.

Understanding these technical aspects of AI systems is important for internal auditors to assess algorithms within an automated decision-making process. The following section investigates the processes involving algorithmic decision-making and how it can be used in the public sector.

5.1.2 Algorithmic or automated decision-making

Algorithmic decision-making involves the use of algorithms or AI to make decisions or recommendations based on data captured in applications such as finance, healthcare, education, criminal justice, and employment (Kossow et al., 2021; Metaxa & Hancock, 2022; Waldman & Martin, 2022). These algorithms can analyse and process large amounts of data and use statistical models to identify patterns or relationships to facilitate more efficient and effective decision-making processes (Bannister & Connolly, 2020). Examples are credit scoring algorithms, used to assess an individual's creditworthiness, and predictive policing algorithms to identify areas that are at a higher risk for crime (Bannister & Connolly, 2020).

Using algorithmic decision-making has benefits, disadvantages, and risks (Bannister & Connolly, 2020; Waldman & Martin, 2022). It can increase efficiency, reduce costs, and provide more accurate and reliable decision-making. Utilising AI can improve conducting due diligence by detecting any gaps present in the regulatory frameworks more efficiently and accurately (Kossow et al., 2021).

Alternatively, it can perpetuate biases and discrimination if the underlying data is incorrect or biased (Galdon Clavell et al., 2020; Kossow et al., 2021) or if the algorithm is not designed to account for potential biases. Waldman and Martin (2022) highlighted the effect on the government's legitimacy when technology and AI are used to violate privacy and circumvent accountability, which could lead to authoritarian or unfair outcomes. Several sources of bias within AI and ML systems contribute to unfair automated decision-making processes. These biases can originate from previously corrupted data containing human and societal biases (Brown et al., 2021), such as biased recruitment practices. Similarly, a skewed sample can result in a harmful feedback cycle where future observations validate past predictions, reinforcing the accuracy of projections based on biased data, such as in the case of a police record. Additionally, limited features can hinder gathering reliable information from minority groups, leading to unfair outcomes (Koene et al., 2019). Furthermore, sample size disparity, where training data from minority groups is significantly smaller than that from the majority group (Brown et al., 2021), can amplify bias and lead to unfair decision-making.

5.1.3 Risks of using algorithms in the public sector

A lack of transparency and accountability and discrimination against specific groups are only a few of the risks and potential damages that AI and the associated technological tools pose for individuals and societies in the public sector (Floridi et al., 2018; Martin, 2019; Bannister & Connolly, 2020; Dignum, 2020; Hayes et al., 2022; Minkkinen et al., 2022). These risks emphasise the importance of algorithmic audits and AI governance (Minkkinen et al., 2022; Schneider et al., 2022). In the public sector, algorithms within decision-making processes pose the following risks (Kossow et al., 2021; Rocco, 2022; Schneider et al., 2022):

I *Bias and discrimination:* Algorithms can be biased or discriminatory if trained on data that is not representative, or if the algorithm is designed without considering the potential for bias, or when purposefully designed to discriminate (Ebers & Gamito, 2021:3; Waldman & Martin, 2022). AI-powered automated decision-making can result in discriminatory outcomes, especially in areas like the judicial system, credit access, and the insurance industry (Bannister & Connolly, 2020; Kossow et al., 2021). AI in decision-making may reinforce discrimination and raise concerns about "*income distribution and public trust in government*" (Kossow et al., 2021:2).

II *Complex systems or processes:* Algorithms rely on complex analytical processes to produce their outputs, which are often difficult for humans to understand (Cobbe et al., 2021; Kossow et al., 2021; Schneider et al., 2022). Lacking technical knowledge and "*dedicated resources*" poses a challenge in detecting erroneous results or outputs (Kossow et al., 2021:1; Rocco, 2022:6).

III *Lack of transparency:* Individuals struggle to understand complex algorithms used in the public sector and how the decisions are being made, hindering their ability to challenge decisions they disagree with (Hayes et al., 2022). The public's trust in government decision-making processes can be influenced by this lack of transparency, interpretability, and explainability (Bannister & Connolly, 2020; Kossow et al., 2021).

IV *Errors and inaccuracy:* Algorithms can be prone to misuse (abuse) (Brown et al., 2021; Rocco, 2022), errors, and inaccuracies, particularly if the data used to train them is incomplete or contains errors (Kossow et al., 2021). This can result in incorrect decisions or information being provided to the public.

V *Security and privacy:* Algorithms used in the public sector may handle sensitive or personal data (Koshiyama et al., 2021), and there is a risk that this data could be compromised or misused if the algorithms are not properly secured or there are vulnerabilities in the software. Data privacy laws within a "*socio-political context*" can be complex, particularly the release of information using "*training data*" (Kossow et al., 2021:1).

VI *Lack of human oversight:* Algorithms may be used for automated decision-making that was previously made by humans, reducing the opportunity for human oversight or intervention (Koene et al., 2019). This can result in decisions being made that have not accounted for contextual or individual factors.

VII *Inflexibility:* Algorithms can be inflexible and may not take into account changing circumstances or new information (Koene et al., 2019), resulting in decisions being made that are irrelevant or ineffective.

5.1.4 Ethical algorithms for decision-making

There are growing concerns about algorithmic decision-making used in areas such as criminal justice and employment, where the potential for bias and discrimination can have serious consequences for individuals and communities (Bannister & Connolly, 2020; Galdon Clavell et al., 2020). As a result, there is increasing interest in developing methods for auditing and regulating algorithmic decision-making to ensure that it is fair, ethical, transparent, and accountable (Galdon Clavell et al., 2020; Koshiyama et al., 2021).

By identifying and implementing specific measures in the public sector, ethical algorithms can be developed to enhance the use of fair and transparent algorithms in automated decision-making:

I   *Identify and mitigate potential biases:* Algorithms could perpetuate biases if the data used to train the algorithm is biased or if the algorithm is not designed to avoid potential biases (Brown et al., 2021). Identifying and mitigating potential biases in the data and algorithm design is important to ensure that decisions made by the algorithm are fair and unbiased.

II *Ensure transparency and access to data:* Transparency is essential to ensure that the decision-making process of an algorithm can be understood and scrutinised (Koene et al., 2019). Providing explanations for decisions made by the algorithm and making the results of audits and assessments publicly available is essential for promoting transparency. Organisations should provide transparency into the development (architecture) and use of algorithms (Brown et al., 2021). This includes documenting the data being used in training and testing algorithms, providing explanations for decisions made by the algorithm, and making the results of audits and assessments of the algorithm accessible to auditors and other stakeholders (e.g., researchers) (Brown et al., 2021).

III *Establish regulatory frameworks and standards:* Governments and regulatory bodies should establish regulatory frameworks, ensuring algorithms are designed, implemented, and used responsibly and ethically (EC, 2019; Kossow et al., 2021; Schneider et al., 2022). Standards include guidelines and policies for developing, processing (OGL, 2022), and using algorithms (Kossow et al., 2021). Performance standards to measure outputs are required, as well as standards for auditing and monitoring algorithmic decision-making (OGL, 2022).

IV *Conduct ethical impact assessments:* Organisations should assess the potential ethical impact of algorithms to identify and manage the risks and ethical concerns associated with using algorithms (Raji et al., 2020). This includes assessing the nature and potential impact of the algorithm on different stakeholders (OGL, 2022), identifying potential biases, and developing strategies to mitigate the associated risks.

V   *Establish governance frameworks:* Organisations should establish clear governance frameworks for developing and using algorithms (Bannister & Connolly, 2020; Schneider et al., 2022). This requires introducing policies and procedures for developing and implementing algorithms, identifying and mitigating risks associated with using algorithms (Schneider et al., 2022), and ensuring appropriate training and expertise are in place. Training and resources should be provided for individuals to become adequately proficient in using algorithms responsibly.

VI *Promote human oversight:* Adequate oversight is necessary to ensure that the algorithm considers crucial contextual or individual factors that may have been excluded during its training (Koene et al., 2019). Human involvement in decision-making is essential to ensure ethical implications are considered.

VII *Establish accountability mechanisms through auditing and testing:* Organisations should establish clear lines of responsibility and accountability for developing and using algorithms (Bannister & Connolly, 2020). Mechanisms should be established to hold individuals and organisations accountable for using algorithms and appropriate consequences and penalties for noncompliance. Algorithms should be regularly or continuously audited and tested for biases and inaccuracies, and the results of these audits should be made public.

The abovementioned measures can improve algorithm transparency, promoting greater accountability and trust in automated decision-making processes.

5.1.5 Algorithmic transparency (trustworthiness)

Transparency in "*automated decision-making*" (algorithmic) systems requires a component of human involvement to identify the objectives of the algorithm and involves the data; variables or assumptions in the algorithms (the model); compliance requirements; and lastly, the results, impact, and usage of the algorithm (Koene et al., 2019:5; Kossow et al., 2021). The level of detail required for transparency will vary depending on the audience, i.e., the general public, regulatory bodies, assurance providers, forensic analysts, or researchers. The extent of transparency available in an algorithmic system is determined by a combination of governance processes and specific technical features (Koene et al., 2019).

Transparency is crucial in ensuring reliability, fairness, and accountability (Koene et al., 2019) in algorithmic systems; identifying potential biases; and building public trust in automated decision-making processes (OGL, 2022). Algorithmic transparency is essential in detecting biases in data and algorithms that impact system fairness (Koene et al., 2019). Transparency involves the extent to which an algorithm's decision-making process can be understood, accessed, and assessed in audits (Mittelstadt, Allo, Taddeo, Wachter & Floridi, 2016).

Transparency involves various dimensions, including the transparency of the intended goal, the translation of the goal into machine language, and the provision of performance and impact metrics (Hayes et al., 2022). Giving assurance that ethical algorithms promote fairness, transparency, and accountability in AI or automated decision-making is crucial. The areas of transparency required within algorithmic systems and ML are (Koene et al., 2019; Hayes et al., 2022):

I *Value and goal transparency:* Algorithmic systems often have multiple goals, and transparency about the "*reasons and motivations*" behind the "*intended goals*" is essential (Hayes et al., 2022:7). The disclosure of the algorithm's priorities helps stakeholders understand the intentions and relative importance of different objectives (Koene et al., 2019), ensuring clarity in the automated decision-making process. The decisions behind its objectives will determine whether the goals align with societal values and ethical considerations (Kossow et al., 2021). The algorithm's purpose should be valuable and serve the intended purpose without biases or discriminatory outcomes (Raji et al., 2020).

II *Data transparency:* Understanding the sources, processing, verification (authentication), and representativeness (inclusivity) of the data used by ML algorithms is essential (Koene et al., 2019). The processes involve updating the datasets and retraining the system on the updated version (Koene et al., 2019). It helps identify biases and ensures the data is impartial and suitable for the intended purpose in the decision-making process (Koene et al., 2019).

III *Algorithm transparency:* Testing the actual outputs against the known inputs and expected results (outcomes) is essential to promote algorithmic transparency (Kossow et al., 2021). Auditors can assess the algorithms' effectiveness, accuracy, and fairness by comparing the actual outputs with the expected outcomes. To ensure that the algorithms are appropriate and relevant for their intended purpose, the auditor should validate and examine the internal functions of the variables used in the algorithm. Third-party code reviews, bug reports, and assurance of sound software development processes all contribute to understanding and verifying the algorithms.

IV *Translation transparency:* Focuses on the transparency of translating the algorithm's intended goal into machine language (Hayes et al., 2022). It involves understanding how the algorithm functions, the logic behind its decision-making processes, and the data it relies on. Translation transparency ensures that the algorithm's implementation accurately represents its intended purpose and reduces the risk of unintended biases or errors in the translation process.

V *Performance transparency:* Performance and impact metrics are necessary to assess the effectiveness of an algorithm and evaluate its impact on various individuals or groups (Hayes et al., 2022; Yu & Li, 2022). These metrics include classification accuracy (Brown et al., 2021) and comparing false-positive and false-negative rates between different groups (Hayes et al., 2022). Performance transparency enables auditors and stakeholders to understand how well the algorithm performs, its potential biases, and any unequal impacts it may have on different population groups.

VI *Outcome or results transparency:* Involves transparency regarding the outcomes (results) of algorithmic systems, including the functioning of the internal system and the impact on external systems and interfaces with other algorithmic systems. Understanding the impact and consequences of these systems is essential for accountability and achieving legitimacy (Yu & Li, 2022).

VII *Compliance or consistency transparency:* Transparency about overall and consistent compliance and adherence to regulations, rules, and standards is essential (Hayes et al., 2022).

VIII *Influence/impact transparency:* Transparency is required to identify and disclose any intentional influence or bias in the AI process (Ebers & Gamito, 2021). Users and regulators should be aware of any manipulation or favouritism that may occur, such as paid placements in search results, to maintain fairness and trust in algorithmic systems (Koene et al., 2019).

IX *Usage transparency:* Users should have insight into the personal data used by algorithmic systems for personalisation or system improvement (Koene et al., 2019). Understanding and controlling the usage of personal data is essential to address privacy concerns and empower users in decision-making processes (Koene et al., 2019).

By promoting transparency in these dimensions, algorithmic auditing aims to uncover biases, ensure accountability, and address potential ethical and societal concerns related to algorithmic systems. Transparency relating to the algorithm's functions is imperative to fully comprehend the impact its outcomes may have on individuals and society. Although modern computing systems are highly advanced, it remains a technical challenge to achieve complete transparency on how the outcomes are reached (Koene et al., 2019). Advanced technological tools and techniques, e.g., AI, can be used for assurance purposes but may be significantly restricted due to regulatory requirements for transparency (Koene et al., 2019), especially in the public sector.

5.1.6 Algorithmic accountability and governance

The OECD (2023) identified several opportunities and challenges in using AI and algorithmic systems to achieve good governance, offering opportunities to improve accountability. Introducing algorithmic or automated decision-making processes into governance systems can reduce the risk of corruption and inefficiencies and provide more trustworthy results compared to previous manual discretionary processes (Kossow et al., 2021).

Algorithmic systems can be utilised in data analysis in large datasets to detect irregularities, predict patterns of fraud and corruption, flag a transaction for further investigation, or deter transactions before they occur (Breslow et al., 2017). However, the effectiveness of algorithms depends on the data they are based on and requires specific standards and regulations in the public sector that are not yet in place (Kossow et al., 2021).

The challenges of algorithmic accountability originate from complex interactions between integrated systems and data sources under the control of different organisations and/or circumstances (Koene et al., 2019); therefore, the system's performance cannot be assessed. Further challenges are the difficulty in understanding the outputs produced from the algorithmic system, information asymmetries, and difficulty in detecting harmful data injections (Koene et al., 2019), which will, therefore, require algorithmic audits.

5.2 AUDITING AND REPORTING IN THE PUBLIC SECTOR

Equivalent to governance, auditing AI and algorithms is necessary to manage risks by requiring specific criteria and adequate controls for AI systems (Koshiyama et al., 2021; Minkkinen et al., 2022). Technical audits form part of regulatory assessments and should be incorporated into a more comprehensive regulatory assurance, including interviews and access to policies, documentation, processes, and outcomes. This will allow assurance providers to assess the outcomes or impact of policies, including the algorithmic system's behaviour that could expand or moderate content. Assurance providers and regulators will require specific authority to use these assurance methods, which might need continuous monitoring and auditing instead of a once-off audit. To conduct these audits, regulators will need the resources and skills. Policymakers will need to enable regulators and assurance providers to conduct algorithmic audits.

5.2.1 Types of algorithmic audits

Different types of algorithmic audits will need to be performed by assurance providers to audit the complete system and related data, as suggested by ADA (2021):

I   Code audits: Assurance providers will have direct access to the AI system's code and codebase, which is useful in understanding algorithms and ML objectives (Bandy, 2021). However, codebases can be extensive, and the engineers sometimes fail to understand how all parts of the AI platform operate, making predicting the impact or outcomes difficult. Concerns regarding intellectual property (IP) and security require specific regulations.

II   User surveys: Gathering descriptive data on user experience and identifying problematic behaviour, auditors carry out surveys and conduct interviews with the users (Bandy, 2021). Concerns could arise about pressure on users to respond in a specific manner, the unreliability of human recollection, and difficulty attributing the actual cause to findings.

III   Application programming interface (API) or scraping audit: Assurance providers can automate data collection by writing code with software through an API platform to send and receive data (Bandy, 2021). Publicly available APIs may not provide regulators or assurance providers with the necessary information, which would require additional engineering work by API platforms. This data is used to understand the content presented on the platform but requires the development of a custom tool for each platform.

IV   Sock-puppet audit: Assurance providers use "sock puppets" to "*impersonate users*" on a platform, recording and analysing the data generated by the platform (Bandy, 2021:6). These puppets are not real users and are a proxy for individual user activity and experience to test the algorithm (Bandy, 2021).

V   Crowd-sourced audit: A "mystery-shopper" audit uses real users to collect information from a platform during use to "*test the algorithm*" (Bandy, 2021:6). It is useful in observing content and profiles but requires a custom data collection approach for each media platform. It has only been demonstrated on desktops, not mobile devices, which may skew results.

5.2.2 Legal and regulatory requirements and challenges to conduct algorithmic audits

Specific laws or regulations can affect algorithm audits in the public sector (OGL, 2022), such as financial institutions or healthcare providers. These requirements can affect the scope and methodology of the audit. The Digital Services Act (DSA) introduced by the EU in 2022 requires audits and provisions to grant access to data for regulators and researchers (DSA, 2022). According to EU regulations, high-risk AI system providers must create "*post-market monitoring plans*" to document and continuously monitor performance throughout the entire life cycle after its implementation (Mökander, Axente, Casolari & Floridi, 2022:241).

Apart from the legal considerations, several other factors can affect algorithm audits, including:

I   Access to data: Algorithmic audits require access to the algorithms' underlying training and test data. Data privacy or difficulty in obtaining the data (i.e., secrecy) (Koene et al., 2019) can limit the outcome in terms of efficiency and effectiveness (Kossow et al., 2021).

II   The complexity of the algorithm and related risks: The more complex the algorithm, the more difficult it may be to conduct a thorough audit (Kossow et al., 2021). Some algorithms may be difficult to interpret, and the audit may require specialised expertise in a particular domain or programming language.

III   Changes to the algorithm: Algorithms can change over time as new data becomes available or the algorithm is updated or modified. This can make it difficult to conduct a consistent audit, as the algorithm being audited may differ from the one tested initially.

IV   Bias and subjectivity: Algorithm audits can be influenced by the biases and subjectivity of the auditor (Raji et al., 2020), e.g., having a particular perspective or agenda that affects their interpretation of the data and findings. Audit integrity by meeting the appropriate ethical standards and following a procedural just audit process to avoid any subjectivity in the conduct of the audit would be required (Raji et al., 2020).

V   Time and resources: Algorithm audits can be time-consuming and resource-intensive, particularly for complex algorithms or large datasets, affecting the feasibility of conducting an audit or the depth of the analysis that can be performed.

VI   Nature of AI technologies: Technologies continuously evolve, as well as the related regulatory requirements (Minkkinen et al., 2022).

5.2.3 Steps in the algorithmic auditing process

Algorithmic audits have emerged as a response to concerns about the potential biases and errors that may be present in algorithms used for automated decision-making (Minkkinen et al., 2022). The abilities and enhanced powers of AI systems impact people and organisations and increasingly require algorithmic audits (Galdon Clavell et al., 2020).

Other factors requiring algorithmic audits are the increasing reliance on algorithms in many areas of life and the need for regulatory compliance (OGL, 2022) and continuous assurance of controls. Various organisations are now requesting algorithmic audits, including government and regulatory agencies, academic researchers, and private companies (AI Now, 2023). These audits can help identify algorithm problems before negatively impacting individuals or society.

As decisions are increasingly being made using automated processes, there is a growing need for transparency and accountability in these processes (Cobbe et al., 2021). Algorithmic audits involve a systematic review of the algorithm's architectural design, development, and implementation to identify any biases or errors that may be present. Brown et al. (2021), Galdon Clavell et al. (2020), and Koshiyama et al. (2021) refer to algorithmic audits as methods to detect and mitigate biases and other negative or discriminatory consequences of algorithms. Such audits may include examining the data used to train the algorithm, analysing the code used to implement the algorithm, and evaluating the outcomes or impact of the algorithm in practice.

Algorithmic auditing gives assurance that algorithms and algorithmic systems are reliable, accurate, and free from biases. It assesses AI's legal, ethical, and security implications (Koshiyama et al., 2021) by examining factors such as fairness, transparency, accountability, and adherence to regulations. Algorithmic audits help mitigate risks, identify biases, and promote responsible and trustworthy algorithmic practices. There is a growing need for formal assurance through algorithmic audits in the public and private sectors to ensure that algorithms are legally compliant, ethical, and secure (Koshiyama et al., 2021).

Ensuring trustworthy AI in decision-making is essential to verify that algorithms are predictable, fair, lawful, responsible, verifiable, transparent, and ethical (EC, 2019; Brundage et al., 2020; Ebers & Gamito, 2021; Koshiyama et al., 2021). Accountability for algorithmic decision-making can be assessed during an algorithmic audit to verify data and algorithms' transparency (Koene et al., 2019). The main steps that form part of algorithm auditing suggested by Koshiyama et al. (2021) are:

I DEVELOPMENT

a. *Defining and documenting the objectives and human involvement in an algorithmic system (audit purpose)*
The objectives and criteria used to develop the algorithm should be clearly defined and documented, including the data sources used, the purpose (intent), the design and functionality of the algorithm, and the decision-making criteria (Kossow et al., 2021).

b. *Verify the quality, accuracy, completeness, relevance, and representativeness of data* (Kossow et al., 2021)
The auditor examines whether the algorithm draws conclusions from relevant data, representing the problem or current situation. This confirms that the algorithm makes informed and objective decisions based on appropriate data sources. The algorithm should explain the decisions it makes, including the reasoning and factors considered in the decision-making process (Brown et al., 2021). This ensures that decisions made by the algorithm are aligned with the objectives and related criteria.

c. *The model architecture and identifying meaningful relationships*
The auditor investigates the algorithm's approach, features, variables, or assumptions for connecting and weighting the data (Kossow et al., 2021). This evaluation can reveal any unexpected or previously unknown relationships that may impact the system's outcomes. Identifying these relationships can lead to a deeper understanding of how the algorithm functions and whether it introduces any biases.

d. *Examine virus detection and correction*
The audit includes thoroughly examining the algorithm's code and implementation to identify and fix any viruses or programming errors (bugs) that may affect the accuracy or fairness of the system. This step is essential in ensuring the reliability and integrity of the algorithmic system.

e. *Investigate safeguards against malicious data injection*
The auditor assesses the algorithmic system's safety and security against malicious or adversarial data input or manipulation by assessing the system's resilience to attacks that may intentionally introduce biases or disrupt the algorithm's functioning (Brundage et al., 2020).

II ASSESSMENT

a. *Assessment and levels of access for algorithmic auditing*
Evaluating the algorithm's behaviour and capacities (capabilities) during an algorithm audit involves seven levels of access to the system (Koshiyama et al., 2021). The highest level is the *white box*, where model architecture details are disclosed, and the lowest is *process-access*, where only "*indirect observation*" is possible (Koshiyama et al., 2021:4). Access to the learning process involves insight into the objective function model architecture, and input data, which is limited by the intermediate levels. Level 7 encompasses all "*assessment, monitoring and mitigation strategies*" from the lower levels (Koshiyama et al., 2021:4). Reports become

less detailed and less accurate as levels decrease and a certain level of inaccuracy can be assumed and accepted (Koshiyama et al., 2021).

b. *Assess the continuous monitoring of performance, robustness, and human oversight*
Algorithms should be monitored regularly through human oversight to ensure they perform as expected (Bannister & Connolly, 2020). Such interventions include auditing the data used to train the algorithm, monitoring the outcomes of decisions made by the algorithm, and assessing the accuracy and fairness to ensure that important contextual or individual factors are considered.

III *MITIGATION*

Mitigation strategies are identified during the audit process and through feedback or output received from the audit. Necessary interventions can be made to reduce or eliminate risks and inefficiencies and to adjust or improve the outcomes of the system across the key levels and stages. The scope/extent of access to the algorithmic system influences the mitigation strategy in terms of being more targeted, technical, diverse, and effective (Koshiyama et al., 2021).

IV *ASSURANCE*

The objective of the algorithm audit is to give assurance that the underlying AI system complies with predetermined standards, practices, or regulations, thus improving confidence and trust (Koshiyama et al., 2021). The internal audit process gives assurance that the system complied with *"regulatory, governance, and ethical standards"* after assessing the system design and implementing mitigation strategies (Koshiyama et al., 2021:22). The AI or algorithmic audit process involves different elements and steps to provide assurance of the trustworthiness of the algorithms (Koshiyama et al., 2021; OGL, 2022):

a. *General national regulation and standards and sector-specific assurance* to ensure compliance and accountability across various sectors such as financial services, education, and healthcare (Koshiyama et al., 2021).

b. *Governance* involves technical assessments to evaluate the robustness, privacy, fairness, verifiability, and impact assessments, which consider risks and compliance (Koshiyama et al., 2021).

c. *Risk management assurance* through risk management processes, risk identification during risk assessment workshops, and implementing strategies *"to mitigate unknown risks"* (Koshiyama et al., 2021:22).

d. *Monitoring interfaces* and risk assessments to monitor and track the performance and safety of AI systems, generating an audit trail for assurance, certification, and insurance purposes. A risk-based approach should be followed (Koshiyama et al., 2021).

e. *Certification* by AI engineers or professionals involved in the development and implementation of AI technologies and systems (Koshiyama et al., 2021). This would be conducted by a third party to indicate confidence that the required standards were followed (OGL, 2022).

f. *Insurance* is an emerging service to address anticipated risks related to AI (Koshiyama et al., 2021).

By incorporating these steps above into the algorithmic audit process, auditors can uncover biases, enhance transparency, and ensure the fairness and reliability of algorithmic systems.

5.2.4 AI and algorithms in blockchain and smart contracts

Combining AI and blockchain within the audit process could enhance the audit through automation and a *"traceable"* and transparent *"audit trail"* (Deloitte, 2016:3). Blockchain technology aims to establish trust by providing transparent and auditable data using a distributed architecture and consensus protocols (Han, Shiwakoti, Jarvis, Mordi & Botchie, 2023). The decentralised nature of blockchain technology allows every node to maintain a copy of the complete blockchain, enhancing the security, transparency, and integrity of the system (Batubara, Ubacht & Janssen, 2019).

The transparency, accountability, and auditability qualities of blockchain could enhance the reliability of data, and the ML tools provide an audit trail of the decision-making process (Han et al., 2023). Blockchain-enabled ML systems simplify the audit of the decisions, being recorded on a *"tamperproof, real-time"* and datapoint-by-datapoint basis (Cong, Du & Vasarhelyi, 2018:1782).

Auditing blockchain-based accounting systems in the public sector is presented in more detail in Chapter 3.

5.2.5 Ethics-based auditing

Ethics-based auditing (EBA) of automated decision-making systems was defined by Mökander, Morley, Taddeo and Floridi (2021:1) as *"a structured process"* by which the current or previous behaviour of an organisation is evaluated in accordance with *"relevant principles"* or standards. The EBA audit focuses on the algorithms, the AI systems, or the organisations. Alternatively, Brown et al. (2021) described an ethical algorithm audit as an assessment of the negative impact of algorithms on stakeholders' rights and interests, including identifying the algorithm's properties and characteristics that contribute to these detrimental effects.

When conducting ethical algorithm audits, the emphasis is placed on the impact of the algorithm itself rather than the underlying principles and ethical norms in EBA. The EU High-Level Expert Group identified three components of trustworthy AI, being lawful, ethical, and technically robust (European Commission, 2019). The components are dependent on each other in that ethical concerns could have legal consequences, and a lack of technical robustness can raise ethical concerns (Mökander et al., 2022).

The ethical focus of audits is based on the economic incentives for companies to develop high-performing AI systems and to achieve legitimacy. However, for EBA to ensure safe and ethically responsible AI systems, further research is required on the development and implementation of standards, tools, and frameworks.

5.3 CONTINUOUS AUDITING (CA) IN ALGORITHMS

Audits have traditionally been conducted periodically and ad hoc, therefore covering only parts of systems, processes, and data. CA is an automated assurance system that continuously audits an AI system in real-time to assess its compliance with rules and standards relevant to the activity (Minkkinen et al., 2022:21). CA can continuously audit the AI system's updates and provide real-time and more accurate data on its performance according to standards and criteria (Dai & Vasarhelyi, 2017).

CA of AI systems follows the same logic and methods and appears to be more relevant to internal audit functions (Raji et al., 2020; Tronto & Killingsworth, 2021) as to external audit, although this may change as the audit and assurance environment continues to evolve (Mökander et al., 2021). The EU identified the potential of continuous AI auditing approaches, proposing the provisions in the AI Act (EC, 2021) for the mandatory monitoring of high-risk AI systems. The AI Now Institute (AI Now, 2023) suggests combining different types of audits and impact assessments, which is necessary to adequately monitor and assess AI systems, such as auditing system performance. The adoption and implementation of continuous audit methodologies are slow and are mostly used in internal auditing (Cong et al., 2018).

5.4 CHAPTER SUMMARY/LESSONS LEARNED

The chapter explores the audit of algorithms and AI systems in the public sector, which involves continuously auditing the performance, quality, and impact of algorithmic or automated decision-making systems. The definition and overview of algorithms and algorithmic systems are discussed, and the benefits and risks of implementation in public sector information systems. The chapter further examines the ethical principles and values that should guide the design and use of algorithms for decision-making, such as fairness, accountability, transparency, and explainability. Current practices and standards of auditing and reporting in the public sector are then reviewed to describe the types and methods of algorithmic audits, such as functional, compliance, impact, and ethical audits. The chapter also analyses the legal requirements and challenges of algorithmic auditing, such as data protection, privacy, security, liability, and human rights. The role and potential of AI and blockchain technologies in enhancing the efficiency and effectiveness of algorithmic auditing are explored, as well as the ethical issues and dilemmas that they pose.

The chapter concludes by proposing the enhanced implementation of continuous auditing of algorithms and AI systems in the public sector, which consists of four phases: planning, conducting, reporting, and follow-up. The chapter also provides recommendations and opportunities for future research in implementing continuous auditing of algorithms and AI systems in the public sector. Recommendations include establishing clear goals and criteria, ensuring stakeholder participation and communication, and adopting a multidisciplinary and combined assurance approach.

REFERENCES

Ada Lovelace Institute, AI Now Institute & Open Government Partnership. 2021. Algorithmic accountability for the public sector. Learning from the first wave of policy implementation. (D. Joshi, T. Basu, J. Brennan, & A. Kak, Eds.) [online]. Available from: www.opengovpartnership. org/documents/algorithmic-accountability-public-sector/. [Accessed 16 February 2023].

AI Now Institute. 2018. Algorithmic accountability policy toolkit. [online]. Available from: https://ain owinstitute.org/aap-toolkit.html. [Accessed 8 June 2023].

Association for Computing Machinery (ACM). 2017. Statement on algorithmic transparency and accountability. [online]. Available from: www.acm.org/binaries/content/assets/public-policy/ 2017_joint_statement_algorithms.pdf. [Accessed 28 October 2023].

Bandy, J. 2021. Problematic machine behavior: A systematic literature review of algorithm audits. *Proceedings of the ACM on Human-Computer Interaction*, 5 (74) (April 2021). https://doi.org/ 10.1145/3449148.

Bannister, F., & Connolly, R. 2020. Administration by algorithm: A risk management framework. *Information Polity*, 25 (2020), 471–490. https://doi.org/10.3233/IP-200249.

Batubara, F.R., Ubacht, J., & Janssen, M. 2019. Unravelling transparency and accountability in blockchain. *Proceedings of the 20th Annual International Conference on Digital Government Research*, June, 204–213. https://doi.org/10.1145/3325112.3325262.

Breslow, S., Hagstroem, M., Mikkelsen, D., & Robu, K. 2017. The new frontier in anti-money laundering. [online]. Available from: www.mckinsey.de/~/media/McKinsey/Business%20Functions/Risk/Our%20Insights/The%20new%20frontier%20in%20anti%20money%20laundering/The-new-frontier-in-anti-money-laundering.pdf. [Accessed 13 June 2023].

Brown, S., Davidovic, J., & Hasan, A. 2021. The algorithm audit: Scoring the algorithms that score us. *Big Data & Society*. http://dx.doi.org/10.1177/2053951720983865.

Brownlee, J. (2011). *Clever Algorithms: Nature-Inspired Programming Recipes*. ISBN: 978-1-4467-8506-5.

Brundage, M., Avin, S., Wang, J., Belfield, H., Krueger, G., & Hadfield, G. 2020. Toward trustworthy AI development: Mechanisms for supporting verifiable claims. [online]. Available from: http://arxiv.org/abs/2004.07213. [Accessed 28 October 2023].

Burrell, J. 2016. How the machine "thinks": Understanding opacity in machine learning algorithms. *Big Data & Society*. http://dx.doi.org/10.1177/2053951715622512.

Cobbe, J., Lee, M.S.A., & Singh, J. 2021. Reviewable automated decision-making: A framework for accountable algorithmic systems. *Conference on Fairness, Accountability, and Transparency (FAccT '21)*, March 3–10, 2021, Virtual Event, Canada. https://doi.org/10.1145/3442188.3445921.

Cong, Y., Du, H., & Vasarhelyi, M.A. 2018. Technological disruption in accounting and auditing. *Journal of Emerging Technologies in Accounting*, 15(2), 1–10. https://doi.org 10.2308/jeta-10640.

Dai, J., & Vasarhelyi, M.A. 2017. Toward blockchain-based accounting and assurance. *Journal of Information System*, 31(3), 5–21. https://doi.org/10.2308/isys-51804.

Deloitte. 2016. Blockchain technology: A game-changer in accounting? [online]. Available from: www2.deloitte.com/content/dam/Deloitte/de/Documents/Innovation/Blockchain_A%20game-changer%20in%20accounting.pdf. [Accessed 27 July 2023].

Digital Services Act (DSA). 2022. European Union Digital Services Act, 27 October 2022, Section 28 and 31. [online]. Available from: https://eur-lex.europa.eu/legal-content/EN/TXT/PDF/?uri=CELEX:32022R2065. [Accessed 27 October 2023].

Dignum, V. 2020. Responsibility and artificial intelligence. In M. D. Dubber, F. Pasquale, & S. Das (Eds.), *The Oxford Handbook of Ethics of AI* (pp. 213–231). Oxford University Press.

Ebers, M., & Gamito, M.C. 2021. *Algorithmic Governance and Governance of Algorithms*. Springer. https://doi.org/10.1007/978-3-030-50559-2.

European Commission (EC). 2019. AI HLEG (High-Level Expert Group on Artificial Intelligence). 2019. A definition of AI: Main capabilities and scientific disciplines. [online] Publications Office of the European Union. Available from: https://ec.europa.eu/futurium/en/system/files/ged/ai_hleg_definition_of_ai_18_december_1.pdf. [Accessed 28 October 2023].

European Commission (EC). 2021. Proposal for a regulation of the European Parliament and of the council laying down harmonised rules on artificial intelligence (Artificial Intelligence Act) and amending certain union legislative acts com/2021/206 [online]. Available from: https://digitalstrategy.ec.europa.eu/en/library/. [Accessed 1 August 2022]

Floridi, L., Cowls, J., Beltrametti, M., Chatila, R., Chazerand, P., Dignum, V., … Vayena, E. 2018. AI4People – An ethical framework for a good AI society: Opportunities, risks, principles, and recommendations. *Minds and Machines*, 28(4), 689–707. https://doi.org/10.1007/s11023-018-9482-5.

Galdon Clavell, G., Martín Zamorano, M., Castillo, C., Smith, O., & Matic, A. 2020. Auditing algorithms: On lessons learned and the risks of data minimization. *Proceedings of the AAAI/ACM Conference on AI, Ethics, and Society*, 265–271. https://doi.org/10.1145/33756 27.33758 52.

Han, H., Shiwakoti, R.K., Jarvis, R., Mordi, C., & Botchie, D. 2023. Accounting and auditing with blockchain technology and artificial Intelligence: A literature review. *International Journal of*

Accounting Information Systems, 48 (2023), 100598 https://doi.org/10.1016/j.accinf.2022.100 598.

Hayes, P., van de Poel, I., & Steen, M. 2022. Moral transparency of and concerning algorithmic tools. *AI Ethics*, 3, 585–600. https://doi.org/10.1007/s43681-022-00190-4.

Koene, A., Clifton, C., Hatada, Y., Webb, H., Patel, M., Machado, C., LaViolette, J., Richardson, R., & Reisman, D. 2019. *A Governance Framework for Algorithmic Accountability and Transparency*. European Union. https://doi.org/10.2861/59990.

Koshiyama, A., Kazim, E., Treleaven, P., Rai, P., Szpruch, L., Pavey, G., … Lomas, E. 2021. Towards algorithm auditing: A survey on managing legal, ethical and technological risks of AI, ML and associated algorithms. *Social Science Research Network*. http://dx.doi.org/10.2139/ssrn.3778 998.

Kossow, N., Windwehr, S., & Jenkins, M. 2021. Algorithmic transparency and accountability. [online]. Available from: https://knowledgehub.transparency.org/assets/uploads/kproducts/Algo rithmic-Transparency_2021.pdf. [Accessed 4 July 2023].

Liu, S., Wei, K., & Gao, B. 2020. Power of information transparency: How online reviews change the effect of agglomeration density on firm revenue. *Decision Support Systems*, 153. https://doi.org/ 10.1016/j.dss.2021.113681.

Martin, K. 2019. Ethical implications and accountability of algorithms. *Journal of Business Ethics*, 160(4), 835–850. https://doi.org/10.1007/s10551-018-3921-3.

Merriam-Webster Dictionary. 2020. Artificial intelligence. [online]. Available from: www.merriam-webster.com/dictionary/artificial%20intelligence. [Accessed 1 August 2022].

Metaxa, D., & Hancock, J. 2022. *Using Algorithm Audits to Understand AI*. Stanford University Human-Centered Artificial Intelligence.

Minkkinen, M., Laine, J., & Mäntymäki, M. 2022. Continuous auditing of artificial intelligence: A conceptualization and assessment of tools and frameworks. *Digital Society*. https://doi.org/ 10.1007/s44206-022-00022-2.

Mittelstadt, B.D., Allo, P., Taddeo, M., Wachter, S., & Floridi, L. 2016. The ethics of algorithms: Mapping the debate. *Big Data & Society*. https://doi.org/10.1177/2053951716679679.

Mökander, J., & Floridi, L. 2022. Operationalising AI governance through ethics-based auditing: An industry case study. *AI and Ethics*. https://doi.org/10.1007/s43681-022-00171-7.

Mökander, J., Axente, M., Casolari, F., & Floridi, L. 2022. Conformity assessments and post-market monitoring: A guide to the role of auditing in the proposed European AI regulation. *Minds and Machines*, 32, 241–268. https://doi.org/10.1007/s11023-021-09577-4.

Mökander, J., Morley, J., Taddeo, M., & Floridi, L. 2021. Ethics-based auditing of automated decision-making systems: Nature, scope, and limitations. *Science and Engineering Ethics*, 27(44). https://doi.org/10.1007/s11948-021-00319-4.

OECD. 2023. Recommendation of the council on artificial intelligence, OECD/LEGAL/0449. [online]. Available from: https://legalinstruments.oecd.org/api/print?ids=648&lang=en. [Accessed 27 October 2023].

Open Government Licence (OGL). 2022. Auditing algorithms: The existing landscape, role of regula-tors and future outlook. [online]. Available from: www.gov.uk/government/publications/findi ngs-from-the-drcf-algorithmic-processing-workstream-spring-2022/auditing-algorithms-the-existing-landscape-role-of-regulators-and-future-outlook. [Accessed 1 August 2022].

Raji, I.D., Smart, A., White, R.D., Mitchell, M., Gebru, T., Hutchinson, B., Smith-Loud, J., Theron, D., & Barnes, P. 2020. Closing the AI accountability gap: Defining an end-to-end framework for internal algorithmic auditing. *Conference on Fairness, Accountability, and Transparency (FAT* '20)*, January 27–30, 2020, Barcelona, Spain. ACM, New York, NY, 12 pages. https://doi.org/ 10.1145/3351095.3372873.

Rocco, S. 2022. Implementing and managing algorithmic decision-making in the public sector. https:// ideas.repec.org/p/osf/socarx/ex93w.html [Accessed 15 May 2024].

Schneider, J., Abraham, R., Meske, C., & Vom Brocke, J. 2022. Artificial intelligence governance for business. *Information Systems Management*. https://doi.org/10.1080/10580530.2022.2085 825.

Tronto, S., & Killingsworth, B.L. 2021. How internal audit can champion continuous monitoring in a business operation via visual reporting and overcome barriers to success. *The International Journal of Digital Accounting Research*, 21(27), 23–59. https://doi.org/10. 4192/1577-8517-v21_2.

Waldman, A., & Martin, K. 2022. Governing algorithmic decisions: The role of decision importance and governance on perceived legitimacy of algorithmic decisions. *Big Data & Society* January, June:1–16 https://doi.org/10.1177/20539517221100449.

Yu, L., & Li, Y. 2022. Artificial Intelligence decision-making transparency and employees' trust: The parallel multiple mediating effect of effectiveness and discomfort. *Behavioural Sciences*, 2022(12), 127. https://doi.org/10.3390/bs12050127.

Chapter 6

The organizational needs and future expectations of public sector internal auditors

Thakane E. Rampai

6.1 INTRODUCTION

e-Government is continually evolving and aims to achieve the public sector strategic goals and objectives efficiently and effectively. As technology evolves and the level of adoption of e-Government increases to support the achievement of service delivery objectives, significant changes occur in the structures of public sector internal auditing, along with the traits and characteristics of internal auditors. Hence, the need for internal auditors to position themselves to respond to the challenges and opportunities provided by the technological advancements in the public sector environment. This chapter investigates how internal audit could adapt its organizational structure and address the future needs of internal auditors in the evolving public sector landscape. It further provides strategic recommendations for public sector internal auditors to navigate the dynamic public sector e-Government environment and maintain their "trusted advisor" role.

6.2 OVERVIEW OF THE CURRENT NEEDS OF PUBLIC SECTOR INTERNAL AUDIT

Internal audit plays a crucial role in providing reasonable assurance, advise, insight, and foresight on the prudent use of resources for transparency and accountability in the public administration. As governments across the world embrace e-Government and new expectations and needs for internal audit emerge, the role of internal audit in public administration becomes crucial. In South Africa, this role is enshrined in the country's constitution and supports the principles of public administration, namely, accountability, transparency, efficiency, economy, and effectiveness in the use of resources (RSA, 1996). In fulfilling its mandate, internal audit is to consider the impact of the seven public sector contexts as identified by the Institute of Internal Auditors (IIA), namely, accountability for public funds, the nature of politics, the public good and interest, governance, compliance, integrity and transparency, and also the efficiency and effectiveness of the delivery of public services (IIA, 2022). As a result, the scope of internal audit in the public sector is diverse and encompass broad services such as assurance, advisory, compliance, performance audits, and fraud investigations (IIA, 2022a). However, in delivering these services, the public sector internal auditors experience unique challenges and obstacles as compared to their private sector counterparts due to the political landscape and legal and/or regulatory requirements in this environment (IIA, 2024). In addition, the advancement in technology, increasing volume of data, implementation of e-Government practices, and frequent changes in regulation have increased the demand for internal audit as well as its scope and

DOI: 10.1201/9781003382706-6

responsibilities. To effectively respond to the demand and deliver on its expanded scope and responsibilities, it is important for the public sector chief audit executives (CAEs) and internal audit stakeholders to understand specific legal provisions and the key characteristics that underpin internal audit effectiveness (IIA, 2024; Lufti & Alqudah, 2023; Usman et al., 2023; Matshona, 2020). This understanding enables an assessment of whether the current organizational structure of public sector internal audit aligns with the strategic goals and service delivery objectives. In addition, it identifies how internal audit can adapt to the realities of the dynamic environment to meet the future organizational needs and expectations from stakeholders.

The efficiency and effectiveness of internal audit is affected by legal and/or regulatory provisions and characteristics such as: organizational status and reporting relationship; adoption and conformance with professional standards; independence of the internal audit function and objectivity of internal auditors; competencies of internal auditors, adoption of technology tools, and continuing professional development (CPD); governing body and management support regarding resource allocation; and collaboration with stakeholder and good understanding of the political environment. Although the IIA issued various supplemental guidance, including the unique aspects of internal auditing in the public sector, internal audit still faces challenges in delivering effectively on its mandate in the current public sector environment (IIA, 2022b). The challenges with these regulatory provisions and characteristics are discussed in the next section.

6.2.1 Organizational status and reporting relationship

Every public sector entity needs an independent internal audit function with the necessary power and authority to assess the full range of public sector activities. For internal audit function to remain effective, it needs to be placed in a high-ranking status within the organization and avoid any conditions that may hinder its ability to carry out its responsibilities with objectivity and integrity (IIA, 2022a). Various studies indicate how legislation and governance framework play a key role in enhancing the independence of internal audit function within the public sector (Langella, Vannini & Persiani, 2023; Khelil & Khlif, 2022; Moodley, Ackers & Odendaal, 2022; Lipunga, Tchereni & Bakuwa, 2021; Kahyaoğlu, Sarikaya & Topal, 2020).

The importance of organizational independence is emphasized in the Global Internal Audit Standards (GIAS) and must be formally adopted in the internal audit charter. Principle 7 of the GIAS requires that the CAE be qualified, directly report to the board, and holds a position within the organization that enables the internal audit function to discharge its services and responsibility without interference (IIA, 2024). The reporting lines of the internal audit function, namely, administrative and functional reporting, refer to the organizational structure where the CAE is appointed and governed, often dictated by legal and/or regulatory provisions and the internal audit charter. Functional reporting to the governing body or audit committee allows for approval and independent oversight over the CAE's appointment, compensation, performance evaluation, and termination, including the approval and oversight of internal audit charter, methodologies, budget, and resource plan. On the other hand, the administrative reporting entails reporting of administrative matters such as budgeting, human resources, internal audit methodologies, among other things, to the head of department or an equivalent (IIA, 2024). In addition, an internal audit charter empowers the internal audit function to have unrestricted access to assets, records, and personnel in the execution of internal audit services. However, in the public sector, legal and/or regulations provisions may influence the mandate, organizational position, scope of work, and methodologies of the internal audit function (IIA, 2024).

Furthermore, while other countries continue to face challenges in ensuring the independence of internal audit function, notable examples of countries such as Turkey, South Africa, Canada, and Malawi, among others, have acknowledged the importance of positioning the internal audit function to maintain its independent status within the organization (Liston-Heyes & Juillet, 2023; Kahyaoğlu et al., 2020; RSA, 1999, 2003). While literature suggests that the position of internal audit within the organization and reporting relationship is crucial to its independence, there is significant variation in how internal audit is positioned within the organization in different countries. This is as a result of the nature of the internal audit structure being founded under a legal framework in a jurisdiction within which it operates (IIA, 2024). These variations in legal and/or regulatory framework in different jurisdiction are discussed in the next section.

6.2.2 Legal and/or regulatory framework and conformance with professional standards

The GIAS and its related public sector publications are the foundation of the internal audit profession designed to offer comprehensive guidance on how internal auditors should fulfill their responsibilities effectively, and further seek to promote consistency and quality of internal audit services within the public sector (IIA, 2024). Although the IIA has issued guidelines on how to govern internal audit function, the varying legal and/or regulatory framework by country significantly impacts on the organizational structure and independence of the internal audit function, including the objectivity of internal auditors (IIA, 2024). Table 6.1 demonstrate notable examples of how a legal framework for the establishment of internal audit function and adoption of the International Professional Practice Framework (IPPF) varies by country.

Table 6.1 demonstrate notable examples of how a legal framework for the establishment of internal audit function and adoption of the International Professional Practice Framework (IPPF) varies by country.

- **Low level of adherence with professional standards**: While the standards are essential and provide best practice guidance for the internal audit, implementation and adherence are voluntary. Countries that support the establishment of internal audit through legal and/or regulatory framework generally adhere to professional standards (Langella et al., 2023; Alzeban & Gwilliam, 2014; RSA, 2009).
- **Role ambiguity**: In the absence of, or lack of understanding of a legal and/or regulatory framework, public sector internal audit function tend to face the challenge of conflicting expectations from its stakeholders, including the citizens, managers, and audit committees (Khelil & Khlif, 2022).
- **Lack of autonomy and independence**. When internal audit function operates under the direct control of managers, there are challenges with reporting of irregularities, leading to prioritization of top management's interest at the expense of other stakeholders (Khelil & Khlif, 2022). However, when internal audit function is independent within the organization, it creates an atmosphere of objectivity, unrestricted appraisal, and unbiased reporting of findings (Motubatse, 2019). The Ukraine public sector is an example of how reporting lines can impact the independence of internal audit function. The National Internal Audit Standards of Ukraine gives the head of the institution

Table 6.1 Examples of application of legal and/or regulatory provisions in various countries

Country	Legal and/or regulatory framework	Application
South African public sector	Public Finance Management Act (PFMA) for national and provincial spheres of government/ Municipal Finance Management Act (MFMA) for the local sphere of government (RSA, 2003, 1999). Internal Audit Framework (RSA, 2009).	The organizational status of internal audit is further supported by dual reporting wherein the CAE reports administratively to the accounting officer and functionally to the audit committee. Section 65(2) of the MFMA also requires the internal audit function to report to the audit committee. This is supported by MFMA Circular 65 which explicitly requires that CAE report functionally to the audit committee and administratively to accounting officer (IIA, 2024; RSA, 1999, 2003). Furthermore, National Treasury issued a regulation that compelled internal audit function to adopt and implement International Standards for the Professional Practice of Internal Auditing (IAS), which consequently requires conformance with the IPPF (Moodley et al., 2022; RSA, 2009).
Italian public sector	National legislation.	Internal audit's establishment results from coercive pressure of national legislation requiring accounting harmonization of financial statements, followed by normative pressure where regional and organizational resolutions adopted the IPPF. Although legislation influenced its establishment, there is no harmonization due to the regional governments' exclusive power over regulations (Langella et al., 2023).
Malawian public sector	Finance Management Act and the Local Government Act.	Internal audit is established in terms of the Finance Management Act and the Local Government Act. However, its governance frameworks do not refer to internal audits (Lipunga et al., 2021).
Canadian public sector	Financial Administration Act.	The Canadian reform between 2006 and 2009 played a significant contribution to the independence of internal auditors. The Financial Administration Act requires administrative heads of public agencies to ensure internal audit function has adequate resources to discharge its responsibility. In addition, the Treasury Board appoints audit committees and requires dual reporting. Furthermore, to strengthen independence, the CAE is required to submit annual reports to the Office of Comptroller General (OCG) (Liston-Heyes & Juillet, 2023).
Tunisia public sector	No formal legislation except "Guide to Good Corporate Governance Practices".	Aside from the "*Guide to Good Corporate Governance Practices*", there is no evidence of formal legislation requiring the establishment of an internal audit function nor defining its responsibilities. A study on "Internal auditors' perceptions of their role as assurance providers" indicated that the absence of legal frameworks that protect internal auditors hinders their ability to fulfill their role as assurance providers (Khelil & Khlif, 2022).

(Continued)

Table 6.1 (Continued)

Country	Legal and/or regulatory framework	Application
Malaysian public sector	Treasury Circular No. 2 of 1979 and Circular No. 9 of 2004.	Internal audit is established through Treasury Circular No. 2 of 1979 and Circular No. 9 of 2004 for implementation in "Federal Ministries and Departments and State Governments" (Ahmi, Saidin, Abdullah, Ahmad & Ismail, 2016).
Saudi Arabian public sector	State Directive: Resolution No.235 (2004) and Resolution No. 129 (2007).	Internal audit is established through a mandate documented in State Directive: Resolution No.235 (2004). Later on, Resolution No. 129 (2007) provided additional guidance and regulation outlining requirements for objective internal audit, adherence to standards, and scope of work (Alzeban & Gwilliam, 2014).
Swedish local government	Swedish Municipal Act.	Internal audit is established in terms of Swedish Municipal Act. However, internal auditors are appointed by, work for, and report to the Council. The fact that politicians appoint internal auditors indicates independence challenges in the Swedish system (Thomasson, 2018).
Turkish public sector:	Public Financial Management and Control Law No. 5018 (2004),	Internal audit is established in terms of Public Financial Management and Control Law No. 5018 (2004), with the Internal Auditing Coordination Board (The Board) playing a vital role in the administration and coordination of internal audit services for different public entities (Kahyaoğlu et al., 2020).
Ukrainian public sector	Article 26 of the new Budget Code, 2008. National Internal Audit Standards of Ukraine (UA Standards).	Internal audit is established in terms of Article 26 of the new Budget Code, 2008. Internal audit interacts with the Accounting Chamber of Ukraine, the head of the institution (manager), and the audit committee. However, it is subordinated and accountable directly to the head of the institution, the budget holder. The National Internal Audit Standards of Ukraine (UA Standards) allow the manager to sign internal audit documents such as assurance and quality improvement programs, internal audit workload, and strategic and operational plans, while the audit committee's role is to discuss management, control, and audit issues (Volodina, Grossi & Vakulenko, 2022).

Source: Prepared by author from literature reviewed

authority and functions generally performed by the CAE and the audit committee, while the audit committee's role is to discuss management, control, and audit issues. Ukraine's new legislative framework, aimed at changing the role of internal audit, created independence issues (Volodina et al., 2022). However, this legislative framework, overlooked an important aspect that, organizational independence is achieved when the CAE reports functionally to the board and is granted the necessary status within the organization to fulfil internal audit responsibilities without interference (IIA, 2024).

- **Attack on the quality of internal audit work**: The absence or lack of understanding of the authority in the legal and/or regulatory framework by internal auditors regarding their mandate to execute internal audit services results in the quality of internal audit work being attacked by auditees (IIA, 2020).
- **Insufficient resource allocation and senior management support**: Internal audit function that is not supported by the legal and/or regulatory framework is often centralized and allocated insufficient staffing to execute its mandate (Lipunga et al., 2021). The varying funding processes for internal audit in the public sector tend to limit the ability of the CAE to fully resource the internal audit function (IIA, 2024).

These factors, among others, suggest that legal and/or regulatory framework and the GIAS are important inputs or variables that affect the organizational status of internal audit function, thus impacting on its independence and objectivity (IIA, 2024). This aspect is discussed in the next section.

6.2.3 Independence and objectivity of internal auditors

The GIAS includes a code of ethics that serves as a valuable tool to ensure that internal auditors execute their mandate with integrity and objectivity (IIA, 2024). The IIA defines objectivity as "an unbiased mental attitude that allows internal auditors to make professional judgments, fulfill their responsibilities, and achieve the purpose of internal auditing without compromise" and, GIAS 2: Maintaining Objectivity requires "internal auditors maintain an impartial and unbiased attitude when performing internal audit services and making decisions" and further emphasizes the importance of individual objectivity, safeguarding of objectivity, and disclosing impairments to objectivity (IIA, 2024). Meaning, when an internal audit is independent within the organization, it creates an atmosphere of objectivity, unrestricted appraisal, and reporting of findings (Motubatse, 2019). However, while objectivity is a critical attribute for any internal auditor, the public sector internal auditors experience challenges of impairment of objectivity due to low organizational status and improper reporting lines (Khelil & Khlif, 2022). This is inclined to have a negative impact on the stakeholders' confidence on the work of the public sector internal audit, as stakeholders such as external auditors often use objectivity as one of the factors to make reliance decision on internal audit work. Usman, Rohman and Ratmono (2023) found a positive correlation between objectivity and external auditors' reliance on internal audit work in the Indonesian public sector and linked it to source credibility theory, which explains that higher credibility leads to greater objectivity. Therefore, the demonstration of independence and objectivity may be an essential prerequisite for securing management support regarding adequate resources allocation and successful adoption of technology tools; these are discussed in the next section.

6.2.4 Resource allocation and adoption of technology tools

6.2.4.1 Resources

The GIAS 8.2: Resources requires the "CAE to evaluate whether internal audit resources are sufficient to fulfill the internal audit mandate" (IIA, 2024). In general, the internal audit function is allocated an annual budget and typically needs to be proportionate to the scope of work (Matshona, 2020). However, insufficient budget is identified as one of the factors impacting internal audit effectiveness (Suleiman, Hamad & Yussuf, 2021; Matshona, 2020). A study conducted by the IIA revealed that, since the Covid-19 pandemic, budget cuts have become persistent in the public sector due to decreased tax revenues, and that internal audit is normally among the first to be affected when budget cuts are necessary (IIA, 2020). Consequently, this trend has the potential to limit the CAE's ability to effectively execute the internal audit plan (IIA, 2024).

6.2.4.2 Adoption of technology tools

The GIAS 10.3: Technological Resources requires the internal audit function to pursue opportunities to improve efficiency and effectiveness through the adoption of technology tools such as audit management system, data science and analytics, governance, risk management, and control process mapping applications (IIA,2024). This drive toward digitalization of business processes through technology and automation is credited for its data analysis ability at a level that surpasses human cognitive abilities and uncovers more results than manual assessments (Jarva & Zeitler, 2023). These include new technological methods such as blockchain, algorithms, cognitive computing, robotic process automation, artificial intelligence, data analytics, and machine learning, among others, which require a different set of skills (KPMG, 2020; Mujalli & Almgrashi, 2020; Wang, Zipperle, Becherer, Gottwalt & Zhang, 2020). One of the skills necessary to navigate new technological methods is the ability to use computer-assisted audit tools and techniques (CAATTs) in conducting internal audit engagements. However, insufficient resources allocation, shortage of technical expertise, and an organizational culture that is not conducive to the use of technology hinder the adoption and implementation of CAATT (Lufti & Alqudah, 2023; Islam & Stafford, 2022). A study in Jordan's public sector found that IT knowledge has a positive moderating effect on the relationship between CAATTs usage and internal audit effectiveness. This implies that the level of IT skills possessed by internal auditors influences the relationship between the use of technological tools and internal audit effectiveness (Lufti & Alqudah, 2023). In addition, research suggests that the lack of knowledge and use of CAATTs and the acquisition of necessary IT resources and infrastructure can impede the effectiveness of audits in a digital environment; conversely, the high level of competency serves as an indication to management that the internal auditors can proficiently execute their mandate (Polizzi & Scannella, 2023; Mosweu & Ngoepe, 2019).

Furthermore, there is a growing expectation from stakeholders that internal auditors need to conduct real-time (continuous) audits. However, complexity and institutional rigidity are some of the challenges that threaten the effective implementation of continuous auditing (Polizzi & Scannella, 2023). The GIAS 10.3: Technological Resources also highlights that in the public sector, the funding challenges may require internal audit function to use only software approved by the organization, which places limitations on the effective execution of internal audit services (IIA, 2024). Addressing these challenges is imperative in reducing uncertainties regarding the implementation of continuous auditing (Kahyaoğlu et al., 2020). Furthermore, a competency development programs to enhance and develop knowledge, skills, and abilities for auditing the technological-enabled environments is necessary; these are discussed in the next section.

6.2.5 Competencies and continuing professional development (CPD)

6.2.5.1 Competencies

Competency encompasses a range of attributes required of internal auditors to be deemed proficient in effectively performing their duties. The IIA defines competency as "knowledge, skills and abilities", and in terms of the GIAS: 3.1: Competency, the "internal auditors are required to possess knowledge, skills and abilities to perform their job and responsibilities in relation to their job position and level of experience" (IIA, 2024). The IIA's commitment to promoting education is illustrated by the introduction of the competency framework to strategically address the professional development and competencies of internal auditors. This framework outlines professionalism, performance, environment, leadership, and communication as pivotal components of internal audit expertise (Aldemİr & Uçma Uysal, 2024; IIA, 2022c).

Therefore, as a foundation, knowledge and skills can be acquired by obtaining qualifications through institutions of higher learning, practical training in industry, and professional certifications (IIA, n.d). A study in the Ministry of Finance in Zanzibar asserts that auditors' professional qualifications are essential to effectively perform internal audit services (Suleiman et al., 2021). In addition, institutions endorsed by the IIA as Internal Auditing Education Partnership (IAEP) schools to offer undergraduate and/or postgraduate internal audit programs equip students with knowledge and skills required to perform internal audits. Furthermore, they lay a foundation for students planning to follow the Certified Internal Auditor (CIA) route (IIA, n.d). However, country-specific factors such as governance system and legal and/or regulatory framework for higher learning and qualifications influence the selection of skills. An example is the Republic of Kosovo, where knowledge of finance and legislation is still considered critical skills of successful auditors over other skills (Vokshi & Xhemajli, 2022). Furthermore, the evolution of technology, the speed of change, and the implementation of e-Government have an impact on internal auditing in the public sector. This requires investment in training of internal auditors to upskill and/or develop new skills to conduct internal audit services effectively using technology (IIA, 2024; Mujalli & Almgrashi, 2020). Therefore, continuing professional development (CPD) plays a pivotal role in enhancing internal audit competencies.

6.2.5.2 Continuing professional development

The investment in CPD is crucial as it ensures that internal auditors stay abreast of the new developments. Accordingly, the GIAS:3.2 advocates for internal auditors' enhancement of knowledge, skills, and other competencies through CPD (IIA, 2024). However, an investment in skills development requires the board and senior management supports through the allocation of sufficient funds (IIA, 2024; Vokshi & Xhemajli, 2022). When internal auditors' knowledge and skills are maintained, it leads to enhanced quality and effectiveness of their output (IIA, 2024). Furthermore, enhancing competencies through upskilling and staying abreast with industry developments may improve the ability of internal auditors to effectively engage with stakeholders (Mosweu & Ngoepe, 2019). The need for enhanced collaboration is discussed in the next section.

6.2.6 Collaboration and engagement with stakeholders

6.2.6.1 Combined assurance

As business processes become more complex, specialized, and interdependent, it is important to heighten collaboration and coordination across roles and disciplines to achieve desired performance outcomes (Bolton, Logan & Gittell, 2021). In the absence of coordination and effective communication among assurance providers and governance structures, there is a potential for duplication of effort and overlooking the management of critical risks (Bantleon, d'Arcy, Eulerich, Hucke, Pedell & Ratzinger-Sakel, 2021). The GIAS:9.5: Coordination and Reliance advocates for collaboration between internal audit, management, audit committee, and other assurance providers for efficient and effective risk management (IIA, 2024). In addition, the IIA introduced the Three Lines Model, previously known as "*The Three Lines of Defense Model*" and an integrated combined assurance concepts in the standards to clarify the roles of different governance functions and to provide a simple and effective way of coordinating and communicating risk management and control activities (Bantleon et al., 2021; IIA, 2015, 2024). However, while the IIA prefers the Three Lines of Defense Model, alternative models have emerged that incorporate additional lines of defense, this includes four-line and five-line models that recognize the importance of including governance structures in assurance mapping (Vousinas, 2021; Minto & Arndorfer, 2015). However, the purpose of this section is not to prefer a certain model against the other but rather to highlight the importance and roles of different structures in coordinating with public sector internal audit. Furthermore, a closer collaboration between internal audit and senior management enables internal audit to understand the public sector policy and strategic direction of the organization, strategic risks, and possibly those that are not formally documented in the risk registers (Moodley et al., 2022).

Importantly, this collaboration is enhanced through the initiative between the IIA and the International Organization of Supreme Audit Institutions (INTOSAI) which extended the combined assurance model to the public sector with the aim of clarifying the key roles and relationship of various stakeholders and their contribution to organization governance and risk management processes (IIA, 2022c). The Report on corporate governance for South Africa (King IV) also advocates for combined assurance and issued guidelines for its implementation (IoD, 2016). However, despite the presence of these guidelines and frameworks, the implementation of combined assurance in the public sector is lagging (Moodley et al., 2022). The essential principles of internal audit collaboration and cooperation with stakeholders, together with combined assurance, are discussed next.

6.2.6.2 External and internal audit

The internal and external auditors are mandated in terms of their respective professional standards to coordinate their activities with the aim of enhancing the efficiency and effectiveness of assurance efforts. The GAIS:9.5 requires the CAE to coordinate with internal and external providers of assurance and consider relying upon their work (IIA, 2024). Similarly, external auditors are required in terms of International Standard of Auditing: 610 to consider using the work of internal auditors, provided that specific requirements are fulfilled by the internal audit function (IAASBA, 2021). These principles of coordinated assurance have been widely adopted by management and the audit committee alike. Consequently, these stakeholders require these assurance providers to work closely and collaboratively to reduce possible duplication of their efforts. Accordingly, Usman et al. (2023) and Motubatse (2019) found that management expects external auditors to rely on the work performed by internal auditors when conducting their audit engagement.

In addition, cooperation between internal and external audits is identified as one of the factors affecting internal audit efficiency and effectiveness (Usman et al., 2023). However, it is important to understand that internal and external auditing plays different roles in the public sector; therefore, the existence of each is not expected to diminish the existence of the other. Hence, a study on "factors preventing internal audits from effectively contributing to improved public sector performance and service delivery" cautions that, internal auditors often dilute their influence within the organization by competing with external auditors instead of leveraging access to internal information and their insight to complement other functions and enhance collaboration with other lines of defense (Moodley et al., 2022). Internal audit further plays a crucial role in fostering a collaborative approach to risk management; this role is discussed in the next section.

6.2.6.3 Risk management

The internal audit function is traditionally responsible for providing assurance on the adequacy design and operational effectiveness of the risk management process. This includes assurance that risks inherent in the organization's operations are managed within the adopted appetite and tolerance levels, and provide advisory services with safeguards in instances where the organization's risk management is inadequate (IIA, 2009). This role has been expanded to include insights and foresight on the enterprise-wide risk management (ERM) philosophy and the activities of the organization (IIA, 2024).

Although the IIA issued a position paper aimed at guiding internal auditors in executing their ERM responsibilities, there is potential risk when internal audit function assumes a central role in risk management which in turn may compromise its independence and the objectivity on internal auditors (IIA, 2009). Ukraine's public sector is an example of conflicting expectations from internal audit between the governing authority and senior management. The governing authority expects internal audit to improve governance and internal control to prevent ineffective use of public resources, while senior management perceives internal audit as "watchdogs" and "revisors" of financial information. These contrasting expectations create pressure for internal auditors, resulting in ineffective collaboration and coordination of risk management activities (Volodina et al., 2022). Despite the challenges, internal audit has more role to play in assisting the organization to manage the risks that has potential to affect the achievement of strategic objectives. The role of internal audit in collaborating with stakeholders in organizational strategic process is discussed in the next section.

6.2.6.4 Strategic process

The internal audit function generally has an ariel view of an organization and the ability to assess alignment of organizational performance with its strategic objectives (IIA, 2024). Therefore, for the internal audit function to effectively execute its mandate, the CAE must have a good understanding of the strategic posture and direction of an organization. Accordingly, Moodley et al. (2022) is of the view that active participation by internal audit in the strategic formulation and management process of the organization has the potential to significantly improve its understanding of the organization's strategy, thus enabling it to drive positive outcomes of the organization's strategic framework. This view is supported by the "relational coordination theory" which advocates for a better integration within the organization to achieve improved outcomes through interactions, effective communication, and positive relationships among individuals or groups (Bolton et al., 2021). In particular, when this collaborative approach is embraced by assurance providers, it minimizes fatigue, reduces costs, and eliminates duplication of effort (Moodley et al., 2022). However, the political environment in the public sector poses another hurdle that can impede an effective collaboration between public sector internal auditors and its stakeholder. The intricacies of the public sector political environment are discussed in detail in the next section.

6.2.7 Political environment

Politics plays a key role in the public sector and may shape the decision-making process. Depending on the specific structure, a governing party is typically elected by citizens, and heads of organizations are appointed by government leaders or governing bodies of the organization itself. These political appointments influence various processes and communication with governance structures; therefore, an understanding of the political process is important for public sector internal auditors to effectively contribute to the achievement of service delivery objectives (IIA, 2022a, 2022e). The IIA cautions that political interference within the public sector poses a major threat to the independence of the internal audit function and objectivity of internal auditors when those charged with authority impose scope limitation for personal gain which impact on the trust and confidence of the citizens. Therefore, unfamiliarity with these intricacies of the public sector by internal auditors can potentially affect internal audit independence and erode trust in the profession (IIA, 2022a).

The Swedish public sector is a typical example of how political interference and biases may affect the credibility of the audit process when political parties play a significant role in the appointment of internal auditors and management of audit outcomes. The implications are that, the more open the process is to political influence, the more the risk of losing credibility (Thomasson, 2018). A study by the IIA (2020) also found that the political environment creates a climate where the quality of internal audit work is attacked by auditees to safeguard their interest or avoid criticism. Therefore, it is important that public sector internal auditors possess sufficient independence to resist any form of political influence. Independence empowers the internal audit function to hold politicians and public servants accountable for their actions in enhancing the democratic principles of accountability and transparency. However, should the audit process be susceptible to political influence, the credibility and legitimacy of the internal audit function will be questioned by its stakeholders (Thomasson, 2018).

It is evident that various challenges facing public sector internal audit functions as indicated in Table 6.2, may potentially undermine the objectivity of internal auditors and compromise the independence, efficiency, and effectiveness of the internal audit functions.

6.2.8 Discussion

Based on the preceding sections, literature suggests that organizational independence of internal audit influences how senior management views and values internal audit, which determines the level of support internal audit received from management and the board (Langella, Vannini & Persiani, 2023; Liston-Heyes & Juillet, 2023; Khelil & Khlif, 2022; Moodley, Ackers & Odendaal, 2022; Lipunga, Tchereni & Bakuwa, 2021; Kahyaoğlu, Sarikaya & Topal, 2020). The support from senior management and the board provides a

Table 6.2 Summary of challenges with current organizational structure and impact on the internal audit function

Internal audit challenges	Impact on internal audit effectiveness
Organizational status and reporting relationship.	• Independence • Objectivity
Legal and/or regulatory framework and conformance with professional standards.	• Credibility • Adherence to GIAS • Independence • Allocation of resources
Independence and objectivity of internal auditors.	• Credibility • Allocation of resources
Allocation of resources and adoption of technology tools.	• Effectiveness • Efficiency
Competencies and continuing professional development (CPD).	• Credibility • Implementation of technology tools • Efficiency
Collaboration with stakeholders.	• Credibility • combined assurance • risk management • Strategy misalignment
Political environment.	• Credibility • Independence

Source: Prepared by the author.

platform to resource internal audit function with skilled and competent internal auditors, acquire necessary technology tools, and contribute to continued professional development. An adequately resourced internal audit function has the capability to meet the expectations of stakeholders, contribute effectively and efficiently to combined assurance, and assist in the achievement of the service delivery goals and objectives. In addition, the adoption and use of audit technologies has the potential to improve transparency and credibility of the audit process and effectively respond to the demand of e-Government, thus enhancing the relevance and effectiveness of the public sector internal audit. Furthermore, the adoption of technology can also enhance the credibility of the public sector internal audit activities as the efficiencies associated with the use of technology will ensure timely assurance and advise that support decision-making. Therefore, the future public sector internal audit needs to be characterized by key attributes advocated in this section. However, achieving this requires that the challenges identified receive attention from the relevant authorities and management. The next section identifies and recommends the focus areas for future organizational structure for an internal audit function and key attributes of future internal auditors.

6.3 THE FUTURE ORGANIZATIONAL STRUCTURE AND EXPECTATION OF PUBLIC SECTOR INTERNAL AUDITORS

As organizations change, the risk landscape evolves and expands the audit universe of the internal audit (IIIA, 2024; Betti & Sarens, 2018). To effectively respond to these changes, internal audit functions are required to adjust their organizational structures and address the needs of auditors. Accordingly, Lenz and Jeppesen (2022) viewed the future of internal audit metaphorically as the "Gardener of Governance" and suggested the Five Ps (5P) model (planet, public, prosperity, profession, and people) illustrated in Figure 6.1 as a possible solution to effectively respond to the ever-increasing expectations and demand for internal audit services.

The 5Ps model relates to (Lenz & Jeppesen, 2022):

- **Planet**: The growing importance of environmental, social, and governance (ESG) objectives, requires internal audit to play a more active role and provide value to organization and society.
- **Public**: Advocating for internal auditing to regulators, boards, and stakeholders to create awareness and heightened legitimacy.
- **Profession**: Creation of a unique internal audit value proposition and be the gardener of governance.
- **Prosperity**: Serving the overall strategy of the organization, protecting and enhancing public welfare by internal auditors.
- **People**: The need for internal auditors to continuously learn, remain flexible, adapt to change, and adopt technology.

Lenz and Jeppesen (2022) view the 5Ps model as a foundation for shaping the future of internal audit due to its relevance, legitimacy, and significance to the organization and society. Based on the preceding discussions and informed by literature review, below

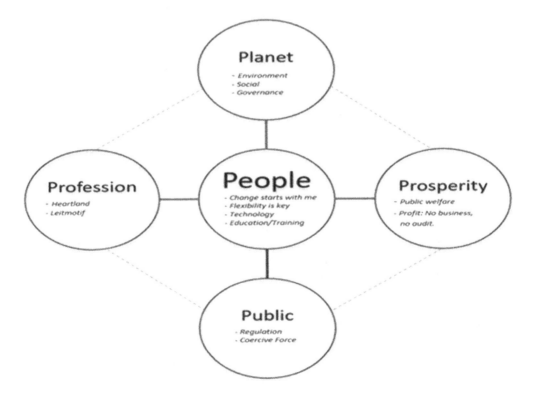

Figure 6.1 The 5Ps model.

Source: Lenz and Jeppesen (2022).

recommendations are presented in two categories, namely, the future organizational structure of internal audit and future needs of internal auditors.

6.3.1 Future organizational structure of internal audit function

The public sector organizations may consider the following focus areas to establish sustainable internal audit function of the future. These focus areas are regarded as a means to prepare the internal audit function to maintain relevance by adapting to the changing organisational needs and technological advancement, and ensure alignment with the organizational strategic goals.

a. **An autonomous internal audit function**: With the public sector becoming more complex due to technological evolution and regulatory changes, the need for a formally defined legal framework that supports the establishment of the internal audit function is instrumental in heightening the legitimacy of internal audit (Lenz & Jeppesen, 2022). An autonomous internal audit function ensures that internal audit services are conducted without pressure or interference. Countries with no legal and/or regulatory provision to support internal audit should consider the development and implementation of such framework. Internal audit functions that are founded on the regulatory framework are likely to conform to professional standards, thus observing the independence requirements (Langella et al., 2023; Alzeban & Gwilliam, 2014; RSA, 2009). However, the regulatory framework should include provisions for reinforcing independence and resource support to ensure the effective functioning of internal audit. In addition, countries, in collaboration with regulators and boards, should carry out sustained education that champion the role and status of internal audit to heighten the awareness and appreciation of internal auditing's value proposition (Lenz & Jeppesen, 2022).

b. **Response to legislative and regulatory changes:** To raise the stature of the internal audit function within the organization, internal auditors must stay abreast of the changing environment within their jurisdiction and share insights with stakeholders (KPMG, 2020). A change in the organization due to a new piece of regulation or shift in political leadership requires the CAE to be flexible and assess whether necessary skills are available to address the associated risk, and adapt the audit plan and resources to address them (Vokshi & Xhemajli, 2022). This may also require the internal audit function to upskill or effectively collaborate with compliance and legal experts for insight on new legislation.

c. **Contribute to sustainability and ESG initiatives:** The global efforts to mitigate the impact of climate change compel organizations to reflect on how their operations affect society and the environment (Lenz & Hoos, 2023). According to the World Economic Forum: Global Risk (WEF) 2023 report, failure to mitigate climate change is ranked the fourth global risk over period of two years, and it is predicted that it will rank number one over a period of ten years (WEF, 2023). Therefore, there is an urgent need for organisations to understand and manage ESG risks, and internal audit is well-positioned to assist the organization in this area (IIA, 2021). The contribution by internal audit in ESG may signify venturing into unknown territory requiring collaboration with expert and upskilling (Lenz & Hoos, 2023). To assist with this challenge, the IIA has issued a guide for internal audit function on auditing ESG reporting. Its role includes assisting management and the governing body with

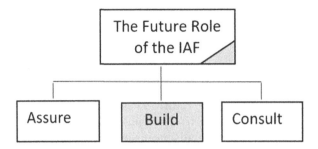

Figure 6.2 ABC model.

Source: Lenz and Hoos (2023).

the establishment of an ESG control environment and assurance on ESG risk assessments, responses, and controls (Lenz & Hoos, 2023; Lenz & Jeppesen, 2022; IIA, 2021). Furthermore, internal audit could integrate ESG in its audit process or could provide advisory services by adopting an "ABC Model" indicated in Figure 6.2.

The ABC model expands the "assurance" and "advisory" role of internal audit and broadens its value proposition to "building" the ESG. This involves co-creating the ESG program with management (Lenz & Hoos, 2023). Although the recommendation to "build" seems to assume management responsibility, GIAS:7.: Organisational Independence allows the CAE to assume roles that fall outside of internal auditing with safeguards to limit impairments to independence or objectivity (Lenz & Hoos, 2023; IIA, 2024).

d. **Strategic insight and alignment**: For the internal audit function to remain relevant, it is important for the public sector internal auditors to understand the mandate and the service delivery objectives of the public sector. To better understand these, the CAE must secure a seat at the strategic table and effectively participate in the organization's strategic processes to provide recommendations that increase the chances of organizational success. In addition, internal audit must be agile and flexible to adapt its plans for alignment with the organization's strategic direction and changes in the risk profile (Moodley, 2022). Betti and Sarens (2018) concur that internal audit needs to adapt their plans regularly and shorten the time between the risk assessment and the beginning of the audit. Additionally, increased focus on IT risks will enable close alignment with organizational strategy, particularly in times of strategic change. Furthermore, collaborating with strategy and performance function during strategic process can enhance internal audit's understanding of the organisational strategy and align it with the internal audit strategy and plan (Moodley et al., 2022).

e. **Digital and data-driven transformation**

e-Government, advanced technology audit tools, and approach

According to the World Economic Forum, technology adoption, big data, cloud computing, and artificial intelligence rank high on the list of technology adoption by organizations (WEF, 2023). As the business environment becomes more digitized, internal audit stakeholders expect the internal audit services and practices to align with e-Government strategies. This includes an understanding of risks associated with automation and digitalization, including data privacy and cyber security risks. The organizational structure of internal audit will have to incorporate technology tools and new approaches to auditing such as robotic process automation, artificial intelligence, and machine learning (KPMG, 2020; Mujalli & Almgrashi, 2020; Wang et al., 2020). In addition, advanced technology tools such as control self-assessment at the planning stage of the audit has the potential to reduce time spent on testing controls that are inadequate, and rather use the time to assist management in designing effective controls.

Furthermore, the rise of artificial intelligence also introduces new opportunities for internal audit to enhance the efficiency and effectiveness of audit processes and represents a crucial strategic shift which goes beyond staying abreast of technological advancements but reshaping the scope and value of internal audit (Aldemİr & Uçma Uysal, 2024). Hence, public sector organizations need to invest on reliable and advanced technologies that mimic auditors for accurate and timely audits, and enable continuous audits (Kahyaoğlu et al., 2020). However, this shift requires commitment to continuous learning, adaptation, and innovation to effectively use technology tools and add value (Aldemİr & Uçma Uysal, 2024; Motubatse, 2019).

Importantly, the big data that is generated through the adoption of e-Government strategies in the public sector, compels internal audit to leverage data analytics and artificial intelligence tools to derive insight from the data and efficiently perform trend analysis, identify anomalies and potential fraud (Aldemİr & Uçma Uysal, 2024). As a result, the public sector internal audit functions must upskill their personnel to use audit technologies, like CAATTs, machine learning and artificial intelligence. Alternatively, these functions must collaborate with data scientist within their organisations or co-source the data analytics skills to effectively derive value from big data.

f. **Continuous auditing and continuous assurance:** The introduction of e-Government makes real-time data accessible, thus enabling continuous monitoring and auditing. Implementation of continuous monitoring in an organization renders traditional auditing irrelevant. This shift necessitates internal audit to adopt advanced approach to auditing such as continuous auditing to align with changes in the organization and enable continuous assessment of risk and control. When continuous monitoring is implemented by management and continuous auditing adopted by internal auditing, continuous assurance is enabled (IIA, 2015). However, adoption of continuous auditing is technology based; therefore, internal auditors will need to acquire skills and competencies to enable the implementation of continuous auditing approach.

g. **Integrated risk management:** The changing risk landscape in the public sector is expanding due to notable disruptions associated with the changes in the legal and/ or regulatory framework, technological advancement, and dynamic political environment. Although internal audit is mandated to provide assurance on organization's risk management processes, among other things, the traditional approach has not kept pace with the era of the real-time economy (Wang et al., 2020). The organisational structure of internal audit function will require the adoption of improved technological methods of risk management such as the use of artificial intelligence to make precise risk assessment and derive meaningful insights from data (Aldemİr & Uçma Uysal, 2024). The continuous compliance awareness framework is an example of a risk management technology designed to automatically prompt timely audit procurement activities by intelligent interpretation of compliance policies and extracting the necessary information from procurement documents (Wang et al., 2020). In addition, as advanced risk assessment approaches and tools become available, internal audit will need to adapt or collaborate with the risk management division.

h. **Collaboration and coordinated assurance**: Duplication of effort, auditing fatigue, increased costs, and inefficiencies are the result of uncoordinated assurance efforts (IIA, 2015). The GIAS: 9.5: Coordination and Reliance recommend that internal audit function embraces its leading role in combined assurance. This could be achieved through developing strategies such as, establishing regular communication channels, leveraging technology for real-time collaboration, and developing a performance matrix to foster participation (IIA, 2024; Moodley et al., 2022).

i. **Remote auditing and virtual teams**: The Covid-19 pandemic has transformed how businesses are conducted, and it also acted as a catalyst for increased digitalisation and adoption of technology within the internal audit profession. Although there are limitations in conducting specific procedures remotely, and the benefits, such as cost savings and improved time management, are derived from remote auditing, the value of on-site presence cannot be replaced (Jarva & Zeitler, 2023). The future organizational structure of internal audit function should integrate a hybrid approach combining the benefits of on-site and remote audits. Such integration could benefit both the auditing profession and the public sector (Jarva & Zeitler, 2023; Wang et al., 2020). Hence, technological-enabled internal audit function is a catalyst to remote auditing, an approach credited with flexibility which contribute to good mental health.

j. **Agile and adaptive internal audit structures**: The risk landscape in the public sector requires internal audit function to adopt flexible structure and teams that can adapt to the rapidly changing environment. In instances where internal audit is not well resourced, agility may be achieved through outsourcing or co-sourcing areas of specialization to ensure internal audit is empowered to respond to the key risks facing the organization.

k. **Governance and fraud mitigation**: In the public sector, the most significant losses are due to misuse of public funds through fraud and corruption. The Pulse of Internal Audit 2022 found that CAEs spend 70% of the time in conducting investigations, an indication of an expanding role on internal audit in combating fraud and is supported by the GIAS 9.4 and 13.2 (IIA, 2022b, 2024). Therefore, internal auditors must adopt advanced techniques and approaches to fraud prevention and detection. Furthermore, as one of the pillars of good governance, internal audit is trusted with the assessment of ethical conduct within the organization and compliance with law and regulation. Adopting advanced technological approaches and tools such as continuous auditing, CAATTs, and due diligence systems has the potential to enhance effectiveness of internal audit in combating fraud.

l. **Enhancing transparency and fostering accountability**: The public sector internal audit is fundamental in promoting accountability, transparency, and responsible use of public resources. The citizens and businesses are the primary stakeholders and fund contributors through taxes, and therefore, demand accountability and transparency in utilizing funds (IIA, 2022a). As a result, adherence to governance requirements is fundamental for ensuring the protection of public resources, and one mechanisms to assist with public management is internal audit (IIA, 2022a). Internal audit can enhance its contribution to accountability, transparency, and responsible use of public resources through performance auditing; auditing of in-year and annual financial, performance reports'; and the general assurance provision on the governance, risk management, and internal controls. This includes assurance of the achievement of public sector strategies.

This section illustrate that, the dynamic public sector environment requires a future internal auditor that is equipped to effectively support public administration. These internal auditors must possess distinct qualities and capabilities as proposed in the next section.

6.3.2 Future needs of internal auditors

The internal auditors may consider the below attributes to ensure they are empowered to adapt and thrive in the evolving public sector landscape.

a. **Acquisition of necessary skills**: Integration of technological tools and new auditing methods requires internal auditors with advanced skills such as data analytics, artificial intelligence, and analytical skills. It is thus crucial for the internal audit function to collectively possess the necessary information technology skills for data interpretation, analysis, and reporting as required by the GIAS (IIA, 2024). In terms of GIA 3.1 and 10.3, internal auditors should develop competencies relating to the following (IIA, 2024):

- Communication and collaboration skills;
- Understanding of governance, risk management, and control processes;
- Expertise in business functions, such as financial management and information technology;
- Data gathering, analysis, and evaluation skills;
- Awareness of various risk and their potential (economic, environmental, legal, and social);
- Knowledge of relevant law, regulation, and practices;
- Understanding of emerging trend and issues;
- Capabilities in supervision and leadership; and
- Technology skills.

Additionally, internal auditors must also acquire relevant skills and competencies to enable the evaluation of processes at a strategic level since internal audit recommendations often influence management decisions (Moodley et al., 2022). The internal audit teams may need to acquire other certification in addition to the certified internal audit (CIA) designation as CIA alone will not be sufficient to deliver value-adding services in the future.

Furthermore, communication and engagement with stakeholders from engagement planning to reporting are fundamental to the internal audit process. Hence, the importance of effective communication skills by internal auditors. Effective communication skills enable unbiased, actionable, and courageous reporting of findings to management (Moodley et al., 2022). The contemporary internal auditors are also required to possess critical thinking and problem-solving skills. These skills combined with business acumen are necessary as organisations rely on internal auditors to thoroughly interrogate data and provide insights that support better decision-making (Islam & Stafford, 2022). According to the World Economic Forum: The Future of Jobs Report, analytical thinking and creative thinking are ranked as the most important skills for workers in 2023 and remain a core skill needed by organisations above all other skills (WEF, 2023). This aligns GIAS:4.3: Professional Skepticism, which requires internal audit to exercise professional skepticism, that is to critically assess the reliability of information when planning and performing internal audit services (IIA, 2024). As a result, internal auditors need to possess these soft skills to enable seamless engagement with stakeholders and provide insightful reports.

   b. **Ethics and integrity:** The GIAS: Principle 1 requires "internal audit to demonstrate integrity in their work and behavior" (IIA, 2024). It is essential that public sector internal auditors uphold integrity and comply with ethical principles when performing their duties. Internal auditors are required to always demonstrate honesty and professional courage; uphold organizational ethical expectations; and abide by legal and/or regulatory requirements when performing their duties (IIA, 2022a, 2024). Consequently, ethics and integrity affect objectivity and contribute to the quality and credibility of audit engagements (Usman et al., 2023). Therefore, internal auditors need to uphold integrity and demonstrate moral excellence even outside of their professional duties as this attribute is a core element of the IPPF and various public sector frameworks.

   c. **Continuous professional development (CPD):** Knowledge, professional skills, and ethics are the foundation of any organization that provide professional judgment. The absence of these attributes negatively impacts the competences of those providing this professional judgment. Therefore, internal auditors need to prepare for the megatrends of digitalization and sustainability through education and training (Lenz & Jeppesen, 2022; ALfrijat, 2020). The practicing internal auditors must, through CPD programs, acquire new knowledge and advanced technical skills to remain relevant. Development in specific skills is necessary as they contribute to the quality of internal audit (ALfrijat, 2020).

Furthermore, the Competency Framework for Internal Auditing as issued by the IIA implores internal auditors to enhance their skills through CPD program to reach higher levels of expertise in their field (IIA, 2022d). However, to ensure auditors view professional development as motivation rather than a critique of their work, a performance appraisal should form part of their career development plan (Vokshi & Xhemajli, 2022). The World Economic Forum: Future Jobs Report 2023 indicated that 6 in 10 workers will require training before 2027, but only half have access to adequate training opportunities (WEF, 2023). Therefore, management's support in terms of CPD budgets is necessary to address internal auditors' future needs (Islam & Stafford, 2022).

6.4 MAPPING 5PS MODEL WITH FUTURE ORGANISATIONAL STRUCTURE AND NEEDS OF PUBLIC INTERNAL AUDITORS

The 5Ps model in Figure 6.3 was mapped with the recommended focus areas for future organisational structure and the needs of public internal auditors. This model is also applicable to the public sector internal audit and essential to position the public sector internal audit as a Gardener of Governance and strengthen its value proposition (Lenz & Jeppesen, 2022). This model illustrates that, central to the implementation of the proposed focus areas is, the autonomy of the internal audit function and allocation of adequate resources as enablers. Therefore, for internal audit to be relevant in the current and future public sector environment, all focus areas under the 5Ps require full support of management and the governing body. Furthermore, mapping these areas with the IIA public sector context illustrates the applicability of the 5Ps and proposed focus area for internal audit in enhancing public sector administration.

The proposed focus area is expanded to include corresponding actions to be taken by the public sector internal audit functions in Table 6.3. These proposed actions are designed to assist the internal audit function to effectively respond to technological advancement and align its plans with organizational strategic goals. The implementation of these, has the potential to enable the public sector internal auditors to adapt and thrive in the complex and evolving public sector environment.

6.5 CONCLUSION

The advancement in technology, digital transformation, and implementation of e-Government has a direct impact on the value proposition and execution of internal audit mandate in the public sector, including methodologies used to conduct audit engagements. Literature identifies various challenges with legal provisions in the current organisational structure and characteristics of internal audit. These challenges negatively impact the credibility, effectiveness, and efficiency of the internal audit function. The absence of these attributes in any internal audit function has the potential to render internal audit irrelevant.

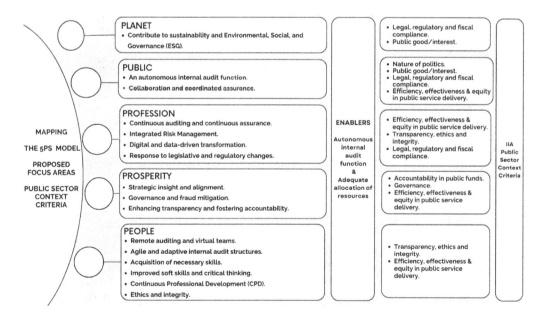

Figure 6.3 Mapping of the 5Ps model with proposed focus areas for future organisational structure and needs of public sector internal auditors and the IIA public sector context criteria.

Source: Lenz and Jeppesen (2022); IIA (2022) and author inputs prepared by the author).

Table 6.3 Summary of proposed focus areas and action

Proposed focus areas	Proposed action
• Contribute to ESG.	• Upskill and collaborate with management to co-create ESG program and provide assurance on existing ESG program.
• An autonomous internal audit function.	• Sustained awareness campaign to regulators, boards, and stakeholders on internal audit value proposition.
• Collaboration and coordinated assurance.	• Establishing regular communication channels, leverage technology for real-time collaboration and develop a performance matrix to foster participation.
• Response to legislative and regulatory changes.	• Collaborate with compliance and legal function/co-source or outsource.
• Continuous auditing and continuous assurance.	• Awareness campaign on benefits of continuous monitoring and auditing and collaborate with management to introduce both approaches.
• Integrated risk management.	• Adopt advanced risk assessment technology tools and collaborate with risk management division in ERM initiatives.
• Digital and data-driven transformation.	• Adopt technology-based tools and services of data scientists or collaborate with data center functions within the organisation.
• Strategic insight and alignment.	• Collaboration with strategy and performance function during strategic process to ensure alignment with the internal audit strategy.
• Governance and fraud mitigation.	• Adopt advanced fraud detection tools and collaborate with investigation units.
• Enhancing transparency and fostering accountability.	• Use specialist in performance audits and contribute to the governance of e-Government (cyber security and data privacy assurance).
• Remote auditing and virtual teams	• Structure audit plans in categories of virtual and on-site audits for efficiency and cost saving.
• Agile and adaptive internal audit structures.	• Determine services that can be outsourced through cost-benefit analysis.
• Ethics and integrity.	• Develop training program to empower staff with necessary skills.
• Acquisition of necessary skills.	
• Continuous professional development (CPD).	• Link career development plans with performance appraisal.

Source: Prepared by the author.

Credibility, ineffectiveness, and inefficiency are closely linked to resource allocation, as lack of advanced internal audit tools has the ability to hamper effective, unbiased, and timely assessments. Therefore, internal audit needs to shift into a new paradigm that can swiftly adapt to the dynamic public sector environment and better align with organizational strategic goals and objectives.

Accordingly, Lenz and Jeppesen (2022) view the future of internal audit metaphorically as the "Gardener of Governance" and developed the 5Ps model which consists of the five main action and focus areas to safeguard relevance and legitimacy of internal audit profession in the future. This model was adopted and used as the basis for identifying focus areas for internal audit function to position itself and empower the internal auditors to adapt and thrive in the evolving public sector landscape. A total of 16 focus areas are identified, of which 13, relate to the organizational structure of internal audit function while three relate to the future needs of internal auditors. The mapping of the 5Ps and proposed focus area for internal audit functions to the IIA public sector context demonstrate how the model can enhance public sector administration if adopted effectively. It is concluded that the successful implementation of all 16 focus areas requires a strong collaboration between internal audit, senior management, the governing body, and regulators. Internal audit also needs to heighten its education awareness and campaign to its stakeholders on the value of internal audit and its relevance in the public sector. The awareness initiatives will not only enhance the credibility, effectiveness, and efficiency of internal audit but will also improve collaboration among stakeholders. Such collaboration will culminate in improved transparency, combined assurance, effective risk management, and achievement of the public sector objectives and service delivery goals. Future research could consider the practical implementation of the proposed action.

REFERENCES

Ahmi, A., Saidin, S.Z., Abdullah, A., Ahmad, A.C. and Ismail, N.A., 2016. State of information technology adoption by internal audit department in Malaysian public sector. *International Journal of Economics and Financial Issues*, 6(7), pp.103–108.

Aldemİr, C. and Uçma Uysal, T., 2024. AI competencies for internal auditors in the public sector. EDPACS, pp.1–19.

ALfrijat, Y.S., 2020. Compliance with continuing professional development (IES7) of internal auditor and quality of internal audit function. *Accounting and Finance Research*, 9(1), pp.1–28.

Alzeban, A. and Gwilliam, D., 2014. Factors affecting the internal audit effectiveness: A survey of the Saudi public sector. *Journal of International Accounting, Auditing and Taxation*, 23(2), pp.74–86.

Bantleon, U., d'Arcy, A., Eulerich, M., Hucke, A., Pedell, B. and Ratzinger-Sakel, N.V., 2021. Coordination challenges in implementing the three lines of defense model. *International Journal of Auditing*, 25(1), pp.59–74.

Betti, N. and Sarens, G., 2018. Aligning Internal Audit Activities and Scope to Organizational Strategy (No. UCL-Université Catholique de Louvain).

Bolton, R., Logan, C. and Gittell, J.H., 2021. Revisiting relational coordination: A systematic review. *The Journal of Applied Behavioral Science*, 57(3), pp.290–322.

Institute of Directors in South Africa. IoD (Institute of Directors). 2016. *Report on Corporate Governance for South Africa 2016*. [Online.] Available from: https://cdn.ymaws.com/www.iodsa.co.za/resource/collection/684B68A7-B768-465C-8214-E3A007F15A5A/IoDSA_King_IV_Report_-_WebVersion.pdf [Accessed 17 July 2023].

International Auditing and Assurance Standards Boards, 2021. *Handbook of International Quality Control, Auditing, Review, Other Assurance, and Related Services Pronouncements* [Online] Available from: www.ifac.org/_flysystem/azure-private/publications/files/IAASB-2021-Handbook-Volume-1.pdf [Accessed 07 May 2024].

Islam, S. and Stafford, T., 2022. Factors associated with the adoption of data analytics by internal audit function. *Managerial Auditing Journal*, 37(2), pp.193–223.

Jarva, H. and Zeitler, T., 2023. Implications of the COVID-19 pandemic on internal auditing: A field study. *Journal of Applied Accounting Research*. https://doi.org/10.1108/JAAR-12-2021-0333

Kahyaoğlu, S.B., Sarikaya, R. and Topal, B., 2020. Continuous auditing as a strategic tool in public sector internal audit: The Turkish case. *Selçuk Üniversitesi Sosyal Bilimler Meslek Yüksekokulu Dergisi*, 23(1), pp.208–225.

Khelil, I. and Khlif, H., 2022. Internal auditors' perceptions of their role as assurance providers: A qualitative study in the Tunisian public sector. *Meditari Accountancy Research*, 30(1), pp.121–141.

KPMG. 2020. *Internal Audit Key Risk Areas 2021*. [Online]. Available from: https://assets.kpmg. com/content/dam/kpmg/nl/pdf/2020/services/internal-audit-key-risk-areas-2021.pdf [Accessed 28 July 2023].

Langella, C., Vannini, I.E. and Persiani, N., 2023. What are the determinants of internal auditing (IA) introduction and development? Evidence from the Italian public healthcare sector. *Public Money & Management*, 43(3), pp.268–276.

Lenz, R. and Hoos, F., 2023. The future role of the internal audit function: Assure. Build. Consult. *EDPACS*, 67(3), pp.39–52.

Lenz, R. and Jeppesen, K.K., 2022. The future of internal auditing: Gardener of governance. *EDPACS*, 66(5), pp.1–21.

Lipunga, A.M., Tchereni, B.H. and Bakuwa, R.C., 2021. Auditing in executive agencies: A case of public hospitals in a developing country. *International Journal of Interdisciplinary Organizational Studies*, 16(1), pp. 13–31.

Liston-Heyes, C. and Juillet, L., 2023. Does increasing auditors' independence lead to more forceful public auditing? A study of a Canadian internal audit reform. *Public Administration*, pp. 1–24.

Lutfi, A. and Alqudah, H., 2023. The influence of technological factors on the computer-assisted audit tools and techniques usage during COVID-19. *Sustainability*, 15(9), p.7704.

Matshona, F.S., 2020. Barriers to effective internal auditing within the South African Police Services: case of Northern Gauteng (Doctoral dissertation, Cape Peninsula University of Technology).

Minto, A. and Arndorfer, I., 2015. The four-line-of-defence model for financial institutions. Taking the three-line-of-defence model further to reflect specific governance features of regulated financial institutions. *Financial Stability Institute Working Paper-BIS*, 11, pp.1–26.

Moodley, A., Ackers, B. and Odendaal, E., 2022. Internal audit's evolving performance role: Lessons from the South African public sector. *Journal of Accounting & Organizational Change*, 18(5), pp.704–726.

Mosweu, O. and Ngoepe, M., 2019. Skills and competencies for authenticating digital records to support audit process in Botswana public sector. *African Journal of Library, Archives & Information Science*, 29(1), pp.17–28.

Motubatse, K.N., 2019. Audit committee expectations on the work of internal audit in the South African National Treasury: A case study. *Journal of Public Administration and Development Alternatives (JPADA)*, 4(1–1), pp.117–131.

Mujalli, A. and Almgrashi, A., 2020, December. A conceptual framework for generalised audit software adoption in Saudi Arabia by government internal auditing departments using an integrated institutional theory-TOE model. In *2020 IEEE Asia-Pacific Conference on Computer Science and Data Engineering (CSDE)* (pp. 1–8). IEEE.

Polizzi, S. and Scannella, E., 2023. Continuous auditing in public sector and central banks: A framework to tackle implementation challenges. *Journal of Financial Regulation and Compliance*, 31(1), pp.40–59.

Republic of South Africa (RSA). 1996. *The Constitution of the Republic of South Africa, 1996*. [Online]. Available from: www.justice.gov.za/legislation/constitution/saconstitution-web-eng. pdf [Accessed 13 February 2024].

Republic of South Africa (RSA). 1999. *Public Finance Management Act 1 of 1999. Government Gazette,19814:28 and 56, 2 March*. [Online]. Available from: www.treasury.gov.za/legislation/ pfma/PFMA%201999%20as%20amended%20March%202017.pdf [Accessed 13 July 2023].

Republic of South Africa (RSA). 2003. *Municipal Finance Management Act 56 of 2003. Government Gazette, 26019:152, 13 February*. [Online]. Available from: www.energy.gov.za/files/policies/ act_municipalfinancemanagement_56of2003_2004.pdf [Accessed 13 July 2023].

Republic of South Africa (RSA). 2009. *National Treasury. 2009. Internal Audit Framework*. [Online]. Available from: www.treasury.gov.za/publications/other/treasury%20internal%20audit%20fr amework%20revised%202009.pdf [Accessed 13 July 2023].

Suleiman, Z.A., Hamad, A.U. and Yussuf, S., 2021. Factors influences the effectiveness of internal audit services at Ministry of Finance and Planning in Zanzibar. *Research Journal of Finance and Accounting, 12*(2), pp.8–13.

The Institute of Internal Auditors (IIA) Public Sector Knowledge Brief. 2020. *Public Sector Audit under Attack: Current Political Climate Intensifies Criticism.* [Online]. Available from: www.the iia.org/globalassets/documents/response-to-regulators/iia-ps-kb-public-sector-auditors-under-attack.pdf [Accessed 11 July 2023].

The Institute of Internal Auditors (IIA). 2009. *IIA Position Paper: The Role of Internal Auditing in Enterprise-Wide Risk Management.* [Online]. Available from: www.theiia.org/globalassets/documents/resources/the-role-of-internal-auditing-in-enterprise-wide-risk-management-january-2009/pp-the-role-of-internal-auditing-in-enterprise-risk-management.pdf [Accessed 5 February 2024].

The Institute of Internal Auditors (IIA). 2015. *GTAG: Global Technology Audit Guide: Continuous Auditing: Implications for Assurance, Monitoring, and Risk Assessment.* [Online]. Available from: www.theiia.org/globalassets/documents/content/articles/guidance/gtag/gtag-3-continu ous-auditing/gtag-3-continuous-auditing-2nd-edition.pdf [Accessed 13 February 2024].

The Institute of Internal Auditors (IIA). 2021. *Internal Audit's Role in ESG Reporting- Independent assurance is critical to effective sustainability reporting* [online]. Available from: www.theiia. org/globalassets/documents/communications/2021/june/white-paper-internal-audits-role-in-esg-reporting.pdf [Accessed 07 May 2024].

The Institute of Internal Auditors (IIA). 2022a. *Unique Aspects of Internal Auditing in the Public Sector.* [Online]. Available from: www.theiia.org/globalassets/documents/content/articles/guidance/practice-guides/unique-aspects-of-internal-auditing-in-the-public-sector/pg_unique_aspects_of_internal_auditing_in_the_ps_newbrand.pdf [Accessed 11 July 2023].

The Institute of Internal Auditors (IIA). 2022b. *The Role of Auditing in Public Sector Governance*: Second Edition. [Online]. Available from: www.theiia.org/globalassets/documents/standards/public_sector_governance1_1_.pdf [Accessed 11 July 2023].

The Institute of Internal Auditors (IIA). 2022c. *Applying the Three Lines Model in the Public Sector.* [Online]. Available from: www.theiia.org/globalassets/site/content/articles/applying_the_three_lines_model_in_the_public_sector.pdf [Accessed 11 July 2023].

The Institute of Internal Auditors (IIA). 2022d. *The IIA's Internal Audit Competency Framework.* [Online]. Available from: www.theiia.org/globalassets/documents/standards/ia-competency-framework/2022-4103-sem-competency-framework-graphics-table_fnl.pdf [Accessed 30 July 2023].

The Institute of Internal Auditors (IIA). 2022e. *Building an Effective Internal Audit Function.* [Online]. Available from: www.theiia.org/globalassets/documents/content/articles/guidance/practice-gui des/unique-aspects-of-internal-auditing-in-the-public-sector/pg_unique_aspects_of_internal_auditing_in_the_ps_newbrand.pdf [Accessed 11 July 2023].

The Institute of Internal Auditors (IIA). n.d. *Internal Auditing Education Partnership (IAEP) Program: Program Guidelines and Operating Framework.* [Online]. Available from: www.the iia.org/globalassets/documents/about-us/initiatives--awards/academic-relations/iaep-program-requirements-and-operating-framework.pdf [Accessed 13 February 2024].

The Institute of Internal Auditors (IIA). 2024. *Global Internal Audit Standards.* [Online]. Available from: www.theiia.org/globalassets/site/standards/globalinternalauditstandards_2024january9_printable.pdf [Accessed 14 February 2024].

Thomasson, A., 2018. Politicisation of the audit process: The case of politically affiliated auditors in Swedish local governments. *Financial Accountability & Management, 34*(4), pp.380–391.

Usman, R., Rohman, A. and Ratmono, D., 2023. The relationship of internal auditors' characteristics with external auditors' reliance and its impact on audit efficiency: Empirical evidence from Indonesian government institutions. *Cogent Business & Management, 10*(1), p.2191781.

Vokshi, B. and Xhemajli, A., 2022. Internal audit in the public sector in Kosovo: Promoting good governance and improving performance. *Calitatea, 23*(189), pp.160–164.

Volodina, T., Grossi, G. and Vakulenko, V., 2022. The changing roles of internal auditors in the Ukrainian central government. *Journal of Accounting & Organizational Change*, *19*(6), pp.1–23.

Vousinas, G.L., 2021. Beyond the three lines of defense: The five lines of defense model for financial institutions. *ACRN Journal of Finance and Risk Perspectives*, *10*, pp.95–110.

Wang, K., Zipperle, M., Becherer, M., Gottwalt, F. and Zhang, Y., 2020. An AI-based automated continuous compliance awareness framework (CoCAF) for procurement auditing. *Big Data and Cognitive Computing*, *4*(3), p.23.

World Economic Forum (WEF). 2023. *Future Jobs Report*. [Online]. Available from: www3.weforum.org/docs/WEF_Future_of_Jobs_2023.pdf [Accessed 3 August 2023].

Chapter 7

New audit reporting tools with AI-based implementation in the public sector

Babalwa Ceki

7.1 INTRODUCTION

The quality of audit reports shapes the most concrete indicator of the effectiveness of audit activities. Performing audits and presenting findings based on digitalisation and artificial intelligence (AI)-based audit analytics applications is gaining importance in the public sector. This chapter emphasises the use of newly developed auditing tools based on AI and analytical applications in audit activities. By integrating audit tools and techniques with audit reports, the findings obtained through AI are presented in a more effective, efficient, and economical way based on new technological developments. In this chapter, the main benefits and challenges of using AI-based audit tools such as text analysing and natural language processing, machine learning, and data analytics in the public sector, and how internal auditors can better use them to increase their effectiveness are discussed.

7.2 MACHINE LEARNING AND DOCUMENT ANALYSES TOOLS

The public sector has recently started implementing audit tools based on AI to improve the efficacy and precision of their auditing procedures. By analysing vast amounts of data and identifying potential fraud, errors, and other anomalies, AI-based audit tools can significantly reduce the time and resources auditors need. However, since using AI in auditing is still a relatively new concept, many problems must be fixed before these tools can be regarded as trustworthy and useful.

The KPMG Contract Abstraction Tool is an example of an AI-based text analysing tool that helps auditors review contracts (Arrowsmith, 2018). To do this, it analyses lease data using a platform for cognitive exploration and content analysis to spot trends, patterns, anomalies, and relationships. This tool's main benefit is that converting the leasing file into a machine-readable format can shorten the time required for an auditor to audit a lease agreement.

The tool first transforms the contract into a readable file and then detects particular traits present in various leasing contracts, which vary depending on the contract type, in the process's second step. The extracted attributes are then formatted and exported into the lease accounting tool (Tsao, 2021). It is comparable to the Halo AI tool that PwC uses, which can scan and analyse a lot of data and interactively display the results on a single platform (Eilifsen, Kinserdal, Messier & McKee, 2020). This tool can help internal auditors learn important details about the opportunities and risks associated with the auditees (Eilifsen et al., 2020).

DOI: 10.1201/9781003382706-7

Deloitte has been using a tool for AI contract analysis called Kira (Yakimova, 2020). It analyses what matters in contracts and pinpoints crucial details in many agreements. Kira has been taught to recognise thousands of different types of data. It has been applied to more than 100,000 documents thus far. More than just utilising, the tool is involved in Deloitte and Kira Systems' collaboration. It is an opportunity for Deloitte to create tailored solutions for document analysis projects like audits, mergers, and contract management. As a result, the auditing process will involve more thorough analysis, better risk assessment, and wiser decision-making. The potential rewards are enormous and internal auditors can use this tool in the public sector.

7.2.1 Machine learning audit tool

Artificial intelligence includes machine learning, which enables computer systems to learn and form hypotheses or judgements without explicit programming. Machine learning has the potential to revolutionise the field of internal auditing. Like GL.ai from PwC, it can be trained on historical audit data to spot patterns or anomalies that may require further investigation, analyse large volumes of data, and spot areas of high risk and potential fraud (PWC, 2022, 2017).

Internal auditors can use machine learning to automate repetitive tasks, prioritise audit areas based on risk assessment, and improve fraud detection. By utilising the power of machine learning, auditors can gain insightful information, increase audit effectiveness, and make decisions that align with their organisation's objectives (PWC, 2017).

Auditing firms are actively investigating machine learning. For instance, Kira, a machine learning tool, is used by Deloitte USA (Yakimova, 2020). This tool analyses contracts for sales, derivatives, and leases. Algorithms that have been programmed enable Kira to recognise key contract clauses, identify trends, and spot any unusual outliers (Ranjith et al., 2021). The use of machine learning technology improves the effectiveness and precision of audits. The advantages of automation, improved risk assessment, and enhanced fraud detection can be utilised by auditors (Yakimova, 2020). Auditors can improve their skills and help their organisations succeed by embracing machine learning.

7.3 MACHINE LEARNING ALGORITHM BENEFITS

Internal auditors can benefit from cutting-edge algorithms that take into account crucial factors like transaction size, frequency, and significance by incorporating AI. By carefully choosing audit samples, auditors can concentrate on audits more likely to turn up errors, fraud, or noncompliance.

AI algorithms can analyse large data sets to find patterns and anomalies. With the help of this analysis, auditors can effectively allocate their resources and identify the areas that need more in-depth investigation (PWC, 2017). Auditors can increase the effectiveness and efficiency of the auditing process by focusing on samples that are more likely to reveal crucial insights (PWC, 2022). Furthermore, AI-driven intelligent sampling gives the audit results high confidence. Auditors can reach precise and solid conclusions by creating representative samples based on the identified variables.

Internal auditors are empowered to make data-driven decisions, thanks to the use of AI in intelligent sampling, which helps them save time and money. Quickly identifying insights and risks improves the audit process's overall quality. As a result, organisations experience increased compliance, risk management, and operational efficiency.

In contrast to conventional methods, Alles (2018) found that AI-based audit tools can assist auditors more quickly and accurately in identifying risks and anomalies in financial data. Li and Yu (2019) also point out that the accuracy of financial reporting can be increased using AI-based tools as well as increase the effectiveness and efficiency of government operations (U.S. Government Accountability Office, 2020).

AI in auditing can improve accuracy and decrease the likelihood of mistakes. AI algorithms can quickly and accurately identify patterns, making it easier to spot irregularities in financial data and allowing auditors to concentrate on areas that need closer inspection (Fedyk et al., 2022; Mirzaei et al., 2022). AI in auditing aids in fraud detection as well. Auditors can be alerted to suspicious activity using AI algorithms, which can help shorten the time required to complete an audit. By automating data analysis, auditors can examine financial data quickly and find any issues or irregularities, finishing their audits much faster than conventional techniques (Mirzaei et al., 2022).

Auditor evaluations can be performed on all data rather than just a sample. In the future, AI has the potential to be used to audit all financial transactions made by the company (Meek, 2017). AI-based tools in audit reporting in auditing are still in their early stages. However, auditors can increase audit activity efficiency through the use of AI and machine learning in a cost-effective manner (Jooman, 2019).

7.3.1 Challenges with AI algorithms reporting

The hiring and training of qualified personnel is the main barrier to the widespread adoption of AI (Fedyk et al., 2022). The assurance of the accuracy of the data used to train the AI algorithms presents another difficulty when using AI in auditing. It is crucial to ensure the data used is accurate, relevant, and current because AI algorithms are only as good as the data they are trained on. This is crucial for auditing because the accuracy of the results produced by AI algorithms can be affected by the data quality.

Another issue is the potential for AI dependence. Although AI can significantly improve audit process accuracy and efficiency, auditors may become overly dependent on AI, preventing them from exercising human judgement and critical thought. This might cause auditors to miss important issues that might have been found during a manual review (Mitchell & Ziegler, 2019).

Transparency and accountability concerning AI algorithms are other problems. Because AI algorithms are developed to predict outcomes based on complex mathematical models, they are frequently called "enigmas" because it is difficult to understand how they make decisions. This opacity can lead to worries about accountability and loss of faith in the results generated by AI algorithms (Rai, 2022). A challenge with AI algorithms is also their need for standardisation. Since AI is still in its infancy, no set method or guidelines exist for creating AI algorithms. This may result in inconsistent results and make it challenging for testers to compare the output of various AI algorithms (Gobbin, 2020).

The public sector has difficulty adopting AI due to potential automated decisions that could be biased or incorrect regarding service eligibility and entitlement, complex ethical problems, regulations regarding human control of AI that are unclear, intricate service delivery and risk management processes, privacy and cybersecurity issues, legal matters that are unclear, concerns about public trust and how public funds are used, and complex workflows between the federation (Desouza et al., 2020; Yigitcanlar & Cugurullo, 2020).

7.4 NATURAL LANGUAGE PROCESSING (NLP)

NLP is a fundamental component of AI, encompassing various functions related to processing and communication. Sullivan and Hannis (2017) define natural language processing as utilising natural language to transmit messages and signals with intelligent systems. According to Samadi (2017), NLP is a prominent technological tool in AI. It focuses on the emulation of human natural languages and aims to communicate in a manner that is similar to human communication. The efficient operation of NLP data processing and communication capabilities improves the quality of audits and enhances the veracity of audit reporting (Wu, Xu, Lou & Chen, 2018).

One illustration of AI use in auditing is the partnership between KPMG and IBM's Watson analytics service in the USA. IBM's Watson is a data analytics engine that employs NLP, a tool that examines the meaning and syntax of spoken language (Kokina & Davenport, 2017). IBM Watson uses analytics to quickly and accurately respond to questions from humans by processing huge amounts of data. They analyse enormous amounts of financial data with this powerful tool to look for odd patterns or anomalies (Kokina & Davenport, 2017).

7.5 BENEFITS OF AI-BASED AUDIT REPORTING TOOLS

In summary, AI in auditing is revolutionising how auditors perform their work and causing an exponential change in the audit process. It gives auditors a more effective and precise method for conducting audits and spotting fraud and anomalies in financial data. Due to its reduced resource and labour requirements, AI in auditing contributes to lower audit process costs. However, there are some problems with using AI in auditing, including the accuracy of the data applied, reliance on AI too much, a lack of accountability and clarity, and a lack of standardisation.

Internal auditors should adopt a collaborative approach to tackle these issues, working with data experts and AI experts to ensure the integrity of the data used and create transparent, accountable AI algorithms. To ensure they are making well-informed decisions, internal auditors should also be trained in AI and familiar with the underlying mathematical models used by AI algorithms. Robotic process automation is yet another cutting-edge tool used in the auditing industry.

7.6 ROBOTIC PROCESS AUTOMATION (RPA)

The primary objective of auditing is to provide clients with the results and discrepancies identified during the audit process, formulate an audit conclusion based on the conducted tests, and offer recommendations upon the completion of the audit (Kapur & Singh, 2022). Historically, the reports have been characterised by their extensive length and excessive use of words. They significantly consume the auditors' working hours. Implementing RPA can be advantageous in managing reporting and dashboarding tasks. RPA facilitates the arrangement and organisation of data for the auditor's report, adhering to predefined templates or internal audit's balanced scorecard.

These software bots imitate human beings and reproduce rule-based, repetitive, and manual tasks, including analytical and substantive audit tasks (Kapur & Singh, 2022). For the software to effectively conduct audit tests, the audit-related data from various sources must be standardised. Subsequently, the software should be programmed to execute the audit tests in an automated manner, as Moretti et al. (2019) suggested (Figure 7.1).

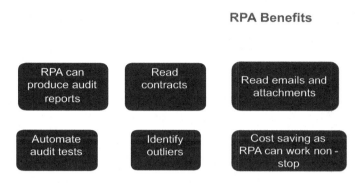

Figure 7.1 RPA benefits.
Source: Author's compilation.

According to Moffitt et al. (2018) and Huang and Vasarhelyi (2019), RPA can perform repetitive manual tasks such as reconciliations, internal control testing, and detailed inspections. RPA can execute repetitive manual tasks, such as reconciliations, internal control testing, and thorough reviews (Moffitt et al., 2018; Huang & Vasarhelyi, 2019). RPA leverages autonomous computer programs to streamline and automate monotonous tasks (Eulerich, Pawlowski, Waddoups & Woods, 2022). Omitting technology tools can lead to ineffective audit practices, whereas utilising technology, mainly through automation, has decreased expenses (Vasarhelyi & Romero, 2014).

7.7 DATA ANALYTICS IN PUBLIC SECTOR AUDITING

Data analysis is the process of scrutinising, purifying, transforming, and portraying data to unearth relevant information, guide conclusions, and assist decision-making (INTOSAI, 2019). Data analysis technology enables auditors to audit an entire data set to analyse connections and associations between data sets, identify patterns and trends, and graphically display results (ICAEW, 2016). This technique is most effective with other methods, such as statistical analysis. Big data analysis can be defined as performing data analytics on large amounts of data, measured in the hundreds of gigabytes, terabytes, or petabytes, with frequent and rapid growth and change, sometimes in real time (ISACA, 2013).

According to some definitions, big data analytics is the process of looking at information and patterns from large data. A system architecture for data collection, transmission, storage, processing, analysis, and mechanisms for visualising data is required (Bendre & Thool, 2016).

Data analytics for audit is a practice adopted widely by public sector auditing organisations in developed countries. For example, the National Audit Office of the UK uses a future model for data analytics workflow (INTOSAI, 2022).

To conduct pertinent scenario testing, the European Court of Auditors has established an audit innovation laboratory that brings together data scientists, experts in AI, and auditors interested in technology. The creation of a big data audit team, the promotion of data awareness, and the formation of an entire data analysis team have all been stressed by the Netherlands Court of Audit. The State Audit Office of the Kingdom of Thailand introduced a guideline on efficiently integrating big data into auditing and applying big data and data analytics in auditing collaboration and capacity building for big data audits (WGBD, 2019).

For auditors to use data analytics, they must satisfy the following requirements that have been noted. Assess the value and advantages that the use of data analytics will bring to audits to identify opportunities for its use. Strategic and operational goals, as well as a clear mission and vision, are required. To ensure that the right investments are made, they must identify the priorities that need to be in place, such as financial or strategic plans, big data governance, and management. Analytics involving large amounts of data call for big data processing platforms and applications in sufficient network architecture (Al Nuaimi, Al Neyadi, Mohamed, & Al-Jaroodi, 2015).

Organisations in the public sector must be aware of how to use ICT solutions and provide information, especially for smart cities. To keep the exchange and flow of big data under control, it is the role of the government to establish guiding principles of openness, transparency, participation, and collaboration (Al Nuaimi et al., 2015).

7.7.1 Benefits of data analytics in public sector auditing

Due to the enormous amounts of time and effort required to review all relevant data, auditing traditionally only uses a sample basis for testing. Traditional methods must advance to keep up with the expanding data and parameters. Data analytics enables auditors to examine all the data and visually display the results, making spotting discrepancies easier (Agnew, 2016; Raphael, 2017). To draw conclusions and gain a deeper understanding, auditors can use data analytics for risk analysis, control testing, and analytical procedures (Eulerich et al., 2022). Data analytics can be helpful but necessitates a significant and sustained commitment. For instance, KPMG Clara combines data analytics, collaboration, and a global auditing process into one platform, allowing for more profound and valuable insights. PwC Halo for Journals uses algorithms to identify high-risk journaled transactions.

Data analytics assists internal auditors in audit reporting and lessens the risk of reaching wrong conclusions (Cardinaels et al., 2021). Stanisic et al. (2019) suggest that internal auditors use predictive tools such as machine learning to analyse and predict audit conclusions. The following are some applications of big data analytics: Finding new correlations through data set analysis can be used to identify business trends, user behaviour analytics, and predictive analytics; to aid in delivering services for smart cities (Al Nuaimi, Al Neyadi, Mohamed, & Al-Jaroodi, 2015) and detection of fraud and malpractice in auditees (Kropp, 2018). In compliance and other audits, risks are identified (OCAGI, 2017).

Data analytics can be used by internal auditors in the public sector creatively to report and advise on Sustainable Development Goals (SDGs), including agriculture, health, and poverty alleviation (Mpatisha, 2019), and examining and reporting on the SDGs' progress, such as SDG 4 aims (Vehkasalo, 2018).

Predictive modelling, cluster analysis, and the analysis of unstructured data, such as texts and videos, can all be done using data analytics (Kuenkaikaew & Vasarhelyi, 2013; Agnew, 2016: IAASB, 2017; Raphael, 2017). Data analytics can be used to efficiently audit the unstructured textual data generated by public procurement, public tendering, and performance audits (Zhang, 2019).

Data analytics can completely revamp audit processes by significantly reducing the contrast between analytical procedures and meaningful testing (Titera, 2013). Additionally, data analytics may reduce the chance of failing to spot an existing false statement, improving the audit's quality and effectiveness while increasing the value for all parties involved (Agnew, 2016; Raphael, 2017). Anomaly models use distributional analysis to identify outliers that may require further investigation (Koreff, 2018). Predictive models employ analytical models that examine existing issue patterns and compare them to current ones to identify issues before they arise (Koreff, 2018). These analytical models can examine unstructured non-financial data.

Finding audit-related information can be done using data analytics. Process mining, for instance, involves tracking computer system activity over time (Jans et al., 2014; Jans et al., 2010). This technique was used by Jans et al. (2014) to examine the sequence of events in a computer system's logs, and they discovered that it could spot payments that were made without authorisation. This outcome demonstrates how data analytics can be used to spot accounting mistakes and internal control violations.

7.8 DISCUSSION

The technologies mentioned above work best when data is accurate, complete, and reliable and when technology controls are properly implemented. The International Auditing and Assurance Standards Board (IAASB) revised auditing standards to include guidance on using advanced auditing technologies because using these technologies in audits requires professional scepticism (IAASB, 2017). The South African Institute of Chartered Accountants (SAICA) suggested that future auditors' academic curricula should include instruction in technology skills (IAASB, 2017). This reflects Ceki's (2019) argument that auditors should be trained in performing audits using cutting-edge technologies and should have technical skills.

The public sector can gain a lot from adopting AI-based audit tools. Compared to conventional techniques, these tools can assist auditors in more quickly and accurately identifying risks and anomalies in financial data. AI-based audit tools can analyse vast data and spot patterns and errors that auditors might overlook immediately. As a result, auditors may be better able to identify potential fraud or errors early and take corrective action before any harm is done.

Second, AI-based audit tools can make the auditing process more efficient. These tools can reduce the time and resources needed for audits by automating some tasks, like data extraction and analysis. This can free up auditors to concentrate on more complex tasks like risk evaluation and fraud detection. Lastly, using AI-based audit tools can increase financial reporting accuracy. These tools can assist organisations in ensuring that financial statements are free of material misstatements and comply with relevant regulations by spotting errors and anomalies more quickly and accurately.

For public sector auditing, AI-based audit tools are crucial, but implementing them can be difficult due to issues with data quality, specialised knowledge, and organisational culture. Data quality is essential for accurate and thorough analysis and efficient use of calls for specialised knowledge and skills. The adoption of new technologies can also be difficult for some organisations.

AI-based audit tools have drawbacks, including bias in the data being analysed, the sizeable investment in new infrastructure and technologies, and the possibility of unreliability because of highly developed algorithms and machine learning capabilities. However, since they can enable auditors to identify potential issues more quickly and precisely, AI-based auditing tools for the public sector have a bright future. One area where AI-based audit tools can significantly improve performance is fraud detection. These tools can assist auditors in spotting potential fraud more quickly by analysing enormous amounts of data in real time, lowering the risk of monetary losses and reputational damage. Another area where

AI-based audit tools can assist auditors is in staying current and in compliance with the most recent regulations in compliance.

The likelihood of bias in the data being analysed, errors or inaccuracies in the algorithms being used, and abuse or improper handling are just a few of the risks connected with AI-based audit tools in the public sector. Specialised training and experience are essential to the success of AI-based audit tools in public sector auditing. Staff members should receive training to ensure they are comfortable using these tools and can effectively interpret results. Additionally, support for resolving any issues arising during the implementation process should be given to the staff.

7.9 CONCLUSION

Using AI-based audit tools in the public sector can potentially revolutionise auditing. By quickly and accurately analysing large volumes of data, these tools can help auditors identify potential issues more quickly and accurately. However, careful consideration and planning must go into their implementation to guarantee that these tools are trustworthy and efficient. There are many obstacles to overcome. As technology develops, AI-based audit tools will become more sophisticated and effective, playing a larger and larger role in auditing.

The public sector has recently started implementing audit tools based on artificial intelligence to improve the efficacy and precision of their auditing procedures (AI). By analysing vast amounts of data and identifying potential fraud, errors, and other anomalies, AI-based audit tools can significantly reduce the time and resources auditors need. However, since using AI in auditing is still a relatively new concept, many problems still need to be fixed before these tools can be regarded as trustworthy and useful.

REFERENCES

Agnew, H. (2016). Auditing: Pitch battle. *Financial Times*, May 9.

Al Nuaimi, E., Al Neyadi, H., Mohamed, N. & Al-Jaroodi, J. (2015). Applications of Big Data to Smart Cities. *Journal of Internet Services and Applications*, 8(9), 1–15.

Alles, M. (2018). AI in Auditing: Opportunities and Risks. *Journal of Business Finance & Accounting*, 45(3–4), 469–499.

Arrowsmith, R. (2018). KPMG offers new IBM Watson-enabled accounting tools. Retrieved from www.accountingtoday.com/news/kpmg-offers-new-ibm-watsonenabled-accounting-tools. Accessed 9 February 2023.

Bendre, M. R. & Thool, V. R. (2016). Analytics, Challenges and Applications in Big Data Environment: A Survey. *Journal of Management Analytics*, 3, 206–239.

Cardinaels, E., Eulerich, M. & Salimi Sofla, A. (2021). Data analytics, pressure, and self-determination: Experimental evidence from internal auditors, pp. 3–7, 22–24. Available at: http://dx.doi.org/10.2139/ssrn.3895796. Accessed 06 November 2023.

Desouza, K., Dawson, G., & Chenok, D. (2020). Designing, Developing, and Deploying Artificial Intelligence Systems: Lessons from and for the Public Sector, *Business Horizons*, 63, 205–213.

Eilifsen, A., Kinserdal, F., Messier Jr, W. F., & McKee, T. E. (2020). An Exploratory Study into the Use of Audit Data Analytics on Audit Engagements. *Accounting Horizons*, 34(4), 75–103.

Eulerich, M., Pawlowski, J., Waddoups, N. J., & Wood, D. A. (2022). A Model for Using Robotic Process Automation for Audit Tasks. *Contemporary Accounting Research*, 39(1), 691–720.

Fedyk, A., Hodson, J., Khimich, N. et al. (2022). Is Artificial Intelligence Improving the Audit Process? *Review of Accounting Studies*, 27, 938–985. https://doi.org/10.1007/s11142-022-09697-xk

Gobbin, C. (2020). Artificial Intelligence in Accounting and Auditing: Opportunities and Challenges. *Journal of Accounting and Taxation*, 2(6), 27–31.

Huang, F., & Vasarhelyi, M. A. (2019). Applying robotic process automation (RPA) in auditing: A framework. *International Journal of Accounting Information Systems*, 35, 100433.

IAASB (2017). Exploring the growing use of technology in the audit, with a focus on data analytics. www.iaasb.org/publications/exploring-growing-use-technology-audit-focus-data-analytics. Accessed 25 July 2020.

Institute of Chartered Accountants in England and Wales. Audit and Assurance Faculty (ICAEW) (2016). Data analytics for external auditors. ICAEW. www.icaew.com/technical/audit-and-assurance/audit/risk-assessment-internal-control-and-response/6-data-analytics-in-external-audit. Accessed 10 June 2023.

INTOSAI Working Group on Big Data (2022). Development overview of big data audits performed by supreme audit institutions from 2016–2021. www.audit.gov.cn/en/n749/c10296921/part/10296937.pdf. Accessed 15 February 2023.

INTOSAI Working Group on IT Audit (2019). *Data Analysis Guideline*. Vienna: INTOSAI.

ISACA (2013, March). Big Data Impacts and Benefits. An ISAXA white paper. Isaca.org

Jans, M., Alles, M. G., & Vasarhelyi, M. A. (2014). A Field Study on the Use of Processmining of Event Logs as an Analytical Procedure in Auditing. *The Accounting Review*, 89(5), 1751–1773.

Jans, M., Lybaert, N., & Vanhoof, K. (2010). Internal Fraud Risk Reduction: Results of a Data Mining Case Study. *International Journal of Accounting Information Systems*, 11(1), 17–41.

Jooman, S. (2019). *The influence of artificial intelligence on the future of the internal auditing profession in South Africa* (Doctoral dissertation).

Kapur, N., & Singh, A. K. (2022). Robotics Process Automation and Internal Audit: A Transformation. *The Management Accountant Journal*, 57(7), 58–63.

Kokina, J., & Davenport, T. H. (2017). The Emergence of Artificial Intelligence: How Automation is Changing Auditing. *Journal of Emerging Technologies in Accounting*, 14(1), 115–122.

Koreff, J. (2018). *Three studies examining auditors' use of data analytics* (Electronic theses and dissertations). 5949. https://stars.library.ucf.edu/etd/5949.

Kropp, T. (2018). *HHS OIG Fraud Analytics*. Washington DC: HHS OIG.

Kuenkaikaew, S., & Vasarhelyi. M. A. (2013). The Predictive Audit Framework. *The International Journal of Digital Accounting Research*, 13, 37–71.

Li, L., & Yu, S. (2019). The Application of Artificial Intelligence in Auditing: A Literature Review. *Journal of Accounting Literature*, 42, 1–20.

Meek, T. (2017). How humans and AI will share the auditing function of the future. Retrieved from www.forbes.com/sites/workday/2017/07/10/how-humansand-ai-will-share-the-auditing-function-of-the-future/#7764b. Accessed 6 February 2023.

Mirzaei, A., Hajizade, M., & Hajizade, H. (2022). Studying the Effect of Artificial Intelligence on Improvement of Various Quality Criteria in Relation to Audit Work in Iran. *International Journal of Health Sciences*, 6(S1), 12623–12635. https://doi.org/10.53730/ijhs.v6nS1.8181

Mitchell, S., & Ziegler, R. (2019). Artificial Intelligence in Auditing: Opportunities and Challenges. *Journal of Information Systems*, 33(2), 235–240.

Moffitt, K. C., Rozario, A. M., & Vasarhelyi, M. A. (2018). Robotic Process Automation for Auditing. *Journal of Emerging Technologies in Accounting*, 15(1), 1–10.

Moretti, R. L. (2019). The future of audit embracing technology and change. www.accountingtoday.com/opinion/the-future-of-audit-embracing-technology-and-change. Accessed 27 July 2020.

Mpatisha, B. (2019). *Big Data: A Case of China. AFROSAI-E Technical Update*. Cape Town: AFROSAI-E.

Office of the Comptroller and Auditor General of India (OCAGI) (2017). *Office of the Comptroller and Auditor General of India*. New Delhi: Office of the Comptroller and Auditor General of India.

PWC (2017). Harnessing the power of AI to transform the detection of fraud and error. Available at: www.pwc.com/gx/en/about/stories-from-across-the-world/harnessing-the-power-of-ai-to-transform-the-detection-of-fraud-and-error.htm

PWC (2022). Technology-driven fight against financial crime. Available at www.pwc.com/gx/en/issues/risk-regulation/financial-crime-managed-services/technology in financial crime prevention.html. Accessed 23 June 2023

Rai, N. (2022). Why Ethical Audit Matters in Artificial Intelligence? *AI and Ethics*, 2(1), 209–218.

Ranjith, P. V., Madan, S., Jian, D. A. W., Teoh, K. B., Singh, A. S., Ganatra, V., & Singh, P. (2021). Harnessing the Power of Artificial Intelligence in the Accounting Industry: A Case Study of KPMG. *International Journal of Accounting & Finance in Asia Pacific (IJAFAP)*, 4(2), 93–106.

Raphael, J. (2017). Rethinking the Audit. *Journal of Accounting*, 223(4), 29–32.

Samadi, S. (2017). The Social Costs of Electricity Generation—Categorising Different Types of Costs and Evaluating Their Respective Relevance. *Energies*, 10(3), 356. https://doi.org/10.3390/en10030356

Stanisic, N., Radojevic, T., & Stanic, N. (2019). Predicting the Type of Auditor Opinion: Statistics, Machine Learning, or a Combination of the Two? *The European Journal of Applied Economics*, 16(2), 1–58. DOI:10.5937/EJAE16-21832.

Sullivan, S., & Hannis, M. (2017). Mathematics Maybe, but Not Money: On Balance Sheets, Numbers and Nature in Ecological Accounting. *Accounting, Auditing & Accountability Journal*, 30(7), 1459–1480. https://doi.org/10.1108/aaaj-06-2017-2963

Titera, W. R. (2013). Updating Audit Standard—Enabling Audit Data Analysis. *Journal of Information Systems*, 27(1), 325–331.

Tsao, G. (2021). *What are the factors that influence the adoption of data analytics and artificial intelligence in auditing?* (UCF theses and dissertations, University of Central Florida).

U.S. Government Accountability Office (2020). Artificial intelligence in federal agencies. www.gao.gov/artificial-intelligence. Accessed on 30 July 2023.

Vasarhelyi, M. A., & Romero, S. (2014). Technology in Audit Engagements: A Case Study. *Managerial Auditing Journal*, 29(4), 350–365. https://doi.org/10.1108/MAJ-06-2013- 0881.

Vehkasalo, V. (2018). Auditing sustainable development goals using data analysis: Dropout prevention program in Finnish vocational education. National Audit Office of Finland.

WGBD (2019). *Summary of Big Data Audit Experience. 3rd Meeting of the INTOSAI Working Group on Big Data*. Copenhagen: WGBD

Wu, X., Xu, Y., Lou, Y., & Chen, Y. (2018). Low Carbon Transition in a Distributed Energy System Regulated by Localized Energy Markets. *Energy Policy*, 122, 474–485. https://doi.org/10.1016/j.enpol.2018.08.008

Yakimova, V. A. E. (2020, April). AI-Audit: The Perspectives of Digital Technology Application in the Audit Activity. In *III International Scientific and Practical Conference "Digital Economy and Finances"* (ISPC-DEF 2020) (pp. 138–142). Atlantis Press. Yigitcanlar & Cugurullo. (2020). The sustainability of artificial intelligence: An urbanistic viewpoint from the lens of smart and sustainable cities. *Sustainability*, 12(20), 8548.

Zhang, C. (2019). Intelligent Process Automation in Audit. *Journal of Emerging Technologies in Accounting*, 16(2), 69–88.

Chapter 8

Digital skills of public sector auditors

Cameron Modisane

8.1 INTRODUCTION AND BACKGROUND

The evolution of technology over the years has resulted in the transformation of industries, including the public sector. As a result, accounting and auditing professions have been challenged to adapt this new era. The emergence of the Fourth Industrial Revolution (4IR) can be characterised as the fusion between physical processes and digitalisation in decentralised systems. Companies are changing their business processes, they are making changes in their strategic direction, sales and branding, supply change management, and information technology (IT) by incorporating progressively digital technologies into their business practices (Verhoef et al., 2021). The speedy development and uptake of Fourth Industrial Revolution (4IR) technologies such as big data and artificial intelligence (AI) are the main drivers of digitisation acceleration.

The public sector is not spared from these technology advances that are happening. Many governments around the world are also learning to adapt to this advent of technology. Electronic Government (e-Government) is what many governmental organisations are starting to change due to the digital transformation that is taking place globally (Radwan, 2021). The main aim of governments using e-Government is to benefit from technology by reducing the human mistakes, through improvement of the accuracy, quality and effectiveness of work performed which would generally be time consuming (Radwan, 2021). The auditing profession has digitally transformed due to the technology improvements that have occurred over the years. The digital transition from traditional auditing to continuous auditing is that transactions are now reviewed real-time as the activities occur. Information systems have transformed the manner that auditors perform their audits (Radwan, 2021). This necessitates that there should be transformation of the skills of auditors in general, including those in the public sector. In this context, the internal auditing profession has been playing a gradually essential role within organisations and in the public sector. Internal auditing plays a critical role in organisations not only limited to verifying the accounting system and the accuracy of the presented financial statements but also assist to recommend control systems improvement and key processes that are imbedded in the activities of any organisation. The Institute of Internal Auditing defines internal auditing as an "independent, objective assurance and consulting activity designed to add value and improve an organisation's operations" (IIA, 2021). Internal auditing assists an organisation to achieve its goals by bringing an organised, controlled approach to assess and advance the effectiveness of risk management, control, and governance procedures.

Financial transactions in the private and public sectors are widely computerised, and manual processes in these financial transactions have changed mainly due to the roles,

DOI: 10.1201/9781003382706-8

responsibilities, and qualifications needed to execute them (Vanbutsele, 2018). This requires the skills of the public sector auditors to be improved to keep up with the current changes occurring in the technology space (Vanbutsele, 2018). The auditing profession is confronted with regular updates and digitalisation of organisations' business operations; therefore, the auditing process should keep abreast with the improvements and innovations with auditors being adequately equipped. The private sector usually takes the lead when it comes to innovation, whereas the public sector is at times left behind as updates often occur. Numerous supreme audit institutions (SAIs) especially in places such as the United Kingdom (UK) and Australia are drastically changing public sector auditing due to the emergence of technological transformation as cited by INTOSAI (2018) and Victorian Auditor-General's Office (VAGO) (2018).

Previously the training and education of auditors has failed to take into account factors such as the recognition of patterns and evaluation of anomalies. These critical skills can only be learnt after many years of experience (Earley, 2015). According to Vanbutsele (2018), IT skills and expertise are critical for any auditor to acquire. There has been an increase in the investment of skills of auditors by the public sector in general over time. This has been seen in various SAIs (Bump, 2015) and Victorian Auditor-General's Office (VAGO) (Jiang, 2019). There are many advantages in the implementation of technology in the auditing process; however, in the advancement of technology, it is not always easily implemented and accepted by various organisations due to the high costs of implementing the technologies. The lack of qualified professionals in digital and information systems auditing make it difficult to implement these systems and document the necessary procedures and practices of the control system (Santos et al., 2019). Therefore, it is important to detail how digitalisation and technology advancements affect the requirements profile regarding the knowledge and skills of auditors. Based on Halar's (2020:78) assessment, a number of internal auditors do not possess the required skills and competencies for evaluating organisations' digitally changing business operations.

8.2 THE DIGITALISATION OF THE ENVIRONMENT

This section aims to distinguish between "digitisation" and "digitalisation". "Digitisation" is defined as the technical process of altering an analogue signal towards a digital nature and finally converting to binary digits (Legner et al., 2017:301). While "digitalisation" refers to the multiple sociotechnical experiences and processes of implementing and utilising these technologies in wider individual, organisational, and societal settings (Legner et al., 2017:301) and exclusively links to the manner that these technologies change active business processes (Verhoef et al., 2021). Consequently, the technical practice of digitisation deals specifically with one portion of digitalisation. Certainly, digitalisation relates to the universal use and wider advancement of technologies in organisations and society in general (Bloem et al., 2014).

To expand further, digitalisation involves an array of changes for organisational practices and activities (Verhoef et al., 2021) leading to business practices that are more digitised and computerised (Bouwman et al., 2018; Brennen & Kreiss, 2016; Canning et al., 2018; Tschakert et al., 2016). It is not enough to consider digitalisation only as advanced digitisation (Ross, 2017; Unruh & Kiron, 2017). Due to the advancement of technology, a number of organisations have tried to implement new digital solutions in order to update their business practices and to further develop their digital environment through the use of emerging digital technologies (Laudien & Pesch, 2019; Parviainen et al., 2017). Therefore, the digitalisation of organisations is about the advancement of digital resources and a responsive organisational structure (Gupta et al., 2020; Verhoef et al., 2021). Staff members would be required to incorporate and integrate digital technologies into their daily working activities (Kane et al., 2015). Consequently, "digitalisation" is about the readiness of organisations to employ digital technologies in their practices and business strategy.

Digitalisation could result in the audit function to integrating data analytics in its business practices, but internal audit shops are confronted with the challenge of implementing digital technologies due to the costs of implementation and utilisation. The other challenge is acquiring the right IT skills by the internal auditors for using this digital technology such as the use of data analytics (Betti & Sarens, 2021). When organisations attempt to implement these new technologies, they are faced with a number of challenges. There are high costs of implementation that need to be absorbed by the organisation which creates uncertainty. There are further issues of change management which need to be considered. Organisations and internal audit staff should accept the use of new technology and should also adapt to the digital environment (Betti & Sarens, 2021; Gupta et al., 2020). With the adoption of these new technologies, it becomes important for the practicing internal auditors to have the required level of digital expertise. Some of these internal auditors would need to be appropriately trained with these new digital skills required. The correct IT knowledge and skill training programmes would have to be specifically developed to upskill these internal auditors with the appropriate digital skills to meet the current need. Therefore, the newly recruited internal auditors would need to possess a higher digital awareness and expertise to meet the workplace demands. Ultimately, this could expand the global degree of digital and IT skills of internal auditors employed. Furthermore, this would also increase the requirement for internal audit departments to recruit and maintain high-quality digital profiles of internal auditors (Bartlett et al., 2017; Burton et al., 2015). These digital profiles are more likely to be vested in far more technology-driven jobs than internal audit roles. Consequently, the internal audit function could first incorporate digital activities into the daily activities of internal auditors.

8.3 FRAMEWORK FOR CATEGORISING DIGITALISATION AND TYPES OF ACTIVITIES

Figure 8.1 shows an overview of three different stages of digitisation in the context of accounting, each of which is disruptive to a different degree for activities and thus competences (Bleiber, 2019; Hübl, 2020): *substitution*, *process change*, and *innovation*. While in stage 1, analogue data or activities are substituted by digital ones, new technologies lead to changes in processes in stage 2. Stage 3 addresses innovation, both processes and their respective outcomes are changed. An insightful framework of digitalised activities is suggested by Aepli et al. (2017), who adopted the classification from Spitz-Oener (2006) and validated it in expert interviews. The framework was chosen because digitalisation is more likely to change activities in a profession rather than erase it in their entirety (Aepli et al., 2017; Autor, 2015; Seeber & Seifried, 2019). In addition, some activities are more prone to digitalisation than others.

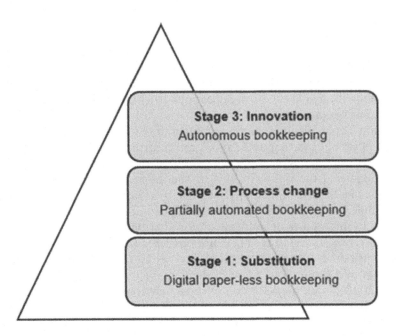

Figure 8.1 Digitisation of accounting processes.

Source: Aepli et al. (2017).

8.4 THE IMPACT OF DIGITALISATION ON THE INTERNAL AUDIT PROFESSION

In Tone at the Top (IIA, 2017), AI is presented as the future of internal audit. The research article is considered important as it brings to the agenda various views on whether the internal audit profession will continue to exist in the future (The Institute of Internal Auditors, 2017). Blockchain, which is one of the most important innovations brought by digitalisation today, leads to many radical changes in audit and control procedures and even renders many of them invalid and unnecessary due to its features such as transparency, traceability, and immutability (Rooney et al., 2017). This necessitates a review of professional standards and procedures. Rooney et al. (2017) questioned whether internal audit is ready for blockchain and all that it brings with it. Although blockchain offers unwavering security, transparency, and many new digital solutions, the article states that the structure of internal audits and the qualifications of internal auditors need to change in certain directions, internal auditors should be subjected to detailed training on innovations, internal auditors should be involved in any project where blockchain infrastructure is installed in businesses, and the concept of continuous auditing should be adopted by all circles with blockchain adaptation.

Rooney et al. (2017) also emphasised that internal auditors, who are cautious by the nature of their profession, should not have problems in adapting to the technology developing at a dizzying pace. Lee et al. (2018) examined the relationship between internal audit and blockchain. In their article, the authors state that blockchain is not just about bitcoin or other virtual currencies, adding that internal auditors have a lot to learn about the systematics of the chain and how it works. In this context, the authors state that the scope of internal auditors' duties will change with the blockchain, especially the testing of the information in the chain in many ways will bring new obligations and job descriptions to internal auditors.

Research conducted by Brender et al. (2019) based on interviews with auditors indicated that all respondents expected a significant transformation in the nature of the profession in the medium term, with more than half expecting the professional orientation to be IT auditing in general. This suggests that the current profile structure of auditors may undergo a radical change. In addition to this radical change, it is obvious that blockchain will change many processes for businesses. This will ensure that one of the main focuses of internal auditors is already realised, and auditors will no longer have the obligation to guarantee the accuracy and integrity of the data. In contrast, the new focus of auditors will shift to more complex areas such as systematic assessment and fraud detection (Karahan & Tüfekçi, 2019).

Establishing and using indicators of whether technological factors are working properly will always keep internal audits one step ahead. For all this to happen, internal audit experts need to adopt and master all these automation processes. In addition, senior management, which will be fed by internal audit, should be tasked with injecting new perspectives throughout the business (Deloitte, 2019). In another study questioning what the functions and roles of internal audit will be in a digitalised world, it is stated that the digital knowledge of auditors should increase due to the fact that IT risks, including cyber threats, are expected to come to the forefront in the coming years, the demand for consultancy activities of internal auditors will increase, and accordingly, internal auditors will undertake consultancy roles related to digital transformation activities in enterprises (Betti & Sarens, 2021).

The Institute of Internal Auditors (2018a) has proposed five things that auditors can perform in tackling the disruptive era, which include seeking advice from experts in their field, increased focus on assurance, training investment on disruptive technology, using updated technology, and pre-empting risks that could be realised during audit activity. Auditors would be required to perform preparatory and preventive measures in embracing the Fourth Industrial Revolution. The skills of auditors should be transformed immensely in a digital world that is filled with automated process control improvement and intense automation as indicated by Appelbaum, Kogan and Vasarhelyi (2017). Business processes should be created with untrained users in mind, but at the same time, auditors need to be trained to function in a technology-driven environment. Byrnes et al. (2018) has indicated that to use clustering by auditor's, there should be simple business processes created that all the use of statistical expertise to assist the auditor's skills, knowledge, and competence.

Auditors need to go for further education and training to attain supplementary skills such as the use of IT in their daily work. We live in a digital era; therefore, such education and training is required to ensure that the competence and skills of auditors remain relevant. Therefore, the modern auditor will need to have requisite skills to master the methods, theories, and knowledge of processes pertaining to using IT when executing auditing assignments. Auditors should be literate in the latest technology in order to take advantage and leverage the opportunities provided by the digital era and also be ready to tackle the challenges posed by the Fourth Industrial Revolution. Auditors are required to process data and analyse big data sets, therefore being technologically literate would assist them as they perform their monitoring services. The auditor should use digital technology for data and information processing; therefore, technology literacy and capability become important in the execution of their duties. The information processing would have to be executed properly by the audit team and the technology skills required for the Fourth Industrial Revolution would come in handy (Rosa et al., 2019).

8.5 IMPLEMENTATION OF COGNITIVE TECHNOLOGY SKILLS FOR AUDITORS

According to Deloitte (2018a), the real challenge to implementing new technology changes into the work environment is due to the limited knowledge in technology in the workplace and poor understanding of cognitive technologies as required by business processes. The cognitive technologies have indeed revolutionised auditing and the manner of how financial reporting is done; therefore, large companies are increasingly investing in the latest technology. Cognitive technologies bring about new technology that allows for a wider view of financial processes; this is done through the visualisation of business strategies and models or business processes that might be updated for the auditors' own understanding (Deloitte, 2018a). There are control deficiencies that exist, and cognitive technologies can aid in the improvement of audit processes and the quality of the audit mission delivered. This can be achieved through a thorough analysis and understanding of the risks that are prevalent in any organisation (Deloitte, 2018a). The auditors would then focus their efforts in understanding the weaknesses (i.e., risk sectors) of the organisation, and venturing the next level (more in-depth) of big data evaluation, through the use of data analytics tools; this can be done alongside AI technologies such as machine learning, robotics process automation (RPA), and blockchain (Deloitte (2018a).

Once fully implemented by organisations and government agencies, these cognitive technologies would assist to bring about to lasting technology transformation in the audit sector (KPMG, 2017a). Organisations that offer audit services and do not take advantage of investing in new technology solutions face the risk of failing on their status to other players in the market (e.g., IBM, Microsoft) who have already successfully implemented these technologies.

Therefore, technology does not compete or replace an audit specialist but rather supports and complements the auditor's way of working activities (Castka et al., 2020). The main goal or "intention" of implementing advanced IT is to further expand human capabilities, not to duplicate it (Deloitte, 2018a, 2018b). The digital changes create a challenge for auditors to understand the big data phenomenon, due to the fact that data meets different formats. Therefore, auditors are making use of analytic tools to ensure heterogeneity in client's data (Moffitt et al., 2018; Cohen & Rozario, 2019; Vasarhelyi et al., 2020). Auditors are charged with making the final conclusion and they are the ones who have the specialist role in coordinating the audit mission (Castka et al., 2020). In this respect, learning about machine learning, analysing data using data analytics, applying AI, evaluating blockchain accounting transactions, recognising situations, and technological advantages establish the considered facets for a compliance opinion (Cristea, 2020).

8.6 CHANGING ROLE OF AUDITORS DUE TO TECHNOLOGY RISKS

According to Betti and Sarens (2021), the introductions of new areas such as IT and cybersecurity has increased the risk universe for the audit function scope due to the major implications created. The increased focus on digital channels has changed and shifted the priorities at a rapid pace. The key ones include the following:

- To address the new risks, new competencies are therefore required. Auditors are required to have an appreciation of how technology functions;

- Due to system malfunctions and cyber-crime, the auditor would have to possess the required level of awareness of both internal and external risks. The auditor would have to collaborate business to ensure that the audit function remains alert to issues; and
- Due to the new threats that may materialise, there needs to be increased agility to allow for a faster and more effective response to those threats and risks. The audit function need to be better prepared to change the processes to enable more effective risk management within an ever changing digital environment, and this can be done through agile comprehension and planning.

Digitalisation has the capability to change the role of the audit function. Management committees are of the considered view that the audit function is an ideal business partner due to the knowledge and capabilities. This is shown in the ever-growing need for the audit function to gradually adopt a consulting function, which is seen to add more value to the organisation. During times of major change such as the implementation of technology, the consulting role become more important for the audit function (Betti & Sarens, 2021).

Betti and Sarens (2021) further state that internal auditors remain hesitant due to the fact that their role and function needs to be seen as independent and do not want to compromise their role. The tasks that internal auditors carry out create a dilemma based on the expectation and the reality on what needs to be done. It is suggested that the internal audit function should embrace a more consultative role to assist management. Due to the indirect nature of providing advisory services to management, the internal audit function retains some independence, since offering advice distances it from allegations of involvement in implementing organisational strategy.

8.7 IMPACT OF BLOCKCHAIN TECHNOLOGY ON AUDITORS

Silva et al. (2021) evaluated the existing stage of blockchain application on auditing area, analysing scholastic publications since the advent of distributed ledger technology (DLT), recognising its implication that has already become reality, and the potential effects. There will no longer be a need for auditors to request a number of documents as part of the audit process when blockchain is implemented for the accounting transactions. The study elaborated that audits will be completed simply through the information of accounts, portfolios, and smart contract codes associated with the blockchain systems. Therefore, a third-party would still be required to determine whether the physical world is accurately represented in the ledger of the companies, and what should remain to the auditor's role as a reality certifier once blockchain has been fully implemented and embraced for information recording.

Elommal and Manita (2021) studied how modern auditors need to prepare for blockchain technology and the impact that this technology will have on the audit profession. They noted five areas where practices need to change to better service audit clients and to ensure that the audit is more relevant. Furthermore, it was indicated that the audit processes would be required to change towards a continuous audit where the focus would change from historical data, but there would be strong focus on recent and current data. The audit process should also transform towards evaluating and testing all datasets not only a sample that represents a smart extract of the entire data. The audit process should also significantly ease the information validation tests and place more emphasis on existing control tests and provide a comprehensive analysis that brings significant benefits to clients and reduces the audit risks. Blockchain will bring about evolution whereby the auditor's role will move from a simple control evaluator to a real strategic advisor who would support organisations in the development of their business and their information and control systems. Audit firms should create an ethos of innovation and client satisfaction at all levels of their services.

Lombardi et al. (2022) examined the significance of blockchain technology on the audit profession to note the trends and research areas and created an agenda for future research. The analysis was done to categorise past research, and the agenda for future research, into three main research themes: (1) Blockchain as a technique for auditing professionals to further advance business information systems to save time and prevent fraud; (2) Smart contracts enabling Audit 4.0 efficiency, reporting, disclosure, and transparency; and (3) Cryptocurrency and initial coin offerings (ICOs) as a springboard for corporate governance and new venture financing. The research findings had a number of significant implications for practice and theory. Abad-Segura et al. (2020) found that the global research on blockchain technology for secure accounting management shows an upward trend in the number of papers and schools of thought. This indicates the interest among the academic/scientific community worldwide on the subject. The research focused on publications that contribute to the knowledge of blockchain accounting discipline link.

Baiod et al. (2021) revealed that blockchain has shown its potential for facilitating complex processes such as transaction verification, reconciliation and settlement, and dispute resolution through its design features. Besides, blockchain may also change traditional business with its vital characteristics, including distribution, anonymity, immutability, and audibility. As blockchain was created to remove intermediaries' role, particularly in the financial transaction space, it uses a decentralised consensus protocol for transaction processing and validation.

Bonyuet (2020) reviewed blockchain technology and the significance of blockchain on the audit profession, including the introduction of new risks, transformation in processes and additional opportunities. The key ideas were gathered from prior research to assess the feasibility of employing blockchain when executing audits. Based on the expanded focus and talks around blockchain, it is important for auditors to appreciate how this technology affects the profession, and more importantly, how it can be employed for the benefit of the audit process. The study further revealed that as the business world continues to be complicated, the auditors would need to perform their audits smarter and more effectively through the use of reliable tools that would give them a chance to provide the assurance that is required and is expected from them. In addition, auditors are also viewed as business advisors, and therefore, there is an expectation that they should also be experts in all relevant technologies. Hence, when the effect of blockchain on auditing is small, auditors will need to have an appreciation of how such technology affects a client's business operations.

Barandi et al. (2020) revealed that blockchain technology brings about numerous advantages that are going to revolutionise the audit profession, from improving on the efficiency of audit processes to developing new tasks and activities for auditors. The study investigated numerous approaches in which auditors might circumvent the restrictions of legacy auditing by using the latest blockchain technology. While the advantages of blockchain-enabled auditing are visible, the study also examined some of its restrictions and concluded that instead of focusing on the limitations, auditors should welcome this emerging technology and ready themselves for the new tasks and activities provided by the emergence of blockchain technology. A healthy level of uncertainty towards new technologies is always good, but the future of the audit profession looks exciting in the new area of blockchain.

Spoke (2015) stated that auditors are required to be aware with the blockchain and how it works. Real-time auditing and the application thereof may be a possibility and auditors need to be familiar with this. The idea behind real-time auditing is to examine financial transactions closer and closer when they actually occur and are processed. Real-time auditing is a huge advantage to the firms who are providing services; at the point of occurrence, authentic data makes predictive analytics more beneficial. The true value is derived from the predictive analytics correlated with higher quality audits, as deviations from informed predictive analytics can be examined further. While a full real-time audit will not be achieved due to the likelihood that only a portion of transactions will be recorded on the blockchain, a part of the substantive procedures related to the blockchain-recorded transactions can be shifted to the present, rather than near the end of the quarter. Blockchain allows for real-time auditing by granting auditors access to the permissioned network. The auditors have the ability to investigate and select transactions as they occur. This also frees up time for auditors at year end to spend their attention to more complex accounting matters involving valuation or classification, or to inspect transactions that have been highlighted as unusual.

According to Shaw (2017), auditors are required to put resources and measures in place to allow for implementation blockchain by companies. It could well be that the hype around blockchain is exaggerated due to the fact that it would not necessarily remove the audit or the auditor (Shaw, 2017). The biggest contributor of blockchain is that it would allow auditors to use their professional judgement. The auditors will be required to use critical thinking and use professional scepticism due to the emergence and use of new technologies in the audit process (Franzel, 2017). Advanced technical skills would be required to be used by auditors with the use of the latest technology tools and approaches. It is challenging to determine audit risks without knowledge of how technology works (Franzel, 2017). Auditors would thus need to upskill themselves in areas such as computer science and statistical inference, due to the fact that these areas will become predominant and integrated into auditing procedures through blockchain. With great improvement in these aspects, i.e., developing a deeper understanding of blockchain technology and concentrating on the new regulations, this will result in auditors being better prepared for any implications that blockchain will have in the future (Ortman, 2018).

8.8 ROBOTICS AND AUTOMATION IN THE AUDITING PROCESS

The word "robot" comes from the Czech word "robota"; this is translated into forced labour and has further progressed referring to dumb machines, machines that execute menial, monotonous activities and highly smart anthropomorphic robots of popular culture (Lanfranco et al., 2004). Robots function through software that allow them to communicate with systems by mimicking human behaviour to execute certain activities (Syed et al., 2020). Robots can thus execute certain activities or tasks which include moving or assembling objects to delivering customer and legal service, diagnosing medical conditions, sensing hazards in physical environments, and providing financial advisory services (Avery, 2019; Cheng, 2019; Lay, 2019). Kokina and Davenport (2019) further add that robotics reduces the completion time for activities and there is a further reduction in costs associated with processing data. Thus, this further improves the correctness and reliability of the data, and this aids in the decision-making process. From an auditing point of view, robotics are able to assist auditors to computerise monotonous activities of extracting and preparing data to be evaluated so that auditors can focus their energy on more value-added activities such as testing the quality and the correctness of the data (Gotthardt et al., 2020; Lombardi, Bloch & Vasarhelyi, 2015).

The progress in technology advancement brings about new challenges and opportunities for the auditors and the profession (Tiberius & Hirth, 2019). For internal auditors, the predicament is how the audit profession can assist with companies to comprehend, organise, and implement adequate controls around the new risk presented by the innovation of these technologies (Rose et al., 2018). Public accounting firms are making use of emerging technologies such as RPA when advancing future software audit tools to enhance efficiencies (Harris, 2017). RPA is preconfigured software that performs a sequence of procedures, tasks, transactions, and activities to computerise tasks that have coordinated data, rule-based procedures, and a single, correct outcome (Lacity & Willcocks, 2016). From an auditing point of view, robotics can be utilised to execute repetitive tasks such as carrying client's data from the previous year within the accounting firm's audit platform and evaluating of the benefits plan, to mention but a few (Cooper et al., 2019; Huang, 2018). Despite the importance of using data analytics and robotics in audit engagements to improve audit quality and practical needs for leveraging big data to gain insights, the use of technology in audit engagement is still limited (Wang & Cuthbertson, 2015).

In a study by Sethibe and Naidoo (2022), it was found that it is critical to understand the challenges and possible enablers of implementing the use of technology in the auditing profession. The research showed that age may be a contributing factor to take into account, predominantly from a social influence standpoint. Possible obstacles in the implementation of robotics are lack of funds and adequate skills for adoption in auditing. Adequate training interventions and management support could be possible solutions to this challenge (Sethibe & Naidoo, 2022).

The authors of this study found that the performance management system and the business case for robotics in the auditing process should be allied to the activities of auditors, and the infrastructure, environment, culture, and legislation should be favourable to technology adoption in the profession (Sethibe & Naidoo, 2022). Secondly, adequate resources be mobilised and availed to aid the use of technology in the profession. What is critical is that there be a readiness and belief by top management that technology will add a positive impact on the effectiveness and efficiency of the auditing operations. Consequently, management is required to take into account the strategic direction of their organisation by ensuring that sufficient budget is allocated towards skills development, investment in technology, and improved data infrastructure to increase operational efficiency (Sethibe & Naidoo, 2022).

8.9 ADVANCED DIGITAL SKILLS REQUIREMENTS FOR AUDITORS

The current Fourth Industrial Revolution introduces new technologies such as AI, the internet of things, blockchain, biotechnology, 3D printing, and drones (Mahomed, 2019). Mahomed (2019) argues that with the Fourth Industrial Revolution, automation will disregard jobs and change the nature of jobs and competencies required for success in the labour market.

In the internal auditing sector, advances in new technologies and the drive for innovation and digital transformation are upturning industries and challenging internal audit functions to remain relevant (IIA, 2018b). Most businesses have also started to invest in RPA, data analysis, predictive analysis, advanced technologies, data analysis, AI, and machine learning to automate work (Furtună & Ciucioi, 2019).

Internal auditors are required to apply data analytics and IT (including IT control frameworks) in performing audit activities and identifying and assessing various risks related to IT, information security, and data privacy (IIA, 2020a). The IIA IPPF standards 1210 states that internal auditors must have sufficient knowledge of key IT risks and controls and available technology-based audit techniques to perform their assigned responsibilities.

According to Deloitte (2018b), it is critical to have internal auditors who understand risk exposures created by emerging technologies in particular, AI and RPA applications. The increase in digitalisation will require organisations to pay more attention to inherent risks such as cybersecurity, privacy, and data security (Saul, 2018). Boulianne (2016) states that it is important that auditors have an advanced level of IT education and acknowledges that challenges to incorporating increased IT education into Higher Education Institutions (HEI) programs me continue to be a problem. Internal auditors require the analytics acumen to master new audit techniques leveraging different sources of data (Jackson, 2020). Refer to Table 8.1 for required IT skills for auditors in relation to IT.

In the current business environment, financial auditors are entrusted to be professionals who give assurance to the existence of transactions; confirm their evidence, accuracy, and completeness; and present related information in financial statements (Hayes et al., 2014). To fulfil these objectives, auditors:

- Are required to fully understand their client's business, including its nature, environment, internal controls and IS – such as blockchain, if in use – related to business processes and financial reporting (ISA 315; AS 2110).
- Are required to employ various types of audit tools, which include new technologies such as data analytics. According to Cao et al. (2015), data analytics can be explained as the process of evaluating, purifying, transforming, and modelling big data to uncover and communicate relevant information and patterns, which suggests that conclusions for decision-making; with big data being large and unstructured data sets produced by people, transactions, and machines (Bender, 2017). For purposes of auditing, data analytics allows for auditors to test the complete population being

Table 8.1 Required IT skills for auditors (own compilation)

Competency category	Competency required based on literature	Key reference
Information technology (including data analytics, security and privacy, and IT control frameworks)	IT knowledge IT infrastructure – computer operations Cybersecurity Data privacy/security Data analytics and visualisation Data mining CAATs Electronic working papers Data risk assessment Robotics, blockchain, and AI Cloud computing Continuous auditing IT control frameworks	Deloitte (2018b), Furtună and Ciucioi (2019), Hirth (2020), IIA (2020a), Janesko (2020) and Jackson (2020)

100% of their clients' transactions and in order to get a deeper insight into their processes and recognise not only errors but also anomalies in the data patterns, which would increase audit quality (Liddy, 2014; Earley, 2015; Murphy & Tysiac, 2015).

- Are required to adhere to auditing standards in the course of their work. The auditing standards are there to ensure that there are measures to validate the performance quality and must provide clear, concise, and definitive imperatives for auditors to follow (Carmichael, 2014).

Overall, there is no doubt that the role of accountants and auditors will evolve under the advancement technology such as machine learning, AI, blockchain, and data analytics. Therefore, public auditors and accountants are not going to lose their jobs. Their roles are expected to change with time and shift in the recording and reconciliation of firms' daily operations from manual to progressively computerised procedures (Schmitz & Leoni, 2019). Therefore, the role of accountants and auditors will be reengineered with the progress of the adoption of these advanced technology systems. A new generation of accountants and auditors with different skills will be required to respond to the changes in the current accounting and auditing paradigm (CPA & AICPA, 2017; KPMG, 2017b).

8.10 CRITICAL IT SKILLS FOR AUDITORS TO ADDRESS EMERGING IT RISKS

In 2015, the Institute of Internal Auditors Research Foundation (IIARF) contracted a study to evaluate the Top 10 technology risks confronted by internal auditors under the Global Internal Audit Common Body of Knowledge (CBOK) (IIA, 2015:3). These Top 10 Risks included the following:

1. Cybersecurity
2. Information security
3. IT systems development projects
4. IT governance
5. Outsourced IT services
6. Social media use
7. Mobile computing
8. IT skills among internal auditors
9. Emerging technologies
10. Board and audit committee technology awareness (IIA, 2015:3).

This CBOK 2015 Global Internal Audit Practitioner Survey displayed a network of complex current and emerging IT issues confronted by the internal audit professional in general. Foremost, the risks confronted by organisations were showed due to the limited IT skills possessed by auditors within the internal audit department. This was largely due to the poor awareness among the board of directors (IIA, 2015:3). This study further indicated the important IT skills which were needed from internal audit professionals that these auditors do not possess.

In a research report, Deloitte (2018b:6) assembled a list of key IT topics and competences needed by internal auditors in financial services. Companies all over the word are required to keep up with the latest financial technology in the market. This will enable them to better manage the risks they are confronted with; furthermore, the auditor professionals are required to be knowledgeable and possess the expertise to evaluate those financial technology risks. The 2018 hot topics for IT internal audit in financial services that internal auditor professionals are required to be skilled in include the following:

1. Cybersecurity
2. Strategic change
3. Data management and data governance
4. IT disaster recovery and resilience
5. Information security/identity and access management
6. Third-party management
7. IT governance and IT risk management
8. Cloud computing
9. Digital and mobile risk
10. Enterprise technology architecture (Deloitte, 2018b:3).

It is worth mentioning that the CBOK 2015 Global Internal Audit study is similar to the 2018 IT Internal Audit Hot Topics study by Deloitte (2018b:6) as there is similarity in matters like data management, cybersecurity, IT governance, third-party/outsourced IT services, information security, and mobile computing risk. This is indicative that current internal auditors should have the needed IT knowledge, skills, and expertise in order to audit the current technology risk confronted by organisations that they service.

The chief audit executive must fully understand the extent of IT knowledge, skills, and expertise that are required to audit the successful implementation of the controls over the known business risks (GTAG, 2012:3). The IIA's Standards and Professional Knowledge department released a new Global Technology Audit Guide (GTAG) to provide a baseline of IT knowledge for internal auditors. This guideline was created to assist auditors for all experience levels. The IIA's IT essentials for internal auditors' guide discusses foundational and baseline IT topics along with possible challenges, risks, and opportunities within this increasingly growing and intensifying area that impacts all organisations (IIA, 2020b).

This IT guide for internal auditors touches on crucial topics such as IT governance activities (including high-level, cross-functional IT activities and the IT and business relationship), IT service delivery, monitoring, and the three main IT technical domains: network, infrastructure, and applications (IIA, 2020b). It is designed to enable internal auditors to grasp technical topics so they can continue to provide valuable organisational assistance through risk-based auditing in a variety of areas that require greater understanding and expertise (IIA, 2020b).

This IT guide is designed to ensure that internal auditors can understand:

• The relationship between IT and the business, including associated challenges and risks.
• Various network structures, components, and related concepts.
• IT infrastructure, including hardware, software, and databases.
• How organisations use, implement, and develop applications.
• Topics such as data analytics, social media, RPA, machine learning, Internet of things (IoT), and other emerging technology issues.

Table 8.2 IIA's IT essentials for internal auditors'

Emerging IT trends and topics	Essential IT-related activities and concepts that internal auditors should know
Relationship with the business and overall IT governance	Business enablement – the Goal of IT IT governance IT as a business Process oversight: IT service delivery and project portfolio management Ongoing monitoring: quality and compliance needs/activities Challenges and risks for IT governance and the IT and business relationship
IT infrastructure	Main components Infrastructure challenges and risks
IT network	Defining a network Network components and concepts Remote network access Network defence Network challenges and risks
Applications	Application architecture Application development and maintenance Applications challenges and risks
Additional and emerging IT topics	Data management Data analytics Social media Robotic process automation Machine learning and artificial intelligence Internet of things (IoT) Challenges for additional and emerging IT topics

Source: IIA (2020b) adapted.

Table 8.2 illustrates the emerging IT trends and topics together with essential IT-related activities and concepts that internal auditors should know in terms of skills and competencies to execute the audit.

According to the IIA (2020b), they see IT as an essential part of every company, including public sector entities. Therefore, it becomes critical for the chief audit executive and their internal audit team to have a foundational understanding and knowledge of IT and the management of important data within their organisations. Protecting enterprise data, supporting IT operations, and safeguarding technology are some of the myriads of the issues that most organisations are confronted with today. While these issues may seem discouraging, they are more than offset by the potential opportunities IT allows an entity, such as optimising its operations, innovating product development, and leveraging processes, including data analytics and technologies such as RPA or AI (IIA, 2020b). IT is an integral part of an organisation's strategy, and understanding the effects of technology on business processes and risk management will help elevate internal audit as a trusted advisor and value creator. Figure 8.2 shows the significant IT areas in which internal auditors should have a baseline understanding.

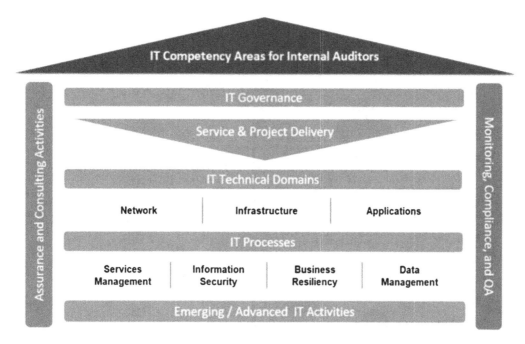

Figure 8.2 The IIA's IT competencies for internal auditors.
Source: IIA (2020b).

The Deloitte (2020) Internal Audit 3.0 framework presents an assembly aimed at assisting organisations creating the next generation of internal auditors as a function well adapted to the issues of emerging risks, technologies, and "disruption". This framework aims to bring a philosophy of innovation, assists functions in terms of keeping up with technological advancements, and increases their impact and influence throughout the organisation. The vision that arises differs from organisation to organisation and will be governed by the need to get adapted to the strategic organisational direction and overall business change.

To successfully lead that transformation, the internal audit function will be required to focus on areas such as: skills and capabilities (people), ways of working (processes – agile models are quite popular options recently), and digital assets and solutions (technology). Numerous leading internal audit functions have already embarked their process into the world of automation by expanding their use of traditional analytics to include predictive models, RPA, and AI (Deloitte, 2020). These programmes have started to see benefits such as audit risk reduction, audit quality enhancements, as well as increased risk intelligence. With automation technologies advancing at a rapid rate, and early adopters demonstrating their effectiveness, it is believed that this is the right time for internal audit to understand and prioritise the use cases for automation and take critical measures to prepare for thoughtful, progressive deployment (Deloitte, 2020).

Figure 8.3 shows the size of the bubble and reflects the ordering in the list, while the horizontal axis shows the threat environment (internal or external to the organisation). The vertical axis shows the range of emerging, new, or existing risks.

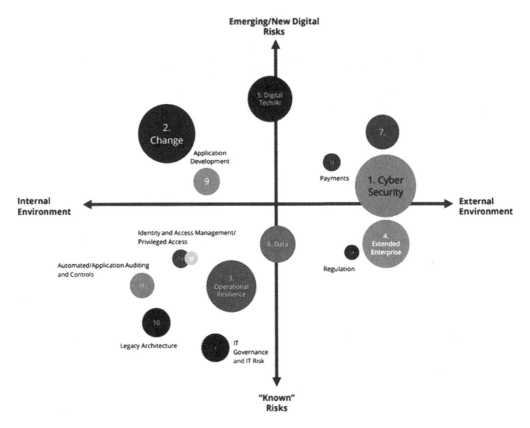

Figure 8.3 Classification of the top-15 IT internal audit hot topics for 2020.

Source: Deloitte (2020:15).

8.11 IT AND DIGITAL COMPETENCIES REQUIRED FOR AUDITORS BY GOVERNMENT AGENCIES AND PROFESSIONAL BODIES

8.11.1 AFROSAI-E Integrated Competency Framework

The AFROSAI-E (2022) Integrated Competency Framework outlines the knowledge, skills, behavioural, and leadership competencies for audit and other professional roles in the SAIs. SAIs are known to perform the independent audit function of governments around the world. The expertise, knowledge, and skills in the framework are associated with the INTOSAI Standards for Supreme Audit Institutions (ISSAIs) on financial, performance, and compliance auditing. The behavioural and leadership competencies are aligned with the five fundamental values of ISSAI 130 (code of ethics). To develop an all-encompassing framework for a SAI, the AFROSAI-E adapted a section of roles from across the SAI, to ensure that the widest range of relevant knowledge and skills are captured in the framework. The updated comprehensive framework was released in January 2022 with knowledge and skills for the following roles such as compliance audit, financial audit, performance audit, specialised audit (consisting of IT, forensic, and environmental audit) as stated by AFOSAI-E (2022).

Table 8.3 Competencies for audit staff at supreme audit institutions (SAIs)

Competency statement	Digital skills and procedures to be executed by a public sector auditor
Information systems, computerised information systems, and computer-assisted audit techniques.	• Knowledge of information systems and computerised information systems and environments, internal controls relating to it, and computer-assisted audit techniques.
Enabling IT tools	• To use IT tools and computer-assisted auditing techniques effectively and efficiently in the general conduct of the business of the SAI and individual engagements.
IT environments at clients	• To evaluate computerised information systems and environments and to develop, perform, and document audit procedures for computerised information systems and environments.
IT audit	Ability to examine and evaluate an organisation's information technology infrastructure, policies, and operations to determine whether IT controls to protect assets, ensure data integrity, and are aligned with the organisation's overall goals. Understand business and financial controls that involve information technology systems. To perform and/or use the following appropriately in an IT audit context: • Analytical skills, • data visualisation skills, • Big data tools, • Programming and algorithms, • Data structures and object-oriented languages, • Coding quantitative and statistical analysis, • Problem-solving, • SQL, • Data mining, • Data value chain.

Source: Adapted from AFROSAI-E (2022).

AFOSAI-E (2022) developed the knowledge requirements and competencies which were recognised for audit professionals to serve and execute effectively in the SAI environment. Operational knowledge is gained through experience, tuition, or formal education and is founded on the theoretical understanding of the SAI environment. This includes specialised audit professionals who should possess IT and digital skills. Table 8.3 indicates the IT competencies and knowledge requirements for auditors who work in the public sector such as the SAI environment.

8.11.2 Registered government auditor competency framework

According to SAIGA (2022), the competency framework was established by the Southern African Institute of Government Auditors (SAIGA) to give the members of the public with the knowledge and skills of a Registered Government Auditor (RGA) professional in Southern Africa. The purpose of the framework is to serve as a guide and standard not only to a prospective RGA but also to the institutions of higher learning and training, skills development providers (SDPs), and registered workplace providers who prepare, train, educate, and develop prospective RGA professionals. It is a framework for all public sector

Table 8.4 Registered government auditor competency framework

Competency statement	Digitals skills and procedures to be executed by a public sector auditor
Technology and digital acumen (An RGA demonstrates the know- how to leverage digital innovations and technology to assist in improving efficiency and effectiveness in conducting audits)	• Describe the use of digital innovation and technology to improve efficiency and effectiveness in audits. • Use digital innovation and technology in audit activities. • Utilise digital techniques and processes to support audit decision-making and analysis.

Source: Adapted from SAIGA (2022).

institutions and audit and accounting firms that perform any business dealings with public sector organisations in the auditing and accounting domain (SAIGA, 2022). Table 8.4 provides the SAIGA's high-level competencies required by IT audit specialist.

8.11.3 ACCA competencies required by IT audit specialists

According to ACCA (2023), the job profile of an auditor is that one who possesses proven audit experience together with knowledge and skills in IT systems, infrastructure, and applications. These audit professionals should also have exceptional analytical and communication skills to correctly document and present data in non-technical terms. Discretion is also paramount as this job profile ordinarily engages with confidential and sensitive information. Table 8.5 provides the ACCA's high-level competencies required by IT audit specialist.

8.11.4 CGMA competency framework: Digital skills

According to AICPA & CIMA (2023), IT knowledge and skills are included into the Chartered Global Management Accountant (CGMA) designation from the Chartered Institute of Management Accountants (CIMA). AICPA and CIMA have appreciated that it was fundamental to adopt emerging technologies at an early stage, and this elevated the importance of digital skills. As these emerging technologies are implemented by organisations, AICPA and CIMA have had a legacy of developing the professional standards that guide features of adoption and implementation. The CGMA designation separates accounting and finance professionals with advanced proficiency in technical, business, digital, people, and leadership skills (AICPA & CIMA, 2023). Table 8.6 provides AICPA and CIMA's high-level competencies required by IT audit specialist.

8.12 KEY LESSONS LEARNT

Public sector auditors need to show that they have the skills to test the control environment and security of information systems with an auditing point of view and know how to apply computerised auditing tools and techniques in executing their duties. Public sector auditors need to possess the required technology-based audit techniques in order to execute their assigned audit responsibilities. This also includes the emerging technologies such as blockchain, AI, RPA, robotics, IoT, and machine learning that are ever evolving to address the

Table 8.5 High-level IT competencies required for auditors

Competency statement	Digitals skills and procedures to be executed by a public sector auditor
Strategy and innovation	A. Applies business acumen and commercial awareness to deliver business objectives. B. Recommends a range of suitable strategic options from which to develop sustainable plans and objectives. C. Evaluates, justifies, and implements suitable strategic options. D. Adopts and applies innovative methods to implement strategy and manages change.
Data, digital, and technology	A. Identifies strategic options to add value, using data and technology. B. Analyses and evaluates data using appropriate technologies and tools. C. Applies technologies to visualise data clearly and effectively. D. Applies scepticism and ethical judgement to the use of data and data technology.
Audit and assurance	A. Advises on and effectively communicates the role and scope of audit and assurance engagements to relevant stakeholders. B. Applies regulatory, legal, professional, and ethical standards relating to audit and assurance engagements. C. Plans and prepares for audit and assurance engagements. D. Performs effective audit and assurance engagements. E. Reviews and reports on the findings of audit and assurance engagements. F. Guiding efficient and effective operations.
Stakeholder relationship management	A. Positively develops relationships with internal and external stakeholders. B. Communicates and gains commitment from internal and external stakeholders. C. Uses emerging technologies to collaborate and communicate effectively with stakeholders. D. Applies professional and ethical judgement when engaging with stakeholders. E. Aligns organisational strategic objectives with stakeholder needs and manages expectations.

Source: ACCA (2023).

key technology risks at their clients. Table 8.7 displaces the key digital skills and knowledge that a public sector auditor should possess.

The world is constantly involving and the key driver for the changes that are occurring in technology. Therefore, now more than ever, the public sector auditors need to be capacitated with the correct digital skills to remain relevant in a fast pace changing world. To better service the emerging risks in any governmental organisation and public sector entities, it is critical for public sector to upskill themselves with the correct skills needed to provide assurance and to ensure that controls are operating as intended.

For public sector auditors to continue adding value to the clients they service, they need to be as agile as the organisations that they are operating in through digital skills development and improvement. These auditors need to evolve as these emerging technologies

Table 8.6 CGMA competency framework digital skills

Competency statement	Digitals skills and procedures to be executed by a public sector auditor
Information and digital literacy (This is the process of understanding information, data, and content in a digital environment.)	• Search for data, information, and content in a digital environment. • Create and update personal records. • Articulate what information is needed. • Organise, store, and retrieve data, information, and content in a digital environment • Analyse and compare sources of data, information, and digital content. • Analyse and interpret data, information, and digital content. • Assess data, information, and digital content and navigate between them • Critically evaluate credibility and reliability of sources of data, information, and digital content. • Critically evaluate data and digital content.
Digital content creation (This is the process of creating, editing, and improving digital content, including copyright and licences.)	• Create content in different formats. • Edit and improve existing content. • Modify, refine, and integrate new information and content into existing body of knowledge to create new, original and relevant content and knowledge. • Advise on how copyright and licences apply to digital information and content.
Problem-solving (This is the process of identifying and resolving technical issues when using digital tools.)	• Identify technical problems when operating devices and/or using digital environments. • Solve technical problems when operating devices and/or using digital environments. • Evaluate and select digital tools to resolve different technical problems. • Use digital tools to create knowledge and to innovate processes and products.
Data strategy and planning (This is the process of developing and managing a set of choices and decisions that align the organisation's data strategy to its business strategy.)	• Demonstrate knowledge of data management techniques. • Manage policies on data protection and privacy. • Develop and implement relevant data models. • Ensure data quality, accessibility, interoperability, and compliance to standards • Develop overall data strategy. • Define metadata using common standards. • Develop policies on data protection, privacy, intellectual property rights, and ethical issues in data management.
Data analytics (This is the process of quality-checking data from multiple sources, choosing appropriate metrics measurements, and developing analytics and verification applications to provide the organisation with analytics-based solutions.)	• Develop and plan required data analytics for organisational tasks, e.g., evaluating requirements and specifications of problems to recommend possible analytics-based solutions. • Verify data quality and veracity. • Define policy and manage intellectual property rights issues. • Plan, design, develop, and implement analytics for organisational tasks. • Develop whole data processing workflows and integrate them into the organisational workflow.

Table 8.6 (Continued)

Competency statement	Digitals skills and procedures to be executed by a public sector auditor
Data visualisation (This is the process of applying existing and developing new visualisation solutions and dashboards to provide solutions for specific business techniques.)	• Apply visualisation techniques and tools for existing data sets and applications. • Use multiple visualisation techniques and languages for existing and new analytics applications and processes. • Develop simple dashboards. • Develop new visualisation solutions and advanced dashboards. • Define best visualisation approach and solutions for specific business issues. • Use multiple techniques to create interactive dashboards.

Source: Adapted from AICPA & CIMA (2020).

Table 8.7 Digital skills and knowledge that a public sector auditor should possess

Competency statement	Digitals skills and procedures to be executed by a public sector auditor
Review of IT systems	• Understand and apply the COBIT Framework • Evaluate the systems documentation • Understand how to document IT system risks • Identify and test general and application controls
Evaluate system security	• Understand and know to test firewalls and access controls • Understand and know how to test encryption • Understand data centre security and procedures
Review of the internet and E-business	• Understand and know how to test Electronic Data Interchange (EDI) • Understand and know how to test web infrastructure • Understand and know how to test e-commerce • Understand and know how to test EFT • Understand and know how to test sys-trust (privacy frameworks)
Evaluate system implementations	• Evaluate the cost of implementation (cost of ownership) • Evaluate the decision process in system implementation • Understand how the choosing systems occurs • Understand who is responsible for system implementations
Review of the ERP systems	• Understand what ERP systems are and the types of companies that use them • Identify the people responsible for the implementation decision • Identify the risks specific to ERP systems • Understand how business processes are mapped (translated) into enterprise system software and how managerial decisions integrate across disciplines • Understand enterprise system modules, including navigation and information access for management • Understand differentiation between enterprise system transactions, queries and reports within a manager's role-specific need-to-know access • Transform raw data into management information that drives managerial analyses and decisions.

(Continued)

Table 8.7 (Continued)

Competency statement	Digitals skills and procedures to be executed by a public sector auditor
Auditing a computerised system	• Auditing the general control environment • Perform CAATs for continuous auditing • Perform CAATs using tools such as ACL • Perform CAATs using tools such as IDEA • Perform data analysis and data mining
Review of database environments	• Identify the risks within a database environment • Identify and test controls to manage these specific risks • Understand the process of auditing of databases
Review of emerging IT technologies	• Understand and know how to test contingency planning • Understand and know how to test software licensing • Understand and know how to test application development • Understand and know how to test cloud computing • Understand and know how to use AI and understand the risks associated with AI • Understand and know how to use blockchain as part of testing • Understand and know how to test cybersecurity and evaluate technology risks • Understand and know how to test the IoT and evaluate technology associated with IoT • Implement continuous auditing as part of the auditing process • Understand and know how to test robotics and machine learning

through making use of data analytics, RPA, AI, machine learning, blockchain and implementing continuous auditing as part of the audit process for early detection of risks and errors in the system.

REFERENCES

Abad-Segura, E.; González-Zamar, M.-D. (2020). "Research Analysis on Emerging Technologies in Corporate Accounting", *Mathematics*, Vol. 8, p, 1589.

Aepli, M., Angst, V., Iten, R., Kaiser, H., Luthi, I., and Schweri, J. (2017). *Die Entwicklungen der Kompetenzanforderungen auf dem Arbeitsmarkt im Zuge der Digitalisierung: Schlussbericht.* Eidgenossisches Hochschulinstitut fur Berufsbildung, Zollikofen

AFROSAI-E. (2022). AFROSAI-E Integrated Competency Framework. Retrieved online at https://afrosai-e.org.za/wp-content/uploads/2022/02/AFROSAI-E-Integrated-Competency-Framework-October-2022.pdf. (Accessed on 29 August 2023).

AICPA & CIMA. (2020). CGMA Competency Framework Digital Skill. Retrieved online at www.aicpa-cima.com/resources/download/cgma-competency-framework-digital-skills. (Accessed on 29 August 2023).

AICPA & CIMA. (2023). Why Digital Skills Are Vital for Accountants. Retrieved online at https://myfuture.cimaglobal.com/career-insights/why-digital-skills-are-vital-for-accountants/. (Accessed on 29 August 2023).

Appelbaum, D., Kogan, A. and Vasarhelyi, M.A. (2017). "Big data and analytics in the modern audit engagement: Research needs", *Auditing*, Vol. 36 No. 4, pp. 1–27, 2017, https://doi.org/10.2308/ajpt-51684.

Association of Chartered Certified Accountants (ACCA). (2023). IT audit specialist. https://careernavigator.accaglobal.com/gb/en/job-profiles/expert/it-audit-specialist.selector.Leader.html#:~:text=IT%20audit%20specialists%20require%20expertise,operating%20system%20and%20application%20level. (Accessed on 29 August 2023).

Autor, D.H. (2015). "Why are there still so many jobs? The history and future of workplace automation", *Journal of Economic Perspectives*, Vol. 29 No. 3–30. https://doi.org/10.1257/jep.29.3.3.

Avery, H. (2019). Private Banking: Wealthtech 2.0 – When Human Meets Robot. Retried online www.euromoney.com/article/b1cygh7rdnlqk1/ private-banking-wealthtech-20-when-human-meets-robot. (Accessed on 23 June 2023).

Baiod, W., Light, J. and Mahanti, A. (2021). "Blockchain technology and its applications across multiple domains: A survey", *Journal of International Technology and Information Management*, Vol. 29, No. 4, https://scholarworks.lib.csusb.edu/jitim/vol29/iss4/4.

Barandi, Z., Lawson-Body, A., Lawson-Body, L. and Willoughby, L. (2020). "Impact of blockchain technology on the continuous auditing: Mediating role of transaction cost theory", *Issues in Information Systems*, Vol. 21, No. 2, pp. 206–212, https://doi.org/10.48009/2_iis_2020_206-212.

Bartlett, G.D., Kremin, J., Saunders, K.K. and Wood, D.A. (2017). "Factors influencing recruitment of non-accounting business professionals into internal auditing", *Behavioral Research in Accounting*, Vol. 29 No. 1, pp. 119–130.

Bender, T. (2017). The Effect of Data Analytics on Audit Efficiency. Retried online from https://thesis.eur.nl/ pub/38929. (Accessed on 23 June 2023).

Betti, N. and Sarens, G. (2021). "Understanding the internal audit function in a digitalised business environment", *Journal of Accounting & Organizational Change*, Vol. 17 No. 2, pp. 197–216.

Bleiber, R. (2019). *Digitalisierung in der Finanzbuchhaltung: Vom Status quo in die digitale Zukunft*. Haufe, Freiburg.

Bloem, J., van Doorn, M., Duivestein, S., Excoffier, D., Maas, R. and Van Ommeren, E. (2014), The Fourth Industrial Revolution. Retrieved online at: www.fr.sogeti.com/globalassets/global/downloads/reports/vint-research-3-the-fourth-industrial-revolution. (Accessed on 7 August 2023).

Bonyuet, D. (2020). "Overview and impact of blockchain on auditing", *The International Journal of Digital Accounting Research*, Vol. 20, pp. 31–43, http://rabida.uhu.es/dspace/bitstream/handle/10272/17766Overview.pdf?sequence=2#:~:text=Blockchain%20adoption%20may%20result%20in,such%20transactions%20can%20be%20generated.

Boulianne, E. (2016). "How should information technology be covered in the accounting programme", *Canadian Journal of Administrative Sciences*, Vol. 33, No. 4, pp. 304–317.

Bouwman, H., Nikou, S., Molina-Castillo, F.J. and de Reuver, M. (2018). "The impact of digitalization on business models", *Digital Policy, Regulation and Governance*, Vol. 20 No. 2, pp. 105–124, https://doi.org/10.1108/DPRG-07-2017-0039.

Brender, N., Gauthier, M., Morin, J.-H. and Salihi, A. (2019). "The potential impact of blockchain technology on audit practice", *Journal of Strategic Innovation and Sustainability*, Vol. 14 No. 2. https://doi.org/10.33423/jsis.v14i2.1370.

Brennen, J.S. and Kreiss, D. (2016), "Digitalization", *The International Encyclopedia of Communication Theory and Philosophy*, pp. 1–11, https://doi.org/10.1002/9781118766804.wbiect111.

Bump, S.M. (2015). "Powering up: How we began with data analytics", *The Journal of Government Financial Management*, Vol. 64, No. 2, pp. 54–56.

Burton, F.G., Starliper, M.W., Summers, S.L. and Wood, D.A. (2015). "The effects of using the internal audit function as a management training ground or as a consulting services provider in enhancing the recruitment of internal auditors", *Accounting Horizons*, Vol. 29 No. 1, pp. 115–140, https://doi.org/10.2308/acch-50925.

Byrnes, P.E., Al-Awadhi, A., Gullvist, B., Brown-Liburd, H., Teeter, R., Warren, J.D. and Vasarhelyi, M. (2018). "Evolution of Auditing: From the Traditional Approach to the Future Audit", In Chan, D.Y., Chiu, V. and Vasarhelyi, M.A. (Ed.) *Continuous Auditing (Rutgers Studies in Accounting Analytics)*, Emerald Publishing Limited, Leeds, pp. 285–297, https://doi.org/10.1108/978-1-78743-413-420181014.

Canning, M., Gendron, Y. and O'Dwyer, B. (2018). "Auditing in a changing environment and the constitution of cross-paradigmatic communication channels", *Auditing: A Journal of Practice and Theory*, Vol. 37 No. 2, pp. 165–174, https://doi.org/10.2308/ajpt-10577.

Cao, M., Chychyla, R. and Stewart, T. (2015). "Big data analytics in financial statement audits", *Accounting Horizons*, Vol. 29 No. 2, pp. 423–429.

Carmichael, D. (2014). "Reflections on the establishment of the PCAOB and its audit standard-setting role", *Accounting Horizons*, Vol. 28 No. 4, pp. 901–915.

Castka, P., Searcy, C. and Mohr, J. (2020). "Technology-enhanced auditing: Improving veracity and timeliness in social and environmental audits of supply chains", *Journal of Cleaner Production*, Vol. 258, p. 120773.

Cheng, A. (2019). 6 Retail Tech Trends to Watch for 2019 That Go Beyond Competing with Amazon. Retrieved online at: www.forbes.com/sites/ andriacheng/2019/01/20/six-key-retail-tech-trends-towatch-for-2019-and-its-not-just-about-amazon. (Accessed on 23 June 2023).

Cohen, M. and Rozario, A. (2019). "Exploring the use of robotic process automation (RPA) in substantive audit procedures", *The CPA Journal*, Vol. 89 No. 7, pp. 49–53.

Cooper, L.A., Holderness, D.K., Sorensen, T.L. and Wood, D.A. (2019). "Robotic process automation in public accounting", *Accounting Horizons*, Vol. 33 No. 4, pp. 15–35. https://doi.org/10.2308/acch-52466.

CPA and AICPA. (2017). Blockchain Technology and Its Potential Impact on the Audit and Assurance Profession. Retrieved online at: www.cpacanada.ca/en/business-and-accounting-resources/audit-andassurance/canadian-auditing-standards-cas/publications/impact-of-blockchain-on-audit. (Accessed on 21 August 2023).

Cristea, L.M. (2020). "Innovations in financial audit based on emerging technologies", *Audit Financial*, Vol. XVIII No. 3(159)/2020, pp. 513–531.

Deloitte. (2018a). Cognitive Technologies. Retrieved from www2.deloitte.com/us/en/insights/focus/cognitive-technologies/ technical-primer.html. (Accessed on 28 July 2023).

Deloitte. (2018b). Internal Audit 3.0 The Future of Internal Audit Is now. Retrieved online at: www2.deloitte.com/mt/en/pages/audit/articles/internal-audit-3-0.html. (Accessed on 30 June 2023).

Deloitte. (2019). Auditing the Risks of Disruptive Technologies Internal Audit in the Age of Digitalization. Retrieved from www2.deloitte.com/content/dam/Deloitte/us/Documents/finance/us-rfa-auditing-the-risks-of-disruptive-technologies.pdf. (Accessed on 23 July 2023).

Deloitte. (2020). 2020 Hot Topics for IT Internal Audit in Financial Services | An Internal Audit Viewpoint. Retrieved online at: www2.deloitte.com/content/dam/Deloitte/uk/Documents/financial-services/deloitte-uk-2020-hot-topics-in-it-internal-audit-in-fs.pdf. (Accessed on 28 August 2023).

Earley, C.E. (2015). "Data analytics in auditing: Opportunities and challenges", *Business Horizons*, Vol. 58, No. 5, pp. 493–500.

Elommal, N. and Manita, R. (2021). "How blockchain innovation could affect the audit profession: A qualitative study", *Journal of Innovation Economics & Management*, https://doi.org/10.3917/jie.pr1.0103.

Franzel, J.M. (2017). "Update on PCAOB Effort to Enhance Audit Quality", Public Company Accounting Oversight Board, Speeches & Statements. https://pcaobus.org/News/Speech/Pages/Franzel-updatePCAOB-efforts-enhance-audit-quality-12-5-17.aspx. (Accessed on 23 June 2023).

Furtună, C. and Ciucioi, A. (2019). "Internal audit in the era of continuous transformation. Survey of Internal Auditors in Romania", *Audit Financiar*, Vol. 17 No. 155, pp. 452–472.

Global Technologies Audit Guide (GTAG). (2012). *Information Technology Risk and Controls* (Global Technology Audit Guide. IPPF Practice Guide). 2nd ed. Institute of Internal Auditors, Lake Mary, FL.

Gotthardt, M., Koivulaakso, D., Paksoy, O., Saramo, C., Martikainen, M. and Lehner, O. (2020). "Current state and challenges in the implementation of smart robotic process automation in accounting and auditing", *ACRN Journal of Finance and Risk Perspectives*, Vol. 9 No. 2020, pp. 90–102. https://doi.org/10.35944/jofrp.2020.9.1.007

Gupta, S., Leszkiewicz, A., Kumar, V., Bijmolt, T. and Potapov, D. (2020). "Digital analytics: Modelling for insights and new methods", *Journal of Interactive Marketing*, Vol. 51, pp. 26–43.

Halar, P. (2020). "The current state and perspectives of the professional development of internal auditors in the age of the digital economy", *Proceedings of the Faculty of Economics and Business in Zagreb*, Vol. 18 No.1. https://doi.org/10.22598/zefzg.2020.1.77

Harris, S.B. (2017). Technology and the Audit of Today and Tomorrow. Retrieved online from: https://pcaobus.org/News/Speech/Pages/Harrisstatement-PCAOB-AAA-4-20-17.aspx. (Accessed on 23 June 2023).

Hayes, R., Dassen, R., Schilder, A. and Wallage, P. (2014). *Principles of Auditing. An Introduction to International Standards on Auditing.* 3rd ed. Pearson, Harlow. Chap 1.

Hirth, B. (2020). Internal Auditors Focused on Identifying and managing Emerging Risks According to New Protiviti Study: Internal Audit Capabilities and Needs Survey Examines Self-Described Strengths, Weaknesses in the Profession. Retrieved online at https://0-www-proquest-com.ujlink.uj.ac.za/business/docview/857347011/A8E94FCBEE324C8APQ/4?accountid=13425. (Accessed 30 June 2023).

Huang, F. (2018). Three Essays on Emerging Technologies in Accounting, viewed 13 June 2021, from https://rucore.libraries.rutgers.edu/rutgers-lib/59927/.

Hübl, L. (2020). "Kritische Erfolgsfaktoren bei der Digitalisierung von Wirtschaftstreuhandkanzleien", In Setnicka, M., Krippner, K., and Rosar, W. (eds) *Digitalisierung im Steuer- und Rechnungswesen.* Linde, Wien, pp 191–203.

International Organisation of Supreme Audit Institutions (INTOSAI) (2018). "Data Analytics at the National Audit Office (UK)". [Online Presentation] Available at: www.pscintosai.org/data/files/D0/71/BD/99/7FB83610AFF59C169B59F9C2/Agenda item_2A_Andy-Fisher_Data%20Analytics%20at%20the%20UK%20NAO.pdf. (Accessed on 23 June 2023).

Jackson, R.A. (2020). "Forming today's internal audit function: Audit leaders must make sure their teams have the right skills to serve their organizations effectively", *Internal Auditor*, Vol. 77 No. 1, p. 36.

Janesko, C. (2020). "The digitally transformed enterprise: As organizations adapt to new ways of doing business, internal audit must expand its understanding of data and technology risk", *Internal Auditor*, Vol. 77, No. 4, p. 25.

Jiang, B. (2019). "Transforming Audit – The Power of Data Analytics", Victorian Auditor-General's Office, Brisbane. [Online Presentation] Available at: https://bit.ly/3KlptRj. (Accessed on 15 June 2023).

Kane, G.C., Palmer, D., Nguyen Phillips, A. and Kiron, D. (2015). "Is your business ready for a digital future?", *MIT Sloan Management Review*, Vol. 56 No. 4, pp. 37–44.

Karahan, Ç. and Tüfekçi, A. (2019). "Blokzincir Teknolojisinin İç Denetim Faaliyetlerine Etkileri: Fırsatlar Ve Tehditler", *Denetişim*, Vol. 0 No. 19, pp. 55–72. Retrieved from https://dergipark.org.tr/tr/pub/denetisim/ issue/46331/585566.

Kokina, J. and Davenport, T.H. (2019). "Early evidence of digital labor in accounting: Innovation with robotic process automation", *International Journal of Accounting Information Systems*, Vol. 35, p. 100431. https://doi.org/10.1016/j.accinf.2019.100431

KPMG. (2017a). *Harnessing the Power of Cognitive Technology to Transform the Audit.* KPMG International, New York City, NY.

KPMG. (2017b). KPMG and Microsoft Blockchain Services. Retrieved online at: https://home.kpmg/xx/en/home/insights/2016/09/kpmg-and-microsoft-blockchain-services.html. (Accessed on 15 July 2023).

Lacity, M.C. and Willcocks, L.P. (2016). A New Approach to Automating Services. Retrieved online from https://sloanreview.mit.edu/article/a-new- approach-to-automating-services/. (Accessed on 23 June 2023).

Lanfranco, A.R., Castellanos, A., Desai, J.P. and Meyers, W. (2004). "Robotic surgery: A current perspective", *Annals of Surgery*, Vol. 239, pp. 14–21. https://doi.org/10.1097/01.sla.0000103020.19595.7d.

Laudien, S.M. and Pesch, R. (2019). "Understanding the influence of digitalization on service firm business model design: A qualitative-empirical analysis", *Review of Managerial Science*, Vol. 13 No. 3, pp. 575–587.

Lay, K. (2019). Robot That's Tuned into Dementia. Retried online: www.thetimes.co.uk/article/robot-that-s-tuned-into-dementia-2m83zq67w. (Accessed on 23 June 2023).

Lee, L., Fiedler, K. and Mautz, R. (2018). "Internal audit and the blockchain: There's more to blockchain than bitcoin, and auditors have much to learn about how it works", *Internal Auditor*, Vol. 75 No. 4, pp. 41–46.

Legner, C., Eymann, T., Hess, T., Matt, C., Böhmann, T., Drews, P., Mädche, A., Urbach, N. and Ahlemann, F. (2017). "Digitalization: Opportunity and challenge for the business and information systems engineering community", *Business and Information Systems Engineering*, Vol. 59 No. 4, pp. 301–308, https://doi.org/10.1007/s12599-017-0484-2.

Liddy, J.P. (2014). "The future of audit", *Forbes*. Retrieved online at: www.forbes.com/sites/realspin/2014/08/04/the-future-of-audit/. (Accessed on 23 June 2023).

Lombardi, D., Bloch, R. and Vasarhelyi, M. (2015). "The current state and future of the audit profession", *Current Issues in Auditing*, Vol. 9 No. 1, pp. 10–16. https://doi.org/10.2308/ ciia-50988.

Lombardi, R., de Villiers, C., Moscariello, N. and Pizzo, M. (2022). "The disruption of blockchain in auditing–A systematic literature review and an agenda for future research", *Accounting, Auditing & Accountability Journal*, Vol. 35 No. 7, pp. 1534–1565.

Mahomed, I. (2019). *The fourth industrial revolution in the workplace*. University of Johannesburg.

Moffitt, K.C., Rozario, A.M. and Vasarhelyi, M.A. (2018). "Robotic process automation for auditing", *Journal of Emerging Technologies in Accounting*, Vol. 15 No. 1, pp. 1–10.

Murphy, M.L. and Tysiac, K. (2015). "Data analytics helps auditors gain deep insight", *Journal of Accountancy*. Retrieved online at: www.journalofaccountancy.com/issues/2015/apr/data-analytics-forauditors.html. (Accessed on 23 June 2023).

Ortman, C. (2018). Blockchain and the Future of the Audit. https://scholarship.claremont.edu/cgi/viewcontent.cgi?referer=&httpsredir=1&article=2903&context=cmc_theses. (Accessed on 23 June 2023).

Parviainen, P., Tihinen, M., KääRiäInen, J. and Teppola, S. (2017). "Tackling the digitalization challenge: How to benefit from digitalization in practice", *International Journal of Information Systems and Project Management*, Vol. 5 No. 1, pp. 63–77, https://doi.org/10.12821/ijispm050 104.

Radwan, H., Zeidan, A. and Elbasuony, H. (2021). "The impact of digital transformation on internal audit", *International Journal of Instructional Technology and Educational Studies (UITES)*, Vol. 2 No. 4, pp 24–27.

Rooney, H., Aiken, B. and Rooney, M. (2017). "Is Internal Audit Ready for Blockchain?" *Technology Innovation Management Review*, Vol. 7 No. 10, pp. 41–44. http://doi.org/10.22215/timreview/1113.

Rosa, R., Rahayu, S., Yudi, Y. and Gowon, M. (2022, January). Internal auditor transformation strategy in the industrial revolution 4.0 era: Literature review. In *Proceedings of the First Lekantara Annual Conference on Public Administration, Literature, Social Sciences, Humanities, and Education, LePALISSHE 2021, August 3, 2021, Malang, Indonesia*.

Rose, M., Rojhani, E. and Rodrigues, V. (2018). "The rise of automation", *Internal Auditor*, Vol. 75, pp. 36–40.

Ross, J. (2017). Don't Confuse Digital with Digitization. Available at: https://sloanreview.mit.edu/article/dont-confuse-digital-with-digitization/. (Accessed on 7 August 2023).

Santos, C., Inácio, H. and Marques, R.P. (2019). "An overview on mobile cloud computing", in Marques, R.P., Santos, C. and Inácio, H. (Eds.), *Organizational Auditing and Assurance in the Digital Age*, IGI-Global, pp. 120–136.

Saul, L. (2018). World Economic Forum and the Fourth Industrial Revolution in South Africa. Retrieved online at: www.dti.gov.za/industrial_development/docs/TIPS.pdf. (Accessed on 30 June 2023).

Schmitz, J. and Leoni, G. (2019). "Accounting and auditing at the time of blockchain technology: A research agenda", *Australian Accounting Review*, Vol. 29 No. 2, pp. 331–342.

Seeber, S. and Seifried, J. (2019). "Herausforderungen und Entwicklungsperspektiven der beruflichen Bildung unter veranderten Rahmenbedingungen", *Zeitschrift für Erziehungswissenschaft: ZfE*, Vol. 22, pp. 485–508.

Sethibe, T. and Naidoo, E. (2022). "The adoption of robotics in the auditing profession", *South African Journal of Information Management*, Vol. 24 No. 1, p. a1441. https://doi.org/10.4102/sajim.v24i1.1441

Shaw, J. (2017). "The Blockchain Transformation of Accounting and Auditing", NJCPA. https://njcpa.org/stay-informed/topics/article/2017/09/14/theblockchain-transformation-of-accounting-and-auditing. (Accessed on 30 June 2023).

Silva, R., Inácio, H. and Marques, R.P. (2021). "Effective and Potential Implications of Blockchain Technology for Auditing", In *Trends and Applications in Information Systems and Technologies: Volume 49*. Springer International Publishing, Cham, Switzerland, pp. 435–451.

Southern African Institute of Government Auditors. (2022). Registered Government Auditor Competency Framework. Retrieved online at: www.saiga.co.za/saiga/wp-content/uploads/2022/12/SAIGA-Competency-Framework-of-an-RGA-Professional-3-1.pdf. (Accessed on 29 August 2023).

Spitz-Oener, A. (2006). "Technical change, job tasks, and rising educational demands: Looking outside the wage structure", *The Journal of Law and Economics*, Vol. 24, pp. 235–270. https://doi.org/10.1086/499972.

Spoke, M. (2015). "How Blockchain Tech Will Change Auditing for Good", *CoinDesk*, www.coindesk.com/blockchains-and-the-future-of-audit/

Syed, R., Suriadi, S., Adams, M., Bandara, W., Leemans, S.J.J. and Ouyang, C. (2020). "Robotic process automation: Contemporary themes and challenges", *Computers in Industry*, Vol. 115, p. 103162. https://doi.org/10.1016/j.compind.2019.103162.

The Institute of Internal Auditors (IIA). (2015). "Navigating Technology's Top 10 Risks: Internal Audit's Role. The Global Internal Audit Common Body of Knowledge". www.iia.nl/SiteFiles/Publicaties/Navigating%20Technology%27s%20Top%2010%20Risks%20_Small.pdf. (Accessed on 14 June 2023).

The Institute of Internal Auditors (IIA). (2017). "Artificial intelligence: The future of internal auditing", *Tone at the Top*, Issue no. 85, 2017.

The Institute of Internal Auditors (IIA). (2018a). "Global Perspectives and Insights: Internal Audit in the Age of Disruption", pp. 1–5. Institute of Internal Auditors, Lake Mary, FL.

The Institute of Internal Auditors (IIA). (2018b). The Next Generation of Internal Auditing – Are You Ready? Catch the Innovation Wave? Retrieved online at: https://chapters.theiia.org/central-iowa/News/ChapterDocuments/Next- FGeneration-Internal-Audit-Protiviti.pdf. (Accessed on 30 June 2023).

The Institute of Internal Auditors (IIA). (2020a). Internal Audit Competency Framework. Retrieved online at: https://na.theiia.org/standards- guidance/Public%20Documents/Internal-Audit-Competency-Framework.pdf. (Access on 23 June 2023).

The Institute of Internal Auditors (IIA). (2020b). GTAG IT Essentials for Internal Auditors. Retrieved online at: https://iia.no/wp-content/uploads/2020/06/2020-GTAG-IT-Essentials-for-Internal-Auditors.pdf. (Access on 18 February 2024).

The Institute of Internal Auditors (IIA). (2021). About Internal Auditing. Available at: https://global.theiia.org/about/about-internalauditing/ pages/about-internal-auditing.aspx. (Accessed on 26 January 2023).

Tiberius, V. and Hirth, S. (2019). "Impacts of digitization on auditing: A Delphi study for Germany", *Journal of International Accounting, Auditing and Taxation*, Vol. 37, p. 1020288. https://doi.org/10.1016/j.intaccaudtax.2019.100288.

Tschakert, N., Kokina, J. and Kozlowski, S. (2016). "The next frontier in data analytics", *Journal of Accountancy*, Vol. 222 No. 2, pp. 58–63.

Unruh, G. and Kiron, D. (2017). Digital Transformation on Purpose. Available at: https://sloanreview.mit.edu/article/digital-transformation-on-purpose/. (Accessed on 7 August 2023).

Vanbutsele, F. (2018). "The Impact of Big Data on Financial Statement Auditing", Master of Science in Business Economics Dissertation, Ghent University.

Vasarhelyi, M.A., Cho, S., Cheong, A. and Zhang, C.A. (2020). "Smart Audit: the digital transformation of audit", *ECA Journal*, Vol. 1, pp.27–32.

Verhoef, P.C., Broekhuizen, T., Bart, Y., Bhattacharya, A., Dong, J.Q., Fabian, N. and Haenlein, M. (2021). "Digital transformation: A multidisciplinary reflection and research agenda", *Journal of Business Research*, Vol. 122, pp. 889–901.

Victorian Auditor-General's Office (VAGO). (2018). "Annual Report 2017–2018", Victorian Auditor-General's Office, Melbourne. [Online] Available at: www.audit.vic.gov.au/sites/default/files/2018-09/VAGO-Annual- Report-2017-18_0.pdf. (Accessed on 30 June 2023).

Wang, T. and Cuthbertson, R. (2015). "Eight issues on audit data analytics we would like researched", *Journal of Information Systems*, Vol. 29 No. 1, pp. 155–162. https://doi.org/10.2308/isys-50955

Chapter 9

Continuous auditing/continuous monitoring

Georges Naoufal

9.1 INTRODUCTION

Due to digital auditing innovation, continuous auditing and continuous monitoring (CA/CM) are revolutionary tools. Ideally, technology has changed risk management, auditing, and accounting in the dynamic business model and service environment. Nevertheless, interconnected CA/CM ideas use technology for real-time audits and monitoring, unlike periodic techniques; therefore, this paradigm change seeks continuous assurance by quickly detecting and fixing faults. Notably, CA/CM in the public sector is important, particularly with artificial intelligence (AI); in fact, remote control, audit, and risk management infrastructure must be solid. However, government organization resistance presents obstacles; hence, overcoming this opposition requires managing job security, procedural changes, and data security and privacy support needs (Polizzi & Scannella, 2023). CA/CM evolved with digital innovation, departing from conventional auditing methods, since modern AI-based technology has boosted CA/CM, enabling real-time monitoring, auditing, and risk management. This chapter aims to explain CA/CM and its public sector applications and problems, whereby, the writers emphasize the importance of digital innovation by separating its implementation challenges. In addition, exploring literature, analyzing it, and synthesizing it will attain the goal, thus this chapter should contribute considerably to public sector CA/CM conversation. Indeed, the authors want to inform practitioners and policymakers by combining literature and emphasizing digital innovation's benefits, because exploring issues, future opportunities, and policy ideas deepens CA/CM knowledge, enabling informed decision-making and field progress.

Digital innovation in modern public sector models means using technology to improve government services and goods. Naturally, digital innovation has a major influence on risk management, auditing, and accounting (Lois et al., 2020). In addition, digital innovation contributed to continuous auditing and continuous monitoring (CA/CM) in the public sector; hence, these methods use technology for real-time audits and government surveillance. Ideally, continuous auditing, unlike periodic audits, continuously evaluates government operations to give confidence and detect concerns as they develop (Lois et al., 2020). In fact, continuous monitoring uses technology to track and assess government actions in real time to discover and resolve issues. Therefore, digital innovation in CA/CM in the public sector improves risk management, decision-making, and audit efficiency and effectiveness, in turn, auditors use AI and data analytics to find abnormalities and exceptions, giving government management ongoing input (Pizzi et al., 2021). Definitely, this strategic approach improves audit quality and reduces fraud and mistakes, enabling government agencies to make quick judgments, thus continuous auditing and continuous monitoring (CA/CM) infrastructure in

DOI: 10.1201/9781003382706-9

the public sector is crucial, particularly with AI-based technology. In sum, a remote control, audit, and risk management infrastructure customized to government activities is essential.

Government agencies may remotely and in real time monitor their activities, thanks to an infrastructure for remote control, auditing, and risk management. The auditing and risk management operations are automated by this infrastructure using cutting-edge AI-based technology (Pizzi et al., 2021). This strategy ensures that operations go as planned and helps agencies see problems and hazards as they materialize and stop them from worsening. Additionally, there could be opposition to reform inside government organizations. It may be difficult to effectively deploy digital innovation and CA/CM projects due to the potential resistance of many government personnel to new procedures or technologies (Pizzi et al., 2021). Concerns about job security or adjustments to current processes may also cause resistance to change. Adopting CA/CM projects may need more support due to data security and privacy concerns. Governmental organizations must ensure that their data collection and storage practices comply with privacy laws. Additionally, they must ensure that data used for CA/CM projects is legal, moral, and open. Failure to do so may seriously affect your reputation and expose you to legal risks.

9.2 BACKGROUND INFORMATION

Accounting records and financial statements are periodically examined in a typical audit to judge the financial statements' fairness. This method depends primarily on sampling approaches and does not offer continuous assurance, which limits its capacity to identify fraud, mistakes, and other problems. As technology developed, auditors looked for ways to use these technologies to improve the auditing process. As a result, two methodologies – continuous auditing and monitoring, or CA/CM – have been developed. Technology is used in CA/CM to automate audit processes, evaluate data in real time, and give management continual assurance and feedback. Although the idea of continuous auditing was initially proposed in the 1970s, it was not until technological improvements in the 1990s that they could be implemented. Since then, AI, data analytics, and other techniques have all advanced how technology is used in auditing (Pizzi et al., 2021). Organizations employ continuous auditing and continuous monitoring (CA/CM) to monitor their operations and transactions to spot and stop fraud, mistakes, and other hazards. The CA/CM concept has been around for a while, with a unique emphasis on using generation to automate the audit procedure (Pizzi et al., 2021). Nevertheless, as new technologies like synthetic intelligence (AI) and devices gaining knowledge of (ML) have emerged, the idea of CA/CM has been modified.

Given the massive chance of fraud and corruption within the public quarter, CA/CM is particularly crucial. Governmental organizations are held to a high standard of scrutiny by the general public and authorities since they handle substantial public monies. Government agencies may enhance their internal control and risk management procedures by implementing CA/CM efforts, ensuring they adhere to rules and standards (Zhang et al., 2022). CA/CM projects must be implemented, necessitating a significant investment in infrastructure, technology, and training. To support the CA/CM objectives, organizations must provide a comprehensive framework for risk management that includes policies, procedures, and controls (Polizzi & Scannella, 2023). Organizations must also ensure that the CA/CM technology is scalable, dependable, and secure (Pizzi et al., 2021). A similar idea called "continuous monitoring" entails continuously observing and analyzing company activity to spot possible problems. Instead of waiting for a routine audit, this strategy enables firms to spot and fix problems immediately. Professional organizations, standard-setters, and regulators are encouraging the implementation of CA/CM methodologies due to the widespread acceptance of digital innovation in auditing (Pizzi et al., 2021). The COVID-19 epidemic in recent years has sped up the adoption of digital innovation as remote work and digital procedures have come to be accepted practices.

9.3 CURRENT ISSUE ON CA/CM

Dai and Vasarhelyi (2020) examine continuous audit intelligence as a service (CAIaaS) and its prospective advantages, providing a complete picture of audit methodology evolution. Ideally, the authors explain how CAIaaS lets auditors monitor transactions in real time and spot irregularities; in fact, this real-time monitoring tool is said to alter audit accuracy and effectiveness. Dai and Vasarhelyi (2020) note that CAIaaS may offer intelligent apps for auditors, helping them choose the best ones for certain audit projects. Naturally, this little feature simplifies and improves audit efficiency and accuracy; hence, the report highlights CAIaaS's ability to speed up fraud and mistake detection, boosting stakeholders' trust in audit results. Notably, CAIaaS's function in auditing is highlighted by its ability to improve audit quality; therefore, a careful reading of the literature shows that the writers propose CAIaaS to address the market's excess of audit applications. Unquestionably, a strategic answer to the difficulty of audit tools is CAIaaS's intelligent app suggestions, because this functionality saves auditors time and optimizes tool use for each audit assignment, according to Dai and Vasarhelyi (2020). Nevertheless, despite its apparent benefits, a critical lens examines CAIaaS's possible drawbacks, where analyzing the wider implications and possible pitfalls of using intelligent app suggestions in audits will help determine CAIaaS's practicality and long-term sustainability in varied audit scenarios. Thus, Dai and Vasarhelyi's (2020) study on CAIaaS and intelligent app recommendations advances audit methodology; hence, the paper's extensive study highlights the possible benefits but urges critical thinking on CAIaaS's implications and limitations in modern audit practices.

Modern auditing, especially the shift from conventional to continuous auditing, is crucial to corporate operations. The article "The transformation of auditing from traditional to continuous auditing in the era of big data", by Çabuk and Aytaç (2019), explores the development of corporate auditing and assurance in the digital age. We get a complete grasp of the shift by critically reviewing this material. Çabuk and Aytaç (2019) explore how auditing procedures have evolved in the setting of big data, where conventional methods must adapt. The relation between traditional and continuous auditing approaches is discussed, highlighting this model shift. The authors methodically analyze big data's difficulties and prospects, arguing that continual auditing is essential to today's dynamic and vast data environments. The critical literature analysis emphasizes continuous auditing's varied significance as a dynamic solution for real-time data evaluation. Çabuk and Aytaç (2019) highlight the benefits of continuous auditing, including timely assurance and early problem detection, whereby technology and data analytics convert continuous auditing into a proactive risk management and fraud detection tool. In addition, Çabuk and Aytaç (2019) demonstrate how these developments enable auditors to identify irregularities and provide ongoing feedback to management; hence, this strategic strategy improves audit quality, eliminates mistakes and fraud, and informs organizational decision-making. Ideally, the critical review highlights the importance of Çabuk and Aytaç (2019) in shedding light on auditing techniques in the big data age. Thus, their blend of historical viewpoints, present issues, and future concerns shows their depth in corporate auditing and assurance discourse. Hence, this literature critically informs the growth of auditing methodology and the strategic positioning of continuous auditing within organizational assurance as businesses struggle with digital transformation.

In their essay, Chaudhuri and Bozkus Kahyaoglu (2023) thoroughly analyze the difficulties and dangers connected to intelligent city cybersecurity assurance. According to the authors, the growing usage of networked technology, which can provide attackers with many access points, makes smart cities vulnerable to cyberattacks (Chaudhuri & Bozkus Kahyaoglu, 2023). Additionally, they raise the possibility that conventional cybersecurity methods may need to be more effective in dealing with the particular difficulties that smart cities provide. The essay outlines the dangers that could result from cybersecurity breaches in clever cities, including the robbery of private facts, interruption of critical offerings, and feasible bodily harm to residents (Chaudhuri & Bozkus Kahyaoglu, 2023). The authors contend that as a way to manage these risks properly, cybersecurity warranty needs to take a chance control approach. They propose together with threat management in the making plans and administration of clever city systems, emphasizing identifying and minimizing possible hazards at every step of the machine's lifetime. A framework for cybersecurity guarantee in clever towns is likewise provided in the examination. It incorporates five vital factors: danger evaluation, tracking and response, risk mitigation, governance and amenability, and stakeholder assignation (Chaudhuri & Bozkus Kahyaoglu, 2023). In keeping with the authors, this framework may additionally resource in ensuring that cybersecurity guarantee is included in the planning and control of systems for clever cities in addition to the robust identification and mitigation of possible threats.

In standard, Chaudhuri and Bozkus Kahyaoglu's (2023) article affords a modern and extensive assessment of the difficulties and risks related to cybersecurity guarantees in smart towns. Which will reap a cybersecurity warranty; the authors emphasize the necessity for a hazard management method and offer a methodology to ensure possible risks are acknowledged and decreased. A more excellent thorough examination of the possible costs and difficulties involved in enforcing this approach and additional empirical evidence of its realistic efficacy might also have been furnished in the paper. No matter this, the study offers insightful records for academics, practitioners, and policymakers engaged in clever city cybersecurity warranty.

In their article, Kahyaoglu and Aksoy (2021) summarize the uses of AI in organizational internal audit and risk assessment procedures. The authors note the potential advantages of utilizing AI, including improved audit process efficiency, accuracy, effectiveness, and the capacity to identify risk and fraud (Kahyaoglu & Aksoy, 2021). The authors' thorough discussion of the many AI technologies, including machine learning, natural language processing, and robots, that may be employed in internal audit and risk assessment is one of this chapter's most vital points. They illustrate how that technology is probably used in real-world conditions, highlighting the capacity blessings of incorporating AI into these techniques (Kahyaoglu & Aksoy, 2021). However, the chapter's short exam of the capacity downsides and regulations of employing AI in inner audit and threat evaluation can be one of its main weaknesses. Although the authors make a passing connection with some of the moral and societal aspects of AI, they do not move into outstanding detail on the risks and difficulties which could get up from deploying these technologies, inclusive of the possibility of biased decision-making or the requirement for specialized technical understanding (Kahyaoglu & Aksoy, 2021). The authors also deliver a cursory rationalization of how AI is utilized in inner audit and hazard evaluation.

They point out several AI's feasible advantages and drawbacks in diverse sports. However, they do not offer a thorough or nuanced examination of how AI may be applied to solve particular issues or challenges in these fields. This may restrict the chapter's practical relevance for readers interested in employing AI in their internal audit and risk assessment procedures (Kahyaoglu & Aksoy, 2021). Overall, the chapter offers a helpful overview of the uses of AI in internal audit and risk assessment. However, a more in-depth discussion of these technologies' potential advantages and disadvantages would benefit from a more thorough analysis of how AI can address particular challenges and problems in these fields.

The issues universities confront in the digital age and how internal auditing may be utilized to meet them are the main topics of Kahyaoglu and Coskun's book (Kahyaoglu & Coskun, 2022). The authors address the possible advantages and drawbacks of utilizing digital technology in the audit process while thoroughly reviewing the condition of internal auditing in higher education today (Kahyaoglu & Coskun, 2022). The practical emphasis of this book is one of its advantages. The issues encountered by universities and the methods internal auditing may be utilized to address them are demonstrated by the author's extensive use of case studies and real-world examples. They also provide chief audit executives (CAEs) and higher education experts with helpful advice and direction on creating efficient internal auditing procedures in their firms (Kahyaoglu & Coskun, 2022). The book's thorough treatment of the subject is another asset. In their discussion of internal auditing in higher education, the writers cover various topics, such as governance and risk management, financial and operational audits, and the application of data analytics and other modern technology. Because of this, the book is a helpful tool for anybody working in internal auditing in higher education.

However, the book's somewhat restricted focus on internal auditing might be a shortcoming. Although the writers thoroughly review the role internal auditing plays in resolving the problems colleges face in the digital age, they have yet to discuss any potential alternative solutions (Kahyaoglu & Coskun, 2022). This could reduce the book's usefulness to those seeking a more comprehensive view of the subject. The book is a valuable resource for everyone interested in internal auditing in higher education. It tackles various topics linked to internal auditing in this context and offers helpful information and suggestions on implementing successful internal auditing processes (Kahyaoglu & Coskun, 2022). Readers who want a more comprehensive understanding of colleges' difficulties in the digital age may need to augment what they read with other sources.

In their work, Hines et al. (2022) make the case that current auditing standards cannot adequately address the legal ramifications of analytics-driven auditing. The authors contend that for auditing standards to accurately represent the reality of current auditing operations, auditors and consumers of financial statements must be more active in promoting and improving auditing standards (Kahyaoglu & Coskun, 2022). The argument in this paper is well-written and compelling, which is one of its merits. The authors strongly argue the need to update auditing standards to consider the legal ramifications of analytics-driven auditing. They give specific instances of how the current standards fall short in this respect (Kahyaoglu & Coskun, 2022). Additionally, they make a compelling argument for the necessity of increased advocacy on the part of auditors and users of financial statements.

The article's applicability to current auditing challenges is another strength. Ensuring that auditing standards stay up with these developments is becoming more crucial as auditing methods continue to alter in response to technological advancements. The author's contention that current standards cannot adequately address the legal ramifications of analytics-driven auditing is a relevant and significant contribution to ongoing discussions about the future of auditing. However, the article needs to pay more attention to the legal ramifications of analytics-driven auditing may be one of its weaknesses. The authors strongly argue the need to update auditing standards in this area. However, they neglect to discuss other possible consequences of analytics-driven auditing, such as ethical or social consequences. This can reduce the article's usefulness for those seeking a more comprehensive view of the subject.

The essay "Advocating for Auditors and Financial Statements Users: Revising Standards Based upon Legal Implications of Analytics-Driven Auditing" contributes significantly to the continuing discussions regarding the future of auditing. It is well-written and compelling overall. Despite its potential limitations, it offers a helpful place to explore the legal implications of analytics-driven auditing.

The article by Soedarsono et al. (2019) looks at the elements that affect how well continuous auditing and continuous monitoring are implemented in Indonesia's government sector. The authors use empirical data to examine the connection between information quality, managerial support, and ongoing auditing and monitoring efficacy. This book's practical emphasis is one of its advantages. The issues universities encounter and the methods in which internal auditing might be utilized to address them are well illustrated by the authors' numerous real-world examples and case studies. In addition, they provide CAEs and higher education experts helpful advice and direction on how to put into practice efficient internal auditing procedures in their respective firms. The book's thorough treatment of the subject is another asset. In their discussion of internal auditing in higher education, the writers cover various topics, such as governance and risk management, financial and operational audits, and the application of data analytics and other modern technology. Because of this, the book is a valuable tool for anybody working in internal auditing in higher education.

However, the book's somewhat restricted focus on internal auditing might be a shortcoming. Although the writers thoroughly review the role internal auditing plays in resolving the problems colleges face in the digital age, they have yet to discuss any potential alternative solutions. This could reduce the book's usefulness to those seeking a more comprehensive view of the subject.

A thorough description of continuous auditing and monitoring techniques and their capability benefits for agencies is given within the paper written by Minnaar, Littley and Farineau (2008). By imparting well-timed and correct records on important commercial enterprise methods, the authors contend that those practices may help companies improve their hazard management, compliance, and widespread performance (Minnaar et al., 2008). The essay outlines the essential distinctions between conventional and continuous auditing and tracking tactics and identifies capability issues with imposing these tactics. The writers additionally cover a number of the leading forces behind non-stop auditing and monitoring, which include the complexity of corporate techniques and the rise in demand for real-time information.

On the way to maximizing the value of continuous auditing and tracking procedures, the thing appraises its possible blessings and downsides. It emphasizes the importance of thoughtful making plans, layout, and execution (Minnaar et al., 2008). The authors additionally provide hints for firms considering adopting non-stop auditing and monitoring, setting up precise goals and overall performance metrics and ensuring that group of workers or contributors receive proper schooling and development. On average, this paper provides a notable body of know-how on non-stop auditing and monitoring tactics. It emphasizes the blessings of these processes for organizations seeking to decorate their threat management and compliance approaches (Minnaar et al., 2008). The item may be made higher by giving more specific examples and case studies of agencies that have efficaciously followed non-stop auditing and monitoring practices and speaking about the potential outcomes of emerging technologies like blockchain and synthetic intelligence.

9.4 REVOLUTIONIZING AUDITING PRACTICES

Continuous audit intelligence as a service (CAIaaS), according to Dai and Vasarhelyi (2020), can assist auditors in seeing possible risks and errors in real time, enabling them to give customers more timely and pertinent suggestions. To improve the efficacy and efficiency of audits, they advise businesses to embrace CAIaaS and suggestions from intelligent apps. In addition, Cabuk and Aytaç (2019) contend that to address the problems brought on by big data successfully, auditing must change from conventional to continuous auditing. In order to discover possible risks and abnormalities in real time, they advise businesses to create a continuous auditing framework that incorporates sophisticated analytics, data visualization, and machine learning algorithms. The necessity for a risk management approach to cybersecurity assurance in smart cities is highlighted by Chaudhuri and Bozkus Kahyaoglu (2023). They advocate for including risk management in the planning and administration of smart city systems, emphasizing identifying and minimizing possible hazards at each step of the system's lifetime. The authors offer a framework with five essential elements: stakeholder involvement, governance and compliance, monitoring and response, and risk assessment.

The possible uses of AI in internal auditing and risk assessment are examined by Kahyaoglu and Aksoy (2021). They contend that AI may provide internal auditors with several advantages, such as increased efficacy, efficiency, and accuracy. The authors give examples of how AI might be applied at many phases of auditing, including risk assessment, data analysis, and report preparation. They also go through a few of the difficulties and restrictions associated with using AI in auditing, such as data quality, technical proficiency, and ethical issues (Zhang et al., 2022). In order to remain competitive and raise the value of their services, the authors advise internal auditors to embrace the usage of AI technologies and tools in their job.

The difficulties and possibilities of auditing at higher education institutions in the digital age are discussed by Kahyaoglu and Coskun (2022). They contend that due to the complexity of their organizational structures and the necessity to strike a balance between academic autonomy and responsibility, higher education institutions need help with their auditing procedures. The authors contend that automated auditing technologies, data analytics, and cybersecurity training can benefit higher education organizations. Additionally, they go through some legal and regulatory issues that impact auditing at institutions of higher learning, such as conformity with national and state laws. In order to maintain effectiveness and competitiveness, the authors advise higher education institutions to modify their auditing procedures to the evolving digital context.

According to Hines et al. (2022), auditing standards should be modified to use analytics and AI technology. They assert that analytics can give auditors a more complete and accurate view of financial reporting and that the conventional auditing procedure might need to be revised to handle the volume and complexity of financial data that will only increase. The authors also explore the ethical and legal ramifications of utilizing analytics in auditing, including data security and privacy issues. They advise that auditors take training courses on utilizing these instruments efficiently while still assuring moral and legal observance. The authors generally support changing auditing standards to more accurately reflect the evolving nature of financial reporting and the potential advantages of analytics-driven auditing.

The main elements that influence the effective adoption of continuous auditing and monitoring methods in Indonesia's government sector are examined by Soedarsono et al. in their 2019 study (Zhang et al., 2022). They contend that managerial support and the quality of the information are crucial elements in determining how effective these techniques are. The authors show that managerial assistance and high-quality information can result from more outstanding risk assessment, early fraud and mistake detection, and better decision-making (Zhang et al., 2022). They also go through some of the difficulties and restrictions associated with putting continuous auditing and monitoring procedures into effect, such as the requirement for adequate technological infrastructure, suitable education and training, and efficient stakeholder coordination.

Zhang et al. (2022) offer several suggestions for businesses implementing continuous auditing and monitoring procedures. First, the authors advise firms to ensure that their continuous auditing and monitoring programs have defined objectives and performance measurements and that these objectives align with the organization's broader strategic goals. This will make it easier to guarantee that the ongoing auditing and monitoring procedures are focused and efficient.

In order to promote the effective deployment of continuous auditing and monitoring methods, the authors advise businesses to guarantee proper employee training and development. Developing a continuous learning and improvement culture and mastering crucial technical skills in data analytics and visualization are required (Zhang et al., 2022). In order to ensure that continuing auditing and monitoring procedures align with the requirements and expectations of all relevant parties, firms should develop effective communication channels among stakeholders, according to the authors' final recommendation (Zhang et al., 2022). This necessitates the creation of obvious reporting and comment strategies and dissemination of pertinent and up-to-date information to stakeholders. The authors emphasize the requirement for robust planning, layout, and execution to maximize the benefits of continuous auditing and tracking tactics. This entails appearing a thorough threat evaluation, growing suitable statistics analysis gear, and installing vicinity dependable facts safety and privacy controls. In conclusion, the advice provided in this text can help companies efficiently impose continuous auditing and monitoring techniques and maximize their advantages. Future studies must examine the precise problems and possibilities of implementing those techniques across various organizational contexts and industries.

The study's recommendations for organizations in Indonesia's government sector are meant to improve information quality management and increase the effectiveness of continuous auditing and monitoring methods. The authors advise businesses to invest in creating and executing data management and quality frameworks and ensure that top management gives sufficient funding and support for ongoing audits and monitoring projects. The authors advise enterprises to concentrate on creating the appropriate technological tools, such as data analytics and visualization software, and to provide their people with the necessary training. The article offers insightful information about the elements that lead to the effective adoption of continuous auditing and monitoring procedures in Indonesia's government sector. Organizations in other industries and nations contemplating adopting similar practices may find the study's results and suggestions helpful.

9.5 INSIGHT INTO THE BLESSINGS OF DIGITAL INNOVATION (PUBLIC-REGION VALUE-DELIVERED AUDITING)

The public sector has transformed to digital innovation, which has created new capabilities to enhance the efficacy and performance of public offerings. Public-area value-delivered audits are one region where digital innovation has a sizable influence. Value-introduced auditing within the public quarter has much to benefit from virtual innovation, higher audit consequences, a more excellent perception of organizational overall performance, and elevated stakeholder involvement and openness. One of the primary advantages of digital innovation in public-area fee-introduced auditing is the ability to conduct audits more incredibly efficiently and successfully. Auditor time and assets may be better spent on extra complex, fee-delivered operations by automating mundane techniques using digital gear and platforms. As an end result, auditors can produce audit effects extra quickly and effectively while growing exceptional in their work and decreasing the chance of mistakes.

Virtual strategies like AI, machine gaining knowledge of (ML), and facts analytics, for example, may assist auditors in rapidly and effectively analyzing enormous volumes of information, identifying patterns and tendencies, and recognizing feasible risks and abnormalities in actual time. As a result, auditors might be better equipped to identify areas that need improvement and give clients more current and relevant advice. By adopting digital innovation, auditors may also improve their capacity for information sharing and collaboration with other stakeholders, which will help them operate more productively and provide better results. The capacity to gather and evaluate data from many sources is another advantage of digital innovation in public-sector value-added audits. Auditors can get data from various sources using digital tools and platforms, including financial systems, social media, and other digital channels. By doing so, auditors can get a complete picture of a business's performance and spot possible risks and problems that would not have been obvious using more conventional auditing techniques.

Auditors may better understand organizational performance via digital innovation, which will help them decide where to improve. Auditors may better understand organizational processes, spot inefficiencies and development opportunities, and provide clients with more specialized and pertinent suggestions by analyzing data and using digital tools to display information. Data visualization technologies, for instance, can assist auditors in making complex data easier to access and comprehend so that stakeholders can better understand the audit process and its results. This can improve the audit process's openness and accountability while fostering stakeholder confidence and credibility.

Furthermore, digital innovation may assist auditors in improving stakeholder engagement and the overall accountability and openness of the audit process. Auditors may connect with clients and other stakeholders more effectively by leveraging digital tools and platforms, giving them additional insight into the audit process and its results. This can improve the audit process's openness and accountability while fostering stakeholder confidence and credibility. In order to keep stakeholders up to speed on the audit process and its results, auditors might use digital technologies like web portals and dashboards to exchange information and updates with them in real time. This can improve the audit process's openness and accountability while fostering stakeholder confidence and credibility.

There are many substantial advantages to digital innovation for value-added auditing in the public sector. Auditors may increase the efficacy and efficiency of their job, the caliber of audit outputs, and stakeholder engagement by embracing digital tools and platforms. As a result, digital innovation ought to be a top priority for firms and auditors looking to improve their auditing capacities and stay ahead of the curve in a world that is becoming more data-driven and technologically sophisticated. Nevertheless, it is crucial to remember that technological progress also brings brand-new dangers and difficulties that must be carefully managed. Data breaches, cyberattacks, and other security risks, for instance, pose a danger to the confidentiality and integrity of audit data. Auditors must be conscious of these dangers and take precautions to reduce them, including putting in place strong cyber-security standards, ensuring data is encrypted and safe, and routinely upgrading and testing their systems and procedures.

Additionally, using digital tools and platforms may reduce the usage of critical thinking and human judgment throughout the audit process (Zhang et al., 2022). Digital technologies can offer insightful information and insights but cannot replace an auditor's experience and judgment. Auditors must continue participating in the audit process, applying their knowledge and discretion to evaluate and analyze data and offer insightful observations and recommendations (Zhang et al., 2022). Auditors' need to continuously adapt and grow their skills and expertise to keep up with quickly evolving technology and digital platforms presents another difficulty related to digital innovation. In order to effectively use digital tools and platforms in their job as technology develops, auditors must keep up with the most recent trends and advancements and consistently improve their abilities.

The introduction of AI is one of the most critical changes that digital innovation has made to the public sector. AI describes a computer system's capacity for knowledge acquisition, logical reasoning, and decision-making using data and formulas (Zhang et al., 2022). For value-added auditing in the public sector, AI technology offers several advantages, including Enhanced Efficiency: AI technology may automate tedious processes like data input, data analysis, and report production, giving auditors more time to work on higher-level duties like detailed data analysis and risk identification. Improved Accuracy: AI algorithms can analyze enormous amounts of data and spot trends and abnormalities that manual auditing can find challenging. This may result in audit results that are more precise and trustworthy (Zhang et al., 2022). Savings: The public sector may save money by using AI technology to automate some operations and cut back on the time and resources needed for audits. Greater Transparency: AI technology can provide auditors with a clearer, more accurate image of how the public sector is run, allowing them to spot possible waste, fraud, and abuse. Real-time data analysis is made possible by AI technology, which enables auditors to spot and handle new risks and problems immediately.

Two digital innovation technologies, continuous audits (CA) and continuous monitoring (CM), have completely changed how public sector firms carry out value-added audits. These technology tools help audits be more successful and efficient by allowing real-time detection of mistakes, fraud, and non-compliance. Some of the main advantages of CA/CM are as follows:

- Real-time monitoring: CA/CM enables auditors to keep track of transactions in real time, enabling them to spot and take care of any problems or irregularities immediately. This lowers the possibility of fraud and mistakes and guarantees that government agencies follow all applicable rules and laws.
- Efficiency gain: By automating some audit processes, such as data analysis and report production, CA/CM may free up auditors' time to concentrate on more challenging duties. As a result, audits take less time and use fewer resources overall, increasing efficiency.

- Increased accuracy: CA/CM can evaluate enormous amounts of data fast and correctly by using digital technologies. As a result, there is a lower chance of mistakes, and the audit results are more accurate.
- Better risk management: CA/CM's real-time monitoring and analysis allow auditors to spot possible hazards and take action before they materialize into serious problems. This improves risk management and lowers risk for firms in the public sector.
- Improved compliance: CA/CM guarantees that public sector businesses abide by rules and regulations by providing real-time monitoring and analysis of transactions (Zhang et al., 2022). This lessens the possibility of non-compliance and the resulting fines.
- Transparency: CA/CM offers a more open and visible picture of the activities of public sector organizations, enabling auditors to see possible waste, fraud, and abuse areas. This improves public confidence in governmental institutions and guarantees efficient use of tax dollars (Zhang et al., 2022).
- Scalability: Depending on the size and complexity of the public sector organization, CA/CM can be scaled up or down. It may therefore be customized to match the demands of businesses of different sizes, making it a versatile tool (Zhang et al., 2022).

Value-added auditing in the public sector has been transformed by modern AI tools and technology, enabling more effective and efficient audits. In order to maximize the advantages of digital innovation, public sector enterprises might employ the following essential technologies and implementation strategies:

- Natural language processing (NLP) is an area of AI that focuses on how human language and computer systems interact. Unstructured data from sources like emails, chat logs, and social media postings may be analyzed using NLP technologies to glean valuable insights. This can assist auditors in locating possible risk and non-compliance areas.
- Machine learning (ML): ML algorithms may automate data categorization and anomaly detection processes. ML algorithms can be taught on big datasets to find patterns and abnormalities. This lowers the chance of mistakes and gives auditors more time to work on jobs requiring more extraordinary skills.
- Robotics process automation (RPA): By automating repetitive operations like data input and report production, RPA solutions can reduce the time and resources needed for audits.
- Data visualization tools: By allowing auditors to rapidly spot trends and patterns in massive datasets, data visualization tools like dashboards and heat maps may help them uncover possible risks and areas for improvement.
- Cloud computing: For colossal data volumes, cloud computing may offer safe, scalable, and affordable storage and processing power. This eliminates the need for pricey technology and software and enables auditors to evaluate massive amounts of information fast and effectively.

Public sector organizations must invest in order to properly utilize these tools and technology.

- Determine their requirements and choose the appropriate tools: Organizations must assess their present audit procedures to see where digital innovation might be beneficial. Then, to best serve their unique demands, they should choose the appropriate tools and technology.
- Invest in training and development: Organizations must invest in training and development to guarantee that auditors can utilize these technologies appropriately. This can entail collaborating with outside suppliers or creating in-house knowledge.

- Ensuring data is secure and private: Organizations must ensure data is stored safely and that privacy rules and regulations are followed. This can entail putting in place security safeguards like encryption and access limits.
- Organizations must create policies and processes to enable these tools and technologies, including data management, risk management, and compliance standards.
- To be sure that these tools and technologies are bringing about the desired effects, organizations must constantly monitor and assess their efficacy.

9.6 INTERNAL CONTROL AND RISK FRAMEWORK

Frameworks for internal control and risk are essential parts of every organization's governance structure. They aid in ensuring the safety of the organization's assets, the accuracy of its financial reporting, and the effectiveness of its operations (Zhang et al., 2022). Implementing internal control and risk frameworks has evolved because digital innovation has altered how firms function. Organizations must develop controls to reduce new risks like cyberattacks, data breaches, and fraud due to the growing use of technology. In recent years, the introduction of digital technology has contributed to the popularity of continuous auditing and monitoring (Zhang et al., 2022). These procedures employ automated tools and methods to track and analyze data in real time, which can assist management and auditors in seeing possible risks and problems immediately. Technology is used in continuous auditing to run automated, continuous audit tests regularly. Instead of waiting until the end of the audit period to evaluate data, auditors can see any problems immediately (Zhang et al., 2022). Contrarily, continuous monitoring uses technology to monitor transactions and other data, enabling companies to spot possible problems and take remedial action immediately.

Organizations should concentrate on the following in order to build an efficient internal control and risk framework in the context of digital innovation and ongoing audits and monitoring:

Risk evaluation: Businesses must identify and evaluate the risks related to their digital operations, including cybersecurity, data privacy, and IT infrastructure. This allows them to create and implement suitable measures to reduce these risks.

- Control environment: Businesses must have a solid control environment supporting compliance and risk management culture. This entails establishing rules and processes that adhere to industry standards and best practices.
- Monitoring and testing: To ensure controls are functioning correctly, organizations should establish continuous monitoring and testing of their controls. This entails employing automated tools and procedures to continuously monitor data and evaluating controls regularly to ensure they work as intended.
- Reporting and communication: Businesses must have a robust reporting and communication system to ensure that the appropriate parties are informed about how well their internal control and risk framework works. This entails often reporting to management and the board and corresponding with regulators and external auditors.

Value-added auditing solutions for the public sector must include continuous auditing and monitoring (CA/CM). Significant advancements in CA/CM have been made possible by digital innovation, offering various advantages (Pizzi et al., 2021). Internal control and risk management requirement are leading forces for digital innovation in CA/CM (Goncalves & Imoniana, 2022). Auditors may monitor and analyze enormous volumes of data in real time using CA/CM technologies, data analytics, and BI approaches, finding possible hazards and areas of concern more rapidly and precisely than ever.

Technology essentials include CA/CM, scorecards, and dashboards without numbers or points. These tools give auditors a visual representation of the data, enabling them to identify trouble areas immediately. Key performance indicators (KPIs), such as those for procurement, finance, or human resources, can be found on a dashboard. Monitoring these KPIs in real time enables auditors to identify issues early and take action. BI techniques and data analytics are also crucial to CA/CM (Pizzi et al., 2021). Auditors examine massive datasets for patterns and trends that may indicate potential risks or areas for development (Shiue et al., 2021). For example, data analytics can identify anomalies in financial transactions, such as sharp increases in spending or strange patterns of behavior.

In the subsequent years, CA/CM will be improved even further by combining data analytics, data engineering, cloud computing, and cutting-edge technologies like AI, ML, and RPA (Goncalves & Imoniana, 2022). With these technologies, auditors can automate tedious activities, enhance the quality of their data, and get deeper insights into possible dangers and opportunities for development.

Digital innovation has transformed CA/CM in public-sector value-added auditing by enabling auditors to collect and analyze data in real time, identify potential dangers more accurately and quickly, and provide stakeholders with real-time insights (Goncalves & Imoniana, 2022). Scorecards and dashboards, BI methodologies, and data analytics are crucial instruments in this process. By embracing emerging technology, CA/CM will become significantly more effective and efficient in the upcoming years.

Value-added auditing in the public sector may benefit significantly from digital innovation, especially regarding rules-based automation (Goncalves & Imoniana, 2022). Here are some details on how digital innovation might be advantageous in this situation:

- Real-time auditing improves the accuracy and efficacy of auditing procedures by enabling auditors to conduct audits quickly using digital innovation (Goncalves & Imoniana, 2022). With automated systems, auditors may monitor transactions live and immediately identify any potential issues or threats.
- Diagnostic, Descriptive, Prescriptive, and Predictive Analytics~ Due to technological advancement, analytical solutions that provide these four types of insights are now more widely available than ever (Goncalves & Imoniana, 2022). This can help auditors identify trends and patterns, investigate the causes, and even anticipate new issues.
- Automation in Compliance Assurance/Compliance Monitoring~ Thanks to technological advancement, CA/CM (Compliance Assurance/Compliance Monitoring) may be automated, boosting output, reducing errors, and saving time (Shiue et al., 2021). This includes using rule engines, process workflows, and several automation techniques.
- Rules-Based RPA (Robotic et al.)~ Rules-based RPA (Robotic et al.) may automate regular, rule-based activities, enabling auditors to focus on more challenging and worthwhile tasks. UiPath and Blue Prism are two examples of RPA tools that could be used in this circumstance.

9.7 THE FUTURE CA/CM

Future developments in digital innovation and new technologies will significantly impact CA/CM (Compliance Assurance/Compliance Monitoring). Here are some potential changes and trends that might affect the direction of CA/CM in the future:

- Increased automation: As RPA technology develops, we may anticipate an increase in the automation of regular CA/CM operations. This may entail data collecting, analysis, and reporting (Goncalves & Imoniana, 2022). The advantages of automation are obvious: It may increase productivity, decrease mistakes, and free up human resources to concentrate on more challenging and valuable tasks.
- Various CA/CM fields now use AI and ML technologies, and their use is expected to rise (Goncalves & Imoniana, 2022). In addition, compliance officers and other stakeholders may receive immediate assistance through AI-powered chatbots, which would speed up response times and increase efficiency. For example, ML algorithms may be used to find patterns and anomalies in massive datasets to more quickly and effectively identify potential compliance concerns.
- Blockchain technology is already used in several accounting and financial industries, including CA/CM (Zhang et al., 2022). Blockchain might create a tamper-proof audit trail for transactions relating to compliance, for example, which might increase transparency and reduce the risk of fraud (Han et al. 2023).
- Things connected to the Internet of Things: According to Shiue et al. (2021), the IoT has a positive impact on various businesses and could be helpful to CA/CM. In order to help ensure that items are being transported and maintained in conformity with legal norms, compliance-related attributes like temperature, humidity, and pressure may be monitored by IoT devices (Zhang et al., 2022). Additionally, as more people use mobile devices: We might expect to see them play a more significant role in CA/CM as they become more prevalent in the workplace (Goncalves & Imoniana, 2022). Compliance officers may use mobile applications to access real-time data and insights, allowing them to monitor compliance-related issues away from their offices.
- Big data analytics. As companies and other organizations generate more data, CA/CM must find ways to manage the influx of data (Goncalves & Imoniana, 2022). Big data analytics techniques can be used to analyze large datasets, which makes it simpler for compliance officers to identify potential issues and dangers (Zhang et al., 2022).
- Collaboration and information sharing. As the regulatory environment becomes more complex, compliance officers will likely need to work more closely with other stakeholders, such as legal teams, risk management teams, and internal auditors (Zhang et al., 2022). Collaboration and knowledge-sharing platforms encourage this cooperation and ensure everyone has access to the information they need to make informed decisions.
- The importance of ongoing compliance monitoring has been emphasized historically when it was a typical task carried out at predetermined intervals (for instance, annually). However, this strategy must be modified as the business environment becomes more dynamic (Zhang et al., 2022). Real-time data and analytics tools combined with ongoing monitoring may simplify identifying and addressing compliance issues as they arise.
- Greater emphasis on culture and ethics. Compliance requires more than just following the law and following the rules; it also calls for creating an atmosphere of morality

and ethical behavior (Shiue et al., 2021). The importance of ethics and culture in CA/CM will be emphasized more in the future (Zhang et al., 2022). This could entail undertaking initiatives like staff training programs, employee satisfaction surveys, and whistleblower hotlines.

- Predictive analytics should be used more often since they may be used to spot compliance concerns before they become serious ones (Goncalves & Imoniana, 2022). Predictive analytics algorithms, for instance, might find trends linked to compliance problems by examining previous data, allowing compliance officers to take action to stop those problems from occurring in the future.

- More literary reporting. CA/CM reporting needs to develop to give insightful data as enterprises and other organizations produce enormous amounts of data (Goncalves & Imoniana, 2022). Using interactive dashboards and visualization technologies to portray compliance data in a more approachable way may help compliance officers and other stakeholders quickly spot patterns, anomalies, and potential risks (Pizzi et al., 2021). Personalized reports based on specific user requirements and insights tailored to the needs of various stakeholders may also be created using advanced reporting technologies.

- System integration. The identity and access management (IAM), governance, risk, and compliance (GRC), and enterprise risk management (ERM) systems are just a few parts of a more comprehensive compliance ecosystem that includes CA/CM (Pizzi et al., 2021). Acquiring and evaluating data from diverse sources should become easier for compliance officers as these systems' integration develops.

- Solutions utilizing the cloud. CA/CM solutions are anticipated to go there as more businesses relocate their operations. Reduced expenses, increased scalability, and improved accessibility are only a few benefits of cloud-based systems (Duan & Hu, 2021). Additionally, they can more effectively connect with other cloud-based applications.

- Focus on risk-based compliance. Historically, compliance monitoring has primarily focused on ensuring businesses follow all relevant rules and regulations (Duan & Hu, 2022). This tactic, however, is only occasionally successful and may require reflecting the risks the company faces appropriately (Pizzi et al., 2021). In the future, we expect to see more risk-based compliance, which focuses compliance operations on the areas that pose the greatest danger to the firm.

9.8 POLICY RECOMMENDATIONS AND INVESTIGATIONS ON DEVELOPMENT AREAS

The efficiency and effectiveness of the public sector may be significantly increased in two significant areas: digital innovation and continuous auditing and continuous monitoring (CA/CM) (Duan & Hu, 2022). Policymakers may promote these two areas and aid the public sector in achieving its objectives by pursuing several policy suggestions and studies. First, policymakers should promote a culture of experimentation and learning since digital innovation is essential in the public sector (Duan & Hu, 2022). A specialized team or unit should be established in the public sector to investigate emerging technologies and ideas that might boost the efficacy and efficiency of public services (Acar et al., 2021). For instance, government organizations may employ AI and ML to streamline data management, automate repetitive processes, and respond to public enquiries instantly (Goncalves & Imoniana, 2022). By automating mundane chores, employees may concentrate on high-value jobs that demand human interaction.

Second, governments must embrace big data analytics and cloud computing for better data management, analysis, and decision-making. Government organizations produce massive amounts of data; using the right tools to analyze this data may help identify trends and direct decision-making (Goncalves & Imoniana, 2022). Big data analytics could boost citizen engagement by providing individualized and targeted services (Duan & Hu, 2022). Organizations may use social media analytics, for instance, to assess public sentiment and respond to queries and concerns promptly.

It is also crucial to establish standards and guidelines for implementing digital innovation initiatives in the public sector (Goncalves & Imoniana, 2022). These guidelines guarantee that digital innovation projects are moral, secure, and compliant with data protection laws (Duan & Hu, 2022). The government should also establish a mechanism for monitoring digital innovation programs to ensure they fulfill their goals and assist citizens.

In order to ensure that public sector employees have the skills and knowledge necessary to benefit from technological innovation, it is vital to invest in their education and training (Goncalves & Imoniana, 2022). Government officials should support training programs that equip staff workers with the skills and knowledge necessary to effectively use new technologies (Lois et al., 2020). This training should be tailored appropriately to each agency's needs in order to ensure that it is practical and applicable.

Finally, authorities should consider establishing public-private partnerships to promote digital innovation in the public sector. The public sector may gain fresh perspectives, technologies, and skills through working with private companies (Zhang et al., 2022). Public-private partnerships will make it simpler for smaller government agencies to carry out digital innovation programs, which also helps to reduce implementation costs.

Continuous auditing and monitoring (CA/CM), another area of development, can significantly boost the efficacy and efficiency of the public sector (Zhang et al., 2022). Policymakers might support using CA/CM to improve internal audit practices in the public sector (Lois et al., 2020). CA/CM may help identify and avoid fraudulent activities, improve compliance, and provide real-time insights into the government's financial health.

To promote the use of CA/CM, policymakers should establish clear regulations and guidelines for its use in the public sector. These standards ensure that CA/CM is implemented successfully and consistently throughout all government ministries (Duan & Hu, 2022). The hints have to offer steerage on the information types to be monitored and scrutinized (Lois et al., 2020). Investing within the era and infrastructure needed to guide CA/CM is vital. Government groups want to get admission to records analytics tools and real-time monitoring systems for CA/CM to be efficaciously adopted (Lamboglia et al., 2021). Policymakers must consider investing in those structures and technology to ensure that agencies can utilize them to their total capacity.

It is crucial to offer training applications for internal auditors and different public zone professionals to make sure they have the skills and data required to execute CA/CM efficaciously (Lamboglia et al., 2021). The training should cowl the ideas of CA/CM, inclusive of the significance of facts analytics and how to employ real-time monitoring tools. It should also be mentioned how to utilize CA/CM to identify and halt fraud.

To make specific CA/CM projects have the predicted effect and enhance the public area, it is crucial to routinely display and examine them (Acar et al., 2021). Normal audits of CA/CM packages' overall performance are essential, and policymakers must offer a framework for judging their effectiveness (Lamboglia et al., 2021). The framework should encompass critical overall performance indicators (KPIs) for monitoring the success of CA/CM packages, which include the lower in fraudulent sports, the boom in compliance, and the development in financial reporting accuracy.

According to policymakers, authorities have to be endorsed to accept CA/CM tasks by providing them with investment or other assets to make their implementation less complicated. As a result, agencies might adopt CA/CM programs more quickly and at a lower cost (Acar et al., 2021). In addition, fostering collaboration between government agencies can help to advance the adoption of CA/CM (Lamboglia et al., 2021). Policymakers should encourage agencies to communicate top tips, acquired information, and other CA/CM-related insights. Collaboration could help reduce duplication of effort and ensure that all agencies use the most effective CA/CM techniques.

Authorities must encourage public education and knowledge of the advantages of CA/CM. The efficiency and efficacy of public services, as well as how they help to decrease fraud and enhance financial responsibility, are all things that citizens need to be aware of (Duan & Hu, 2022). This boosts the public's acceptance of CA/CM programs and strengthens public support.

Governments may encourage adopting digital innovation and CA/CM projects in the public sector by defining rules and norms, spending money on infrastructure and technology, creating training programs for staff members, and constantly evaluating their performance (Duan & Hu, 2022). These programs can promote compliance, decrease fraud, and strengthen financial responsibility while enhancing public services' efficacy and efficiency (Maksimovic et al., 2023). Additionally, raising public support for these projects and guaranteeing their successful implementation in the public sector depends on public education and awareness campaigns.

9.9 CHALLENGES AND SETBACK

Despite the benefits of CA/CM projects and digital innovation in the public sector, their execution needs to be improved (Duan & Hu, 2022). One of the main barriers is the cost of performing these services. Due to the significant expenses of adopting new infrastructure and technology, smaller government agencies may require additional financial resources to implement CA/CM initiatives properly (Lamboglia et al., 2021). Also, hiring and training employees to supervise and complete these initiatives could be expensive. Another challenge is the complexity of putting these initiatives into action. Successful CA/CM efforts require a complex collection of processes, procedures, and technologies requiring specialized knowledge and abilities (Duan & Hu, 2022). Government organizations might need more funding or technology expertise to carry out these tasks independently, which could result in delays and more costs.

Additionally, there could be opposition to reform inside government organizations. It may be difficult to effectively deploy digital innovation and CA/CM projects due to the potential resistance of many government personnel to new procedures or technologies (Singh & Best, 2023). Concerns about job security or adjustments to current processes may also cause resistance to change. Implementing CA/CM projects may need more support due to data security and privacy concerns (Acar et al., 2021). Governmental organizations must ensure that their data collection and storage practices comply with privacy laws (Singh & Best, 2023). Additionally, they must ensure that data use for CA/CM projects is legal, moral, and open. Failure to do so may seriously affect your reputation and expose you to legal risks.

There is insufficient governmental support or will for CA/CM projects and digital innovation. Government representatives might not give these initiatives the priority they require, which could leave them without the funding or resources they require to be successful (Duan & Hu, 2022). Additionally, these initiatives might be discontinued or scaled back due to governmental objectives or leadership changes (Sanusi et al., 2023). Singh and Best's case study-based research from 2023 looked at the impact of continuous controls monitoring (CCM) technologies on the internal audit function during the COVID-19 pandemic. The study found that companies that had previously made CCM technology investments could better adapt to the new requirements and constraints imposed by the epidemic (Singh & Best, 2023). The challenges and missteps in implementing CA/CM initiatives and digital innovation in the public sector highlight the significance of careful planning, coordination, and resource allocation.

To ensure these efforts are implemented successfully, policymakers must solve the financial, technological, organizational, and regulatory obstacles (Lamboglia et al., 2021). Furthermore, increasing public acceptance and knowledge of the advantages of these efforts can aid in overcoming opposition to change and strengthen political support for their implementation.

9.10 CONCLUSION

It has been demonstrated that integrating digital innovation with continuous auditing and continuous monitoring (CA/CM) in the public sector is a successful strategy for enhancing governmental organizations' internal control and risk management procedures. Organizations have been able to automate the audit process further, lower the risk of human mistakes, and improve the accuracy and dependability of the audit findings via AI and other cutting-edge technology. The literature analysis has demonstrated that while CA/CM is a concept that has been around for a while, it has considerably changed due to the emergence of new technologies like AI, ML, and data analytics. Organizations can now monitor their operations and transactions in real time, identify possible problems before they become serious, and enhance their risk management procedures. Public-sector value-added auditing has much to gain from digital innovation, including increased efficiency and effectiveness, decreased audit time and effort, and greater accuracy and dependability. The focus on AI and other cutting-edge technologies has facilitated the development of various technology enablers for CA/CM, including real-time insight, dashboards, scorecards, analytics, rules-based systems, and automation.

A thorough risk management comprehensive rework that includes rules, procedures, and controls is necessary for the execution of CA/CM programs. Several common motivations for CA/CM, such as regulatory compliance, enhanced transparency, fraud prevention, and cost reduction, have been discovered by the literature research. Creating solid governance, choosing the right technological solutions, creating a clear business case, and investing in employee training and development are all tactics for implementing CA/CM projects. With the potential to significantly increase the efficacy and efficiency of audit procedures, CA/CM has a bright future. The capabilities of CA/CM are anticipated to be improved, and companies are likely to receive real-time insights into their operations and transactions due to the combination of DA, data engineering, cloud, and BI approaches.

Additionally, enterprises will be able to automate the audit process further and improve the accuracy and dependability of the audit findings thanks to the predicted considerable growth in the usage of AI and ML in CA/CM. The requirement for routine assessments and evaluations of CA/CM programs to ensure they are reaching their intended results and positively influencing the public sector is one of the policy suggestions for developing CA/CM efforts in the public sector. Policymakers should also provide a framework for implementing CA/CM efforts, including a thorough risk management plan, suitable technological options, and spending on personnel training and development.

REFERENCES

Acar, D., Gal, G., Öztürk, M. S., & Usul, H. (2021). A case study in the implementation of a continuous monitoring system. *Journal of Emerging Technologies in Accounting, 18*(1), 17–25. https://doi.org/10.2308/JETA-17-04-29-9

Çabuk, A., & Aytaç, A. (2019). The transformation of auditing from traditional to continuous auditing in the era of big data. In *Organizational Auditing and Assurance in the Digital Age* (pp. 137–152). IGI Global. https://doi.org10.4018/978-1-5225-7356-2.ch007

Chaudhuri, A., & Bozkus Kahyaoglu, S. (2023). Cybersecurity assurance in smart cities: A risk management perspective. *EDPACS*, 1–22. https://doi.org/10.1080/07366981.2023.2165293

Dai, J., & Vasarhelyi, M. A. (2020). Continuous audit intelligence as a service (CAIaaS) and intelligent app recommendations. *Journal of Emerging Technologies in Accounting, 17*(2), 1–15. https://doi.org/10.2308/jeta-10751

Duan, H. K., & Hu, H. (2021). Continuous intelligent pandemic monitoring (CIPM). *Journal of Emerging Technologies in Accounting, 18*(1), 185–194. https://doi.org/10.2308/JETA-2020-061

Goncalves, R. C. M. G., & Imoniana, J. O. (2022). Readiness of low complexity ERP for continuous auditing in SMEs: The Brazilian case study. *Control and Cybernetics, 51*. https://bibliotekana uki.pl/articles/2183483

Han, H., Shiwakoti, R. K., Jarvis, R., Mordi, C., & Botchie, D. (2023). Accounting and auditing with blockchain technology and artificial Intelligence: A literature review. *International Journal of Accounting Information Systems, 48*, 100598. https://doi.org/10.1016/j.accinf.2022.100598

Hines, C. S., Naegle, J. C., Tapis, G., & Tassin, K. (2022). Advocating for auditors and financial statements users: Revising standards based upon legal implications of analytics-driven auditing. *Atlantic Law Journal, 24*, 86.

Kahyaoglu, S. B., & Aksoy, T. (2021). Artificial intelligence in internal audit and risk assessment. In *Financial Ecosystem and Strategy in the Digital Era: Global Approaches and New Opportunities* (pp. 179–192). Cham: Springer International Publishing. https://doi.org10.1007/978-3-030-72624-9_8

Kahyaoglu, S. B., & Coskun, E. (2022). *University Auditing in the Digital Era: Challenges and Lessons for Higher Education Professionals and CAEs.* Boca Raton, FL: CRC Press.

Lamboglia, R., Lavorato, D., Scornavacca, E., & Za, S. (2021). Exploring the relationship between audit and technology. A bibliometric analysis. *Meditari Accountancy Research, 29*(5), 1233–1260. https://doi.org/10.1108/MEDAR-03-2020-0836

Lois, P., Drogalas, G., Karagiorgos, A., & Tsikalakis, K. (2020). Internal audits in the digital era: Opportunities risks and challenges. *EuroMed Journal of Business.* https://doi.org/10.1108/EMJB-07-2019-0097

Maksimovic, S., Vlaskovic, V., Jovic, D., & Zivanovic, N. (2023). Internal audit in the function of corporate management in the public sector of Serbia. *Economic and Social Development: Book of Proceedings*, 232–241. http://dx.doi.org/10.2298/EKA1191123L

Minnaar, D., Littley, J., & Farineau, D. (2008). *Continuous Auditing and Continuous Monitoring: Transforming Internal Audit and Management Monitoring to Create Value.* New York: KPMG LLP.

Pizzi, S., Venturelli, A., Variale, M., & Macario, G. P. (2021). Assessing the impacts of digital transformation on internal auditing: A bibliometric analysis. *Technology in Society, 67*, 101738. https://doi.org/10.1016/j.techsoc.2021.101738

Polizzi, S., & Scannella, E. (2023). Continuous auditing in public sector and central banks: A framework to tackle implementation challenges. *Journal of Financial Regulation and Compliance*, *31*(1), 40–59. https://doi.org/10.1108/jfrc-02-2022-0011

Sanusi, Z. M., Noor, N. F. M., Isa, Y. M., Ghazali, A. W., & Rentah, F. (2023). The implications of digital audit practice, management support and team support on auditor performance. *IPN Journal of Research and Practice in Public Sector Accounting and Management*, *13*(1), 59–79. https://doi.org/10.58458/ipnj.v13.01.04.0088

Shiue, W., Liu, J. Y., & Li, Z. Y. (2021). Strategic multiple criteria group decision-making model for continuous auditing system. *Journal of Multi-Criteria Decision Analysis*, *28*(5–6), 269–282. https://doi.org/10.1002/mcda.1758

Singh, K., & Best, P. (2023). Auditing during a pandemic–can continuous controls monitoring (CCM) address challenges facing internal audit departments? *Pacific Accounting Review*. https://doi.org/10.1108/PAR-07-2022-0103

Soedarsono, S., Mulyani, S., Tugiman, H., & Suhardi, D. (2019). Information quality and management support as key factors in the applications of continuous auditing and monitoring: An empirical study in the government sector of Indonesia. *Contemporary Economics*, *13*(3), 335–351. www.ceeol.com/search/article-detail?id=974395

Zhang, G., Atasoy, H., & Vasarhelyi, M. A. (2022). Continuous monitoring with machine learning and interactive data visualisation: An application to a healthcare payroll process. *International Journal of Accounting Information Systems*, *46*, 100570. https://doi.org/10.1016/j.accinf.2022.100570

Chapter 10

The ethical perspective of digital auditing in public sector

Léandi Steenkamp and Louis A. Smidt

10.1 INTRODUCTION

Applications based on artificial intelligence provide significant benefits and possibilities for adding value to auditing. However, as with many other new technologies and in different sectors, there may also be ethical problems that cause gray areas in using artificial intelligence (AI) as part of the auditing process. This chapter explains ethical violations and conflict areas related to the abuse of AI. It explains what should be done so that auditors are not adversely affected by this situation when using audit tools and techniques based on AI. In particular, the AI-based application examples in the literature and ethical standards of AI are examined. A discussion is presented on the measures to be taken not to impair the ethical compliance of digitalized auditing in the public sector. In particular, using AI in internal auditing in the public sector raises concerns about the accuracy, fairness, and transparency of audit processes, as well as the potential for bias and discrimination.

Several scholars have identified the need for research to address these ethical implications of AI in internal auditing (Kahyaoglu and Aksoy, 2021; Lehner et al., 2022) with specific focus on the ethical implications of using AI in internal audit, particularly in the public sector where accountability and transparency are critical (Fukas et al., 2021; Loi and Spielkamp, 2021; Raji et al., 2022).

10.2 DEFINING ETHICS AND APPLYING ETHICAL THEORIES

As alluded to by Munoko et al. (2020), there is a growing awareness among these stakeholders that valid ethical concerns arise from using AI technologies. Several ethical theories could be applied to studying the ethical implications of using AI in internal auditing in the public sector, including consequentialism, virtue theory, deontological ethics, and care ethics.

Consequentialism is a normative ethical theory that evaluates the morality of actions based on their potential consequences or outcomes (Anshari et al., 2021; Kernaghan, 2014). In the context of AI in internal auditing, consequentialism could be used to evaluate the ethical implications of AI tools in terms of their impact on stakeholders such as auditors, management, regulators, and the public. This could involve assessing the potential benefits and harms of using AI in internal auditing, determining whether the benefits outweigh the disadvantages, as well as considering the distribution of benefits and harms across different stakeholders (Saveliev and Zhurenkov, 2021). The ethical implications of using AI in internal auditing can be evaluated by examining the consequences of its use and determining whether they align with ethical principles such as fairness, impartiality, and accountability.

DOI: 10.1201/9781003382706-10

For example, if using AI in internal auditing improves efficiency, effectiveness, and accuracy, leading to better decision-making and increased public trust in the audit process, this could be seen as a positive consequence. However, on the contrary, if the use of AI leads to job loss or the perpetuation of biases and discrimination in the audit process (see Section 10.4.3), then this could be seen as a negative consequence. For example, if an AI system incorrectly flags audit findings, it could lead to unwarranted investigations, damaging reputations, and wasting resources. Consequentialism further recognizes that ethical judgments may need to evolve as circumstances change (Anshari et al., 2021; Reijers et al., 2016). Auditors must remain flexible and adapt AI systems and ethical guidelines in response to emerging challenges and technologies, with constant, careful examination of both short-term and long-term outcomes, continually refining AI systems and ethical practices to align with the greater public good (Anshari et al., 2021; Saveliev and Zhurenkov, 2021; Stahl, 2021; Zollo et al., 2017).

Applying *virtue theory* to using AI in internal auditing within the public sector emphasizes the cultivation of moral virtues and character traits to guide ethical decision-making and responsible AI use (O'Loughlin and Bukowitz, 2021). Several studies explore the ethical implications of using AI in the public sector from a virtue ethics perspective (Mittelstadt et al., 2016; Plesner et al., 2018; Wirtz et al., 2019, 2021) and emphasize the importance of cultivating virtues such as honesty, integrity, and responsibility in the use of AI, emphasizing that AI should be designed to support virtuous behavior in auditing. They also examine various challenges to implementing virtue ethics in AI design, such as the need for transparency, accountability, fairness, independence, and ethical training for auditors and AI developers, which will be further discussed in Section 10.5. Auditors in the public sector should conduct audits with honesty, accuracy, and a commitment to the truth. Integrity ensures that AI-generated audit results are reliable and trustworthy (Rozario and Vasarhelyi, 2018). Auditors may need courage, standing up for ethical principles, to challenge AI systems if they suspect biases, errors, or ethical concerns (Chi and Chu, 2021; Chisty and Adusumalli, 2022; European Court of Auditors, 2020). Virtue theory encourages auditors to exercise professional skepticism (Harding et al., 2016; Quadackers et al., 2014). This involves critically evaluating AI algorithms, data sources, and audit results to identify potential biases, errors, or ethical concerns (Stahl, 2021). Auditors should make thoughtful decisions that align with ethical principles and serve the public interest (Zollo et al., 2017). Virtue theory values the pursuit of knowledge and adaptability, implying that auditors in the public sector should continually educate themselves about AI developments and ethical best practices, adapting their approaches as technology evolves (Kottler, 2020; Olaitan et al., 2019).

The theory of *deontology* emphasizes the importance of respecting individual autonomy and rights (Nagitta et al., 2022; Vasarhelyi and Kogan Editors, 1997). The theory emphasizes duty-based ethics, and the use of AI by internal auditors in the public sector involves focusing on principles, rules, and moral obligations rather than solely on consequences (Fleischman et al., 2019). Deontological ethics stresses adherence to ethical codes and regulations. Auditors should follow established rules and guidelines, including legal and ethical standards specific to the public sector when using AI, as will be further alluded to in Section 10.5. This ensures that auditing practices align with moral duties and societal expectations (Stahl et al., 2017). Auditors have a duty of care to the public and the organizations they audit and to exercise due diligence when implementing AI systems (Brown et al., 2021). This involves thoroughly assessing the ethical implications and potential risks associated with AI and taking steps to mitigate them. The principle of non-maleficence, inherent in deontology, implies that auditors should take measures to prevent AI systems from producing biased, discriminatory, or harmful outcomes in the auditing process (Anshari et al., 2021). Deontology also places a high value on professional integrity (Loi and Spielkamp, 2021). Auditors in the public sector should maintain their professional integrity by upholding ethical principles and ensuring that AI is used in ways that are consistent with their duties and obligations. Deontology encourages the use of ethical decision-making frameworks that are grounded in principles and duties (Pearson et al., 2021). Auditors should follow such frameworks (see Section 10.6) to assess the ethical implications of using AI in specific audit scenarios, ensuring that actions align with their moral obligations (Wirtz et al., 2019). Auditors must prioritize these duties to ensure that AI is used in ways that uphold individual rights, adhere to ethical regulations, and promote the well-being of the public and organizations under scrutiny.

Ethical theories, as explained in the preceding section, provide a moral compass to guide auditors and organizations as they navigate the ethical landscape of technology-driven audits.

10.3 ETHICAL VIOLATIONS AND CONFLICT AREAS RELATED TO THE ABUSE OF ARTIFICIAL INTELLIGENCE IN GENERAL

Having established the foundational principles of ethics theories, including consequentialism, virtue theory, and deontology, it is imperative to examine how these ethical frameworks are applied in the real-world context of AI-enhanced internal audits.

Ethical violations represent departures from these ethical theories, highlighting instances where the principles of virtue, duty, and consequences are compromised. In AI-augmented internal audits, several key areas demand scrutiny: bias, privacy, transparency, and malice. These ethical violations can have profound implications for the integrity, fairness, and accountability of the audit process. It is essential to understand and address these concerns to ensure that AI is used ethically and responsibly.

10.3.1 Bias

AI systems can potentially reinforce or intensify present prejudices and discrimination. For instance, if an AI system is trained on biased information, it may adopt and reproduce those biases, resulting in discriminatory consequences (Alaa, 2021; Kossow et al., 2021). This could be incredibly challenging where historically marginalized individuals may already confront obstacles to fair treatment (Baird and Schuller, 2020). It is essential to acknowledge that AI systems are only as unbiased as the data they are trained on (Martin, 2019; Wang et al., 2022). Therefore, it is crucial to ensure that the data used to train these systems is diverse and representative of all individuals, regardless of race, gender, or ethnicity (Fonseka et al., 2022; Ryan and Stahl, 2021; Taiwo et al., 2019; Wirtz et al., 2019). Additionally, implementing ethical guidelines for AI development can help prevent discriminatory outcomes (Mökander et al., 2021; Mökander and Floridi, 2023). This will be further discussed in Section 10.5. Ultimately, it is crucial to prioritize fairness and safety in the development and deployment of AI systems to prevent perpetuating existing prejudices and discrimination (Kossow et al., 2021; Pedrosa et al., 2020; Uglum, 2021).

10.3.2 Privacy violations

Another area of concern is *privacy violations*. With the ability to collect and process vast amounts of personal data, there is a risk that AI systems could be used to invade individuals' privacy (Mökander and Floridi, 2023; La Torre et al., 2019). For example, AI algorithms could monitor individuals' online activities, track their movements, or even collect biometric data without their knowledge or consent (Saleh et al., 2022). This could result in significant harm to individuals, including potential discrimination or stigmatization based on their personal information (Capurro et al., 2021; Eulerich and Lenz, 2020). To avoid these risks, it is vital to establish clear ethical guidelines for using AI and to ensure that appropriate safeguards are in place to protect individuals' privacy.

10.3.3 Lack of transparency

Transparency is another important ethical issue when it comes to using AI. It refers to the extent to which the decision-making processes of AI systems are open and understandable to humans (Baird and Schuller, 2020; Fuhrman et al., 2022). AI systems can be complex and opaque (Buhmann et al., 2020), making it difficult for individuals to understand how decisions are being made (Bednarek, 2018; Burrell, 2016). This lack of transparency can lead to a lack of accountability, potentially enabling unethical or illegal behavior (Baykurt, 2022; Martin, 2019). Lack of transparency can also lead to a lack of trust in AI systems (Alaa, 2021; Lopez and Alcaide, 2020). Therefore, it is crucial to establish clear guidelines for transparency in the development and use of AI systems and to ensure that appropriate measures are in place to promote transparency (Fedyk et al., 2022; de Laat, 2021).

10.3.4 Malice

There is also the potential for AI systems to be used for *malicious* purposes, such as cyberattacks or the spread of disinformation. Malice refers to the intentional use of AI systems to cause harm or disadvantage to individuals or groups (Moffitt, 2018). Malicious use of AI can take many forms, such as using AI to abuse power, spread false information, or manipulate public opinion or using AI to discriminate against certain groups of people. Malice in using AI is a serious concern, as it can have significant negative impacts on society and individuals (Gotthardt et al., 2020). It is therefore essential to promote the development of AI systems that prioritize the well-being and safety of individuals and communities, rather than being used solely for personal gain or malicious intent (Misuraca and van Noordt, 2020).

In summary, using AI carries ethical implications and potential for conflict areas, particularly bias, privacy violations, lack of transparency, and potential for malicious use. These risks must be addressed through appropriate regulations, safeguards, and ethical considerations.

10.4 ETHICAL CHALLENGES OF USING ARTIFICIAL INTELLIGENCE IN INTERNAL AUDITING

The four components identified by Rest (1986, 1994) are widely considered to be one of the most important models that can be used to guide moral processes when making ethical decisions (Fleischman et al., 2019; Lehner et al., 2022). According to Rest's model, a sound ethical decision is made when individuals follow four psychological processes.

The first step in making ethical decisions is *moral sensitivity*. It requires recognizing when a situation has moral implications and requires ethical consideration. In essence, it's about being aware of the ethical dimension of a problem (Kernaghan, 2014; Zollo et al., 2017). Once an individual recognizes the ethical nature of a situation, they proceed to make a *moral judgment*. This involves evaluating the problem from an ethical perspective and determining what the right course of action should be. Ethical beliefs, values, and principles influence moral judgment (La Torre et al., 2019). After making a moral judgment, individuals must be motivated to act in accordance with their ethical assessment. This component considers whether an individual is willing to prioritize ethical considerations over other factors, such as personal gain or peer pressure. *Moral motivation*, as a third component, is crucial because it drives ethical behavior (Srinivasan and San Miguel González, 2022). The final part is *moral character* (Alaa, 2021) which relates to a person's ability to act on their ethical judgment and motivation. It involves having the courage and integrity to follow through with the chosen ethical course of action, even in the face of challenges or resistance. Lehner et al. (2022) used the structure of Rest's four-component model as a framework for ethical decision-making to evaluate specific ethical challenges in human-machine collaboration in accounting.

10.4.1 Lack of transparency and understanding of how auditing decisions are made

In the context of digital auditing in the public sector, the lack of transparency pertains to a deficiency in providing clear information about how decisions are made within the auditing process. This absence of transparency can have significant implications, particularly in understanding how decisions are reached (often referred to by scholars as explainability) (Alaa, 2021; Kay et al., 2021; Wilson and van der Velden, 2022), and it gives rise to several challenges and consequences, such as ambiguity in decision-making, reduced accountability, concealing ethical concerns, impairing public trust, and challenges with identifying and taking corrective action. The lack of transparency can cause *ambiguity* (Kemper and Kolkman, 2019) in the decision-making process. In traditional auditing, human auditors follow specific procedures and guidelines that can be relatively transparent. However, in digital auditing, primarily when powered by complex AI and machine learning algorithms (sometimes referred to as a kind of black box (Appelbaum and Vasarhelyi, 2017)), the decision-making process may become obscure, making it challenging to discern how certain conclusions or findings were reached (Kossow et al., 2021; Wilson and van der Velden, 2022). This ambiguity and inscrutability can raise questions about the validity and reliability of audit outcomes (Busuioc, 2021; Minkkinen et al., 2022; Mittelstadt et al., 2016; Tabassi, 2023). Public sector organizations, auditors, and oversight bodies rely on transparency to ensure that audit processes align with ethical standards, regulations, and government policies. The lack of transparency may erode this *accountability*, creating doubts about whether decisions were made following established rules and ethical guidelines. This will be further discussed in Section 10.4.4. Public sector auditors often encounter complex and *opaque* AI systems that generate difficult-to-decipher findings and conclusions (Kossow et al., 2021). Without transparency, auditors may find it challenging to understand how the AI system arrived at its decisions and the reliability of those decisions (Burrell, 2016; Greif, 2022). When stakeholders, including citizens and government officials, are unable to comprehend how audit decisions are made, trust in the fairness, objectivity, and integrity of the audit process may be adversely impacted. Additionally, it can lead to conflicts of interest if AI is used to conceal or manipulate information during the audit process. Furthermore, suppose auditors are unaware of the algorithms and data used in the AI system. In that case, they may be unable to identify or address ethical issues related to the system's use (Fukas et al., 2021). When the decision-making process or auditors lack transparency, it becomes more challenging to pinpoint and rectify errors, biases, or inaccuracies in the audit results (Srinivasan and San Miguel González, 2022). (See also Section 10.4.3. for further detail on the concepts of bias.)

A lack of transparency in auditing processes can hinder *reproducibility* (Akula and Garibay, 2021; European Court of Auditors, 2020; Fischer et al., 2021; Misuraca and van Noordt, 2020) of audit procedures, and the capacity to take corrective actions, which are vital for improving future audits and ensuring fairness and accuracy.

To address these concerns, it is essential to ensure transparency in auditing procedures using AI systems, as discussed in Section 10.5.1.

10.4.2 Privacy, security risks, and inappropriate use of data in auditing

AI systems employed in public sector auditing often handle vast amounts of personal and sensitive data associated with the individuals and organizations (the public) under scrutiny (Nagitta et al., 2022). This raises concerns regarding how such data is acquired, stored, and utilized (Sookhak et al., 2018). For instance, there may be instances where AI systems are utilized to access confidential information that should remain beyond the purview of auditors (Hazar, 2021). Ethical red flags are raised when auditors use data to infringe upon the privacy or confidentiality of the individuals or entities whose information is being processed (Dwivedi et al., 2021; Spina Alì and Yu, 2021). Such breaches can have severe consequences for individuals, including harm to their reputation or a loss of trust in the audited public sector organization (Buhmann et al., 2020; Tsai et al., 2015). When AI systems are integrated into public sector audits, they become potential targets for cyberattacks. As briefly alluded to in Section 10.3.4, malicious actors may exploit vulnerabilities within these systems to gain unauthorized access to sensitive data or tamper with the auditing process to manipulate results (Moffitt, 2018; Moffitt and Vasarhelyi, 2013). Public sector auditors therefore bear a substantial responsibility in safeguarding sensitive data, maintaining ethical standards, and fortifying cybersecurity measures to ensure the integrity, transparency, and reliability of the auditing process. To mitigate security risks in the public sector auditing process, it is imperative to implement robust cybersecurity measures. This will be further discussed in Section 10.5.2.

10.4.3 Objectivity, bias, and discrimination in auditing procedures

In the context of the public sector, the utilization of AI systems in auditing procedures presents a unique set of challenges related to objectivity, bias, and discrimination. These challenges can have far-reaching consequences, including conflicts of interest and ethical concerns when AI systems are employed to make decisions that directly impact the rights and opportunities of individuals or groups (Gotthardt et al., 2020; Lehner et al., 2022).

Public sector auditing procedures involving AI systems are particularly susceptible to bias and discrimination when the data used to train these systems exhibits prejudice or when the algorithms guiding decision-making harbor discriminatory elements (Ingrams et al., 2022; Mökander and Floridi, 2023). For instance, if an AI system is trained on data that inadvertently reflects biases against certain demographic or socio-economic groups, such as minority communities, there is a heightened risk of flagging these groups for potential issues, even if the problems are trivial or inconsequential (Martin, 2019). Such scenarios can lead to conflicts of interest and ethical concerns, especially when the audit outcomes influence the allocation of public resources or government policies that affect the rights and opportunities of these groups (Waldman and Martin, 2022). Moreover, AI systems within the public sector can unintentionally perpetuate or amplify pre-existing biases and discrimination if their algorithms are inadvertently programmed with discriminatory elements. For example, suppose an AI system is designed to prioritize certain types of data over others without a comprehensive and objective rationale. In that case, it may inadvertently introduce bias and discrimination into the auditing process (Munoko et al., 2020). This raises ethical concerns about equal opportunity and human rights violations within the public sector (Rozario and Issa, 2020).

To address these critical issues within the public sector, it is imperative to prioritize diversity and representation in the data used to train AI systems (Raji et al., 2020). Additionally, it is crucial to ensure that the algorithms guiding these systems are transparent, fair, and free from any form of discrimination (Gepp et al., 2017). This will be further discussed in Section 10.5.3.

10.4.4 Lack of accountability in AI-enabled internal audits within the public sector

The multifaceted nature of AI-enhanced auditing often leads to questions about where ultimate responsibility lies (Dalla Via et al., 2019). Determining who should be held accountable for AI-driven audit outcomes can be complex (Brown-Liburd et al., 2015; Ryan and Stahl, 2021), raising questions as to whether the developers of the AI system, the auditors who use it, or the management that oversees the process is the ultimately accountable party. Uncertainty about responsibility can result in delayed or ineffective responses to audit findings (Bol et al., 2016; Roussy, 2015) and can deter individuals or entities from taking ownership of the audit process (Liston-Heyes and Juillet, 2019). Lack of oversight is a further challenge, as public sector organizations may not always have the necessary oversight processes in place to monitor AI-augmented audits adequately, which can lead to unmonitored and potentially unethical decisions (International Auditing and Assurance Standards Board, 2018; Raji et al., 2022). Auditors may struggle to understand the complex decisions made by AI algorithms, making it challenging for them to justify and defend those decisions to stakeholders and oversight bodies (Mäntymäki et al., 2022; Minkkinen et al., 2022). Ensuring that audit staff possess the necessary skills and competence to use AI systems ethically can be a complex undertaking (Agostino et al., 2022; Kandeh and Alsahli, 2020; Modisane, 2019). Inadequate training may lead to auditors making decisions without a comprehensive understanding of AI technology (Ta and Doan, 2022) and can result in ethical violations due to errors, biases, or lapses in moral judgment. Addressing these accountability challenges requires the development of clear guidelines, comprehensive ethical training for auditors, robust oversight mechanisms, and transparent audit process documentation, which will be alluded to in Section 10.5.5.

10.4.5 Challenges of trustworthiness of the audit processes

Trustworthiness is a fundamental principle in AI-augmented public sector internal audits (Estella, 2023). Maintaining public trust in AI-augmented audits is vital and misconceptions or distrust can hinder the acceptance of AI-generated audit findings (Mosweu and Ngoepe, 2020). Ensuring stakeholders, including government officials and the public, comprehensively understand AI's capabilities and limitations is a complex task (Mökander and Floridi, 2021; Wilson and van der Velden, 2022). Misinformed or underinformed stakeholders can impact trustworthiness. If stakeholders are unaware of AI's specific functions and limitations, they may either overestimate or underestimate the system's capabilities, leading to unwarranted trust or skepticism. Mazzù et al. (2022) explains that trust in AI-augmented algorithms follows a four-stage process: formation, extension, comprehension, and resolution, each stage presenting its own challenges. Formation involves initial preconceptions and judgments about AI's reliability, which can be influenced by biases or prior (often negative) experiences. The extension stage requires stakeholders to accept AI's role. Comprehension involves understanding AI's decision-making processes, and resolution implies the final resolution of trust issues (Alaa, 2021). Ensuring trust in a complex ecosystem of AI, blockchain, bots, cloud computing, and the Internet of Things (IoT) used in audits can be intricate. The trustworthiness of the audit process relies on the security and accuracy of the data generated by these devices and the interplay of these technologies (Chisty and Adusumalli, 2022; Liu et al., 2015). If data sources used in audits are unreliable, it can undermine systemic trust (Lehner et al., 2022) and cast doubt on the accuracy and integrity of the entire audit process.

Establishing a harmonious human-machine relationship is therefore critical (Bach et al., 2022). Auditors' distrust of AI systems can disrupt the audit process (Kontos, 2021; Lehner et al., 2022; Minkkinen et al., 2022). If audit practitioners resist using AI systems, believing that they may undermine their role or job security, it can hinder the effective integration of AI into the audit process. Several influencing factors, such as industry standards, technological advances, and the actions of other organizations, can enhance the trustworthiness of AI-augmented audits. If a regulatory body sets rigorous AI audit standards, organizations that do not meet these standards may face trust issues from stakeholders (see also Sections 10.4.4 and 10.6.), Trustworthiness can also be influenced by the emotions evoked by AI systems' actions, their virtual appearance, and the interface's user-friendliness (Aslan, 2021; Keyes and Austin, 2022). If an AI system lacks a user-friendly interface or appears unprofessional, it may lead to negative emotions and reduced trust among auditors and stakeholders (Wright and Schultz, 2018; Yu and Li, 2022; Zollo et al., 2017). Striking the right balance in humanizing AI systems can be challenging (Criado and O.de Zarate-Alcarazo, 2022; Lenz and Jeppesen, 2022). Over-humanizing may lead to misplaced trust, while under-humanizing can potentially create distrust. For example, if an AI system's interactions mimic human behavior too closely, auditors may assume it has human-like decision-making capabilities, potentially leading to unwarranted trust (Munoko et al., 2020).

Understanding the dual role of trust, as both influencing stakeholder behavior and as a moderator of AI performance, is essential for ensuring trustworthiness (Otia and Bracci, 2022). Building and maintaining trust is an ongoing process, vital for effectively integrating AI in the public sector audit landscape (Ingrams et al., 2022; Masood and Lodhi, 2015; Rikhardsson and Dull, 2016).

10.4.6 Lack of human judgment in auditing procedures

Auditors are responsible for making judgments based on the information gathered during the auditing process. However, AI systems are typically programmed to make decisions based solely on the available data and algorithms. As a result, it may lack the context and human judgment needed to make ethical decisions during the auditing process (Bernier et al., 2023; Sun and Vasarhelyi, 2017). This can create conflicts of interest and ethical concerns if the AI system is used to make decisions requiring ethical considerations or over-rides human judgment inappropriately during the auditing process (Brown-Liburd et al., 2015; Hamdam et al., 2021). Additionally, the reliance on AI systems for decision-making can lead to a lack of accountability for ethical violations (Gotthardt et al., 2020; Holt and Loraas, 2021). As mentioned in Section 10.4.4 above, if an ethical breach occurs due to an AI system, it may be challenging to determine who is responsible for the decision-making process. There is a need to ensure that AI systems used in auditing procedures are designed to recognize and account for the importance of human judgment and ethical considerations (Raji et al., 2020, 2022). This requires careful consideration of the ethical implications of using AI systems in auditing procedures and developing appropriate safeguards to ensure that ethical standards are upheld.

In summary, using AI in internal auditing can lead to ethical violations and conflicts of interest, particularly in transparency, data use, bias, security, and human judgment. It is essential for internal auditors to carefully consider these risks and take appropriate steps to address them in their auditing procedures to ensure the integrity and fairness of the auditing process.

10.5 ETHICAL STANDARDS FOR AI IN INTERNAL AUDIT

When using AI for internal audit, it is essential to adhere to specific ethical standards to ensure that the technology is being used in a responsible and trustworthy manner. These ethical standards include transparency, privacy, fairness, independence, accountability, and continuous monitoring.

10.5.1 Transparency

Transparency in AI-enhanced internal audits within the public sector is pivotal to main taining public trust and upholding the integrity of government processes (Simbeck, 2022). It encompasses openness in data collection, handling, and usage; clarity in AI decision-making; and transparent reporting of audit findings (Soh and Martinov-Bennie, 2015). Public sector organizations employing AI in internal audits must be transparent about the data they collect. This transparency involves clearly articulating the *types* of data gathered, including financial records, citizen information, and government documents. Auditors and stakeholders should comprehensively understand the data's sources, scope, and purpose (Baykurt, 2022; Buttigieg and Ellul, 2021; Lopez and Alcaide, 2020). Transparency demands that public sector entities understand *how* collected data is managed and stored (Mosweu and Ngoepe, 2020). This includes robust data protection measures to safeguard sensitive information (Sookhak et al., 2018; Thompson et al., 2015). Transparency further extends to the decision-making processes of AI systems (Piscopo et al., 2017). Public sector auditors should be able to discern how AI algorithms arrive at their conclusions. This involves providing visibility into AI systems' algorithms, methodologies, and criteria in reaching audit findings (Mittelstadt et al., 2016). Public sector auditors must be able to explain the methods underpinning AI-enhanced audits, specifically how AI systems are inte-grated into the audit workflow, the criteria used for risk assessment, and the specific audit objectives they support (Al-Okaily et al., 2022; Dowling and Leech, 2014; Issa et al., 2016; Mahzan and Lymer, 2014; Turetken et al., 2020). Transparency further requires public sector organizations to provide clear and accessible audit findings. Auditors should communicate the results in a manner that is understandable to stakeholders, including government officials, oversight bodies, and the public (Kend and Nguyen, 2022). Public sector auditors should openly address ethical considerations associated with AI use (Endaya and Hanefah, 2016). This includes transparency regarding efforts to prevent bias, discrimination, and other ethical concerns in AI-augmented audits. Transparent communication regarding the steps taken to ensure ethical auditing practices enhances public trust (Aslan, 2021). Another important consideration is that public sector auditors should maintain a comprehensive audit trail (Van Dyk and Goosen, 2017), recording actions taken by AI systems during audits (Han et al., 2023; Tiron-Tudor et al., 2021). This ensures transparency and facilitates accountability in cases where confidential information is accessed or modified (Axelsen et al., 2017; Bresser et al., 2014; Singh et al., 2014).

Transparency extends to compliance with relevant laws and regulations governing data privacy, security, and AI usage. By prioritizing transparency, public sector internal auditors can reinforce their commitment to ethical, accountable, and trustworthy auditing practices.

10.5.2 Privacy

Ensuring the privacy and confidentiality of individuals and organizations undergoing audits is paramount in the public sector's adoption of AI systems (Han et al., 2023; Lehner et al., 2022; Tarek et al., 2017). This commitment involves several critical facets. This involves designing AI systems to adhere to rigorous data privacy standards and safeguarding the personal and sensitive information of citizens and entities under audit (Gupta et al., 2013; Squio and Hoffmann, 2021). Robust confidentiality safeguards within AI systems must encompass the secure handling and storage of confidential data, ensuring it remains inaccessible to unauthorized personnel (Zhang et al., 2015). AI systems employed in the public sector's internal audits must be programmed to use data ethically by implementing stringent controls to prevent data misuse or unauthorized access, enhancing public trust in the ethical handling of sensitive information (Ross et al., 2023). These measures limit disclosure to essential individuals, minimizing the risk of unauthorized exposure (Mangiuc, 2012; Tan, 2016). In certain instances, public sector audits may require informed consent from individuals or organizations whose data is being audited (Loi and Spielkamp, 2021). Transparency (as per Section 10.5.1 above) in seeking consent and communicating the purpose of data usage is essential to uphold privacy and confidentiality standards (Mantelero, 2014; Saleh et al., 2022). Public sector auditors should regularly audit the privacy and confidentiality measures implemented within AI-augmented audits to ensure ongoing compliance and identifies areas for improvement (Buhmann et al., 2020). Public sector organizations must align their AI-augmented audits with not only legal standards but also ethical principles. This includes upholding the fundamental rights of individuals and entities under audit, maintaining their trust and confidence in the audit process (Baird and Schuller, 2020).

10.5.3 Fairness

Ensuring fairness and non-discrimination is fundamental when deploying AI systems in internal audits within the public sector (Stumpf et al., 2021; Van Veenstra et al., 2020). Public sector organizations must proactively mitigate bias in AI systems used for internal audits. This involves rigorous data analysis to identify and rectify any biases in the training data or algorithms. Auditors should ensure that AI systems are as impartial and unbiased as possible (Kokina and Davenport, 2017; Koshiyama et al., 2021). AI systems must be programmed to treat all individuals and entities equally. Public sector auditors should strive to eliminate any potential for preferential treatment or undue advantage in the audit process, ensuring equitable treatment across all groups and individuals. To minimize the risk of underrepresentation or overrepresentation of specific groups, public sector organizations must ensure that the data used for training AI systems includes a broad cross-section of society. Proactive measures must be taken to maintain fairness and equity in audit findings. Public sector organizations should implement regular audits of AI outputs to identify and rectify any instances of bias or discrimination (Kossow et al., 2021). Public sector auditors must consider the social impact of audit findings. They should ensure that AI-generated conclusions do not perpetuate disparities or injustices and that audit outcomes are fair for all groups and individuals (Brown et al., 2021). Public sector auditors must adhere to legal and ethical standards related to non-discrimination and equal treatment. This involves upholding anti-discrimination laws and ethical guidelines that prohibit bias in auditing processes (Castka et al., 2020; Wilson and van der Velden, 2022). By prioritizing data diversity, regular auditing of AI outputs, sensitivity to social impact, transparent decision-making, and strict adherence to legal and ethical standards, public sector organizations can ensure equitable and unbiased audit processes.

10.5.4 Independence

Within the public sector, upholding professionalism and independence is of paramount importance when integrating AI systems into internal audit processes. Public sector internal auditors should steadfastly uphold their professional judgment as a cornerstone of audit practice (Walker and Brown-Liburd, 2019). While AI systems offer valuable insights, auditors should rely on their expertise to interpret AI-generated data and findings, ensuring that decisions are guided by their deep knowledge of public sector operations, regulations, and policies (Kandeh and Alsahli, 2020; Kend and Nguyen, 2022). Maintaining independence in the auditing process is essential. Public sector auditors must ensure they are not unduly influenced by AI technology, thus preserving their objectivity and impartiality throughout the audit (The Association of Chartered Certified Accountants, 2017). This necessitates ongoing training and skill development to ensure that auditors can harness AI's capabilities while preserving their professional judgment and independence (Sun and Vasarhelyi, 2017). Auditors should proactively identify and mitigate conflicts of interest that may arise when utilizing AI systems (Salijeni et al., 2021). Public sector organizations should have mechanisms to detect, address, and disclose potential conflicts, ensuring that audit decisions remain impartial and objective (Bumgarner and Vasarhelyi, 2015; Roussy, 2015). The use of AI in public sector internal audits should be subject to supervision and review by competent authorities or oversight bodies. This oversight ensures that audit processes remain aligned with professional standards and principles of independence (Fischer et al., 2021; Hasan, 2022).

10.5.5 Accountability

Internal audit functions using AI for internal audit should be accountable for the decisions made by the AI system and should be able to explain the reasoning behind those decisions (Leitner-Hanetseder et al., 2021). In the public sector, auditors must maintain a solid commitment to normative accountability, ensuring that AI applications align with ethical and regulatory frameworks (Loi and Spielkamp, 2021; Petrakaki, 2018). Public sector auditors and AI system designers should collaborate to ensure that AI systems are designed to meet ethical and audit-specific requirements, fostering trust and reliability (Bracci, 2022; Dillard and Vinnari, 2019). In the public sector, delegation of accountability involves the allocation of responsibilities among stakeholders engaged in AI-augmented audits. Clear assignment of roles and responsibilities ensures that each party is accountable for their specific tasks and outcomes (Dillard and Vinnari, 2019). Public sector auditors should engage AI experts to oversee and validate AI-augmented audit processes. This expert involvement (Griffith, 2020) helps ensure the accuracy and integrity of AI-driven results. Shared accountability recognizes that accountability is not limited to a single entity but is distributed among various stakeholders (Appelbaum et al., 2021). Accountability is shared among auditors, government agencies, oversight bodies, and the public in the public sector, and effective communication and collaboration among these stakeholders enhance accountability (Cooley, 2020; Cooper et al., 2019). Responsibility involves acknowledging obligations and duties tied to AI-augmented audits (Bebbington et al., 2020) and involves adhering to norms and ethical guidelines (Bol et al., 2016), collaborating with AI designers, delegating responsibilities, leveraging experts, sharing accountability among stakeholders, and recognizing the inherent public accountability of government audits. Public sector auditors play a pivotal role in upholding accountability (Agostino et al., 2022), ensuring the responsible and transparent use of AI technology to enhance the effectiveness and integrity of audit processes.

10.6 BEST PRACTICES AND FRAMEWORKS

Stakeholders, including auditors, management, and oversight bodies, collaborate to ensure ethical and responsible use of AI in internal auditing within the public sector (Dwivedi et al., 2021; Estella, 2023; Leitner-Hanetseder et al., 2021). Several governance frameworks have been developed to ensure that decision-making related to AI auditing is transparent, accountable, and in line with ethical principles (Buttigieg and Ellul, 2021). These include the IIA's Artificial Intelligence Auditing Framework (The Institute of Internal Auditors Global, 2017) and guidance issued by the IAASB (International Auditing and Assurance Standards Board, 2018), a governance framework for AI by the EPRS (European Parliamentary Research Service, 2019). These frameworks provide a comprehensive set of guidelines for auditors to ensure that AI is used ethically and responsibly in the audit process. Other frameworks that have been developed include the General Data Protection Regulation (GDPR) (The European Parliament and the Council of the European Union, 2014), which includes provisions related to the use of AI, and the Principles for AI developed by the Organisation for Economic Co-operation and Development (OECD), which guide the ethical and responsible use of AI (Organisation for Economic Co-operation and Development, 2019). In addition to these frameworks, regulatory bodies such as the Securities and Exchange Commission (SEC) and the Public Company Accounting Oversight Board (PCAOB) have also issued guidance on the use of AI in auditing (Public Company Accounting Oversight Board, 2023) to ensure that auditors are adhering to ethical principles and legal requirements.

10.7 CONCLUSION AND LESSONS LEARNED

As AI continues to play a more significant role in digital audits in the public sector, these audits mustn't be only efficient and accurate but also trustworthy. Auditors must navigate an increasingly complex web of automated auditing processes while keeping important ethical principles in mind.

This discussion covered a range of ethical theories, from consequentialism to virtue ethics and deontology. These theories can serve as a guide, helping auditors to ensure transparency, fairness, and accountability. However, applying these theories in practice is an ongoing process that requires constant reflection and adaptation.

There are several challenges to achieving trust in AI-augmented audits, of which lack of transparency, privacy issues, security risks, bias, and lack of judgment are paramount.

To overcome these challenges, it is essential to integrate ethical standards, educate stakeholders on the capabilities and limitations of AI, and carefully design accountability frameworks. Additionally, auditors must remain committed to fairness, transparency, privacy, accountability, and the unbiased pursuit of truth. This requires collaboration and vigilance as we move forward toward a future where AI and humans work together.

While the path may be fraught with complexities, the commitment to upholding these ethical principles in digital auditing is the compass that will steer the public sector toward a future of heightened accountability, credibility, and, most crucially, public trust.

REFERENCES

Agostino, D., Saliterer, I. and Steccolini, I. (2022), "Digitalization, accounting and accountability: A literature review and reflections on future research in public services", *Financial Accountability and Management*, 1 May, doi: 10.1111/faam.12301.

Akula, R. and Garibay, I. (2021), "Audit and assurance of AI algorithms: A framework to ensure ethical algorithmic practices in artificial intelligence", *International Conference on Human-Computer Interaction 2021*. arXiv preprint arXiv:2107.14046.

Alaa, M. (2021), "Artificial intelligence: Explainability, ethical issues and bias", *Annals of Robotics and Automation*, pp. 034–037, doi: 10.17352/ara.000011.

Al-Okaily, M., Alqudah, H.M., Al-Qudah, A.A. and Alkhwaldi, A.F. (2022), "Examining the critical factors of computer-assisted audit tools and techniques adoption in the post-COVID-19 period: Internal auditors perspective", *VINE Journal of Information and Knowledge Management Systems*, doi: 10.1108/VJIKMS-12-2021-0311.

Anshari, M., Almunawar, M.N., Masri, M. and Hrdy, M. (2021), "Financial technology with AI-enabled and ethical challenges", *Society*, Vol. 58 No. 3, pp. 189–195, doi: 10.1007/s12115-021-00592-w.

Appelbaum, D. and Vasarhelyi, M. (2017), "Public auditing, analytics, and big data in the modern economy", *Rutgers, The State University of New Jersey*, pp. 1–355.

Appelbaum, D., Scott Showalter, D., Sun, T. and Vasarhelyi, M.A. (2021), "A framework for auditor data literacy: A normative position", *Accounting Horizons*, Vol. 35 No. 2, pp. 5–25, doi: 10.2308/HORIZONS-19-127.

Aslan, L. (2021), "The evolving competencies of the public auditor and the future of public sector auditing", *Contemporary Studies in Economic and Financial Analysis*, Vol. 105, pp. 113–129, doi: 10.1108/S1569-375920200000105008.

Axelsen, M., Green, P. and Ridley, G. (2017), "Explaining the information systems auditor role in the public sector financial audit", *International Journal of Accounting Information Systems*, Vol. 24, pp. 15–31, doi: 10.1016/j.accinf.2016.12.003.

Bach, T.A., Khan, A., Hallock, H., Beltrão, G. and Sousa, S. (2022), "A systematic literature review of user trust in AI-enabled systems: An HCI perspective", *International Journal of Human-Computer Interaction*, doi: 10.1080/10447318.2022.2138826.

Baird, A. and Schuller, B. (2020), "Considerations for a more ethical approach to data in AI: On data representation and infrastructure", *Frontiers in Big Data*, Vol. 3 No. 25, doi: 10.3389/fdata.2020.00025.

Baykurt, B. (2022), "Algorithmic accountability in U.S. cities: Transparency, impact, and political economy", *Big Data and Society*, Vol. July-Dec, pp. 1–12, doi: 10.1177/20539517221115426.

Bebbington, J., Österblom, H., Crona, B., Jouffray, J.B., Larrinaga, C., Russell, S. and Scholtens, B. (2020), "Accounting and accountability in the Anthropocene", *Accounting, Auditing and Accountability Journal*, Vol. 33 No. 1, pp. 152–177, doi: 10.1108/AAAJ-11-2018-3745.

Bednarek, P. (2018), "Factors Affecting the Internal Audit Effectiveness: A Survey of the Polish Private and Public Sectors", in *Efficiency in Business and Economics*, Springer, Cham, pp. 1–16, doi: 10.1007/978-3-319-68285-3.

Bernier, A., Raven-Adams, M., Zaccagnini, D. and Knoppers, B.M. (2023), "Recording the ethical provenance of data and automating data stewardship", *Big Data and Society*, Vol. January-J, pp. 1–11, doi: 10.1177/20539517231163174.

Bol, J.C., Kramer, S. and Maas, V.S. (2016), "How control system design affects performance evaluation compression: The role of information accuracy and outcome transparency", *Accounting, Organizations and Society*, Vol. 51, pp. 64–73, doi: 10.1016/j.aos.2016.01.001.

Bracci, E. (2022), "The loopholes of algorithmic public services: An 'intelligent' accountability research agenda", *Accounting, Auditing and Accountability Journal*, doi: 10.1108/AAAJ-06-2022-5856.

Bresser, L., Kohler, S. and Schwaab, C. (2014), "The development of an application for data privacy by applying an audit repository based on IHE ATNA", *Studies in Health Technology and Informatics*, Vol. 198, pp. 219–225, doi: 10.3233/978-1-61499-397-1-219.

Brown, S., Davidovic, J. and Hasan, A. (2021), "The algorithm audit: Scoring the algorithms that score us", *Big Data and Society*, Vol. January-, pp. 1–8, doi: 10.1177/2053951720983865.

Brown-Liburd, H., Issa, H. and Lombardi, D. (2015), "Behavioral implications of big data's impact on audit judgment and decision making and future research directions", *Accounting Horizons*, Vol. 29 No. 2, pp. 451–468, doi: 10.2308/acch-51023.

Buhmann, A., Paßmann, J. and Fieseler, C. (2020), "Managing algorithmic accountability: Balancing reputational concerns, engagement strategies, and the potential of rational discourse", *Journal of Business Ethics*, Vol. 163 No. 2, pp. 265–280, doi: 10.1007/s10551-019-04226-4.

Bumgarner, N. and Vasarhelyi, M.A. (2015), "Continuous Auditing – A New View", in *Audit Analytics and Continuous Audit: Looking Toward the Future*, American Institute of Certified Public Accountants, Inc., New York, pp. 3–52.

Burrell, J. (2016), "How the machine 'thinks': Understanding opacity in machine learning algorithms", *Big Data and Society*, Vol. 3 No. 1, doi: 10.1177/2053951715622512.

Busuioc, M. (2021), "Accountable artificial intelligence: Holding algorithms to account", *Public Administration Review*, Vol. 81 No. 5, pp. 825–836, doi: 10.1111/puar.13293.

Buttigieg, R. and Ellul, L. (2021), "Benefits and challenges of applying data analytics in government auditing", *Journal of Accounting Finance and Auditing Studies (JAFAS)*, Vol. 7 No. 3, pp. 1–33, doi: 10.32602/jafas.2021.017.

Capurro, R., Fiorentino, R., Garzella, S. and Giudici, A. (2021), "Big data analytics in innovation processes: Which forms of dynamic capabilities should be developed and how to embrace digitization?", *European Journal of Innovation Management*, doi: 10.1108/EJIM-05-2021-0256.

Castka, P., Searcy, C. and Fischer, S. (2020), "Technology-enhanced auditing in voluntary sustainability standards: The impact of COVID-19", *Sustainability (Switzerland)*, Vol. 12 No. 11, doi: 10.3390/su12114740.

Chi, D.J. and Chu, C.C. (2021), "Artificial intelligence in corporate sustainability: Using LSTM and GRU for going concern prediction", *Sustainability (Switzerland)*, Vol. 13 No. 21, doi: 10.3390/su132111631.

Chisty, N.M.A. and Adusumalli, H.P. (2022), "Applications of artificial intelligence in quality assurance and assurance of productivity", *ABC Journal of Advanced Research*, Vol. 11 No. 1, doi: 10.18034/abcjar.v11i1.625.

Cooley, A. (2020), "Comparative analysis of online accountability practices in three sectors: Private, public and nonprofit", *Accounting, Auditing and Accountability Journal*, Vol. 33 No. 6, pp. 1423–1445, doi: 10.1108/AAAJ-03-2019-3919.

Cooper, L.A., Holderness, D.K., Sorensen, T.L. and Wood, D.A. (2019), "Robotic process automation in public accounting", *Accounting Horizons*, Vol. 33 No. 4, pp. 15–35, doi: 10.2308/acch-52466.

Criado, J.I. and de Zarate-Alcarazo, L.O. (2022), "Technological frames, CIOs, and artificial intelligence in public administration: A socio-cognitive exploratory study in Spanish local governments", *Government Information Quarterly*, Vol. 39 No. 3, doi: 10.1016/j.giq.2022.101688.

Dalla Via, N., Perego, P. and van Rinsum, M. (2019), "How accountability type influences information search processes and decision quality", *Accounting, Organizations and Society*, Vol. 75, pp. 79–91, doi: 10.1016/j.aos.2018.10.001.

de Laat, P.B. (2021), "Companies committed to responsible AI: From principles towards implementation and regulation?", *Philosophy and Technology*, Vol. 34 No. 4, pp. 1135–1193, doi: 10.1007/s13347-021-00474-3.

Dillard, J. and Vinnari, E. (2019), "Critical dialogical accountability: From accounting-based accountability to accountability-based accounting", *Critical Perspectives on Accounting*, Vol. 62, pp. 16–38, doi: 10.1016/j.cpa.2018.10.003.

Dowling, C. and Leech, S.A. (2014), "A big 4 firm's use of information technology to control the audit process: How an audit support system is changing auditor behavior", *Contemporary Accounting Research*, Vol. 31 No. 1, pp. 230–252, doi: 10.1111/1911-3846.12010.

Dwivedi, Y.K., Hughes, L., Ismagilova, E., Aarts, G., Coombs, C., Crick, T., Duan, Y., et al. (2021), "Artificial intelligence (AI): Multidisciplinary perspectives on emerging challenges, opportunities, and agenda for research, practice and policy", *International Journal of Information Management*, Vol. 57, p. 101994, doi: 10.1016/j.ijinfomgt.2019.08.002.

Endaya, K.A. and Hanefah, M.M. (2016), "Internal auditor characteristics, internal audit effectiveness, and moderating effect of senior management", *Journal of Economic and Administrative Sciences*, Vol. 32 No. 2, pp. 160–176, doi: 10.1108/jeas-07-2015-0023.

Estella, A. (2023), "Trust in artificial intelligence analysis of the European Commission proposal for a regulation of artificial intelligence", *Indiana Journal of Global Legal Studies*, Vol. 30 No. 1, pp. 39–64, doi: 10.2979/gls.2023.a886162.

Eulerich, M. and Lenz, R. (2020), *Defining, Measuring, and Communicating the Value of Internal Audit: Best Practices for the Profession*, The Internal Audit Foundation, Lake Mary, FL.

European Court of Auditors. (2020), "Digital audit checklist", *Journal – European Court of Auditors*, Vol. 1 No. 1, pp. 1–176.

European Parliamentary Research Service. (2019), *A Governance Framework for Algorithmic Accountability and Transparency*, doi: 10.2861/59990.

Fedyk, A., Hodson, J., Khimich, N. and Fedyk, T. (2022), "Is artificial intelligence improving the audit process?", *Review of Accounting Studies*, Vol. 27 No. 3, pp. 938–985, doi: 10.1007/s11142-022-09697-x.

Fischer, C., Heuberger, M. and Heine, M. (2021), "The impact of digitalization in the public sector: A systematic literature review", *Der Moderne Staat – Zeitschrift Für Public Policy, Recht Und Management*, Vol. 14 No. 1–2021, pp. 3–23, doi: 10.3224/dms.v14i1.13.

Fleischman, G.M., Johnson, E.N., Walker, K.B. and Valentine, S.R. (2019), "Ethics versus outcomes: Managerial responses to incentive-driven and goal-induced employee behavior", *Journal of Business Ethics*, Vol. 158 No. 4, pp. 951–967, doi: 10.1007/s10551-017-3695-z.

Fonseka, K., Jaharadak, A.A. and Raman, M. (2022), "Impact of E-commerce adoption on business performance of SMEs in Sri Lanka; moderating role of artificial intelligence", *International Journal of Social Economics*, Vol. 49 No. 10, pp. 1518–1531, doi: 10.1108/IJSE-12-2021-0752.

Fuhrman, J.D., Gorre, N., Hu, Q., Li, H., El Naqa, I. and Giger, M.L. (2022), "A review of explainable and interpretable AI with applications in COVID-19 imaging", *Medical Physics*, 1 January, doi: 10.1002/mp.15359.

Fukas, P., Rebstadt, J., Remark, F. and Thomas, O. (2021), "Developing an artificial intelligence maturity model for auditing", *29th European Conference on Information Systems Research Papers*, ECIS 2021 Research Papers, No. June, p. 133.

Gepp, A., Linnenluecke, M.K., O'Neill, T. and Smith, T. (2017), "Big data techniques in auditing research and practice: Current trends and future opportunities", *SSRN Electronic Journal*, pp. 1–42, doi: 10.2139/ssrn.2930767.

Gotthardt, M., Koivulaakso, D., Paksoy, O., Saramo, C., Martikainen, M. and Lehner, O. (2020), "Current state and challenges in the implementation of smart robotic process automation in accounting and auditing", *ACRN Journal of Finance and Risk Perspectives*, Vol. 9 No. 1, pp. 90–102, doi: 10.35944/JOFRP.2020.9.1.007.

Greif, H. (2022), "Analogue models and universal machines. Paradigms of epistemic transparency in artificial intelligence", *Minds and Machines*, Vol. 32 No. 1, pp. 111–133, doi: 10.1007/s11023-022-09596-9.

Griffith, E.E. (2020), "Auditors, specialists, and professional jurisdiction in audits of fair values", *Contemporary Accounting Research*, Vol. 37 No. 1, pp. 245–276, doi: 10.1111/1911-3846.12506.

Gupta, M., Professor, A. and Mago, J. (2013), "Fuzzy expert system to evaluate the quality of service provider in the implementation of E-government", *International Journal of Computer Applications*, Vol. 67 No. 18, pp. 975–8887.

Hamdam, A., Jusoh, R., Yahya, Y., Abdul Jalil, A. and Zainal Abidin, N.H. (2021), "Auditor judgment and decision-making in big data environment: A proposed research framework", *Accounting Research Journal*, doi: 10.1108/ARJ-04-2020-0078.

Han, H., Shiwakoti, R.K., Jarvis, R., Mordi, C. and Botchie, D. (2023), "Accounting and auditing with blockchain technology and artificial Intelligence: A literature review", *International Journal of Accounting Information Systems*, Vol. 48 No. November 2022, p. 100598, doi: 10.1016/j.accinf.2022.100598.

Harding, N., Azim, M.I., Jidin, R. and Muir, J.P. (2016), "A consideration of literature on trust and distrust as they relate to auditor professional scepticism", *Australian Accounting Review*, Vol. 26 No. 3, pp. 243–254, doi: 10.1111/auar.12126.

Hasan, A.R. (2022), "Artificial intelligence (AI) in accounting & auditing: A literature review", *Open Journal of Business and Management*, Vol. 10 No. 01, pp. 440–465, doi: 10.4236/ojbm.2022.101026.

Hazar, H.B. (2021), "New paradigm in auditing: Continuous auditing", *Accounting, Finance, Sustainability, Governance and Fraud*, Vol. II, pp. 253–268, doi: 10.1007/978-981-15-1928-4_15.

Holt, T.P. and Loraas, T.M. (2021), "A potential unintended consequence of big data: Does information structure lead to suboptimal auditor judgment and decision-making?", *Accounting Horizons*, Vol. 35 No. 3, pp. 161–186, doi: 10.2308/HORIZONS-19-123.

Ingrams, A., Kaufmann, W. and Jacobs, D. (2022), "In AI we trust? Citizen perceptions of AI in government decision making", *Policy and Internet*, Vol. 14 No. 2, pp. 390–409, doi: 10.1002/poi3.276.

International Auditing and Assurance Standards Board. (2018), "Exploring the Growing Use of Technology in the Audit, with a Focus on Data Analytics".

Issa, H., Sun, T. and Vasarhelyi, M.A. (2016), "Research ideas for artificial intelligence in auditing: The formalization of audit and workforce supplementation", *Journal of Emerging Technologies in Accounting*, American Accounting Association, doi: 10.2308/jeta-10511.

Kahyaoglu, S.B. and Aksoy, T. (2021), "Artificial Intelligence in Internal Audit and Risk Assessment", in *Financial Ecosystem and Strategy in the Digital Era. Contributions to Finance and Accounting*, Springer, Cham, pp. 179–192, doi: 10.1007/978-3-030-72624-9_8.

Kandeh, H. and Alsahli, M. (2020), "Effect of big data analytics on audit: An exploratory qualitative study of data analytics on auditors' skills and competence, perception of professional judgement, audit efficiency and audit quality", Master's Thesis in Business Administration Umea School of Business Economics and Statistics, p. 5.

Kay, J., Kuflik, T., Rovatsos, M. and Reports, D. (2021), "Transparency by design", *Dagstuhl Reports*. doi: 10.4230/DagRep.11.5.1.

Kemper, J. and Kolkman, D. (2019), "Transparent to whom? No algorithmic accountability without a critical audience", *Information Communication and Society*, Vol. 22 No. 14, pp. 2081–2096, doi: 10.1080/1369118X.2018.1477967.

Kend, M. and Nguyen, L.A. (2022), "The emergence of audit data analytics in existing audit spaces: Findings from three technologically advanced audit and assurance service markets", *Qualitative Research in Accounting and Management*, Vol. 19 No. 5, pp. 540–563, doi: 10.1108/QRAM-01-2021-0005.

Kernaghan, K. (2014), "The rights and wrongs of robotics: Ethics and robots in public organizations", *Canadian Public Administration*, Vol. 57 No. 4, pp. 485–506, doi: 10.1111/capa.12093.

Keyes, O. and Austin, J. (2022), "Feeling fixes: Mess and emotion in algorithmic audits", *Big Data & Society*, Vol. 9 No. 2, p. 205395172211137, doi: 10.1177/20539517221113772.

Kokina, J. and Davenport, T.H. (2017), "The emergence of artificial intelligence: How automation is changing auditing", *Journal of Emerging Technologies in Accounting*, Vol. 14 No. 1, pp. 115–122, doi: 10.2308/jeta-51730.

Kontos, J. (2021), "Artificial intelligence, machine consciousness and explanation", *Academia Letters*, doi: 10.20935/al1709.

Koshiyama, A., Kazim, E., Treleaven, P., Rai, P., Szpruch, L., Pavey, G., Ahamat, G., et al. (2021), *Towards Algorithm Auditing: A Survey on Managing Legal, Ethical and Technological Risks of AI, ML and Associated Algorithms*. http://dx.doi.org/10.2139/ssrn.3778998

Kossow, N., Windwehr, S., Jenkins, M., Eriksson, D., Vrushi, J. and Millar, L. (2021), "Algorithmic transparency and accountability", *Transparency International Anti-Corruption Helpdesk Answer*. Transparency International, and Laurence Millar, Transparency International New Zealand. https://knowledgehub.transparency.org/assets/uploads/kproducts/Algorithmic-Transparency_2021.pdf

Kottler, N. (2020), "Artificial intelligence: A private practice perspective", *Journal of the American College of Radiology*, Vol. 17 No. 11, pp. 1398–1404, doi: 10.1016/j.jacr.2020.09.029.

La Torre, M., Botes, V.L., Dumay, J. and Odendaal, E. (2019), "Protecting a new Achilles heel: The role of auditors within the practice of data protection", *Managerial Auditing Journal*, Vol. 36 No. 2, pp. 218–239, doi: 10.1108/MAJ-03-2018-1836.

Lehner, O.M., Ittonen, K., Silvola, H., Ström, E. and Wührleitner, A. (2022), "Artificial intelligence based decision-making in accounting and auditing: Ethical challenges and normative thinking", *Accounting, Auditing and Accountability Journal*, Vol. 35 No. 9, pp. 109–135, doi: 10.1108/AAAJ-09-2020-4934.

Leitner-Hanetseder, S., Lehner, O.M., Eisl, C. and Forstenlechner, C. (2021), "A profession in transition: Actors, tasks and roles in AI-based accounting", *Journal of Applied Accounting Research*, Vol. 22 No. 3, pp. 539–556, doi: 10.1108/JAAR-10-2020-0201.

Lenz, R. and Jeppesen, K.K. (2022), "The future of internal auditing: Gardener of governance", *EDPACS*, Vol. 66 No. 5, pp. 1–21, doi: 10.1080/07366981.2022.2036314.

Liston-Heyes, C. and Juillet, L. (2019), "Employee isolation and support for change in the public sector: A study of the internal audit profession", *Public Management Review*, Vol. 21 No. 3, pp. 423–445, doi: 10.1080/14719037.2018.1500628.

Liu, C., Yang, C., Zhang, X. and Chen, J. (2015), "External integrity verification for outsourced big data in cloud and IoT: A big picture", *Future Generation Computer Systems*, Vol. 49, pp. 58–67, doi: 10.1016/j.future.2014.08.007.

Loi, M. and Spielkamp, M. (2021), *Towards Accountability in the Use of Artificial Intelligence for Public Administrations*, AIES 2021 – Proceedings of the 2021 AAAI/ACM Conference on AI, Ethics, and Society, Vol. 1, Association for Computing Machinery, doi: 10.1145/3461702.3462631.

Lopez, B.S. and Alcaide, A.V. (2020), "Blockchain, artificial intelligence, internet of things to improve governance, financial management and control of crisis: Case study COVID-19", *SocioEconomic Challenges*, Vol. 4 No. 2, pp. 78–89, doi: 10.21272/sec.4(2).78-89.2020.

Mahzan, N. and Lymer, A. (2014), "Examining the adoption of computer-assisted audit tools and techniques: Cases of generalized audit software use by internal auditors", *Managerial Auditing Journal*, Vol. 29 No. 4, pp. 327–349, doi: 10.1108/MAJ-05-2013-0877.

Mangiuc, D.M. (2012), "Cloud identity and access management – A model proposal", *Accounting & Management Information Systems*, Vol. 11 No. 3, pp. 484–500.

Mantelero, A. (2014), "The future of consumer data protection in the E.U. Re-thinking the 'notice and consent' paradigm in the new era of predictive analytics", *Computer Law and Security Review*, Vol. 30 No. 6, pp. 643–660, doi: 10.1016/j.clsr.2014.09.004.

Mäntymäki, M., Minkkinen, M., Birkstedt, T. and Viljanen, M. (2022), "Defining organizational AI governance", *AI and Ethics*, Vol. 2 No. 4, pp. 603–609, doi: 10.1007/s43681-022-00143-x.

Martin, K. (2019), "Ethical implications and accountability of algorithms", *Journal of Business Ethics*, Vol. 160 No. 4, pp. 835–850, doi: 10.1007/s10551-018-3921-3.

Masood, A. and Lodhi, R.N. (2015), "Factors affecting the success of government audits: A case study of Pakistan", *Universal Journal of Management*, Vol. 3 No. 2, pp. 52–62, doi: 10.13189/ujm.2015.030202.

Mazzù, M.F., Baccelloni, A., Romani, S. and Andria, A. (2022), "The role of trust and algorithms in consumers' front-of-pack labels acceptance: A cross-country investigation", *European Journal of Marketing*, Vol. 56 No. 11, pp. 3107–3137, doi: 10.1108/EJM-10-2021-0764.

Minkkinen, M., Laine, J. and Mäntymäki, M. (2022), "Continuous auditing of artificial intelligence: A conceptualization and assessment of tools and frameworks", *Digital Society*, Vol. 1 No. 3, doi: 10.1007/s44206-022-00022-2.

Misuraca, G. and van Noordt, C. (2020), *Overview of the Use and Impact of AI in Public Services in the EU*, EU Science Hub, Luxembourg, doi: 10.2760/039619.

Mittelstadt, B.D., Allo, P., Taddeo, M., Wachter, S. and Floridi, L. (2016), "The ethics of algorithms: Mapping the debate", *Big Data and Society*, Vol. 3 No. 2, doi: 10.1177/2053951716679679.

Modisane, T.C. (2019), *Establishing a Competency Framework for the Integration of Workplace Information Technology Knowledge and Skills within an Internal Audit Education Programme and Training, North-West University*. PhD in Accountancy at the North-West University.

Moffitt, K.C. (2018), "A framework for legacy source code audit analytics", *Journal of Emerging Technologies in Accounting*, Vol. 15 No. 2, pp. 67–75, doi: 10.2308/jeta-52269.

Moffitt, K.C. and Vasarhelyi, M.A. (2013), "AIS in an age of big data", *Journal of Information Systems*, Vol. 27 No. 2, pp. 1–19, doi: 10.2308/isys-10372.

Mökander, J. and Floridi, L. (2021), "Ethics-based auditing to develop trustworthy AI", *Minds and Machines*, Vol. 31 No. 2, pp. 323–327, doi: 10.1007/s11023-021-09557-8.

Mökander, J. and Floridi, L. (2023), "Operationalising AI governance through ethics-based auditing: An industry case study", *AI and Ethics*, Vol. 3 No. 2, pp. 451–468, doi: 10.1007/s43681-022-00171-7.

Mökander, J., Morley, J., Taddeo, M. and Floridi, L. (2021), "Ethics-based auditing of automated decision-making systems: Nature, scope, and limitations", *Science and Engineering Ethics*, Vol. 27 No. 4, doi: 10.1007/s11948-021-00319-4.

Mosweu, O. and Ngoepe, M. (2020), "Trustworthiness of digital records in government accounting system to support the audit process in Botswana", *Records Management Journal*, Vol. 31 No. 1, pp. 89–108, doi: 10.1108/RMJ-11-2019-0069.

Munoko, I., Brown-Liburd, H.L. and Vasarhelyi, M. (2020), "The ethical implications of using artificial intelligence in auditing", *Journal of Business Ethics*, Vol. 167 No. 2, pp. 209–234, doi: 10.1007/s10551-019-04407-1.

Nagitta, P.O., Mugurusi, G., Obicci, P.A. and Awuor, E. (2022), "Human-centered artificial intelligence for the public sector: The gate keeping role of the public procurement professional", *Procedia Computer Science*, Vol. 200 No. 2019, pp. 1084–1092, doi: 10.1016/j.procs.2022.01.308.

O'Loughlin, T. and Bukowitz, R. (2021), "A new approach toward social licensing of data analytics in the public sector", *Australian Journal of Social Issues*, Vol. 56 No. 2, pp. 198–212, doi: 10.1002/ajs4.161.

Olaitan, O., Herselman, M. and Wayi, N. (2019), "A data governance maturity evaluation model for government departments of the Eastern Cape province, South Africa", *SA Journal of Information Management*, Vol. 21 No. 1, pp. 1–12, doi: 10.4102/sajim.v21i1.996.

Organisation for Economic Co-operation and Development. (2019), *What Are the OECD Principles on AI?* https://legalinstruments.oecd.org/en/.

Otia, J.E. and Bracci, E. (2022), "Digital transformation and the public sector auditing: The SAI's perspective", *Financial Accountability and Management*, Vol. 38 No. 2, pp. 252–280, doi: 10.1111/faam.12317.

Pearson, S., Lloyd, M. and Nallur, V. (2021), "Towards an ethics-audit bot". arXiv preprint arXiv:2103.15746.

Pedrosa, I., Costa, C.J. and Aparicio, M. (2020), "Determinants adoption of computer-assisted auditing tools (CAATs)", *Cognition, Technology and Work*, Vol. 22 No. 3, pp. 565–583, doi: 10.1007/s10111-019-00581-4.

Petrakaki, D. (2018), "Re-locating accountability through technology: From bureaucratic to electronic ways of governing public sector work", *International Journal of Public Sector Management*, Vol. 31 No. 1, pp. 31–45, doi: 10.1108/IJPSM-02-2017-0043.

Piscopo, A., Siebes, R. and Hardman, L. (2017), "Predicting sense of community and participation by applying machine learning to open government data", *Policy & Internet*, Vol. 9 No. 1, pp. 55–75.

Plesner, U., Justesen, L. and Glerup, C. (2018), "The transformation of work in digitized public sector organizations", *Journal of Organizational Change Management*, Vol. 31 No. 5, pp. 1176–1190, doi: 10.1108/JOCM-06-2017-0257.

Public Company Accounting Oversight Board. (2023), *Proposed Amendments Related to Aspects of Designing and Performing Audit Procedures That Involve Technology-Assisted Analysis of Information in Electronic Form.*

Quadackers, L., Groot, T. and Wright, A. (2014), "Auditors' professional skepticism: Neutrality versus presumptive doubt", *Contemporary Accounting Research*, Vol. 31 No. 3, pp. 639–657, doi: 10.1111/1911-3846.12052.

Raji, I.D., Smart, A., White, R.N., Mitchell, M., Gebru, T., Hutchinson, B., Smith-Loud, J., et al. (2020), "Closing the AI accountability gap: Defining an end-to-end framework for internal algorithmic auditing", *Proceedings of the 2020 Conference on Fairness, Accountability, and Transparency*, pp. 33–44, doi: 10.1145/3351095.3372873.

Raji, I.D., Xu, P., Honigsberg, C. and Ho, D. (2022), *Outsider Oversight: Designing a Third Party Audit Ecosystem for AI Governance*, AIES 2022 – *Proceedings of the 2022 AAAI/ACM Conference on AI, Ethics, and Society*, Vol. 1, Association for Computing Machinery, doi: 10.1145/3514094.3534181.

Reijers, W., Brey, P., Jansen, P., Rodrigues, R., Koivisto, R. and Tuominen, A. (2016), "A common framework for ethical impact assessment", *Stakeholders Acting Together on the Ethical Impact Assessment of Research and Innovation – SATORI*.

Rest, J.R. (1986), *Moral Development: Advances in Research and Theory*, Praeger, New York.

Rest, J.R. (1994), *Moral Development in the Professions Psychology and Applied Ethics*, Psychology Press, Hillsdale.

Rikhardsson, P. and Dull, R. (2016), "An exploratory study of the adoption, application and impacts of continuous auditing technologies in small businesses", *International Journal of Accounting Information Systems*, Vol. 20, pp. 26–37, doi: 10.1016/j.accinf.2016.01.003.

Ross, G.M.S., Zhao, Y., Bosman, A.J., Geballa-Koukoula, A., Zhou, H., Elliott, C.T., Nielen, M.W.F., et al. (2023), "Best practices and current implementation of emerging smartphone-based (bio) sensors – Part 1: Data handling and ethics", *TrAC – Trends in Analytical Chemistry*, 1 January, doi: 10.1016/j.trac.2022.116863.

Roussy, M. (2015), "Welcome to the day-to-day of internal auditors: How do they cope with conflicts?", *Auditing: A Journal of Practice & Theory*, Vol. 34 No. 2, pp. 237–264, doi: 10.2308/ajpt-50904.

Rozario, A.M. and Issa, H. (2020), "Risk-based data analytics in the government sector: A case study for a U.S. county", *Government Information Quarterly*, Vol. 37 No. 2, p. 101457, doi: 10.1016/j.giq.2020.101457.

Rozario, A.M. and Vasarhelyi, M.A. (2018), "Auditing with smart contracts", *International Journal of Digital Accounting Research*, Vol. 18 No. February, pp. 1–27, doi: 10.4192/1577-8517-v18_1.

Ryan, M. and Stahl, B.C. (2021), "Artificial intelligence ethics guidelines for developers and users: Clarifying their content and normative implications", *Journal of Information, Communication and Ethics in Society*, Vol. 19 No. 1, pp. 61–86, doi: 10.1108/JICES-12-2019-0138.

Saleh, I., Marei, Y., Ayoush, M. and Abu Afifa, M.M. (2022), "Big data analytics and financial reporting quality: Qualitative evidence from Canada", *Journal of Financial Reporting and Accounting*, doi: 10.1108/JFRA-12-2021-0489.

Salijeni, G., Samsonova-Taddei, A. and Turley, S. (2021), "Understanding how big data technologies reconfigure the nature and organization of financial statement audits: A sociomaterial analysis", *European Accounting Review*, Vol. 30 No. 3, pp. 531–555, doi: 10.1080/09638180.2021.1882320.

Saveliev, A. and Zhurenkov, D. (2021), "Artificial intelligence and social responsibility: The case of the artificial intelligence strategies in the United States, Russia, and China", *Kybernetes*, Vol. 50 No. 3, pp. 656–675, doi: 10.1108/K-01-2020-0060.

Simbeck, K. (2022), "FAccT-Check on AI Regulation: Systematic Evaluation of AI Regulation on the Example of the Legislation on the Use of AI in the Public Sector in the German Federal State of Schleswig-Holstein", *ACM International Conference Proceeding Series*, Association for Computing Machinery, pp. 89–96, doi: 10.1145/3531146.3533076.

Singh, H., Woodliff, D., Sultana, N. and Newby, R. (2014), "Additional evidence on the relationship between an internal audit function and external audit fees in australia", *International Journal of Auditing*, Vol. 18 No. 1, pp. 27–39, doi: 10.1111/ijau.12009.

Soh, D.S.B. and Martinov-Bennie, N. (2015), "Internal auditors' perceptions of their role in environmental, social and governance assurance and consulting", *Managerial Auditing Journal*, Vol. 30 No. 1, doi: 10.1108/09574090910954864.

Sookhak, M., Richard Yu, F. and Zomaya, A.Y. (2018), "Auditing big data storage in cloud computing using divide and conquer tables", *IEEE Transactions on Parallel and Distributed Systems*, Vol. 29 No. 5, pp. 999–1012, doi: 10.1109/TPDS.2017.2784423.

Spina Alì, G. and Yu, R. (2021), "Artificial intelligence between transparency and secrecy: From the EC whitepaper to the AIA and beyond", *European Journal of Law and Technology*, Vol. 12 No. 3, pp. 1–15.

Squio, C.R. and Hoffmann, M.G. (2021), "Co-production and innovation in public services' assessment: The case of the Citizen Audit Project", *Revista de Administração Da UFSM*, Vol. 14 No. 4, pp. 864–887, doi: 10.5902/1983465963947.

Srinivasan, R. and San Miguel González, B. (2022), "The role of empathy for artificial intelligence accountability", *Journal of Responsible Technology*, Vol. 9, p. 100021, doi: 10.1016/j.jrt.2021.100021.

Stahl, B.C. (2021), *Artificial Intelligence for a Better Future: An Ecosystem Perspective on the Ethics of AI and Emerging Digital Technologies*, Springer. https://library.oapen.org/handle/20.500.12657/48228.

Stahl, B.C., Timmermans, J. and Flick, C. (2017), "Ethics of emerging information and communication technologies: On the implementation of responsible research and innovation", *Science and Public Policy*, Vol. 44 No. 3, pp. 369–381, doi: 10.1093/scipol/scw069.

Stumpf, S., Strappelli, L., Ahmed, S., Nakao, Y., Naseer, A., Gamba, G.D. and Regoli, D. (2021), "Design methods for artificial intelligence fairness and transparency", *CEUR Workshop Proceedings*, Vol. 2903, p. 2903.

Sun, T. and Vasarhelyi, M.A. (2017), "Deep learning and the future of auditing: How an evolving technology could transform analysis and improve judgment", *The CPA Journal*, Vol. June, pp. 24–29.

Ta, T.T. and Doan, T.N. (2022), "Factors affecting internal audit effectiveness: Empirical evidence from Vietnam", *International Journal of Financial Studies*, Vol. 10 No. 2, doi: 10.3390/ijfs10020037.

Tabassi, E. (2023), *Artificial Intelligence Risk Management Framework (AI RMF 1.0)*, doi: 10.6028/NIST.AI.100-1.

Taiwo, S.O., Ayandibu, A.O., Taiwo, M.B. and Vezi-Magigaba, M.F. (2019), "Effect of innovative technology on internal audit using selected municipalities in Nigeria as case study", *Journal of Gender, Information and Development in Africa*, Vol. 8 No. 1, pp. 43–62, doi: 10.31920/2050-4284/2019/8n1a2.

Tan, Ö.F. (2016), "Impact of accounting information systems on internal auditors in Turkey", *Marmara Üniversitesi Öneri Dergisi*, Vol. 12, pp. 245–260.

Tarek, M., Mohamed, E.K.A., Hussain, M.M. and Basuony, M.A.K. (2017), "The implication of information technology on the audit profession in developing country: Extent of use and perceived importance", *International Journal of Accounting and Information Management*, Vol. 25 No. 2, pp. 237–255, doi: 10.1108/IJAIM-03-2016-0022.

The Association of Chartered Certified Accountants. (2017), *Professional Accountants – the Future: Ethics and Trust in a Digital Age*, The Association of Chartered Certified Accountants, London.

The European Parliament and the Council of the European Union. (2014), *Regulations on the Protection of Natural Persons with Regard to the Processing of Personal Data and on the Free Movement of Such Data, and Repealing Directive 95/46/EC (General Data Protection Regulation)*, Legislative Acts, pp. 1–88.

The Institute of Internal Auditors Global. (2017), *The IIA's Artificial Intelligence Auditing Framework: Practical Applications Part A, Global Perspectives and Insights*.

Thompson, N., Ravindran, R. and Nicosia, S. (2015), "Government data does not mean data governance: Lessons learned from a public sector application audit", *Government Information Quarterly*, Vol. 32 No. 3, pp. 316–322, doi: 10.1016/j.giq.2015.05.001.

Tiron-Tudor, A., Deliu, D., Farcane, N. and Dontu, A. (2021), "Managing change with and through blockchain in accountancy organizations: A systematic literature review", *Journal of Organizational Change Management*, Vol. 34 No. 2, pp. 477–506, doi: 10.1108/JOCM-10-2020-0302.

Tsai, W.-H., Chen, H.-C., Chang, J.-C., Leu, J.-D., Chen, D.C. and Purbokusumo, Y. (2015), "Performance of the internal audit department under ERP systems: Empirical evidence from Taiwanese firms", *Enterprise Information Systems*, Vol. 9 No. 7, pp. 725–742, doi: 10.1080/17517575.2013.830341.

Turetken, O., Jethefer, S. and Ozkan, B. (2020), "Internal audit effectiveness: Operationalization and influencing factors", *Managerial Auditing Journal*, Vol. 35 No. 2, pp. 238–271, doi: 10.1108/MAJ-08-2018-1980.

Uglum, M.K. (2021), *Consideration of the Ethical Implications of Artificial Intelligence in the Audit Profession*, University of Northern Iowa.

Van Dyk, H.O. and Goosen, R. (2017), "Developing an internal audit planning framework at a strategic level by integrating continuous auditing", *Southern Journal of Accountability and Auditing Research*, Vol. 19 No. 1, pp. 59–70.

Van Veenstra, A.F., Grommé, F. and Djafari, S. (2020), "The use of public sector data analytics in the Netherlands", *Transforming Government: People, Process and Policy*, Vol. 15 No. 4, pp. 396–419, doi: 10.1108/TG-09-2019-0095.

Vasarhelyi, M.A. and Kogan, A. (editors) (1997), *Artificial Intelligence in Accounting and Auditing*, Vol. 4, Markus Wiener Publisher, New York.

Waldman, A. and Martin, K. (2022), "Governing algorithmic decisions: The role of decision importance and governance on perceived legitimacy of algorithmic decisions", *Big Data and Society*, Vol. 9 No. 1, doi: 10.1177/20539517221100449.

Walker, K. and Brown-Liburd, H. (2019), *The Emergence of Data Analytics in Auditing: Perspectives from Internal and External Auditors through the Lens of Institutional Theory*, Rutgers, New Jersey.

Wang, J., Lu, Y., Fan, S., Hu, P. and Wang, B. (2022), "How to survive in the age of artificial intelligence? Exploring the intelligent transformations of SMEs in central China", *International Journal of Emerging Markets*, Vol. 17 No. 4, pp. 1143–1162, doi: 10.1108/IJOEM-06-2021-0985.

Wilson, C. and van der Velden, M. (2022), "Sustainable AI: An integrated model to guide public sector decision-making", *Technology in Society*, Vol. 68 No. October 2020, p. 101926, doi: 10.1016/j.techsoc.2022.101926.

Wirtz, B.W., Langer, P.F. and Fenner, C. (2021), "Artificial intelligence in the public sector – A research agenda", *International Journal of Public Administration*, Vol. 44 No. 13, pp. 1103–1128, doi: 10.1080/01900692.2021.1947319.

Wirtz, B.W., Weyerer, J.C. and Geyer, C. (2019), "Artificial intelligence and the public sector – Applications and challenges", *International Journal of Public Administration*, Vol. 42 No. 7, pp. 596–615, doi: 10.1080/01900692.2018.1498103.

Wright, S.A. and Schultz, A.E. (2018), "The rising tide of artificial intelligence and business automation: Developing an ethical framework", *Business Horizons*, Vol. 61 No. 6, pp. 823–832, doi: 10.1016/j.bushor.2018.07.001.

Yu, L. and Li, Y. (2022), "Artificial intelligence decision-making transparency and employees' trust: The parallel multiple mediating effect of effectiveness and discomfort", *Behavioral Sciences*, Vol. 12 No. 5, doi: 10.3390/bs12050127.

Zhang, J., Yang, X. and Appelbaum, D. (2015), "Toward effective big data analysis in continuous auditing", *Accounting Horizons*, Vol. 29 No. 2, pp. 469–476, doi: 10.2308/acch-51070.

Zollo, L., Pellegrini, M.M. and Ciappei, C. (2017), "What sparks ethical decision making? The interplay between moral intuition and moral reasoning: Lessons from the scholastic doctrine peer-reviewed version forthcoming in Journal of Business Ethics", *Journal of Business Ethics*, Vol. 145, pp. 681–700.

Chapter 11

The impact of AI on the sustainability in public sector internal auditing

Babalwa Ceki

11.1 INTRODUCTION AND DEFINITION OF KEYWORDS

The concept of sustainability has entered every aspect of our daily life, including audit activities. This chapter focuses on the impact of artificial intelligence (AI) and sustainability on public sector auditing. It explains what needs to be done to achieve the sustainability of audit activities based on AI. The major information and AI-based application examples given in this chapter are presented from the perspective of public sector auditors. Essential information and policy recommendations are presented based on relevant literature. In this way, the author aims to increase the impact of artificial intelligence (AI) for sustainable public sector auditing to become widespread. The effective application of AI in the public sector necessitates strategic design and consideration of numerous factors, including cyber-security risks, AI policy and guidelines, governance, and responsible leadership.

Definition of words

Sustainability refers to the continued and effective use of new technologies in the public sector internal auditing to foster the four e's, being, economical, effective, efficient, and ethical.

Digitalisation refers to "the use of digital technology and data to create revenue and transform business processes (not simply digitise them) and create an environment for digital business, whereby digital information is at the core". Digitisation refers to the conversion of manual or paper-based audit to digital audit (I-SCOOP, 2016). **Digital transformation** focuses on strategy and broad business models; digitisation and digit-alisation emphasise technology (Otia & Bracci, 2022).

Digital transformation in the public sector signifies a change in how decisions are made, carried out, and enforced, as well as how auditing is carried out (Bonsón & Bednárová, 2019; Schmitz & Leoni, 2019). It includes the organisation, strategy, technology, processes, and external technological factors, as well as the people and culture of the SAI (Otia & Bracca, 2022).

Artificial intelligence (AI) is a technology programmed to resemble human decision-making and cognitive abilities and intended to take cues from its surroundings. Based on these hints, AI systems can evaluate risks to decide, predict, or act. Unlike other software, AI systems learn from data and can improve themselves over time without explicit human programming, thanks to exposure to new data (Shaw, 2019). Auditing firms are investing in AI for improved quality of audits and reporting (Munoko et al., 2020).

A combination of hardware and software known as AI can evaluate, make decisions, and carry out intricate decision-making processes based on the information at hand (Puthukulam et al., 2021). By handling repetitive tasks, AI-powered software systems can enhance performance and simplify people's lives. The Oxford English Dictionary defines artificial intelligence as the capacity of computers or other machines to exhibit or mimic intelligent behaviour (OED Online, 2019).

Even though AI was conceptualised in the 1940s, it is still regarded as an emerging technology because the methods used to implement it are undergoing rapid change (Stahl et al., 2017). In addition, businesses are currently spending a lot of money on the advancement and spread of AI. Four types of AI are described by Munoko et al. (2020), first is natural language processing which translates speech into text and is typically integrated into current processes. For instance, a Microsoft research team has disclosed creating an AI program to better translate speech into text than a human (Munoko et al., 2020). Companies can use this application to transcribe customer calls to understand customer needs better and assess support agents' effectiveness (Microsoft, 2019).

The second type is augmented AI systems, which incorporate human decision-making and increasingly learn from their interactions with people and the environment (PwC, 2017). As a result, these systems display the analytical intelligence required for AI to process information for problem-solving and learn from data. Humans and artificial intelligence are co-decision makers in this situation. The third type, autonomous AI systems, can act independently without human intervention and can adapt to various situations. People are beginning to assign decision-making to AI in this situation.

Autonomous AI systems demonstrate both logical and compassionate intelligence. Empathetic intelligence enables AI to recognise human emotions, react to them appropriately, and influence people. Intuitive intelligence enables AI to adapt creatively and successfully to new situations. For autonomous AI to handle unfamiliar situations, more advanced heuristics are required, and even more empathetic intelligence is necessary for AI to interact with humans productively (Huang & Rust, 2018).

AI is used in warranty applications for accounting and auditing tasks like general ledger review, tax compliance, reporting and data analysis, fraud investigation, and judgement. Artificial intelligence promises to quickly and concisely analyse numerical, textual, and visual data while examining unstructured data in real-time. Intelligent systems can successfully point the auditor to high-risk areas in the face of big data (Munoko et al., 2020). AI can make a few important assumptions, though, as businesses and auditors rely on it more and more. A presumption underlying the concept of absolute reliability in AI systems is that they always maintain adherence to desired constraints. Another assumption made is that any deviations from these constraints will be able to be identified and corrected. The universal applicability of these assumptions is subject to scrutiny, thus bearing noteworthy ethical implications.

11.2 AI TRAINING IN THE PUBLIC SECTOR

The use of AI in public internal auditing has many benefits. First, AI-driven auditing techniques can greatly increase the reliability and accuracy of audit findings, lowering the possibility of biases or errors (Hoffman & Zuckerman, 2019). Second, AI makes auditing procedures more efficient, freeing auditors to concentrate on important tasks and strategic analysis (Salleh et al., 2021). Thirdly, proactive risk management and early detection of potential problems are made possible by real-time data analytics and predictive capabilities, encouraging sustainable practices in the public sector (Mohan et al., 2022).

Despite its advantages, applying AI to public internal auditing is challenging. Issues with algorithmic bias, data quality, and privacy raise significant ethical questions. Maintaining public trust and upholding ethical standards in auditing requires ensuring data integrity, transparency, and objective AI decision-making (Wang et al., 2020). Additionally, auditors may encounter difficulties deciphering and interpreting results generated by AI, highlighting the necessity of adequate training and upskilling of internal auditors (Verma et al., 2021).

Investing in public sector internal auditors' AI training is essential to effectively implement AI in the public sector. Training programmes should be created to improve auditors' understanding of AI concepts, capabilities, and constraints. Workshops, seminars, and online courses can be used as part of training initiatives to upskill and promote an innovation culture driven by AI.

Audit institutions internationally are training their auditors on AI use in auditing. For example, in the United Kingdom, supreme audit institutions (SAIs) train their employees through in-house workshops (NAO, 2019). The INTOSAI and several regional SAI have undertaken initiatives for technology training, such as organising conferences and seminars on enhancing the use of digital technology in auditing (Otia & Bracci, 2022).

SAI India has updated the auditors' profiles and competencies to reflect new skills like collaboration, digital literacy, and critical thinking. SAI Chile has implemented a plan to improve its data analytics capabilities (over 600 employees are certified in data analysis, 64 in Python, and 97 in Tableau). Since 2015, SAI Brazil has funded staff members' specialised data analysis training and hired 30 data analysts (INTOSAI, 2021).

Technology is only useful when combined with the appropriate knowledge and abilities. If a company invests in technology without considering its users, it will fail (Andersson et al., 2018). The importance of people, organisational cultures, and other non-technological elements should be considered when adopting new technology. Getting auditors acquainted with digital culture is the first step. Employees will require new skills and technological knowledge (Andersson et al., 2018). The HR division must determine whether hiring is necessary or whether the necessary skills can be found internally. It might be necessary to create and implement training programs for staff, including those for expert data analysts and auditors (AFROSAI-E, 2022).

Since digitisation requires new skill sets from auditors that are even on par with audit technical skills, today's auditors are compared to data scientists with auditing capabilities (INTOSAI, 2022; AFROSAI, 2022). Tech-savvy auditors thrive in an environment with a digital culture (Ceki, 2019).

According to Munoko et al. (2020), accounting professionals have an ethical obligation to possess technical competence and engage in ongoing self-improvement to enhance the quality of their services. This inquiry pertains to the adequacy of the existing auditing and accounting curriculum in incorporating emerging technology to equip future auditors with the necessary skills and knowledge to operate effectively in the evolving technological auditing landscape. Auditors with high technical competence can effectively utilise AI applications without compromising independence. Therefore, the audit profession must contemplate the ramifications of AI in training novice auditors. Critical thinking and professional judgement are a necessity for auditors to be able to increase audit performance while assisted by AI tools (Plumlee et al., 2015).

Challenges related to AI adoption are that it may disrupt routines and behaviours; employees may feel uncertain or stressed due to training requirements and a change from the status quo (Alkhoori, 2022). A lack of involvement and training exacerbates employee resistance to change and readiness to adopt new technologies (Mullins, 2005). Employees frequently object to adopting new technology due to resistance, hesitation, a lack of preparation, ignorance, and opposition. When a company adopts technology gradually, employees are likelier to adopt the new technologies (Alkhoori, 2022). Hence, digital culture is necessary to upskill auditors in digital skills.

11.3 DIGITAL CULTURE

A digital culture must be established for AI to be successfully implemented in the public sector. It entails creating an atmosphere that welcomes technological advancement, promotes experimentation, and aids in incorporating AI solutions into current workflows. It takes leadership commitment, stakeholder involvement, and the creation of collaborative platforms to support knowledge sharing and learning across government agencies to develop a digital culture.

Digital culture plays a critical role in how employees of an organisation understand and use technology. It would be similar to enforcing technology in a possibly resistant workplace without a well-managed digital culture that incorporates technology adoption with the workplace's values (Craig et al., 2014). According to Ahmad et al. (2013), employees' behaviour and attitudes can change and become more open to participating in and joining a new venture when they are prepared to do so (Ahmad et al., 2013). SAIs should have environments encouraging innovative thinking, exploration, and training sessions (Otti & Bacci, 2022). In such a culture, auditors can try new things; even failure might be viewed as a step in improving one's craft (Schlaepfer, Von Radowitz, Koch & Merkofer, 2017). Strong digital leadership that can encourage innovation and is not afraid to take calculated risks is required for an excellent digital culture (Berghaus, Back & Kaltenrieder, 2017).

Digital transformation, like employees, culture, and organisational support, is crucial to successfully adopt and sustain AI use in public sector auditing. People must be motivated to use the technology and see its advantages and higher leadership must support this. A chief technology officer is important in overseeing, implementing, and providing ongoing support for AI adoption and sustainability (Kraus, Jones, Kailer, Weinmann, Chaparro-Banegas & Roig-Tierno, 2021). The ability of an organisation to quickly adopt and use new technology is essential for digital transformation to occur (Hess et al., 2016).

11.4 DATA COLLECTION PLATFORMS AND AI TOOL ACQUISITION/INFRASTRUCTURE

SAIs need to be able to access client information to carry out their mandate. The COVID-19 pandemic made auditors work remotely both during and after it. When auditing, most SAIs needed help connecting to systems and gaining access to information. This was partly attributed to the countries' information systems' infrastructure quality. However, it may also indicate that SAIs still need to automate or carefully choose their technologies (AFROSAI-E, 2022). Although SAIs have automated and chosen technologies, the remote working model imposed by the pandemic revealed to SAIs that they were not technologically ready.

The INTOSAI working group recommends that well-developed big data audit platforms be available for data analytics for big data analytics to be effectively adopted (INTOSAI,

2022). Another suggestion is to create data collection platforms where data from auditees is stored and managed by a big data chief technology officer for audit evidence. Data application regulations are crucial. Working groups of specialists who receive ongoing training from INTOSAI and other experts should exist within SAIs to exchange data analytics knowledge (INTOSAI, 2022). The SAI may discover through its assessment of its capabilities that its infrastructure in terms of network, storage, processing power, and analysis tools needs to be improved. A strategy for the SAI should include a plan for scaling up to the desired level, as technology investments may be expensive (AFROSAI-E, 2022).

Adopting AI in the public sector heavily depends on developing reliable data collection platforms and acquiring the necessary infrastructure and tools. Governments should invest in scalable and secure data collection systems to collect and process large volumes of data from various sources. To efficiently acquire AI tools and infrastructure while ensuring compatibility with current systems and adherence to ethical and privacy standards, procurement processes should also be streamlined.

Internal auditors must use AI to provide the highest quality audit, as the Big 4 audit firms' audit quality was significantly impacted by it (Widuri, Ferdiansyah & Kongchan, 2021). Manita, Elommal, Baudier and Hikkerova (2020) claim that digitisation produces more relevant audits by analysing all consumer data, allowing audit companies to expand their service offerings and raise audit quality. A new auditor profile has emerged due to digitisation, encouraging an innovative culture within audit firms.

In addition to highlighting the benefits of digital technology, the INTOSAI also highlights some of its drawbacks, particularly those related to accessing, storing, and managing complex data generated while implementing governmental policies (INTOSAI, 2019). The amount of data continues to be challenging, particularly in countries with decentralised government systems that are common at the municipal, regional, and subnational levels. There needs to be more empirical research on how public sector audit organisations conceptualise and analyse the phenomena of digital transformation in their planning and day-to-day operations (Eggers & Bellman, 2015). According to Otia and Bracci (2022), the COVID-19 epidemic prompted SAIs to automate several audit processes, particularly data collection, sharing, and analysis. Most tried to increase database connectivity by using online query tools to get information directly from auditees.

Due to restrictions on public organisations' ability to generate, access, and manage data, AI auditing may be challenging. Through their audits, recommendations, and supporting actions, auditors can help to resolve these challenges. For instance, SAI India has advised the government on data collection and handling (INTOSAI, 2021). SAIs have assessed the capacities and skills needed to support these new audit methodologies and the existing capacity gaps. They emphasised the need for new capacity development strategies to replace in-person training and for investments in employee resilience and professional competencies (such as in South Africa and India) (INTOSAI, 2021).

SAIs are reorganising their organisational structures to include new hardware and software to accept disruptive technology. According to Otia and Bracci (2022), SAIs in developed nations have established innovation labs, hired more data scientists, and created and used cloud environments to prepare for technological disruptions. However, regarding how much automation (data analytics) SAIs rely on when making audit decisions, most SAIs viewed data analytics as an auxiliary tool. SAIs used digital auditing techniques and relied heavily on data analytics findings when making audit decisions. The same digital culture and innovation should be adopted by internal audit institutions, especially in developing nations.

11.5 GOVERNANCE OF AI

Implementing regulations pertaining to examining, verifying, and endorsing AI systems would safeguard the well-being of individuals utilising such systems (Anderson, 2008). Additionally, these regulations would ensure that AI systems exhibit fairness, accuracy, and objectivity (Sprigman, 2018). Furthermore, they would demonstrate that the development of such technology adheres to a value-sensitive approach (Wright, 2011; HLEG, 2018). The policies implemented serve to address ethical concerns that arise from the inherent characteristics of AI. For instance, the complexity of AI systems may impede transparency and hinder access to the technology. Additionally, relying on extensive datasets for AI training may give rise to potential data security risks.

When AI systems are used to assist professionals in judgement and decision-making, their effects may be favourable because AI is a robust technology. For instance, intelligent decision systems can successfully direct an auditor towards higher-risk areas when the auditor has a lot of data to analyse (Brown-Liburd et al., 2015). Long-term use of decision aids, however, may result in the auditor concentrating only on issues that the decision aid has identified, neglecting to consider additional factors or issues that the system has not picked up on (Seow, 2011). Auditors should pick up areas AI did not identify and maintain professional scepticism and critical thinking (Munoko et al., 2020).

As we enter the Fourth Industrial Revolution, the auditing profession has a greater awareness of the importance of making ethical decisions. The rapidly emerging technological advances will undeniably positively impact the profession; however, these technologies may also jeopardise critical ethical values. Values such as fairness, privacy, independence, beneficence, accountability, and responsibility have all been flagged as "at risk" by the Big 4 audit firms, Deloitte, KPMG, PricewaterhouseCoopers, and EY. Smaller firms have also echoed these concerns (Munoko et al., 2020).

To ensure AI is used in the public sector responsibly and ethically, governance mechanisms are crucial. To oversee the implementation, monitoring, and evaluation of AI initiatives, governments must create specialised bodies for AI governance or incorporate AI governance into already-existing structures. To provide a variety of viewpoints and guarantee thorough oversight, these bodies should include multidisciplinary experts and representatives from academia, industry, civil society, and government organisations.

The existing governance frameworks about AI lack well-defined and concrete structures. One of the prominent Big 4 audit firms has expressed concern regarding the growing disparity between the advancement of AI and the governance and control mechanisms that regulate its implementation within organisations. Cobey et al. (2018) emphasise the necessity of establishing guiding principles to facilitate the intentional development of ethical AI and the implementation of agile governance strategies in response to the emergence of new technologies.

The governance of AI within the audit profession continues to exhibit significant deficiencies. Munoko et al. (2020) illustrate a set of governance inquiries. To whom should an audit firm disclose its utilisation of AI, including but not limited to its clientele, regulatory bodies, and stakeholders relying on financial statements? What types of monitoring controls should audit firms establish to govern the various tiers of AI? Which individuals possess the requisite technical expertise to audit the AI systems employed by auditing firms? Although the initial plausibility of these inquiries may be debatable, it is essential to consider the implications of the World Economic Forum's (2015) prediction that 30% of auditing will use AI by 2025. Is it necessary to know the specific tasks undertaken by AI in the auditing process, such as documentation or making judgements, as well as the level of reliability and trustworthiness exhibited by the AI system?

At present, it is imperative for the regulator, client, and shareholder to possess comprehensive insight into the audit activities conducted by professionals and the specific tasks delegated to AI systems. Therefore, it is imperative for auditors to take into account the development of suitable monitoring and reporting controls within the AI-infused audit setting (Munoko et al., 2020). According to Wachter and Mittelstadt (2019), the primary objective of data protection law is to safeguard individuals' privacy, identity, reputation, and autonomy. However, the current framework must adequately shield data subjects from the emerging risks associated with inferential analytics.

It has been cautioned that ethical concerns may arise when attempting to offer explanations to AI users, as the content of these explanations could unintentionally reveal confidential information belonging to others. Hence, it is imperative to establish a judicious equilibrium in the governance of AI ethics. Auditing regulatory bodies are recommended to implement verification, validation, and accreditation policies at the technology policy level while tailoring these policies to suit the specific types of AI employed within the auditing field. Implementing this customisation would establish monitoring and reporting mechanisms that govern audit firms' utilisation of AI (Munoko et al., 2020). For instance, continuously monitoring the operation logs of autonomous AI during audit procedures. Another example is documenting the review of assisted and augmented AI by audit professionals to ensure the application of professional scepticism and judgement.

Auditing regulators and standard setters should consider the ethical implications of using AI in auditing and provide practical guidance to firms. This could involve enhancing existing standards, such as ISA 620, to include AI systems (Munoko et al., 2020). These standards already address the assessment of experts' competence and the evaluation of their work, making them a good starting point for developing guidance on AI reliance.

A relevant standard to take into account in AI utilisation is ISA 530, which pertains to audit sampling and testing. Automation tools can facilitate auditors in conducting comprehensive testing of all transactions under consideration, offering a more comprehensive approach than traditional sampling (Byrnes et al., 2018). Regulators should explore how the profession can migrate towards AI to enhance audit quality, while addressing challenges faced by early adopters, such as managing a large number of exceptions flagged by automated systems.

11.5.1 CyberSecurity risks

The African Organisation of English-speaking Supreme Audit Institutions (Afrosai-e) formed a working group on information systems audit and management (WGISM) in response to global technological advancements and cybersecurity risks. Technology is developing quickly; therefore, SAIs and internal audit institutions must ensure that they not only automate but do so correctly.

When integrating AI into the public sector, a proactive approach to addressing cybersecurity risks must be taken. Governments must prioritise cybersecurity measures to safeguard vital infrastructure from online threats and sensitive data. This entails strong encryption techniques, frequent security reviews, and ongoing AI system monitoring to identify and address potential vulnerabilities. Governments can stay ahead of developing cyber threats by working with cybersecurity experts and implementing best practices.

Auditors are expected to articulate the reasons behind their choices and professionally use their knowledge and skills to assess audit evidence ethically and fairly. Auditors should be able to comprehend the reasoning behind AI decisions and actions and to check that ethics are not compromised (Munoko et al., 2020). The AI system should be transparent to enable the auditors to justify their testing methods to avoid automation bias and complacency, meaning they may trust the AI system's accuracy without questioning it too much (Parasuraman & Manzey, 2010). Therefore, creating explainable AI is crucial in ensuring that an AI-enabled audit adheres to professional standards (Samek et al., 2017).

According to current auditing standards, auditors might be held accountable for audit failures resulting from subpar auditing decision aids or erroneous audit judgements that followed (Specht et al., 1991). Hence, ensuring that the AI adheres to auditing standards and is ethically reliable is important. Munoko et al. (2020) suggest accreditation of third-party AI systems that non-technology firms use by an independent technology body as that may increase the confidence of users on it.

11.5.2 AI policy and guidelines

The responsible use of AI in the public sector depends on establishing clear AI policies and guidelines. Governments should create guidelines that cover ethical issues, data privacy, accountability, and transparency in AI systems. To ensure that AI policies are inclusive, aligned with societal values, and balance innovation and regulation, policymakers should engage in multi-stakeholder consultations.

New technologies bring risks to data privacy and cybersecurity; the solution has been to rely on governance (Rojas & Tuomi, 2022). Since AI development is decentralised, global regulation seems necessary to guide developers towards the greater good (Stanford, 2018). However, regulatory responses typically take longer to implement than the actual pace of technological innovation, and it often takes longer for negative effects to become evident before new regulatory frameworks can be developed (Owen et al., 2013). Several AI governance guidelines have been created as a starting point for AI, but some businesses disregard this "soft" governance for action speed and financial gain (Hagendorff, 2020).

The efficacy of compliance guidelines could be better, even when integrated into broader governance ecosystems like policy frameworks and standard professional practices that employ distinct methodologies. Applying ethical principles differs significantly from theory (Schiff et al., 2020). AI system designers and developers struggle to adhere to these standards while simultaneously coming up with new goods and services consumers want and are willing to pay for. Several studies have examined and analysed the AI guidelines to pinpoint the key themes and suggested enhancements to AI application development. Some of them have pointed out the need for more information on cultural sensitivity, sustainability, and operationalisation. AI ethics guidelines usually only offer high-level principles, primarily concerning trustworthiness and privacy, and frequently omit plans for operationalisation (Rojas & Tuomi, 2022). For AI ethics guidelines to be useful for businesses, it is recommended that a more explicit foundation be established within distinct sectors and contextual frameworks. To ensure full implementation, it is imperative to shift from broad-application guidance to governance principles tailored to specific industries.

11.5.3 Responsible leadership

To successfully implement AI in the public sector, responsible leadership is essential. Leaders should prioritise moral issues, encourage a culture of openness, and ensure AI is used in the public interest. To benefit from their expertise and address potential biases and risks related to AI, they should also promote collaboration and partnerships with external stakeholders, such as academia and industry. The potential of AI is maximised, and sustainability is promoted in public internal auditing when implemented responsibly. Public sector organisations need to establish comprehensive frameworks for AI governance that consider accountability, transparency, and fairness. AI audits need human oversight and expertise to address complex ethical issues and ensure regulatory compliance (Gladwin et al., 2019).

Awuah et al. (2021) assert that because management drives AI adoption, a managerial mindset, readiness to accept technology, and a strong IT infrastructure are all necessary. Audit partners should encourage technology adoption and set an example for others and should spend more money on IT infrastructure, more data scientists or engineers, and big data analytics training workshops.

11.6 DISCUSSION

The following recommendations are drawn from literature for public sector organisations looking to integrate AI into their internal auditing processes ethically: Create AI-specific laws and regulations that uphold moral principles and legal requirements (Abdel-Basset et al., 2021). Spend money on skills development and training for auditors to effectively use AI-driven systems and comprehend the insights generated by AI (Soltani et al., 2022). Prioritise data quality and implement strict data governance procedures to prevent biases and maintain data integrity (Kamal & Nandi, 2021).

Work with academia, industry, and civil society professionals to address potential cybersecurity problems related to AI and discover best practices (Mishra et al., 2023). Work with stakeholders to ensure accountability, transparency, and public trust in AI-driven auditing processes, including citizens and civil society organisations (Bansal et al., 2022). The investigation and mitigation of cybersecurity risks necessitate the implementation of governance standards. Additionally, AI developers must enhance the transparency of AI systems. To achieve this, developers should incorporate an explanation facility within the AI, enabling it to communicate the rationale behind its decision-making process to users. The provision of transparent explanations in AI systems can enhance user trust. However, it is essential to consider that if these explanations can be leveraged to derive insights about individuals other than the user, and there is a risk of privacy infringement.

The INTOSAI formed three working groups on digital transformation to promote technology integration into the public sector auditing process (Otia & Bracci, 2022). The internal audit function in organisations can follow INTOSAI's example by establishing working groups on AI and big data in internal auditing.

When choosing which technologies to adopt, the internal audit function should emphasise the technological complexity, compatibility, and cost-benefit factors. IAI should think about implementing technologies that users find simple to use. They should also consider whether the technology they want to implement is compatible with other technologies already used by the IAI and its clients. Additionally, a thorough cost-benefit analysis should be performed to ensure that the best new technology is chosen – cost-effective and appropriate given the initial investment and ongoing maintenance expenses.

Management must be aware of technological advancements in the market (among suppliers and customers) before investing in new technology. This aids in choosing an appropriate AI technology that meets the requirements of the IAI. The overall risk management procedure used by the audit institution should take new technology investments into account.

Before using AI-based tools, an IAI ICT maturity assessment should be completed to determine areas for improvement.

The high implementation costs and the requirement to train internal auditors in AI and ML audits are two significant obstacles to implementing AI and ML in audits. The company will incur additional costs due to the ongoing updating of AI and ML under the most recent developments and the proper training of auditors. Given the contemporary challenges in auditing that have never been encountered before, this will pose a significant challenge to organisations struggling with limited financial situations (Puthukulam et al., 2021). Applications for AI and ML must be implemented with a sound implementation strategy. Most internal auditors concurred that machine learning and AI are crucial to enhancing audits' accuracy, dependability, and general effectiveness. It aids in spotting mistakes and false statements.

Using AI software enables the internal auditor to carry out a thorough assessment, create reports that highlight the most crucial findings, discuss them with management, and propose recommendations and suitable remedial measures to improve the functions of the auditee (Ali et al., 2022). According to Ali et al. (2022), accountants and auditors must be trained for AI use and be familiar with its latest developments for use in their functions. To secure and protect users, new laws and regulations must be published to govern the use of AI in internal audits.

Within IAIs' facilities, a thorough systems analysis is required to identify the organisational, compliance, and technological shortcomings impeding success. Making informed decisions about what to prioritise purchasing and setting up will enable internal auditors to achieve the desired levels of technology adoption impact. This will guarantee that IT goals are in line with overall organisational goals.

11.7 CONCLUSION

The public sector will benefit from implementing AI by receiving better services, more efficient resource allocation, and improved decision-making. However, a comprehensive strategy that considers AI training, digital culture, data collection platforms, cybersecurity risks, policy and guidelines, governance, and responsible leadership is needed to fully enjoy these advantages. Governments must invest in these areas to guarantee that AI is utilised ethically, transparently, and responsibly to serve the public interest. By addressing these crucial factors, governments can fully utilise AI while mitigating potential risks and ensuring public confidence in AI-enabled systems.

Auditors' roles must change for technological innovation to coexist with a shift in culture and society. A digital culture may impact how quickly auditors adopt new technology. Internal audit institutions should be digitally transformed and have tech-savvy auditors, even though the auditee's IT environment may need to be more cutting-edge and up-to-date to support data analytics. An organisation must undergo a digital transformation in order to adopt new technology. Digital transformation involves societal adjustments and giving people the tools to adopt new technologies. A digital technology strategy related to people, processes, and implementation plans is also called digitisation. The impact of culture, tech-savvy auditors, AI governance, and support from leadership is crucial for AI sustainability in the public sector. Internal auditors must set a high standard by aggressively demonstrating that early adopters and leaders experiment with cutting-edge items and concepts to enhance their work.

The potential of AI is maximised, and sustainability is promoted in public internal auditing when implemented responsibly. Public sector organisations need to establish comprehensive frameworks for AI governance that consider accountability, transparency, and fairness. AI audits need human oversight and expertise to address complex ethical issues and ensure regulatory compliance (Gladwin et al., 2019).

REFERENCES

Abdel-Basset, M., Chang, V., & Gaber, S., 2021. Intelligent decision support system for sustainable supply chain management: A survey. *Journal of Cleaner Production, 280*, 124330.

AFROSAI-E, 2022. WGISAM meeting focused on SAIs becoming data-driven. https://afrosai-e.org.za/2022/10/26/wgisam-meeting-focused-on-sais-becoming-data-driven/. Accessed 13 February 2023.

Ahmad, N., Tarek Amer, N., Qutaifan, F., & Alhilali, A., 2013. Technology adoption model and a road map to successful implementation of ITIL. *Journal of Enterprise Information Management, 26*(5), 553–576.

Ali, M.M., Abdullah, A.S., & Khattab, G.S., 2022. The effect of activating artificial intelligence techniques on enhancing internal auditing activities "field study". *Alexandria Journal of Accounting Research, 6*(3), 1–40.

AlKhoori, I., 2022. A Critical Review of Change Management and Technology Adoption Factors to Drive Organisational Performance: A Study of the Abu Dhabi National Oil Company (ADNOC). *PQDT-Global* (Doctoral thesis, Liverpool John Moores University).

Anderson, S.L., 2008. Asimov's "three laws of robotics" and machine metaethics. *AI & Society, 22*(4), 477–493.

Andersson, P., Movin, S., Mähring, M., Teigland, R., & Wennberg, K., 2018. Managing digital transformation. *Stockholm School of Economics Institute for Research (SIR)*. www.hhs.se/contentassets/a3083bb76c384052b3f3f4c82236e38f/managing-digitaltransformation-med-omslag.pdf.

Awuah, B., Onumah, J.M., & Duho, K.C.T., 2021. "Information Technology Adoption within Internal Auditing in Ghana: Empirical Analysis", *Dataking Working Paper Series N° WP2021-04-04*, Available at SSRN: https://ssrn.com/abstract=3824403.

Bansal, P., Bertels, S., Ewart, T., MacInnis, D., & Singh, N., 2022. Harnessing the power of artificial intelligence to improve sustainability. *Journal of Business Ethics, 183*(4), 587–611.

Berghaus, S., Back, A., & Kaltenrieder, B., 2017. Digital maturity and transformation report 2017. St. Gallen. https://officeroxx.de/wp-content/uploads/2019/01/digital-maturity-transformation-report-2017.pdf.

Bonsón, E., & Bednárová, M., 2019. Blockchain and its implications for accounting and auditing. *Meditari Accountancy Research, 27*(5), 725–740.

Brown-Liburd, H., Issa, H., & Lombardi, D., 2015. Behavioral implications of Big Data's impact on audit judgment and decision making and future research directions. *Accounting Horizons, 29*(2), 451–468.

Byrnes, P.E., Al-Awadhi, A., Gullvist, B., Brown-Liburd, H., Teeter, R., Warren Jr, J. D., & Vasarhelyi, M., 2018. Evolution of auditing: From the traditional approach to the future audit. In Chan, D.Y, Chiu, V, and Vasarhelyi, M.A. (Eds.),*Continuous Auditing: Theory and Application* (pp. 285–297). Emerald Publishing Limited, Bingley, UK.

Ceki, B., 2019. Re-purposing audit assurance: The techno-economic implications of blockchain for auditor-client engagements. *International Conference of Accounting and Business 2019*. South Africa: Johannesburg, pp. 30–31. July 2019.

Cobey, C., Strier, K., & Boillet, J., 2018. How do you teach AI the value of trust? Retrieved August 15, 2019 from www.ey.com/en_gl/digital/how-do-you-teach-ai-the-value-of-trust.

Craig, R., Amernic, J., & Tourish, D., 2014. Perverse audit culture and accountability of the modern public university. *Financial Accountability and Management*, *30*(1), 1–24

Eggers, W.D., & Bellman, J., 2015. The journey to government's digital transformation. www2.deloi tte.com/content/dam/insights/us/articles/digital-transformation-in-government/DUP_1081_Jour ney-to-govt-digital-future_MASTER.pdf. Accessed 11 October 2022.

Gladwin, R., Ji, S., & Li, J., 2019. Achieving sustainability in the era of big data analytics: Challenges and opportunities. *Journal of Cleaner Production*, *242*, 117866.

Hagendorff, T., 2020. The ethics of AI ethics: An evaluation of guidelines. *Minds and Machines*, *30*, 99–120.

Hess, T., Matt, C., Benlian, A., & Wiesböck, F., 2016. Options for formulating a digital transform-ation strategy. *MIS Quarterly Executive*, *15*(2), 123–139.

HLEG, A., 2018. Ethics guidelines for trustworthy AI. Retrieved November 16, 2019 from www. euractiv.com/wp-content/uploads/sites/2/2018/12/AIHLEGDraftAIEthicsGuidelinespdf.pdf.

Hoffman, K.M., & Zuckerman, P., 2019. Artificial intelligence in audit: Opportunities and challenges. *Journal of Accounting Literature*, *42*, 23–44.

Huang, M.H., & Rust, R.T., 2018. Artificial intelligence in service. *Journal of Service Research*, *21*(2), 155–172.

INTOSAI Working Group on Big Data, 2022. Development overview of big data audits performed by supreme audit institutions from 2016–2021. www.audit.gov.cn/en/n749/c10296921/part/ 10296937.pdf. Accessed 15 February 2023.

INTOSAI Working Group on IT Audit, 2019. *Data Analysis Guideline*. Vienna: INTOSAI.

INTOSAI, 2021. 25th UN/INTOSAI symposium report. Available at www.intosai.org/fileadmin/ downloads/news_centre/events/un_int_symposia/reports_un_int_symp/en/EN_25_Symp_2021_ report.pdf. Accessed 8 March 2023.

I-SCOOP, 2016. Digital transformation: Online guide to digital business transformation. Available at: www.i-scoop.eu/. Accessed 20 June 2022.

Kamal, M., & Nandi, G., 2021. Governance of artificial intelligence for sustainability in the era of digital transformation. *Sustainable Development*, *29*(2), 238–247.

Kraus, S., Jones, P., Kailer, N., Weinmann, A., Chaparro-Banegas, N., & Roig-Tierno, N., 2021. Digital transformation: An overview of the current state of the art of research. *SAGE Open*, *11*(3), 1–15. http://journals.sagepub.com/doi/10.1177/21582440211047576.

Manita, R., Elommal, N., Baudier, P., & Hikkerova, L., 2020. The digital transformation of external audit and its impact on corporate governance. *Technological Forecasting and Social Change*, *150*, 119751.

Microsoft, 2019. Speech services for telephony data. Retrieved August 17, 2019 from https://docs. microsoft.com/en-us/azure/cognitive-services/speech-service/call-center-transcription

Mishra, S., Poudel, S., & Kweka, I.T., 2023. Artificial intelligence in public internal auditing: A sys-tematic review. *International Journal of Auditing*, *27*(1), 80–101.

Mohan, N., Dash, M., & Pandey, M., 2022. A conceptual framework for the application of artificial intelligence in public auditing. *Journal of Government Information Quarterly*, *39*(1), 101665.

Mullins, L.J., 2005. *Management and Organisational Behavior*. Harlow, England; New York: Prentice Hall/Financial Times.

Munoko, I., Brown-Liburd, H.L., & Vasarhelyi, M., 2020. The ethical implications of using artificial intelligence in auditing. *Journal of Business Ethics*, *167*, 209–234. https://doi.org/10.1007/s10 551-019-04407-1.

NAO, 2019. Applying data analytics to performance and financial audit: The NAO experience. https://bit.ly/4bc5n7E.

OED Online, 2019. Artificial intelligence. Oxford University Press. Retrieved August 15, 2019 from www.oed.com/view/Entry/271625?redirectedFrom=artificial+intelligence.

Otia, J.E., & Bracci, E., 2022. Digital transformation and the public sector auditing: The SAI's per-spective. *Financial Accountability & Management*, *38*(2), 252–280.

Owen, R., Stilgoe, J., Macnaghten, P., Gorman, M., Fisher, E., & Guston, D., 2013. A framework for responsible innovation. In Owen, R., Bessant, J.R. and Heintz, M. (Eds.), *Responsible Innovation: Managing the Responsible Emergence of Science and Innovation in Society* (pp. 27–50). ProQuest Ebook Central, Ann Arbor, Michigan.

Parasuraman, R., & Manzey, D.H., 2010. Complacency and bias in human use of automation: An attentional integration. *Human Factors*, 32(3), 381–410.

Plumlee, D.R., Rixom, B.A., & Rosman, A.J., 2015. Training auditors to perform analytical procedures using metacognitive skills. *The Accounting Review*, 90(1), 351–369.

Puthukulam, G., Ravikumar, A., Sharma, R.V.K., & Meesaala, K.M., 2021. Auditors' Perception on the Impact of Artificial Intelligence on Professional Skepticism and Judgment in Oman. *Universal Journal of Accounting and Finance*, 9(5), 1184–1190.

PwC, 2017. Sizing the prize what's the real value of AI for your business and how can you capitalise? Retrieved August 15, 2019 from www.pwc.com/gx/en/issues/analytics/assets/pwc-ai-analysis-sizing-the-prize-report.pdf.

Rojas, A., & Tuomi, A., 2022. Reimagining the sustainable social development of AI for the service sector: The role of startups. *Journal of Ethics in Entrepreneurship and Technology*, 2(1), 39–54.

Salleh, N.A., Abdul Rahim, A.N., & Jusoh, A., 2021. Artificial intelligence in auditing: A systematic review. *Journal of Accounting Literature*, 45, 100609.

Samek, W., Wiegand, T., & Müller, K.R., 2017. Explainable artificial intelligence: Understanding, visualizing and interpreting deep learning models. Retrieved November 23, 2019 from https://arxiv.org/pdf/1708.08296.pdf.

Schiff, D., Rakova, B., Ayesh, A., Fanti, A., & Lennon, M., 2020. Principles to practices for responsible AI: Closing the gap. arXiv:2006.04707.

Schlaepfer, R., Von Radowitz, K., Koch, M., & Merkofer, P., 2017. Digital future-readiness – How do companies prepare for the opportunities and challenges of digitalization? Available at: www2.deloitte.com/content/dam/Deloitte/ch/Documents/consumerbusiness/ch-cip-en-swiss-transformation.pdf. Accessed 1 April 2022.

Schmitz, J., & Leoni, G., 2019. Accounting and auditing at the time of blockchain technology: A research agenda. *Australian Accounting Review*, 29(2), 331–342.

Seow, P.S., 2011. The effects of decision aid structural restrictiveness on decision-making outcomes. *International Journal of Accounting Information Systems*, 12(1), 40–56.

Shaw, J., 2019. Artificial intelligence and ethics: Ethics and the dawn of decision-making machines. Retrieved August 18, 2019 from https://harvardmagazine.com/2019/01/artificial-intelligence-limitations.

Soltani, Z., Naude, P., & Govender, K., 2022. The impact of artificial intelligence on internal audit work: Perspectives from practitioners. *International Journal of Accounting Information Systems*, 40, 101202.

Specht, L., Trotter, R., Young, R., & Sutton, S.,1991. The public accounting litigation wars: Will expert systems lead the next assault. *Jurimetrics*, 31, 247–257.

Sprigman, C.J., 2018. Will algorithms take the fairness out of fair use? Retrieved August 15, 2019 from https://heinonline.org/HOL/LandingPage?handle=hein.journals/jotwell2018.

Stahl, B.C., Timmermans, J., & Flick, C., 2017. Ethics of emerging information and communication technologies: On the implementation of responsible research and innovation. *Science and Public Policy*, 44(3), 369–381.

The Stanford Human-Centered AI Initiative (HAI), 2018, Introducing Stanford's human-centered AI initiative, available at: https://hai.stanford.edu/blog/introducing-stanfords-human-centered-ai-initiative. Accessed 1 October 2023.

Verma, S., Singh, R.K., & Dey, N., 2021. Artificial intelligence in auditing: A review and future research directions. *Journal of Accounting Literature*, 47, 101586.

Wachter, S., & Mittelstadt, B., 2019. A right to reasonable inferences: Re-thinking data protection law in the age of big data and AI. *Columbia Business Law Review*.

Wang, D., Kung, L., Byrd, T.A., & Dang, Y., 2020. Artificial intelligence in auditing: A meta-analysis of empirical research. *International Journal of Accounting Information Systems*, *38*, 100526.

Widuri, R., Ferdiansyah, I., & Kongchan, P., 2021. The influence of culture, technology, organization and environment on the adoption of computer assisted audit techniques. *PalArch's Journal of Archaeology of Egypt/Egyptology*, *18*(1), 494–504.

World Economic Forum, 2015. Deep shift technology tipping points and societal impact. Retrieved August 15, 2019 from www.weforum.org/reports/deep-shift-technology-tipping-points-and-societal-impact.

Wright, D., 2011. A framework for the ethical impact assessment of information technology. *Ethics and Information Technology*, *13*(3), 199–226.

Chapter 12

Conclusion and future research recommendations

Lourens J. Erasmus and Sezer Bozkuş Kahyaoğlu

12.1 INTRODUCTION

Consideration of the use of artificial intelligence applications in the public sector is increasing day by day, both by researchers in academia and by professionals working in practice. Although there are opportunities identified as a result of these considerations, there are also challenges that have yet to be resolved (Ngwenya and Kakunda, 2014; Okee and Fred, 2021). To solve these challenges and manage risks, it is necessary to review the conventional style of internal audit, internal control, and risk management activities in the public sector. Even to ensure their adaptation to this new era to understand artificial intelligence applications in the public sector correctly and at the same time to develop artificial intelligence implementation, governance, and auditing standards (Bozkuş Kahyaoğlu et al., 2020; Lehman and Thor, 2020).

When we say artificial intelligence, we relate all kinds of applications and machines that imitate human behaviour and thinking (Wirtz et al., 2019). Within this framework, it is observed that many applications have been implemented to train and direct machines, using algorithms. Artificial intelligence applications can increase efficiency and productivity in the public sphere with the construction of smart cities, the manufacturing of smart vehicles, and an approach based on optimising every application, to provide consistent and accurate data. Therefore, artificial intelligence applications are of strategic importance in the new era (Rogger et al., 2023).

When considering the aforementioned, it may be possible to make rapid progress in the field of artificial intelligence through the robust design and application of big data generation processes (GAO, 2021). These smart applications are sorely needed in the public sector due to the widening gap between citizen service expectations and the ability of governments to respond to them effectively and efficiently (OECD, 2019a, 2019b). While, on the one hand, service delivery by the public sector through digitalisation, automation, and robotic applications is becoming widespread, on the other hand, there are challenges, risks, and threats that come with using such systems and tools. It is of paramount importance to detect these challenges, risks, and threats in the public sector early and, at the same time, to support sustainable urbanisation by ensuring trust and stability with legal regulations, policies, and surveillance mechanisms. Needless to say, improving social services and support through the use of smart technology can be backed up by public sector internal auditing based on smart tools and techniques (Bozkuş Kahyaoğlu et al., 2020; Welby, 2019).

Considering the scale of the public sector and the importance of providing public services with scarce resources, significant developments in digitalisation have emerged, in particular artificial intelligence applications, and these developments are expected to occur

DOI: 10.1201/9781003382706-12

incrementally. Considering the range of services offered by the public sector, there is almost no field in which artificial intelligence cannot contribute, which means a huge opportunity to increase efficiency and effectiveness (GAO, 2021; OECD, 2019a). Therefore, it is not a coincidence that most states and governments around the world are renewing their public management policies and setting clear targets regarding artificial intelligence among their strategic goals (Lehman and Thor, 2020). However, it must be accepted that there are social and ethical problems in the digital transformation process. In this context, artificial intelligence projects must be orientated towards transparency, accountability, and social benefit. Despite everything, artificial intelligence applications in the public sector are still being implemented based on pilot projects. Hence, it is accepted that we are at the very beginning of the road. At this stage, there is a need to develop continuous auditing, continuous monitoring, internal audit, internal control, and risk management activities in the public sector to support the spread of artificial intelligence applications and to carry out projects following sustainable service standards (Welby et al., 2019).

Current research findings show that countries using artificial intelligence applications will experience a significant increase in their national income due to increased productivity. We started to hear news of new pioneering works every day in both the private and public sectors to support the workforce and reduce costs through digitalisation, automation, and smart systems. Especially the United States of Amerika (USA) and China, as the first countries to realise how important a tool artificial intelligence is, have initiated important developments in the public sector by making intense investments (GAO, 2021). As the most important example, we can show the preparations for the transition to an artificial intelligence-based education system (IIA, 2017; ISACA, 2018).

The structure of the concluding chapter is presented as follows. First, the lessons learnt from each chapter are given. Second, the research methodology and analysis approach in each chapter is explained. Third, policy recommendations and future research opportunities are presented to add value to the literature and internal auditing stakeholders in the public sector.

12.2 LESSONS LEARNT WITHIN THE SCOPE OF THE CHAPTERS

The chapters of the book are presented in a modular and complementary manner. The methodology and analysis approach used to present the information given in each chapter, its scope, and its contribution to the literature are briefly presented.

Chapter 1 is presented as an introduction to key terms and the major impact of artificial intelligence on the public sector digitalisation process and the public sector internal auditing structure. The scope and aim of the work are explained based on the relevant literature. In this context, the major topics and their value-added points are presented and discussed in subsequent chapters.

Chapter 2 explains artificial intelligence from a historical perspective and provides a context of how accounting and auditing can take advantage of the use of emerging technology. Most importantly, the impact of artificial intelligence on the accounting and auditing practice using literature is presented. The subject of artificial intelligence is closely related to accounting, finance, and auditing as an interdisciplinary field. In this context, the effects of new approaches and developments in the literature are discussed from a strategic perspective. The interacting areas and applications that can guide the future are explained, and background information is provided. This chapter is structured in such a way as to establish strong background information which is critical to understanding the chapters that follow.

Chapter 3 gives an overview of blockchain technology and its possible integration with other applications of artificial intelligence relevant to the public sector. The integration of blockchain with machine learning, smart contracts, the Internet of things, the Internet of services, robotic process automation, intelligent process automation, and data analytics to enhance access to information, performance, and functionality is also discussed. Audit activities are affected by many factors. The most important of these is technology. Technological developments and especially strategically important innovations accelerate the development of new tools and techniques for auditing. In this chapter, blockchain applications in accounting are discussed that support the core values of auditing and facilitate the implementation of international auditing standards. It should be noted that the evaluations and the effects of blockchain-based accounting systems on auditing are explained at the base of the public sector.

Chapter 4 focusses on how innovations in the world affect developments in audit activities and audit ecosystems. The position of the public audit ecosystem among the different ecosystems that emerged with the effect of digitalisation is evaluated. In particular, the definition of the audit ecosystem is made, and how the audit innovations cause effects is explained with a broad perspective. Thus, the main aspects that can add value to public sector auditing are presented to professionals and stakeholders in the digital era. Depending on technological developments, the structure of the audit ecosystem is changing, and it is necessary to support it with a comprehensive digitalisation strategy. Public sector audit innovation examples are determined on the basis of different countries' best practices. These cases are analysed and the benefits and future challenges are explained. Especially in the public sector, the strategic interaction areas that the innovations in the audit ecosystem can cause are examined, and policy recommendations are presented.

Chapter 5 explains the emerging field of algorithmic auditing in the public sector, focussing on the continuous auditing of algorithms and artificial intelligence systems, and hence, what should be understood from the fact that the audit is carried out by algorithms. Looking at the literature: While digital audit and digital audit reporting are among the topics discussed recently, auditing based on algorithms is becoming a basic need at this point. Key definitions and concepts related to algorithms are explained from the perspective of public sector auditing. Accordingly, the basic features of algorithmic auditing are explained, and it is emphasised how the expected public sector auditing can change with the effect of algorithms with the acceleration of artificial intelligence applications in the future. In this regard, policy recommendations are proposed, and discussions are made about the areas of need.

Chapter 6 focusses on how the organisational structure of public sector-specific internal auditing should be in the future. Significant changes occur in the context of the audit structure in the public sector and the characteristics that auditors should have. In e-Government, which is implemented in relation to the strategic goals and objectives in the public sector, basic recommendations are presented for public internal auditors to maintain their existence in the physical and virtual environment effectively and not to lose their "trusted advisor" role. Application examples are given based on the Lenz and Jeppesen 5Ps model (planet, public, prosperity, profession, and people) for an effective audit organisational structure in the public sector. A total of 16 focus areas and relevant proposed actions are explained based on relevant literature.

Chapter 7 emphasises the use of newly developed auditing tools based on artificial intelligence and analytical applications in audit activities. By integrating audit tools and techniques with audit reports, AI findings are presented more effectively, efficiently, and economically, based on new technological developments. The most concrete indicator of the effectiveness of audit activities is shaped by the quality of audit reports. Presenting information based on digitalisation, big data analysis, and audit analytics applications in audit reporting is gaining importance in the public sector. In this chapter, the usage areas of newly developed reporting tools based on artificial intelligence and analytical applications in audit activities are stressed. Different tools are analysed and information is given on their added value. It is a fact that by integrating audit tools and techniques with audit reports, the findings obtained through artificial intelligence are presented in a better quality, more effective, efficient, and economical way, based on new developments in technology.

Chapter 8 explains the needs of internal auditors due to digitalisation and technological developments and the new areas of development that they need to achieve in the public sector. In the age of artificial intelligence, there are significant changes in the basic skills that all internal auditors should have. The challenges, opportunities, and threats experienced in this process are revealed. Policy recommendations are presented on the scope and application areas of digital auditor competencies and digital skills in the context of the future public sector audit.

Chapter 9 examines the advantages and difficulties of adopting digital innovation and continuous auditing and continuous monitoring (CA/CM) programmes in the public sector. Advanced technology is necessary to establish an effective remote control mechanism such as CA/CM. In this chapter, the importance of the CA/CM infrastructure in the public sector is emphasised by introducing the remote control, audit, and risk management infrastructure that has developed with the implementation of new technologies based on artificial intelligence. Especially during the COVID-19 pandemic period, the advantages and development areas of CA/CM are stated based on the relevant literature. As an advanced auditing tool, CA/CM has gained strategic importance during the pandemic period. Discussions are presented as to whether this will continue in the future. In this context, policy recommendations are made and research on development areas is explained as relevant for public sector value-added auditing.

Chapter 10 explains ethical violations and conflict areas related to the abuse of artificial intelligence. Applications based on artificial intelligence provide very important benefits, and a long list can be prepared for the added value areas that artificial intelligence offers to the audit. However, as with many other issues, there may also be ethical problems that cause grey areas in this issue. This chapter explains what should be done so that auditors are not adversely affected by this situation when using artificial intelligence-based audit tools and techniques. In particular, the artificial intelligence-based application examples in the literature and ethical standards of artificial intelligence are examined. A discussion is presented on the measures to be taken to not impair the ethical compliance of digitalised auditing in the public sector.

Chapter 11 focusses on the impact of artificial intelligence and sustainability on public sector auditing. The concept of sustainability has entered every aspect of our daily lives, including audit activities. It explains what needs to be done to achieve the sustainability of AI-based audit activities. The main information and artificial intelligence-based application examples given in this chapter are presented from the perspective of public sector auditors. Essential information and policy recommendations are presented based on the relevant literature. In this way, the authors aim to increase the impact of artificial intelligence for sustainable public sector auditing to become widespread in the future.

12.3 THE RESEARCH METHODOLOGY AND ANALYSIS APPROACH OF CHAPTERS

In addition to the information provided in the book and the evaluations of the future of the auditing profession, the research methods and analysis approaches that form the basis for the preparation of all the topics included in this book are presented below in summary in Figure 12.1. In this way, our aim is to shed light and guide future research.

The authors of the respective chapters of this book were tasked with conducting a literature review as a basis for their contributions. This section provides information on the rigour of the review process followed for each of the chapters.

Chapter 2

A comprehensive and investigative review of the diverse and authoritative international literature was conducted through an explorative and descriptive analysis within a qualitative research approach. A literature search was conducted to identify relevant studies in various

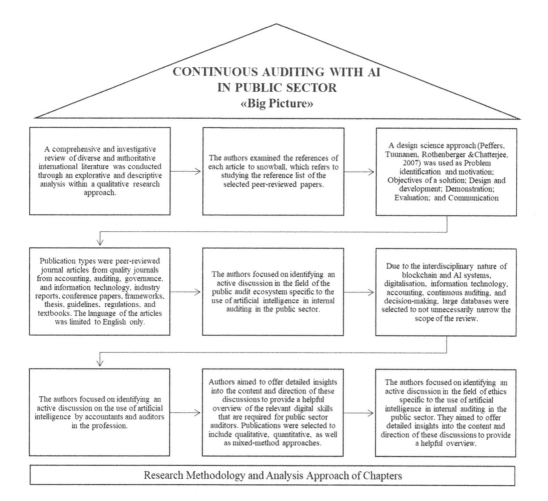

Figure 12.1 The research methodology and analysis approach of chapters.

Source: Prepared by the authors.

databases to obtain a detailed background on the origins of artificial intelligence. Articles and conference papers were searched via the Unisa Library databases and accredited journals, e.g., Google Scholar, Science Direct, Springer, Elsevier, IEEE Xplore Digital Library, LexisNexis, Wiley Online Library, Research Gate, Academia, Emerald Insight, Taylor & Francis Online, SAGE Journals, and IEEE Xplore. Keywords used included "artificial intelligence for auditors and accountants", "history of artificial intelligence", "definition of artificial intelligence", "benefits of artificial intelligence for auditors and accountants", and "AI practice in accounting and auditing", The language of the publications was restricted to English only.

The selected articles were chosen based on the perceived relevance of reading the title, abstract, and occasionally the introduction and conclusion of the article. The time frame selected was from the 1950s to 2023 (to date)—but in most cases, the selected results were from 2017 to 2023. There was a need to go back to the 1950s to understand the background history of artificial intelligence. Peer-reviewed articles were selected for the study.

The authors focused on identifying an active discussion on the use of artificial intelligence by accountants and auditors in the profession. They aimed to provide detailed insights into the content and direction of discussions around how modern accountants and auditors are using the latest AI tools to execute their daily activities. Most importantly, we must understand the true and original definitions of artificial intelligence as we have come to know it today. The publications were selected to include qualitative, quantitative, and mixed method approaches.

Chapter 3

A comprehensive and integrative review of the diverse and authoritative international literature was carried out through an explorative and descriptive analysis within a qualitative research approach. An integrative literature review involves synthesising and analysing existing "representative literature on a particular topic to identify patterns, themes and gaps in knowledge literature in an integrated way such that new perspectives on the topic are generated" (Torraco, 2005:356).

Due to the interdisciplinary nature of blockchain and AI systems, digitalisation, information technology, accounting, continuous auditing, and decision-making, large databases were selected to not unnecessarily narrow the scope of the review. Articles and conference papers were searched via the Unisa Library databases and accredited journals, e.g., Google Scholar, Science Direct, Springer, Elsevier, IEEE Xplore Digital Library, LexisNexis, Wiley Online Library, Research Gate, Academia, Emerald Insight, Taylor & Francis Online, SAGE Journals, and IEEE Xplore. Due to the technical perspectives on AI and algorithmic decision-making and the development of continuous auditing of AI and algorithmic systems, online articles, annual reports, guidelines, and publications from professional bodies (e.g., IIA, ISO, COSO), regulators, institutes (e.g., AI Now Institute), auditing firms, WEF, UN, OECD, media, and business publications were searched.

Themes, concepts, and patterns from the literature were identified as relevant to the study topic and then categorised according to the outline of the chapter. Data were critically analysed and synthesised, using content analysis as a descriptive approach and tool for interpretation within document analysis (Bowen, 2009). ATLAS.ti™ was used to search the keywords in the identified literature to ensure that all relevant literature was included.

The reference lists in the collected articles were examined for additional references to authoritative articles. The relevance and reliability of the literature being consulted were evaluated to meet the quality criteria standards for qualitative research. Sources were limited to publications in the last ten years (2013–2023), except for seminal authors and authoritative publications. Keywords that were searched as a starting point for the literature review were, i.e., "blockchain" and "accounting automation". Keywords digitalisation, AI, robotics, digital economy, public sector accounting, continuous auditing, automated decision-making, Internet of things (IoT), big data, transparency, and governance were added during the next phase of the database search. Alternative forms and synonyms of the words were included in the search. Abstracts were evaluated for relevance to the research topic. The language of the publications was restricted to English only. The types of publications were peer-reviewed journal articles from quality journals from accounting, auditing, governance, and information technology; industry reports, conference papers, frameworks, theses, guidelines, regulations, and textbooks.

Chapter 4

The review of Chapter 4 consisted of search, selection, analysis, and synthesis processes. The databases accessed were EBSCOhost, Emerald Insight, IEEE/IET Electronic Library (Conference Papers), Sabinet Discovery, Sage Journals, ScienceDirect, SpringerLink, Taylor & Francis, and Wiley Online Library. EBSCOhost has a Discovery Service where most of the databases subscribed to by an institution are included, which is why the other databases are listed, as articles from these databases would have been automatically included in the searches, where possible duplicates would have occurred, i.e., the article may have been indexed both on EBSCOhost and another database.

The authors focused on identifying an active discussion in the field of the public audit ecosystem specific to the use of artificial intelligence in internal auditing in the public sector. The aim of the authors was to provide detailed insights into the content and direction of these discussions to provide a helpful overview. Publications were selected to include qualitative, quantitative, and mixed method approaches, where all publications have the following terms, either in the title, abstract, keywords, or body of the article: public audit ecosystem; public auditing ecosystem; innovation and public sector audit ecosystem; innovation and public sector; public audit(ing) ecosystem or public audit and innovation(s); public audit(ing) ecosystem or public audit and transformation(s); public audit(ing) ecosystem or public audit and reorganisation or reorganisation; public audit(ing) ecosystem or public audit and change or alteration; public sector auditing and change or alteration; public sector audit(ing) and innovation(s); public sector auditor auditing and transformation; public sector audit(ing) and reorganisation/reorganisation; public audit ecosystem(s) and government agencies/departments/sectors; public audit system(s) and government agencies/departments/sectors; public audit(s)and government agencies/departments/sectors; public audit ecosystem(s) and regulators/regulatory bodies/entities; public audit system(s) and regulators/regulatory bodies; public audit ecosystem(s)and standards-setting bodies/entities; public audit system(s) and standards-setting bodies/entities; public audit ecosystem(s) and the public/people/citizens/residents/community(ies); public audit system(s) and the public/people/citizens/residents/community(ies); IA digitalisation/digitalisation or internal audit digitalisation/digitalisation; new audit reporting tools and AI/artificial intelligence and public sector; new audit reporting tools and AI/artificial intelligence and municipalities/municipal sector; audit reporting software/tools and AI/artificial intelligence and public sector/municipalities; audit(ing) software/programmes/programmes and AI/artificial intelligence and public sector/municipalities/government departments; new audit(ing) tools; auditing tools or audit software; internal audit(ing) tools/software and public sector/municipalities; impact of AI and sustainability and public internal audit or auditing; AI/artificial intelligence and sustainability and public internal audit(ing); AI/artificial intelligence and viability and public internal audit(ing); AI/artificial intelligence and continuity and public internal audit(ing); AI/artificial intelligence and maintainable systems and public internal audit(ing); E-Government(s)/digital government(s)/online government(s)/ electronic government(s) and United Arab Emirates or UAE; E-Government(s)/digital government(s)/online government(s)/electronic government(s) and Dubai; E-Government(s)/ digital government(s)/online government(s)/electronic government(s) and Singapore; E-Government(s)/digital government(s)/online government(s)/electronic government(s) and Cyprus; E-Government(s)/digital government(s)/online government(s)/electronic government(s) and USA or United States or United States of America or America; E-Government(s)/digital government(s)/online government(s)/electronic government(s) and Europe/European countries/European Union/EU; audit data analytics maturity framework or frameworks; artificial intelligence/AI maturity framework(s) /system(s)/structure(s)/organisation/organisation; internal audit reports/reporting and hindsight; internal audit reports/ reporting and insight; internal audit reports/reporting and foresight; internal audit reports/ reporting and predictive or envisioning; AI/artificial intelligence and policy/policies; AI and schedules/guidelines/systems/strategies/plans; artificial intelligence and schedules/guidelines/ systems/strategies/plans; AI/artificial intelligence and policy regulation(s)/mandate(s)/law(s)/ directive(s)/ruling(s)/dictate(s) and policy controls; AI/artificial intelligence and policy recommendations or advice—additional searches were conducted using these search terms, then adding the following countries to the search string: EU, European Union, European countries, UK, United Kingdom, England, Ireland, Wales, Scotland, US, United States, United States of America, America, North America, Brazil, Egypt, India, Mauritius, and South Africa; AI/artificial intelligence implementation/use/usage/application/employment/ practice; AI/artificial intelligence implementation/use/usage/application/employment/practice in business; AI/artificial intelligence implementation/use/usage/application/employment/ practice in audit(ing(/internal audit(ing)/external audit(ing); AI/artificial intelligence implementation best practices; AI/artificial intelligence implementation success stories; AI/artificial intelligence and successful practices.

Note that Google Scholar, ResearchGate, and Academia were occasionally used to access the full text of a peer-reviewed article where the full text was not available in the research database. The selected articles were chosen based on the perceived relevance of reading the title, abstract, and occasionally the introduction and conclusion of the article. The selected time frame was from January 2017 to 2023 (to date)—the last six years, but in most cases, the selected results were 2020–2023. Peer-reviewed articles were selected.

Chapter 5

A comprehensive and integrative review of the diverse and authoritative international literature was carried out through an explorative and descriptive analysis within a qualitative research approach. An integrative literature review involves synthesising and analysing existing "representative literature on a particular topic to identify patterns, themes, and gaps in knowledge literature in an integrated way such that new perspectives on the topic are generated" (Torraco, 2005:356).

Due to the interdisciplinary nature of artificial intelligence (AI) and AI systems, continuous auditing, algorithmic audits, and decision-making, large databases were selected to not unnecessarily narrow the scope of the review. Articles and conference papers were searched via the Unisa Library databases and accredited journals, e.g., Google Scholar, Science Direct, Springer, Elsevier, IEEE Xplore Digital Library, LexisNexis, Wiley Online Library, Research Gate, Academia, Emerald Insight, Taylor & Francis Online, SAGE Journals, and IEEE Xplore. Due to the technical perspectives on AI and algorithmic decision-making and the development of continuous auditing of AI and algorithmic systems, online articles, annual reports, guidelines, and publications from professional bodies (e.g., IIA, ISO, COSO), regulators, institutes (e.g., AI Now Institute), auditing firms, WEF, UN, OECD, media, and business publications were searched.

Themes, concepts, and patterns were identified from the literature relevant to the study topic and then categorised according to the outline of the chapter. Data were critically analysed and synthesised, using content analysis as a descriptive approach and tool for interpretation within document analysis (Bowen, 2009). ATLAS.ti™ was used to search the keywords in the identified literature to ensure that all relevant literature was included.

The reference lists in the collected articles were examined for additional references to authoritative articles. The relevance and reliability of the literature being consulted were evaluated to meet the quality criteria standards for qualitative research. The period of publication was limited to publications published within the last ten years (2013–2023), except for seminal authors and authoritative publications. Keywords that were searched as a starting point for the literature review were, i.e., "continuous auditing", "artificial intelligence (AI)", and "algorithmic audits". Keywords digitalisation, accountability, public sector, automated decision-making, transparency, and governance were added during the next phase of the database search. Alternative forms, for example, "algorithm audits", and synonyms of the words were included in the search. Abstracts were evaluated for relevance to the research topic. The language of the articles was limited to English only. The types of publications were peer-reviewed journal articles from quality journals of accounting, auditing, governance and information technology, industry reports, conference papers, frameworks, theses, guidelines, regulations, and textbooks.

Chapter 6

The author followed a design science approach (Peffers, Tuunanen, Rothenberger & Chatterjee, 2007). It consists of six stages (problem identification and motivation; objectives of a solution; design and development; demonstration; evaluation; and communication). However, only four stages of design science were used, and as the chapter is nonempirical research, the demonstration and evaluation stages were not considered. The first step was to identify the motivation of the study, which was to understand the organisational needs and future expectations of public sector internal auditors and to recommend the future organisational structure to ensure internal audit position itself in the era of big data and technology. The second stage was to define the objectives of a solution, which was to identify and review the existing literature on the organisational needs and future expectations of public sector internal auditors and make recommendations. The third stage was to design and develop a solution. Review of the literature: In this stage, a literature search was conducted to identify relevant studies in various databases, government reports, and publications by professional associations related to the title. Theoretical framework: Factors that affect organisational needs and future expectations of public sector internal auditors were identified from the literature. These factors were used as input to close the gap and identify opportunities for improvement. Develop a solution: Lenz and Jeppesen (2022) 5Ps model identified from the literature was used as a foundation to identify relevant focus areas that internal auditing should consider. The 5Ps (planet, public, prosperity, profession, and people) were expanded to include various focus areas and proposed actions. The fourth stage was to communicate the solution: This was done in a table and graphic format.

Little literature was found that focused specifically on the "future internal audit needs". Therefore, searches had to be done using a combination of keywords to find relevant literature to review. However, many publications are available from professional associations on the topic. The following databases were used to search for articles: Scopus; ProQuest Central; EBSCOhost; Emerald Insight; IEEE/IET Electronic Library; Google Scholar; Publications: IIA-Research Foundation & Public Sector Knowledge Centre, World Economic Forum, KPMG. PwC. Deloitte, EY; Government documents. Criteria for inclusion were peer-reviewed, full text, period: 2000–2023, language: English. Keywords were public internal auditing; public sector internal auditing; public internal in the public sector; public sector + internal audit; "Public Sector" AND "Internal Auditing"; government AND internal auditing; internal auditing AND public sector or government; public sector AND internal auditing AND governance; public sector AND internal auditing AND regulation; public sector AND internal auditing AND risk management; public sector AND internal auditing AND internal control; public sector AND internal auditing AND information technology; public sector AND internal auditing AND competencies; public sector AND internal auditing AND skills; public sector AND internal auditing AND sustainability; public sector AND internal auditing AND effectiveness; public sector AND internal auditing AND independence; public sector AND internal auditing AND objectivity.

Chapter 7

Studies carried out primarily between 2012 and 2023 and written in English were considered. Scientific search engines collected data from papers and books on the adoption of public sector audit technology for internal auditing and reporting. The search engines used to collect articles and books for review were Google Scholar, Science Direct ProQuest, EBSCOhost, OpenAthens, International Organisation of Supreme Audit Institutions (INTOSAI), and African Organisation of English-Speaking Supreme Audit Institutions (AFROSAI-e) websites and documents. Keywords used to search for the articles were technology adoption in auditing, artificial intelligence in auditing, AI audit reporting, public sector auditing, and AI audit technologies.

The author examined the references of each article to snowball, which refers to studying the reference list of the selected peer-reviewed papers. The articles analysed were chosen on the basis of the following criteria. Articles about the benefits, acceptance, and adoption of 4IR technologies, such as natural language processing, artificial intelligence, information technology adoption, internal auditors' preparation for AI audit technologies adoption, and robotic processing automation, were considered in a public auditing setting for audit reporting and effectiveness.

Chapter 8

A comprehensive and investigative review of the diverse and authoritative international literature was conducted through an explorative and descriptive analysis within a qualitative research approach. Articles and conference papers were searched via the Unisa Library databases and accredited journals, e.g., Google Scholar, Science Direct, Springer, Elsevier, IEEE Xplore Digital Library, LexisNexis, Wiley Online Library, Research Gate, Academia, Emerald Insight, Taylor & Francis Online, SAGE Journals, and IEEE Xplore. Keywords used included "digital skills for auditors", "IT skills for auditors", "4IR skills of auditors", "IT competency framework for auditors", and "IT knowledge of auditors". The language of the publications was restricted to English only.

The selected articles were chosen based on the perceived relevance of reading the title, abstract, and occasionally the introduction and conclusion of the article. The selected time frame was from January 2017 to 2023 (to date)—the last six years, but in most cases, the selected results were from 2020 to 2023. Peer-reviewed articles were selected. Online research articles, annual reports, guidelines, and publications from professional bodies such as IIA, ISO, COSO, ISACA, and IFAC were searched.

The authors focused on identifying an active discussion in the field of IT skills of auditors in the public sector. They aimed to provide detailed insights into the content and direction of these discussions to provide a helpful overview of the relevant digital skills that are required for public sector auditors. The publications were selected to include qualitative, quantitative, and mixed method approaches.

Chapter 9

To compile a comprehensive literature review on continuous auditing and continuous monitoring (CA/CM) in the public sector, a systematic and thorough methodology was employed. In particular, the process involved accessing a diverse range of reputable academic sources and scholarly articles to ensure a well-rounded understanding of the subject matter. Initially, the exploration began by searching various academic databases, including, but not limited to, ResearchGate, ACM Digital Library, and reputable journals in the field of auditing, risk management, and technology adoption in the public sector.

Keywords such as "Continuous Auditing", "Continuous Monitoring", "Digital Innovation in Auditing", and "Public Sector Implementation Challenges" were utilised to identify relevant studies. Selection criteria were applied to choose articles that specifically focused on the integration of CA/CM in the public sector, considering the evolution of digital innovation and the challenges faced by governmental organisations. Only recent peer-reviewed articles were included to ensure the incorporation of the latest insights and developments.

The selected literature was subjected to a critical analysis, dissecting key concepts, methodologies, findings, and implications presented in each source. Attention was paid to distinguishing between traditional auditing methods and the transformative impact of digital innovation, particularly focussing on the role of AI-based technologies. Ideally, to enhance clarity and coherence, the collected information was organised thematically. This involved categorising the literature into subtopics such as the significance of digital innovation, challenges faced in public sector adoption, and the crucial role of AI and real-time monitoring.

To provide a holistic view, various perspectives from different authors were integrated, where this approach ensured that the literature review reflects a comprehensive understanding of the subject matter, incorporating insights from academic researchers and industry practitioners. The methodology extended beyond academic discourse to include literature that addresses policy implications and practical insights for the successful implementation of CA/CM in the public sector. This incorporation aimed to offer actionable recommendations to practitioners and policy makers.

This methodology ensured a thorough exploration of the evolving landscape of continuous auditing and monitoring in the public sector, leveraging digital innovation. The careful selection, critical analysis, and thematic organisation of the literature facilitated the creation of a detailed and informed review of the literature on the subject.

Chapter 10

The review consisted of search, selection, analysis, and synthesis processes. The databases used for the search were EBSCOhost, Emerald Insight, IEEE/IET Electronic Library (Conference Papers), Sabinet Discovery, Sage Journals, ScienceDirect, SpringerLink, Taylor & Francis, and Wiley Online Library. EBSCOhost has a Discovery Service where most of the databases subscribed to by an institution are included, which is why the other databases are listed, as articles from these databases would have been automatically included in the searches, where possible duplicates would have occurred, i.e., the article may have been indexed both on EBSCOhost and another database.

The authors focus on identifying an active discussion in the field of ethics specific to the use of artificial intelligence in internal auditing in the public sector. The aim of the authors was to provide detailed insights into the content and direction of these discussions to provide a helpful overview. The authors selected articles that include qualitative, quantitative, and mixed methods approaches, where all articles have the following terms, either in the title, abstract, keywords, or body of the paper. Note that Google Scholar, ResearchGate, and Academia were occasionally used to access the full text of a peer-reviewed article where the full text was not available in the research database. The selected articles were chosen based on the perceived relevance of reading the title, abstract, and occasionally the introduction and conclusion of the article. The selected time frame was from January 2017 to 2023 (to date)—the last six years, but in most cases, the selected results were from 2020 to 2023. Peer-reviewed articles were selected. The following search terms were used: Ethical perspective(s) or ethics and digital audit(ing) and public sector/government sector; ethical concerns and digital auditing and public sector/government sector/municipalities; ethical behaviour/behaviour and digital audit(ing) and public sector/government; departments/municipalities; ethical implications and digital audit(ing) and public sector/government sector/municipalities; ethics and digital audit(ing) and public sector/government sector/municipalities; ethics and new digital audit(ing) technology and public sector/government sector/municipalities.

Chapter 11
Studies carried out primarily between 2012 and 2023 and written in English were considered. Scientific search engines collected data from papers and books on the adoption of public sector audit technology for internal auditing and reporting. The search engines used to collect articles and books for review were Google Scholar, Science Direct ProQuest, EBSCOhost, OpenAthens, International Organisation of Supreme Audit Institutions (INTOSAI), and African Organisation of English-Speaking Supreme Audit Institutions (AFROSAI-e) websites and documents. Keywords used to search for the articles were technology adoption in auditing, artificial intelligence in auditing, AI audit reporting, public sector auditing, and AI audit technologies.

The author examined the references of each article to snowball, which refers to studying the reference list of the selected peer-reviewed papers. The articles analysed were chosen on the basis of the following criteria. Articles about the benefits, acceptance, and adoption of 4IR technologies, such as natural language processing, artificial intelligence, information technology adoption, internal auditors' preparation for AI audit technologies adoption, and robotic processing automation, were considered in a public auditing setting for audit reporting and effectiveness.

12.4 CONCLUDING REMARKS AND FUTURE RESEARCH RECOMMENDATIONS

The effectiveness of internal audit activities is important in terms of the sustainability of change in the public sector. In this sense, the tools and techniques used and the level of competencies of public sector auditors are decisive. This book deals with the effects of current technological developments in the public sector on auditing and risk management activities. Therefore, it is a resource for public internal auditors to create a digital audit strategy based on artificial intelligence applications. Institutionalisation of their own structures is important for public internal auditors, which is a critical position that ensures institutionalisation. For this, basic requirements, future expectations, and best practices are explained.

This book will be pioneering work based on CA/CM approaches using various AI tools and techniques. We hope that our colleagues who serve as internal auditors, internal controllers, risk managers, and academic staff will benefit from our book project. We hope to add value to the literature and contribute to all internal auditors and stakeholders in the public sector.

REFERENCES

Bowen, G.A. (2009), Document Analysis as a Qualitative Research Method. *Qualitative Research Journal*, Vol. 9 No. 2, pp. 27–40. https://doi.org/10.3316/QRJ0902027

Bozkuş Kahyaoğlu, S., Sarıkaya, R. & Topal, B. (2020). Continuous Auditing as a Strategic Tool in Public Sector Internal Audit: The Turkish Case. *Sosyal Bilimler Meslek Yüksekokulu Dergisi—Journal of Vocational School of Social Sciences*, Vol. 23 No. 1, pp. 208–225.

GAO, United States Government Accountability Office (2021). Artificial Intelligence-An Accountability Framework for Federal Agencies and Other Entities. www.gao.gov/assets/gao-21-519sp.pdf (Access date: 4 February 2024).

ISACA (2018). Auditing Artificial Intelligence. https://ec.europa.eu/futurium/en/system/files/ged/auditing-artificial-intelligence.pdf (Access date: 4 February 2024).

Lehmann, D. & Thor, M. (2020). The Next Generation of Internal Audit Harnessing Value from Innovation and Transformation. *CPA Journal*, February 2020. www.cpajournal.com/2020/02/18/the-next-generation-of-internal-audit/ (Access date: 4 February, 2024).

Lenz, R. & Jeppesen, K.K. (2022). The Future of Internal Auditing: Gardener of Governance. *EDPACS*, Vol. 66 No. 5, pp. 1–21. https://doi.org/10.1080/07366981.2022.2036314

Ngwenya, B. & Kakunda, R. (2014). Challenges of Internal Auditing in the Public Sector Organisations and Their Effect on Internal Auditors Job Satisfaction: A Case Study of Public Institutions in Chingola District, Zambia. *International Journal of Research in Computer Application & Management*, Vol. 4 No. 12, pp. 1–3. http://ijrcm.org.in/

OECD (Organisation for Economic Co-operation and Development) (2019a). Artificial Intelligence in Society, OECD Publishing: Paris, revised August 2019, https://doi.org/10.1787/eedfee77-en (Access date: 4 February, 2024).

OECD (Organisation for Economic Co-operation and Development) (2019b). Going Digital: Shaping Policies, Improving Lives, OECD Publishing, Paris, https://dx.doi.org/10.1787/9789264312012-en (Access date: 4 February, 2024).

Okee, C.F. & Fred, I.S. (2021). A Review of the Challenges with Internal Audit Functions in Public Institutions in Nigeria. *International Journal of Business & Law Research*, Vol. 9 No. (1), pp. 195–207. https://seahipaj.org/journals-ci/mar-2021/IJBLR/full/IJBLR-M-20-2021.pdf (Access date: 4 February, 2024).

Peffers, K., Tuunanen, T., Rothenberger, M.A., & Chatterjee, S. (2007). A Design Science Research Methodology for Information Systems Research. *Journal of Management Information Systems*, Vol. 24 No. 3, pp. 45–77. www.jstor.org/stable/40398896

Rogger, D. & Schuster, C. (editors) (2023). *The Government Analytics Handbook: Leveraging Data to Strengthen Public Administration*. Washington, DC: World Bank. http://hdl.handle.net/10986/39857 License: CC BY 3.0 IGO (Access date: 4 February 2024).

The Institute of Internal Auditors (2017). Global Perspectives and Insights Series, The IIA's Artificial Intelligence Auditing Framework—Practical Applications, Part A, 2017, https://na.theiia.org/periodicals/Public%20Documents/ GPI-Artificial-Intelligence-Part-II.pdf (Access date: 4 February 2024).

Torraco, R.J. (2005). Writing Integrative Literature Reviews: Guidelines and Examples. *Human Resource Development Review*, Vol. 4 No. 3, pp. 356–367. https://doi.org/10.1177/153448430 5278283

Welby, B. (2019). OECD Digital Government Project: The Impact of Digital Government on Citizen Well-Being, Public Governance, No. 32, OECD, Paris, https://doi.org/10.1787/19934351 (Access date: 4 February 2024).

Welby, B., van Ooijen, C., and Ubaldi, B. (2019). A data-driven public sector: Enabling the strategic use of data for productive, inclusive and trustworthy governance, Public Governance Working Papers, No. 33, OECD, Paris, https://doi.org/10.1787/19934351 (Access date: 4 February, 2024).

Wirtz Bernd, W., Weyerer Jan, C., & Carolin, G. (2019). Artificial Intelligence and the Public Sector—Applications and Challenges. *International Journal of Public Administration*, Vol. 42 No. 7. www.tandfonline.com/doi/full/10.1080/01900692.2018.1498103 (Access date: 4 February 2024).

Index

Printed in the United States
by Baker & Taylor Publisher Services